❧ SPEAK TO THE GODS AND GODDESSES ❧

All the planets, signs, gods and goddesses are within you and represent part of your eternal, archetypal self. When you make contact with a particular planet or mythological deity you are really making contact with part of your eternal self.

Perhaps you have identified a planet in your chart which has always represented one of your strengths; you may wish to increase and nurture that archetype within yourself in order to become yet stronger and more whole. Or, on the contrary, maybe you've been having trouble with a particular planet. Maybe you are having difficulty with the "material world" and you need to make friends with Saturn. Maybe your love life is a mess and the problems lie with psychological issues suggestive of your Mars and Venus. Or maybe you've had a dream in which a particular planetary archetype has suddenly emerged with great force; you want to know more about what it means. Or maybe one of the myths and stories in this book or some other has given you that peculiar feeling—common with myth and fairytale, though rare in other forms of literature—which can only be described as "eerie" or "uncanny." Such a feeling indicates that the archetypal world has been activated within you by the myth, and in such cases it is always worth exploring the matter further.

Mythic Astrology will take you on an inner journey like no other. When you finally stand in the presence of the archetype (through the techniques described herein of dreamwork, symbolic amplification, or active imagination), the god or goddess will have something to tell you. If you have come before the deity with a particular problem, you may ask for wisdom or advice on the matter directly. If you have been drawn indirectly to this archetype by a dream or by intuition, you may simply open yourself to whatever the gods wish to tell you. Whatever happens, you will have made a living and vital contact with the world of the deities inside you and with the inner dimensions of your birthchart. When you hear something of value that echoes in the stillness of your imagination, you will know that the gods have spoken.

"Mythic Astrology is a wonderful tool to explore personal myths and integrate the emerging Goddess archetypes into the birthchart."

Dell Horoscope

"Mythic Astrology is a fascinating psychological study of the mythic archetypes represented in the birthchart. It is an intelligent and easy-to-understand-and-use astrology book that gives the reader a clear road map to the unconscious."

The Santa Fe Sun

"This is as comprehensive as anyone could wish, virtually everything you can wish to know about Greek mythology that's become associated with astrological symbols."

Considerations

ABOUT THE AUTHORS

Ariel Guttman has been involved with the study of astrology since 1974. In 1980 she founded an astrological consulting firm, Astro Originals, through which astrological seminars, personal and business consulting, astrological teaching and lecturing are conducted. For several years she has been involved with asteroid research, and by including those asteroids in her astrological work, has found a growing interest in this, "the feminine" aspects of astrology. She has lectured for numerous astrological organizations and conferences both in the United States and in Europe. She is the author of *Astro-Compatibility*, and co-author of *The Astro*Carto*Graphy Book of Maps*.

Kenneth Johnson holds a degree in Religious Studies from California State University Fullerton. His emphasis was in the study of mythology and this interest is reflected in his writing and his astrological practice. Kenneth discovered astrology while traveling in Europe during the summer of 1973. He studied in Amsterdam and London before returning to the United States and developing a practice which focuses on archetypal themes and personal mythologies. In addition to his astrological interests, Kenneth is also a musical theater librettist and a member of the Dramatists Guild.

TO WRITE TO THE AUTHORS

If you wish to contact the authors or would like more information about this book, please write to the authors in care of Llewellyn Worldwide and we will forward your request. The authors and the publisher appreciate hearing from you and learning of your enjoyment of this book and how it has helped you. Llewellyn Worldwide cannot guarantee that every letter written to the authors can be answered, but all will be forwarded. Please write to:

Ariel Guttman and/or Kenneth Johnson
c/o Llewellyn Worldwide
P.O. Box 64383, Dept. L248-9,
St. Paul, MN 55164-0380, U.S.A.

Please enclose a self-addressed, stamped envelope for reply, or $1.00 to cover costs.
If outside U.S.A., enclose international postal reply coupon.

MYTHIC ASTROLOGY

Archetypal Powers in the Horoscope

ARIEL GUTTMAN

AND

KENNETH JOHNSON

1998
Llewellyn Publications
St. Paul, Minnesota, U.S.A. 55164-0383

FIRST EDITION
Fourth Printing,1998

Cover design by Chris Wells
Cover illustration by Randy Asplund-Faith
Chapter title page design by Diane Smirnow and Susan Van Sant
Chapter title page illustrations and graphics by Diane Smirnow except where noted
Book design and layout by Susan Van Sant

Worksheet pages based on a class developed and taught by Ariel Guttman

Library of Congress Cataloging-in-publication Data:

Guttman, Ariel
    Mythic astrology: archetypal powers in the horoscope / Ariel Guttman and Kenneth
    Johnson.
        p.   cm.
    Includes bibliographical references and index.
    ISBN 0-87542-248-9 : $17.95
    1. Astrology and mythology. 2. Archetype (Psychology) — Miscellanea.
    I. Johnson, Kenneth, 1952–   II. Title.
    BF1729.M9G87   1993   93-20514
                                                              CIP

    Acknowledgements/permissions:
        Quotations on pages 53, 89, 97, and 115 from: Athanassakis, Apostolos N., trans.,
        The Homeric Hymns, the Johns Hopkins University Press, Baltimore/London, 1976.
        Quotation on page 141 from: Lattimore, Richard, trans., *Pindaric Odes*, University
        of Chicago Press, Chicago, Illinois, 1947, p. 52.

Publisher's note:
Llewellyn Worldwide does not participate in, endorse, or have any authority or responsibility concerning private business transactions between our authors and the public.
    All mail addressed to the author is forwarded but the publisher cannot, unless specifically instructed by the author, give out an address or phone number.

Printed in the United States of America

Llewellyn Publications
A Division of Llewellyn Worldwide, Ltd.
P.O. Box 64383, St. Paul, MN 55164-0383

❧ ACKNOWLEDGEMENTS ❧

Grateful appreciation is hereby expressed to the astrologers who carved a path into the world of mythic astrology, namely, Liz Greene for her inspired and thought-provoking works. Sorely missed and fondly remembered are Tony Joseph, Richard Idemon, and Howard Sasportas for their insightful perspectives on the myths as applied to the astrological technique. Thanks to astrologers Zipporah Dobyns for illuminating the world of asteroids and to Demetra George for her continued research.

Many thanks to Michael who is always supportive and helpful in my life and in my work; to Maryfrank for her support, friendship and assistance; Diane for her friendship and extraordinary design work in this volume; to our editor at Llewellyn—Susan Van Sant, who has been a joy to work with in every way; and finally, to students and friends alike who have been overwhelmingly supportive of this work.

ARIEL GUTTMAN
April, 1993

I would like to express my appreciation to Michael Bernstein for introducing me to the art of astrology; to Dr. Dorothea Kenny, Professor of Comparative Literature at California State University, Fullerton, who first showed me that mythology constituted a conscious spiritual path; to Carl Jung and Joseph Campbell who have been my principal sources of inspiration; to my mother for introducing me to the world of books in general; to Susan Van Sant for her clear, concise, and helpful editing; and to Marguerite for her continuing support.

KENNETH JOHNSON
April, 1993

OTHER BOOKS BY ARIEL GUTTMAN

Astro-Compatibility

The Astro*Carto*Graphy Book of Maps (co-authored with Jim Lewis)

OTHER BOOKS BY KENNETH JOHNSON

The Pyramid of Time: A Guide to the Mayan Calendar

The Grail Castle: Male Myths and Mysteries in the Celtic Tradition (co-authored with Marguerite Elsbeth) — forthcoming

❧ TABLE OF CONTENTS ❧

PREFACE

How to use this Book

To make use of the myths and archetypes which lie behind the practice of astrology, you may begin from the birth chart itself, or simply from your own inner response to the myths.

To begin with the birth chart is perhaps the most direct approach. If you have enough astrological background to read the chart yourself, you will of course be able to identify the planets or signs which play the largest role in your own "personal myth." If not, you may need to have an experienced astrologer pick out for you the planetary or zodiacal factors which have the strongest resonance in your chart. More often than not, the dominant planets or signs in your birth chart will indicate the myths and archetypes to which you respond most strongly. Begin by studying the chapters which touch upon these, your own personal myths.

Or you may choose to take a more intuitive, less structured approach. You may begin with the book itself, and simply take note of which gods, goddesses, or myths have the greatest impact upon your heart and mind. You needn't worry if a particular planet or sign resonates strongly in your soul but doesn't seem to be that strongly emphasized in the birth chart! After all, you may be gravitating towards a myth which was comparatively absent from your natal chart, but one of which you now have need. (Though we may lean toward identification with particular symbols and myths, we also strive, however unconsciously, to experience all the planetary and zodiacal archetypes, for the ultimate goal is completeness.)

Let us say, for instance, that you find yourself drawn to the archetype of Venus. Maybe you know Venus is important to you because you have always placed a primary value on the relationships in your life; if those relationships have not gone well, then you will know that you need to do some serious work on the love goddess within you. Maybe you have Venus exalted in Pisces, or fallen in Virgo. Maybe you were once struck by the power of Botticelli's famous *Birth of Venus* and have carried the image with you for years. Or maybe you have simply kept an ankh (identical to the astrological Venus symbol) above your bed since the 1960s.

One way or another, you have decided that the goddess of love is an archetype you want to work with—or need to work with. You are now ready to begin that curious and meandering process which Jungian psychology calls symbolic amplification. Study the chapters on Venus, and on her signs, Taurus and Libra. If you are a man, you may wish to ask yourself at this point what kind of women you are attracted to. Are you entranced by the goddess' earthy, sensual aspect (Taurus), or by her distant, glittering perfection (Libra)? If you are a woman, then which aspect of Venus do you embody in your own relationships? Do you think of sex first and foremost, followed perhaps by money and children? Then you are leaning toward the earthier aspect of the goddess. Or do you prefer to dress to the hilt, be romanced with expensive dinners and wine, and then keep him at a distance until you are ready? If so, you are gravitating towards the more Libran aspect of the goddess. (Don't worry too much about where Venus is in your chart, for there are many factors which affect your responses, and this, after all, is an intuitive journey.)

As you explore the different aspects of the love goddess in these pages, you may discover that Venus is exalted in Pisces. Suppose that you go on to study Pisces, then Neptune, its ruler. Now you discover that dream-like, unrealistic relationships are related to the Neptune factor in a chart, and that movie stars frequently have a strong Neptune. So if you're a man who has always had his romantic hopes dashed by harsh realities, and who goes into a trance over the newest Venus on the wide screen, then you will know that Neptune is playing a role in your love life which may be just as important as that of Venus herself. Exploring Neptune, you may find that you have always been a sort of Dionysian dreamer, more interested in your guitar and exotic forms of spiritual wisdom than in holding down a job or being a big success. So Venus has led you to Neptune, and Neptune has opened up issues concerning the meaning and direction of your life itself. So you begin to work with Neptune, and in time Neptune may lead you somewhere else. The process of symbolic amplification has no particular beginning or end; it goes in circles. This is an indirect route. Like alchemy, it mixes and "cooks" various symbols and myths until a whole new image is born by way of a process of transmutation.

The second technique is dreamwork, and in some ways it resembles symbolic amplification. As most of us know, our dreams are filled with stories, characters and themes which are also found in folklore, fairy tales, and mythology—in other words, our dreams embody our personal myths. It is the unconscious psyche which speaks to us through our dreams, and myth is the language of the unconscious. So we can use our dreams to look more deeply into our own personal myths, and into the planetary or zodiacal factors involved.

For instance: a client of one of the authors had a dream in which he was traveling through a great city. In the course of the dream, he and his traveling companions had many adventures in many different locales around the city. Finally, they found themselves in a pet shop. The dreamer looked toward one corner of the pet shop, and beheld a very unusual scene: a dark-haired man, with a snake entwined around his body, was staring at the dreamer and pointing a finger at him. The dreamer then noticed a small puppy escaping from one of the cages. Feeling happy that the dog had escaped captivity, he decided not to tell any of the pet store employees about the fleeing animal.

The motif of the journey might well remind us of the long journeys undertaken by many of the hero figures mentioned in this book: Jason's quest for the Golden Fleece, Odysseus' journey through unknown seas, or Perceval's search for the Grail. We might suspect that the dreamer is actually involved in some sort of quest, as the many adventures he meets along his way would indicate. As a citizen of contemporary America rather than the Middle Ages, he wanders through a great city rather than a dark forest.

What about the pet shop? Clearly, the dreamer is in the "animal kingdom"—a level of consciousness somewhat more primal or "primitive" than his ordinary waking consciousness. But the most striking feature of the dream is obviously the dark man entwined with a snake. Three male figures associated with serpents may be familiar to us from the pages of this book: Hermes, Asclepius, and Pluto. Hermes, of course, held the caduceus, the wand entwined with serpents which has become the emblem of the medical profession. Asclepius, another healer, held a similar wand; he has a place in the sky as the constellation Ophiuchus and is associated with Scorpio and also with Chiron, his legendary teacher. As lord of the underworld, Pluto or Hades rules the home of the serpent wisdom; his female counterparts, Persephone and Ereshkigal, have serpents in their hair. The chapter on Mercury also informs us that Hermes was, among other things, the guide who helped souls journey to the underworld, Pluto's realm.

So we have a collection of symbols here, all of which speak the same language: the dreamer has reached a stage in his quest wherein he has made contact with a realm of consciousness somewhat more primal than his own, i.e., with the "animal kingdom." But he must go deeper still. The dark, serpent-shrouded figure is obviously a guide, come to lead him to the very depths of his spirit where the serpent wisdom is hidden; and yet this process, no matter how fearful, is also a process of healing, as the symbolism clearly shows.

Now we may proceed to examine how the dream and the birth chart combine with each other. Specifically, we would want to look at the dreamer's Mercury, Chiron and Pluto. We would want to see whether he has any planets in Scorpio or the Eighth House, and whether there are any transits involving these planets in his chart. Pluto turns out to provide the answer: at the time of the dream, transiting Pluto was in opposition to the dreamer's Sun. Since the Sun represents the dreamer's deepest self—the heart of his own personal myth—we can see that nothing less than a total transformative descent into the dreamer's private underworld is required. The dark beckoning figure is most probably the God of the Underworld himself, calling the dreamer's conscious ego (another aspect of the Sun) to descend in search of the serpent wisdom. Fortunately, the dreamer has an animal helper like the heroes and heroines of fairy tale—the escaped puppy is clearly a portion of his vital soul which will remain free and alive during his underworld passage.

The third method of contacting the planetary and zodiacal archetypes is the most direct of all. Jungian analysts call it active imagination, but those who have some acquaintance with Wicca, practical Kabbalah, or other forms of magic will recognize this technique as similar to invocation. Perhaps this is why many Jungian therapists warn their clients against attempting this particular exercise without the guidance of a therapist. After all, it is no small matter to invoke the ancient goddesses and gods. But the technique of active imagination is typically undertaken as a free and undirected inner journey wherein the therapist plays the role of guide; hence it differs from invocation, which is firmly directed by the individual who performs the operation. If one allows one's consciousness to journey into archetypal realms with no clear intention of where it is going, one may indeed encounter dangerous images or unpleasant inner realities. But the technique we will describe here is by no means undirected. Choose the planet or goddess or god you intend to activate within yourself. Know where you're going and what you're getting into.

Quite simply, the exercise consists of picking a particular planet or mythological deity you wish to make contact with. Of course, all the planets and signs, gods and goddesses, are within you, and represent part of your eternal, archetypal self. So what you are really doing is contacting part of your eternal self. How do you choose such a planet and/or deity? Perhaps you have identified a planet in your chart which has always represented one of your strengths; you may wish to increase and nurture that archetype within yourself in order to become yet stronger and more whole. Or, on the contrary, maybe you've been having trouble with a particular planet. Maybe you are having difficulty with the material world and you need to make friends with Saturn. Maybe your love life is a mess and the problem lies with psychological issues suggestive of your Mars and Venus. Or maybe you've had a dream in which a particular planetary archetype has suddenly emerged with great force; you want to know more about what it means. Or maybe one of the myths and stories in this book or some other has given you that peculiar feeling—common with myth and fairy tale, though rare in other forms of literature—which can only be described as eerie or uncanny. Such a feeling indicates that the archetypal world has been activated within you by the myth, and in such cases it is always worth exploring the matter further.

Find a calm, quiet place to sit. Begin your meditation with the specific intent of contacting a particular archetype—your own Mars, or Moon, or Chiron, or whatever it may be. You may already know what form you wish this archetype to take. For instance: a woman who seeks to contact her inner Mars or Sun will probably already know what her ideal or inner man, her *animus*, looks like, for she has met him in her fantasies and dreams many times. She may therefore build up an image of the inner archetypal force based on her own personal knowledge of that which powerful symbolic images that lie at the heart of our deepest psychological process-es and which Jung called archetypes.

Because the planets are named for the gods and goddesses of mythology, and because the signs of the zodiac also have mythic associations, we might suspect that these astrological factors are archetypes, and that their influence upon us is based as much upon symbolic reality as it is upon any astrophysical force. Jung believed that symbolic or archetypal realities interact with the events of our everyday lives through a process called synchronicity. He described this as "an acausal connecting princi-ple," meaning a process which links two factors (the cosmic symbol and the worldly event) without any *apparent* or physical cause for that link. The union between reality and symbol takes place on an internal, psychological level, and the unconscious is the active agent which shapes the union. Jung used the principle of synchronicity as a rationale for other divinatory tools such as the Tarot and the *I Ching*.[5]

Building upon Jung's thesis, astrologer Dane Rudhyar argued that the moment of an individual's birth is perhaps the most synchronistic moment of all, for it marks our entry into a larger cosmos, both physically and symbolically. As a diagram or image of that moment, the natal horoscope or birth chart is also the image of our symbolic relationship with the cosmos around us; it places us, as individuals, in the archetypal scheme of things.[6] The birth chart diagram itself lends credence to this notion, for it is unquestionably a kind of *mandala*.

The word *mandala* is Sanskrit; in India and Tibet, it describes a symbolic picture or diagram used as a tool in meditation. A *mandala* is a symbol of wholeness, of psy-cho-spiritual unity; to meditate on a *mandala* aids the seeker in the search for that wholeness or unity. A *mandala* is generally circular, since wholeness or oneness is conceived of as a circle, without beginning or end. Often, the circle is divided into four parts—for, as we shall see, wholeness is also conceived of as a fourfold entity or process. True unity, in the psychological or mystical sense, combines the circle and the square.[7]

The horoscope diagram that we use in astrology today is in the form of a circle. (This is a purely arbitrary or symbolic choice, by the way, for in India they use a square.) This circle is divided into four quadrants, based upon the four cardinal angles of the birth chart: the Ascendant (sunrise), Midheaven (noon), Descendant (sunset), and Nadir (midnight). Some astrologers—primarily those who have been influenced by Rudhyar—correlate these four angles with the four elements or with Jung's four psychic functions (see the Four Elements).[8] Clearly, then, the horo-scope has all the components of a classic *mandala*. It is a circle divided into four symbolic parts, representing a complete whole. But what is the complete whole pic-tured in this astrological *mandala*?

In one sense, the horoscope represents the universe at large. After all, it *is* a dia-gram of the sky above—a cosmogram. But, as we know, the sky is always in motion. A horoscope is a diagram of the sky *at a particular moment in time*. Typically, this moment in time represents that most magical and synchronistic of all moments:

the moment of birth. The birth of what? It really doesn't matter. It could be the birth of an idea, the christening of your new boat, the birth of a litter of puppies or of a corporation—but most often, a horoscope represents the birth of a human being. *You* are the *mandala*.

In Tibet, a *mandala* often includes pictures of various deities, demons, Buddhas, and Bodhisattvas at different points around the circle. Similarly, a horoscope includes planets and zodiacal signs, and, as we have noted, the planets and signs have deep mythological connotations, as do the demons and Bodhisattvas of Tibetan Buddhism.

The planets, however, are never in *precisely* the same relationship with each other from moment to moment. The sky is ever-changing. Thus each horoscope is as individual as a snowflake. It cannot be replicated, even over the course of thousands of years. Like the person it represents, whose DNA is encoded with an individually specific formula, it is entirely unique.

Thus we may say that the horoscope links you, the individual, with the cosmos, a larger frame of reality. Each one of us is fashioned of the same archetypal materials, for the same planets and signs are present in each and every birth chart. But they are never arranged in exactly the same way. We are universal, for we all partake of the self-same archetypes. But we are also unique.

It should be apparent, then, that it is the constant orbital motion of the planets, as well as the revolution of the earth which accounts for the rising and setting of the signs, that makes each chart so individualized. And indeed, it is the arrangement of signs and planets which forms the basis of all astrological interpretation. Where, then, have we derived the meaning of those planets and signs?

While there are many astrology books which address the meanings of the signs, planets, houses and aspects that make up the birth chart, there is very little reference to the origins of these meanings. We have all heard astrologers make statements such as: "You have five planets in Pisces, therefore you will excel in matters of spiritual development, art or music, but worldly affairs keep you somewhat in the dark." "Your Moon in Taurus bodes well for the acquisition of money and property, but doesn't allow for quick, decisive action." "Your Sun in the Fourth House requires the security of a home base, and family matters are much more important to you than most." "So much air in your chart has you constantly swirling ideas around in your head, but they may not get put into action without the grounding element of earth or the energetic motivation of fire." Where do statements like this come from and why are they usually so amazingly accurate?

The planets, as we have noted, are named for the gods and goddesses of Rome, all borrowed from Greek mythology, and each sign is associated with one or more of these gods and goddesses. Though astrology was born in Babylon and influenced by Egypt, it has come down to us primarily through Greek thinkers and writers. When we consider the psychological or archetypal meanings behind planets and signs, we are considering the world-view of Greek myth.

lies within her. Or you may have had a dream: perhaps Mercury appeared to you as a salesman or a petty thief in the dream, and thus you may wish to call him up in that same form. Those who have a taste for the mythological past or a background in other forms of magic may well wish to invoke the gods and goddesses in their customary forms: Athene with her helmet and the owl on her shoulder, Jupiter with his beard and thunderbolt, or the Moon as Isis.

Typically, your imagination will take you to a particular landscape. You may have to wander through this mythic landscape for a little while before the deity you've invoked actually puts in an appearance. But when you finally stand in the presence of the archetype, you may begin your inner dialogue. The god or goddess will have something to tell you—something of value which echoes in the stillness of your imagination. This is how the gods speak to us, as Neoplatonic astrologers and magicians of the Hellenistic era, such as Iamblichus and Porphyry, knew full well. If you have come before the deity with a particular problem, you may ask for wisdom or advice on that matter directly. Or if you have been drawn indirectly to this archetype by a dream or by intuition, you may simply open yourself to whatever the gods wish to tell you.

This is perhaps the most powerful technique of all for making contact with the planets within. It should not be done frivolously. And, as the Jungians warn us, it should never be done in an undirected or unstructured way. Always know who or what you intend to meet with in the archetypal realm. Show respect and honor to the goddesses and gods within. When they choose to depart, allow them to do so. Treat them as real, not as figments of your imagination. You may gain a living and vital contact with the world of the deities within you, and with the inner dimensions of your birth chart.

ARIEL GUTTMAN
KENNETH JOHNSON

INTRODUCTION

Astrology and the Language of Myth

For centuries people have consulted astrologers with questions like: what is my fate, how will I fare in love and money, how will I achieve success, what of my health? The astute astrologer, conversant with the "language of the stars," casts the querent's horoscope, a diagram consisting of symbols and lines referring to planetary placements in the heavens at the time of birth (natal astrology) or at the moment the question is posed (horary astrology), and then proceeds to address those questions. The fact that a piece of paper with some mathematical scribblings and oddly shaped glyphs could provide a person with reasonable and accurate responses to such questions has baffled educated minds for as many years as the practice has been going on. Yet astrology persists and flourishes even now. Today, in the final years preceding the turn of the millennium, when the Age of Reason is being retired (or perhaps integrated into the Age of Intuition), astrology can be understood as never before by the very minds that have challenged it for so long—because it is the integration of reason (mathematics, orbital frequencies, cycles) and intuition (symbolic references to long forgotten myths and deities) that the study of astrology represents.

Debate continues about the "why" of astrology, even among its supporters. Some insist that we are, in fact, under the influence of some kind of magnetism or energy field which emanates from the planets, an energy which has yet to be identified and measured by science. French researchers Michel and Francoise Gauquelin spent years compiling data which indicates that the positions of the planets do indeed influence our lives.[1] The Gauquelins focused their attention on identifying and confirming planetary placements in successful professionals' careers—a more measurable factor than some of the intangibles which form the foundation of astrology. Thousands of birth dates fed into the computer led the Gauquelins to the conclusion that the rising and culmination of the planets (or, at any rate, of the "seven ancient planets") plays a major role in identifying character traits that would lead one to eventually follow a particular career path. British astronomer Percy Seymour, after studying the Gauquelin data, has developed a new theory of celestial magnetism to account for the influence of the planets upon human nature.[2]

An astrologer casting a horoscope, from Robert Fludd's Utriusque Cosmi Historia, *Oppenheim, 1617*

Other astrologers find it unnecessary to seek a rationale for their art in the science of astrophysics. Citing the work of psychologist Carl Jung, they point out that symbolic realities are just as important to human nature as are physical realities (probably *more* important). Jungian psychologist and astrologer Liz Greene notes that in working with a client's birth chart she never questions *why* or *how* astrology works—the important thing is that it does.[3]

Jung argued that the gods and goddesses of ancient mythology were symbolic of deep motivating factors in human psychology, elements which were shared by all humanity. Jung postulated a level of consciousness, which he named the collective unconscious, shared by the entire human race.[4] The concept is familiar to students of the world's spiritual traditions by a variety of names: the astral light, the group mind, the *alaya-vijnana*, and so on. It is the collective unconscious which creates the

The Greeks had a complex mythology which included the story of creation and the birth or appearance of the presiding deities of human affairs. Each god and goddess had a specific function and was honored through celebrations, offerings, holidays, prayers, and rituals. These pagan rituals later came to reflect the sophistication of Greek philosophy, and to embody a metaphysical rather than a purely ritual paganism. With the downfall of Classical Greece and the emergence of the Roman Empire, the Romans borrowed many of their deities from the Greeks. The names and costumes were changed to reflect Roman style, but the meanings changed little. Greek Hermes became the Roman Mercury, Hera became Juno and so on.

The planets whose circular paths in the heavens orbit around one central deity, the Sun, have the Latin names of the gods and goddesses of Rome. In the sky, as on Mt. Olympus, they continue to reside *above* human awareness. Thus the transference from god to planet is established. But how have the characteristics of these gods developed into the meanings associated with particular planets? It is this issue we wish to explore in this volume. In investigating this process we will attempt to unearth the archetypal vision of ancient mythology and proceed to weave it into the interpretations used in modern astrology.

Astrologers have generally been content to link the planets and signs with the Greek deities in a very general way. Mercury is about communication because Hermes/Mercury was the messenger of the gods; Pluto is about the process of death

A medieval woodcut showing Arabian astrologers, from Macrobius' In Somnium Scipionis, *Venice, 1513*

and rebirth because Hades/Pluto was the god of the underworld. We believe that this is only the beginning, and that the key to a proper understanding of all the astrological symbols — planets and signs — lies in a deeper understanding of the mythic archetypes upon which the symbols are based. To richly experience the myths which lie at the heart of astrology is to gain a deeper and more spiritual perspective on the art itself.

After many ages during which astrology has been used, misused, discarded, revised and finally brought into a sensitive and useful application, we have now begun to see a renaissance of the world's ancient mythologies as a factor to consider in understanding the human psyche. It is this approach to astrology that both authors find especially useful today, in a world where advanced technologies and industrialization don't often give people the answers they're looking for. Astrology has indeed evolved into a psychology of myth. "Mythology is a validation of experience, giving it its spiritual or psychological dimension" according to Joseph Campbell.[9] When properly examined and understood, astrology offers the same spiritual and psychological dimension as myth.

*The title page from a Hungarian Gypsy publication (*Egypto-Persian Book
of Planets)*, Austria-Hungary, 1890*

A pre-Copernican view of the solar system with the earth at the center

THE PLANETS

CHAPTER ONE

The senate-house of planets all did sit,
To knit in her their best perfections.

—*Shakespeare*, Pericles, I, I

When they first become interested in astrology, people tend to regard the signs of the zodiac as the most important factors in the astrological arcanum. Professional astrologers, however, know that it is the planets rather than the signs which form the core of the whole system.

The relationship between the planets, the signs and the twelve houses can be expressed through an extended metaphor. Let us examine a theatrical production. This particular production is your life, and you are the playwright—or, more precisely, the divine spark within you is the playwright. The play will, of course, have a number of different scenes. Those scenes or sets—the furniture, props and so on—are represented in our metaphor by the twelve houses of the horoscope. As the actors enter, speak their lines and exit, they will of course wear different costumes, and the zodiacal signs which the planets occupy represent those costumes.

But the actors themselves? The actors are the planets, and the speeches through which they relate to one another are the planetary aspects.

When the Egyptians and Babylonians began to observe the sky, they noted that most of the stars occupied fixed positions. Five of them, however, could be seen to travel through the heavens, just as the sun and moon traveled. These "wandering stars" were, of course, the planets, and in fact the word planet comes from a Greek term meaning wanderer. The zodiac itself probably developed as a way of measuring the motion of the planets.

The earliest Greeks assigned guardians—A Titan and a Titaness—to each of the seven ancient planets. Theia and Hyperion governed the Sun while Phoebe and Atlas presided over the Moon. Dione and Crius guarded Mars; Metis and Coeus were linked with Mercury, Themis and Eurymedon with Jupiter, Tethys and Oceanus with Venus, and finally, Rhea and Cronus with Saturn. A few of these ancient guardians will be recognized as influencing a planet's nature to some degree, just as we are influenced to some degree by the nature of our earliest ancestors.

The Babylonians, who took astrology more seriously than any other ancient people, named the planets after their various gods. The king of the gods, Marduk, was the planet we now call Jupiter, and our Venus was originally named for Ishtar, the love goddess of ancient Babylon. In time, the Greeks imitated the Babylonians: Marduk became Zeus, the Greek king of the gods; Ishtar became smiling Aphrodite. The Romans translated the names of the planets into Latin, and it is these names we use today.

The days of the week are named for the planets. The obvious ones to English-speaking people will be Saturday (Saturn's Day), Sunday (Sun's Day), and Monday (Moon's Day). Tuesday, named after Tiw, the Germanic god of war, corre-

French planetary talismans for the seven days of the week, from Le Petit Albert's Secretes merveilleux de la magie, *Cologne, 1722*

Emblematic representation of the seven planetary gods, from Johann Daniel Milius' Philosophia Reformata, *Frankfort, 1622*

sponds to Mars. Wednesday is named for Odin or Woden, the Norse counterpart to Mercury. Thursday or Thor's Day is named for Jupiter, while Friday or Freyja's Day is the day of Venus.

Though the Greeks of the Archaic Period (800–500 BC) imagined their gods as real entities living on a real mountaintop, the sophisticated intellectuals of the Hellenistic (c. 300 BC–1 AD) and Roman (1 AD–400 AD) periods regarded the gods and planets primarily as psychological entities. Plato called the gods archetypes, and he meant exactly what Carl Jung meant when he too used that term. The gods, according to Plato, were primordial ideas which existed on a plane or in a dimension somewhat removed from our ordinary consciousness, and which we might perceive as being "above" that ordinary consciousness. These primordial ideas were common to all human beings, and were reflected in each of us like images in a mirror—as above, so below. The heavens are the macrocosm; humankind is the microcosm.

Seen from this point of view, we may also suspect that the planets constitute a journey in consciousness. The Greek and Roman astrologers understood this. We still labor under the illusion that ancient (and modern) astrologers thought astrology worked because of mysterious rays emanating from the actual physical planets and influencing us here on earth. But a careful reading of Plato—and especially of his followers, the Neoplatonists—reveals that the ancients actually regarded the planets as archetypes, symbols for internal psychological processes.

Marsilio Ficino, the Renaissance scholar who translated the Hermetic writings, developed a doctrine of the inner planets which held that the astrological planets were, in fact, internal psycho-spiritual entities, and that by means of meditation, talismans, and other sympathetic magical practices, one could enhance or harmonize the influence of those inner planets so as to produce beneficial effects in one's life.[1]

To the Gnostic philosophers of the early Christian centuries, the journey through the planets was a meditative process similar to the shaman's journey to the otherworld. The Gnostics admittedly had a somewhat negative view of astrology: to them, the planets symbolized the harsh regime of human destiny. One overcame the influence of the planets and gained freedom from destiny by "rising above" the archetypal symbols which make up our individual psychology and achieving union with a higher self—a self which was infinite and thus free of all planetary (i.e., psychological) compulsion.

But the Gnostics knew that one could never be free of a planetary affliction or psychological complex until one had mastered it on the inner, psycho-spiritual level. Consequently, they believed that one must journey through each planet successively—a journey which to them symbolized the ascent to higher consciousness. Through meditation, chant, ritual, and talismanic magic they sought to master—or, in Ficino's words, to harmonize—the influence of each planet, and by so doing to rise above it to a higher state of awareness.

The journey remains the same today. Some of the actors, however, have changed—or, more accurately, some new characters have entered the astrological drama. The discovery of new planets, as well as the charting of the major asteroids, has extended our spectrum of astrological awareness beyond the seven planets known to the ancients. This extension of awareness is a matter of choice, and very typical of Western culture. In India, astrologers continue to limit their chartwork to a consideration of the seven ancient planets, plus the Moon's Nodes. They have little or no interest in Uranus, Neptune or Pluto, and certainly no interest in Chiron or the asteroids. We Westerners, on the other hand, approach the discovery of new heavenly bodies with an eager curiosity. Similarly, Western astrologers use the tropical zodiac while Hindu astrologers favor the more ancient sidereal system. A great deal has been written in recent years about the weaknesses of our overly assertive, scientific, analytical civilization. But our willingness to expand our collective consciousness by embracing anything new may well be one of the strengths of such a civilization.

One of the tenets of astrological philosophy is that the discovery of a new planet signals the development of a new stage in humankind's conscious evolution. Jung believed that the collective unconscious would constellate new symbols or archetypes whenever humanity needed them. These new archetypes—which are more often dramatic restatements of old archetypes—emerge into our collective consciousness at sensitive points in history, during times when the paradigms of reality are undergoing a radical shift. Impressed by the archetypal symbolism he observed

The Seven Planets, from Sebastian Münster's Organum Uranicum,
printed by Heinrich Petri, Basle, 1536

❧ 13 ❧

The seven planets as the protectors of farmers, engraved by V. Feil, from Thannstetter's
Wiener Praktik, *Vienna, 1524*

in UFO reports, Jung suggested that UFOs were themselves the manifestation of a
new archetype. Jacques Vallee and Whitley Streiber have reached similar conclu-
sions about the so-called "visitor experience."

From the astrological perspective, we could say that the discovery and naming
of a new planet is a dramatic incidence of synchronicity which has implications for
all the inhabitants of planet earth. It will be observed that new planets (or asteroids,
or comets) are named by the astronomers who discover them, and that these individuals have little sympathy for astrology (they usually abhor it). Yet the mythological names they give to the planets have, in most cases, an uncanny relationship to
the actual functioning of those planets in the birth chart. The discovery of a planet,
the person "chosen" to "discover" it, its naming, and its mythic impact upon human
consciousness all combine in a web of synchronicity which gives birth to a new collective archetype.

All of this has a profound significance for our own time. From antiquity until 1781, there were only the seven planets (i.e., the five visible planets plus the Sun and Moon). Uranus was discovered in 1781, Neptune in 1846, and Pluto in 1930. The major asteroids were charted in the early 1800s, and tables of their motion were published in the 1970s. The comet Chiron was discovered in 1977. It should be clear, then, that new discoveries are being made at an increasingly rapid rate.

This accelerating tempo of discovery symbolizes an equally dramatic acceleration in consciousness. New archetypes are bursting forth from the collective psyche at a truly remarkable rate. The human mind is breaking through its previous boundaries, expanding at a speed which, for many, seems all too fast. We stand upon the threshold of a new collective consciousness—not a surprising situation, inasmuch as we also stand upon the threshold of a new astrological age.

The journey through the planets is indeed a journey towards ever higher states of awareness. We travel the same celestial road the Gnostics traveled; but for us, it is a longer, wider road. As we mentioned earlier, Hindu astrologers are uninterested in using the "modern" planets, let alone the asteroids. Their attitude embodies a very Eastern concept—the idea that the essence of human consciousness is eternal and changeless. And this is true enough. By eagerly adopting new celestial discoveries into our astrological repertoire, we embody an attitude which is intrinsically Western—the idea that human consciousness is in a continual state of evolution. And this is equally true. It is in this spirit of exploration and evolution that we include Gaia (Earth), the four major asteroids, and Chiron in this book, as we feel these orbiting bodies in space are archetypes which have significant meaning for modern times.

As we have observed, the planets constitute the core of our astrological framework. This is one factor which has remained constant through the centuries. But the ideas that have been held about the planets have gone through considerable alteration—perhaps evolution—through the ages. Certainly they have been colored by historical and political realities and have reflected to some extent the way in which astrology itself has been regarded. For instance, the earliest clay tablets from Babylon suggest that "if a child is born when Venus comes forth and Jupiter has set, his wife will be stronger than he."[2] Here, no reference has been made to the sign of the zodiac which was occupied by the planets—or even the Sun sign! Instead, there is a reference to angularity (the rise and set of the planets), which the Gauquelins have confirmed and reconfirmed as a point worth much emphasis in astrological delineation. However, it is likely that few contemporary astrologers would agree with the interpretation, as the way in which we interpret Venus and Jupiter has changed over the centuries.

Our predecessors' interest in the rising and setting of planets was usually related to concerns such as whether there would be enough crops that year to feed the people, or whether the kingdom was in danger from an invading army. Lunar and solar eclipses also figured prominently in this scheme. Records were kept as to which planets were overhead or retrograde at times of natural disasters or invasions. In some instances, these same theories and techniques apply today. Modern astrologers still observe the eclipse cycle very carefully and, with increasingly more sophisticated measuring devices and computers, they are able to pinpoint precise locations of these eclipses upon the earth. But there is a primary difference in assigning a meaning to Saturn, Jupiter, or Mars when analyzing political and climatic patterns as opposed to analyzing a newborn's life. And this is one of the most important considerations in working within the astrological system. In the astrological specialties known as mundane astrology, where political and geographical realities are discussed, or in horary astrology, where a specific answer is given to a specific question, or in economic astrology, where stock market cycles are analyzed against planetary cycles, there are hard and fast rules of interpretation. And maybe even to our ancestors, who lived in a "fixed" world where there seemed to be little if any control over personal destiny, a rising Saturn in a birth chart cast a gloomy shadow over one's life. But today it is different. In a society where we have begun to realize that human evolution is infused with a divine substance, where negative patterns from the past can be transformed into dynamic growth situations, and reality becomes that which is created from moment to moment by our thought patterns and belief systems, Saturn on the Ascendant is no longer merely a dark shadow; it is also the inner dynamic that fuels the individual to reach her or his greatest life achievement—consciousness.

SUN

CHAPTER TWO

... The Sun ariseth in his majesty;
Who doth the world so gloriously behold
That cedar-tops and hills seem burnish'd gold.

Venus salutes him with this fair good-morrow:
"O thou clear god, and patron of all light,
From whom each lamp and shining star doth borrow
The beauteous influence that makes him bright..."

—*Shakespeare,* Venus and Adonis

The Sun occupies a unique position in astrology. It is not an equal with the other planets. It stands out, towering above the rest by virtue of the fact that all planets revolve *around* it. It is the *center* of the pack; its light and warmth allow life to exist, grow, and evolve—at least on earth.

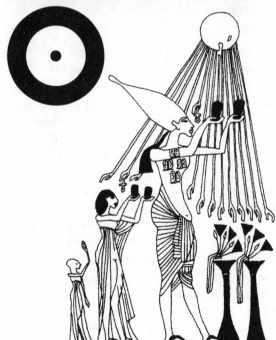

The first truly monotheistic religion in human history was a solar cult, instituted by the Egyptian pharaoh Akhenaten. A hymn composed by this precocious religious thinker still survives, and indicates that for Akhenaten, as for later inhabitants of planet earth, the sun was the source of all life:

O Ra,
at dawn you open each horizon.
Each world of life you've made
*   is conquered by your love.*
Because the daylight follows you,
*   it walks in peace...*

Everything created
was created in your heart:
the earth, the people on it,
the four leggeds, winged ones,
swimming ones, all…

I am your child.
In the greatest of all dawns,
raise me up![1]

The position of the Sun in the horoscopic wheel, along with its sign and aspects, has for many astrologers been the primary reference point. Perhaps this is why sun-sign astrology has become so popular. But despite its importance, the Sun is not the *only* factor in the horoscope, and the emphasis on sun-sign astrology in newspapers and magazines has actually conspired to prevent public awareness of the deeper aspects of astrology as an integrated, holistic system of thought. While the debate may rage for many more decades about the importance of the Sun when weighed against the other planets, most astrologers will probably agree that it is still the first item studied when reading a chart, and, when combined with the Moon and Ascendant, constitutes much of the essential data upon which one bases an astrological reading.

Most cultures have recognized sun gods. In Greece, the earliest solar deity was the Titan Helios, who drove the chariot of the Sun across the sky each day and who was the subject of the famous statue called the Colossus of Rhodes (the sunny island of Rhodes was sacred to Helios). But the sun god most familiar to Western culture is Apollo. His mother, the Titaness Leto, had been impregnated by Zeus, the king of the gods. Zeus' wife Hera, furious over her husband's affair with Leto, issued a celestial proclamation that forbade all sanctuary for the pregnant Leto. Having wandered across the land in search of a place to give birth, Leto finally came to the island of Ortygia and there birthed Artemis, twin sister of Apollo and goddess of the Moon, who sprang forth from her mother's womb and

Helios with the horses of the sun

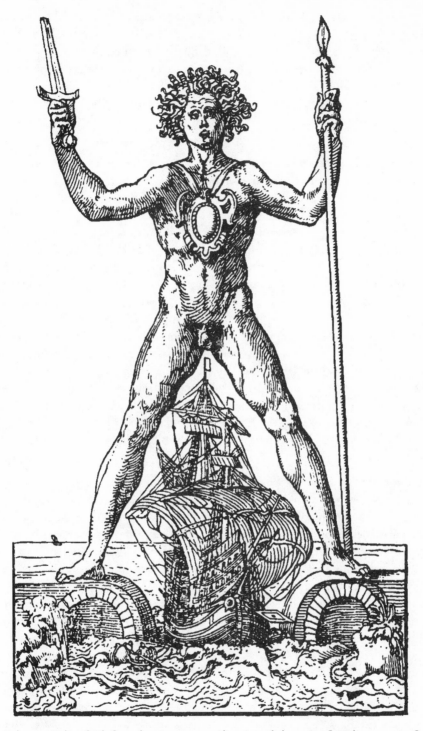

Colossus Solis of Rhodes, the giant personification of the sun god Helios, engraved by Jean Cousin, from André Thevet's Cosmographia de Levant, *printed by Jean de Tournes and Guillaume Gazeau, Lyons, 1554*

promptly ushered the still-laboring Leto to the neighboring isle of Delos, where, on the ninth day, she assisted with the birth of her brother Apollo. Delos subsequently became a holy shrine, celebrating Apollo's birth. No mortal was allowed to be born or die upon this island. Interestingly enough, Delos is considered the *center* of the chain of islands called the Cyclades, just as the Sun is considered the center of the system of orbiting planets. And two lions, emblematic of the solar-ruled sign Leo, guard Apollo's shrine there.

Apollo was the golden child of the Greek pantheon, gifted in music, mathematics, medicine, and prophecy. But at first he wandered all over Greece in search of a holy place upon which to found his shrine. At last he came to the spot we now call Delphi, but found it guarded by a giant serpent, the Python. Apollo did battle with the serpent, slew it, and set up his shrine. Here the priestess known as the Pythoness later had her seat, and people from all stations in life came from throughout the ancient world to ask questions of the Delphic Oracle. The Pythoness chewed sacred laurel leaves, breathed the fumes arising from a fissure in the earth, and prophesied. Whatever message the oracle had decreed was considered to be immutable law. No one could question it or argue with it. Thus Apollo, while not directly dictating the messages, became associated with the laws that were handed down from Delphi. Two messages inscribed upon the temple gates at Delphi were "Know Thyself" and "Nothing in Excess." The first axiom clearly resonates with the astrological concept of the Sun, since this luminary is usually regarded as representing the "true self" of an individual. Most people's introduction to astrology, and to the deeper aspects motivating their personalities, is via information represented by the Sun's position in the horoscope. But what about "Nothing in Excess?" This axiom, too, describes a solar function, but one which involves a much deeper examination of myth.

Legends which describe a god in combat with a mythic serpent or dragon such as the Python are widespread. Some feminist scholars have seen these myths as emblematic of sacred history. The god, they tell us, represents the deity of invading patriarchal tribes, while the serpent represents the Great Mother, who was overcome and driven underground by the new, more warlike religions.[2] But the same myth is found, in almost precisely the same form, among Semites as well as Indo-Europeans—all over the ancient world. In India the god Indra slays the dragon Vritra; Norse Thor fights the Midgard Serpent; in Greece again, Zeus battles a primordial dragon called Typhon; the Babylonian creation epic records Marduk's battle with the sea serpent Tiamat and the Old Testament preserves fragments of an ancient myth in which Yahweh does battle with yet another primordial sea serpent, the Leviathan. Obviously, this dragon-slaying myth is common to all Indo-European peoples as well as among the Jews and Babylonians who fell within the same cultural orbit. It is true that in the Near East the primordial serpent is described as feminine, and we may suspect that in this region the myth did indeed become a metaphor for the conquest of the matriarchy. But its universality suggests that there is yet a deeper, psycho-spiritual meaning behind it.

A detail from "The Delphic Pythia Enrapt," a nineteenth-century engraving

A nineteenth-century wood engraving of Apollo Belvedere with serpent, bow, and arrows

Erich Neumann, in his well-known book, *The Origins and History of Consciousness*, advanced a Jungian interpretation of these dragon-slaying myths.[3] The primal serpent or dragon represents the collective unconscious, as is clearly seen by the fact that it dwells under the ocean (or, in the Apollo story, beneath the earth), a universal symbol for the unconscious. Like the Ouroboros serpent of alchemy, the dragon is possessed of *power*, the vital power of life itself. But this power is still without direction or purpose, without focus. The dragon may occasionally be depicted as feminine because feminine consciousness receives impressions and perceptions in an intuitive, psychic manner, rather than by way of conscious judgment (we are talking in very general terms here, without reference to the chosen

Helios, the sun god

perceptive modes of individual men and women). Hence the dragon-slaying god introduces order into chaos and brings the vital power of the collective mind into the light of day by giving it focus and direction.

The Sun has always been symbolic of that directed will or sense of purpose—a strong Sun in a horoscope equals a strong sense of purpose. But the Sun, as the giver of all life, is also that vast, inchoate life-force which lies beneath focused awareness. This is why all sun gods symbolize a *balance* between the unconscious life-force and the will or purpose which directs it. By studying the attributes of the various solar deities, we may learn how the ancients perceived spiritual balance. Apollo may not have been a sun god originally (this deity has a long and convoluted history),[4] but he became one in Classical times, and it is worth considering the arts and gifts he symbolized. He was the god of science, mathematics, and archery, which are functions of *focused* consciousness, but he was also a god of oracles and prophecy, which are a function of that deeper, more mystical awareness lying beneath directed consciousness. As the god of music and medicine, Apollo shows his true nature as the reconciler of opposites—the musician brings order to the holy chaos of pure sound, as the healer brings order to the life-force itself. "Nothing in Excess,"—this philosophy of balance which found expression on the gates of the Delphic Oracle—may equally signify "everything in balance."

Shamash, the Babylonian sun god, is frequently depicted rising between two mountains.[5] These mountains symbolize the boundaries of the world—or, as we would say today, the polarities of consciousness. The Sun reconciles the opposites and serves as the central point or balance between the *yin* and *yang* of life.

In the Ptolemaic astrological system which was practiced in Roman and medieval times, the Sun was regarded as the king of the planets, and the Emperor Aurelian erected temples to Sol Invictus, the "unconquerable Sun."[6] The Sun is traditionally said to rule Leo, sign of the lion, and the lion is the king of beasts. This concept of the Sun survived in alchemy, which retained a mythological world view well into the 17th century. The alchemists illustrated their treatises with fabulous and magical pictures in which the solar force was often depicted as a king, crowned and robed in purple. The alchemical Sun frequently stood as a metaphor for sulphur, a fiery, burning substance. In psychological terms, "sun" or "sulphur" or the "solar lion" meant the vital commanding life-force, the same force which manifests in our daily lives as the ego.[7]

The Sun, therefore, may be equated with the powerful masculine archetype that Robert Bly calls the "inner king."[8] This inner king, which all of us, male and female alike, possess, is admittedly a very complex archetype and cannot be relegated to the Sun alone—Jupiter, for instance, is also an important component of the inner king. But at its most fundamental level, the inner king is another symbol of that sense of individual purpose which makes our decisions for us, which establishes the road upon which we travel. It is not the Self, the symbol of complete wholeness. Though we have found that potential for completion embodied to some degree in the gods Apollo and Shamash, the Sun or inner king is for most of us what it was to the alchemists—the vital force or masculine directive principle. According to the alchemists, the Self only appears when the king unites with the queen in a mystical or sacred marriage—the *mysterium coniunctionis* of Sol and Luna, the Sun and Moon. The emergence of the Self is dependent upon a union of masculine and feminine qualities.[9]

Emblematic representation of the sun as God, from Boschio's Arte Symbolica, *Augsburg, 1702*

During medieval times, and later on in the 18th century, the king was the visible symbol of the solar life-force. Louis XIV of France was thinking mythologically when he called himself "the Sun King." Is it any wonder, then, that kings were regarded as sacred beings? The Egyptian pharaohs and the Merovingian kings of France were believed to be children of the gods, or of God, and Hebrew kings like Saul and David were "anointed ones."

It is obvious that a single individual is not, in fact, a "sacred" being—except in the sense that we are all sacred beings. In our democratic world, we have moved beyond the concept of absolute monarchy which often kept the mass of humanity oppressed or enslaved by the desires and

A detail from a decorated page by Tobias Stimmer from the Biblische Figuren *printed by Thomas Gwarin, Basle, 1576, shows Eve, who may have originally been a sun goddess*

edicts of a single person. But if we have gained something in terms of freedom, we have lost something in terms of clarity—astrologically, we may note that Uranus, planet of freedom and significator of democratic revolutions everywhere, rules the sign opposite Leo (Aquarius), and that solar clarity is in eternal opposition with the chaos of democratic freedom. Robert Bly points out that few of our American leaders, at least during the past half-century, have embodied a truly solar or kingly archetype that we can relate to on a national level. Instead, they have embodied a perverted form of the warrior archetype—Mars raging on the battlefield.[10] Thus we stand bereft, as a nation, of clear or directed purpose.

But even this apparent loss can have its benefits. We are now forced to seek the king within ourselves rather than through patriotic national archetypes. We are forced to pursue our own self-awareness.

Though the inner king is usually regarded as a male archetype—at least in Europe and the Near East, whence our own culture arose—we use the gender term advisedly. There have been sun goddesses in abundance throughout the world's history, notably in Japan and among the Cherokee. Even in our own cultural sphere, we find that the solar force has sometimes been depicted as feminine. The Hittites reverenced a sun goddess called Hebat; her name in Greek would be Hebe, the goddess of youth who served nectar and ambrosia to the gods on Olympus. (Hercules, the archetypal solar hero whose twelve labors are reminiscent of the signs of the zodiac, married Hebe when he became deified.) Hebat or Hebe also appears to be related linguistically to the Hebrew Eve—the "first woman" may have

Phaethon, son of the Sun

originally been a sun goddess. Eve's name is said to mean "the Mother of All Living." Archetypes, after all, are mutable and fluid—the Babylonians regarded the Moon as a god rather than a goddess.

As the symbol of human will or purpose, the Sun is also the mythic hero; the hero's journey, as Joseph Campbell has demonstrated, is nothing less than the journey of human consciousness towards the Self.[11] We have mentioned Hercules: to the Greeks and Romans, this vigorous and powerful character was the quintessential hero. But Hercules was just as chaotic as he was courageous—he gets drunk, starts fights, rages and rants, and so on. Like life itself, he is a force of nature, unconstrained by social traditions or ethical values.

The wild arrogance of Hercules points out the Sun's more unpleasant side. Consider the myth of Phaethon. This illegitimate "son of the Sun" journeyed to the farthest eastern horizon to confront his father, the sun god Helios. He had only one request: he himself wished to drive the chariot of the Sun. His father tried to dissuade him, but Phaethon insisted. Reluctantly, Helios allowed the boy to mount the solar chariot. But driving the horses of the Sun was beyond young Phaethon's skill; the chariot careened wildly through the sky, burning up the earth when it came too close. At last Jupiter, in anger, sent a thunderbolt to slay Phaethon. The meaning of the myth is clear: *too much* will-power and purpose leads us to arrogance, which can have destructive consequences.

Just how destructive these consequences can be is hinted at by another myth. In this Babylonian story, Nergal, the god of the noonday sun, storms into the underworld and overpowers the goddess who rules there. He sets himself up as the lord of the dead, to rule alongside the dark goddess.[12]

Nergal represents the scorching noonday sun that withers and blights the crops. He also represents the planet Mars. He is yet another symbol of the negative solar force, which equals anger, violence, insolence, and rage. Astrologers will note that this story links Mars, the Sun, and Pluto. The Sun is exalted in a sign ruled by Mars (Aries) and Mars shares rulership of another sign (Scorpio) with Pluto.

Yet another solar myth concerns Icarus, the young son of the master craftsman, Daedalus (see Taurus). Both father and son were imprisoned by King Minos of Crete in the labyrinth that Daedalus himself had constructed. To accomplish their escape, Daedalus fashioned two sets of wings out of wax, strapped them to himself and the boy, and gave Icarus a warning that if he flew too close to the sun the wings

The Flight of Daedalus and the Fall of Icarus, engraved by Albrecht Dürer, from Friedrich Riederer's Spiegel der wahren Rhetorik, *Freiburg, 1493*

would melt. Paying little heed to his father, Icarus flew towards the sun, exhilarated by the feelings he was experiencing. As a result he crash-landed in the sea. His more self-controlled father, however, arrived safely in Sicily.

These stories tell us of the consequences of too much Sun, but there is yet another negative aspect of the Sun, and this is when the solar purpose isn't strong enough. Traditionally, the Sun is in "fall" in Libra, which is the symbolic "sunset point" in the astrological *mandala*. Here the individual's will and purpose is submerged by the desire to compromise or harmonize with others. Though the Sun in Libra is typically considered a "weak" Sun, its symbolism points out one thing which the powerful solar ego isn't very good at: *relating*. Apollo may have been the most handsome and accomplished of the gods, but he was a failure at relationships. He never married. He fell in love with the nymph Daphne, but she rejected him, ran away, and was subsequently turned into a tree by Apollo's wrath—the laurel, Apollo's sacred tree, the leaves of which were chewed by the priestess of Delphi. Why should Daphne have been so reluctant to enter into partnership with the most glorious of the gods? The fact is: solar people are almost entirely self-absorbed. The sense of purpose, the goal to be achieved, means everything to them. They don't really have time for relating to others; they're too busy conquering the world. Hercules was another solar hero who failed miserably at relationships until after he died and was taken up to Olympus (as we have seen, he married Hebe, another solar symbol). There is an arrogance and self-interest about excessively solar people—after all, the Sun rules Leo and is exalted in Aries, two signs renowned for their egotism.

In keeping with the actual mechanics of our solar system, it is important to recognize that the planets *do* revolve around the Sun. Most Westerners practice the form of astrology known as geocentric (earth-centered), where, for all practical purposes, the Sun is seen as a body in space orbiting outside of us like the Moon and the other planets. Recently, more attention has been given to heliocentric astrology, where the Sun is placed in the center and the Earth/Moon point is placed in the horoscope 180 degrees away from the Sun. In geocentric astrology, the Sun might not *literally* be the central force, but it is regarded as such for all intents and purposes, and it is important to note the set-up of the other planets in terms of how they feed energy to or receive energy from the Sun. A careful observation of solar aspects is also important to the analysis of one's individual will. For instance, many people born in the 1940s and 1950s with an Aries Sun have the planet Neptune (which occupied Libra during those years) in exact opposition to their Suns and conjunct their Earth positions (see Gaia). While we normally think of an Aries Sun as the primal expression of fire, altogether unimpeded, we must also think of the watery and turbulent depths of Neptune continually affecting such an individual. Of course, there will still be a profound need to express that primal fire, but the unconscious forces symbolized by Neptune must first be handled before the individual can realize his or her solar destiny (see Neptune). The system of aspects, or geometric links from one planet to another, constitutes a large part of the astrological framework, and those planets that link directly to the Sun will have a profound impact upon the individual's ability to reach his or her conscious aim in life. And inasmuch as vitality and life force are symbolic of good health, let us not forget that Apollo was also the god of healing. Harmony between one's outer world and one's solar purpose is perhaps the best available guarantee of good health.

Mercury and the Artisans *by Hans Sebald Behaim (sixteenth-century woodcut)*

MERCURY

CHAPTER THREE

Be Mercury, set feathers to thy heels,
And fly like thought from them to me again.

—*Shakespeare*, King John, IV, II

Mercury, the smallest planet, is also the planet nearest the sun. A symbol of the rational mind, Mercury is intimately linked with our sense of spiritual direction (the Sun). The mind must serve our sense of purpose. Since Mercury is never found more than twenty-eight degrees of longitude away from the sun, the only possible relationship it can establish with that luminary is conjunction—i.e., union. One's intellect may be somewhat detached from one's central purpose if Mercury is at its maximum distance from the sun, but in the case of a close conjunction it can symbolize that the mind and the will are united.

This relationship between mind and will is imaged mythically by the relationship between Mercury and Jupiter, as well as Mercury and the Sun. Jupiter, a symbol of social purpose or relationship with a larger whole, serves to focus one's consciousness—a mythic role which it shares with the Sun. Thus it has become an astrological dictum that Mercury must be the servant of Jupiter—i.e., the intellect must be directed towards a higher purpose.

Jupiter, of course, was Zeus, the king of the gods, and in Babylon this planet was called Marduk. The god Marduk became king of heaven by slaying the sea monster Tiamat, and thereby establishing order in the universe.[1] Marduk, the heavenly king, was the father of the god Nebo (or Nabu), identified with the planet Mercury. Nebo was the scribe of the gods, who wrote down the laws and edicts of Marduk and communicated them to humankind. During the Babylonian New Year's Festival—which was the most important ceremony of the Babylonian calendar and which recreated Marduk's primal battle with chaos—the image of the god Nebo was ceremoniously removed from its shrine in Borsippa and carried to the Temple of Marduk in Babylon.[2] Nebo was symbolically joined with his father. The mind was ceremonially linked with that sense of directed purpose which is represented by the king of the gods. Mercury served Jupiter.

The Babylonian Nebo was a dignified, solemn god. The Babylonians apparently had great respect for the rational intellect and its role in human consciousness. The Egyptian "scribe of the gods" is likewise a formidable figure—Thoth, the ibis-headed god, lord not only of writing but of magic. And why not? It was the business of the shaman or magician to understand the laws of nature by knowing the *secret names of things*. Thus his function was similar to that of the scribe, who also knew the names of all things. In late classical times, (c. 300 BC–300 AD) Hermes, the Greek Mercury, was symbolically united with the Egyptian Thoth, so that Greek-speaking Egyptians of the early Christian centuries came to worship the god Hermes-Thoth—who, like Hermes, was a god of the mind, and, like Thoth, a god of magic. But we must not press this connection between Mercury and Thoth too far, for Thoth was never associated with the *planet* Mercury. Instead, he was considered to be the god of the Moon.

The connection between Hermes and Thoth, or Mercury and the Moon, is, however, not without its mythic significance. Mercury represents the rational intellect, and the Moon represents instinctual memory. In India, the Moon is the god Chandra, and Mercury, whose name is Budha (*not* Buddha), is the son of the moon god. The Hindus believe that whenever these two, father and son, are united, there is a union between mind (Mercury) and memory (the Moon)—and memory,

Thoth, from a tomb painting at Thebes

in Hindu thought, is merely another aspect of mind. Thus, when the two planets are found in conjunction, a splendid intellect is said to result, for the native has an innate ability to remember (Moon) everything he or she learns (Mercury).[3] When the Moon is in conjunction with Mercury, Hermes and Thoth are truly united, and the astrologer should suspect a sparkling intellect in the client. And as we shall see, Mercury was given rulership over the sign Cancer in the ancient system of Olympian rulerships, a sign that present-day astrologers connect with the Moon.

Though Nebo and Thoth represent the dignified and purposeful aspect of the intellect, there is a devious and playful—and sometimes downright dangerous—side to the mind as well. The Greeks recognized this duality of the mind, for their god Hermes is the god of thieves as well as of communication.

Hermes was a child of Zeus and his mother was the nymph Maia. According

Thoth, illustrated by Diane Smirnow

to the Greek scholar Karl Kerenyi, Maia was once a goddess in her own right, and was linked with the Pleiades.[4] (There is another fascinating link here, for in the sidereal zodiac of India, the Pleiades lie at 3 degrees of Taurus, and this is the exaltation degree of the Moon—which, as we have seen, is intimately connected with Mercury.)[5] In any event, Hermes was a thief almost from the moment of his birth in a cave atop Mt. Cyllene in Arcadia. As the precocious infant emerged into the light, the first thing he beheld was a tortoise. From the shell of this creature he fashioned the lyre, a musical instrument. Continuing on his way, he stole the cattle of Apollo, and, when found out, was hauled up to Olympus to be judged by Zeus. In the final analysis, Zeus and Apollo were both impressed with this infant's ferocious cleverness. Hermes returned the stolen cattle to the sun god, and gave him the lyre as well. The lyre later became a symbol of Apollo as god of music. Apollo made Hermes the conductor of souls from this world to the next—a divine function which had previously been performed by the sun god.

This story, which comes from the *Homeric Hymns*, reveals a great deal about Mercury. He is a thief and was later called the god of thieves. Why should the god of the mind, and of all literary activity, be a god of thieves? Because the human intellect, in and of itself, is amoral. Its function, which is rational thought, is not necessarily connected to any ethical code. The same mental process which leads one individual to write a book on home repair may be used by a different individual to break locks or defuse a burglar alarm — or swindle millions of dollars from an unsuspecting public through the sale of junk bonds (Mercury was also the patron of merchants). Here again, the relationship between Mercury and Jupiter or the Sun is of vital importance: the mind only becomes a strong force for good when directed by a higher sense of awareness. It is no wonder that the ancients called Mercury a "neutral" planet. It has always been an astrological tradition that a strong but afflicted Mercury will be present in the birth chart of a professional thief. Another theme in this Homeric hymn is Mercury's youthfulness. All the actions of Hermes, whether inventive (the lyre) or felonious (stealing the cattle) are performed by an infant, and in medieval astrological works Mercury was a significator of "young people," especially in horary astrology. People with a strong Mercury, or an emphasis on Gemini or the Third House (though not necessarily on Virgo or the Sixth House) often seem to be "Peter Pans." They have the suave, glittering charm of Mercury, but they are not quite "grown up." This youthful quality may mark a highly creative person or a completely undeveloped individual — sometimes both. Jungian analysts call this personality type the *puer aeternus*, the "eternal boy."[6] Possessing all the charm of children, these people float through life without any noticeable purpose, specializing in Don Juan-style love affairs and talking endlessly of the marvelous creative things they will do someday. The female correspondence to this personality type is the *puella aeterna*, who lives for love, cherishes her own physical beauty above all things, and goes through men in record time.[7] She is gen-

erally a stimulating personality, with the usual Mercurial charm, and she may truly inspire the men she loves — and through whom she lives vicariously. But there is an emptiness to her, something insubstantial in her inability to commit. It should be noted, however, that these *puers* and *puellas* may sometimes stop talking about the great achievements in their future and actually get to work making something happen. When they do this, they may become the great artists and writers of this world — and indeed, most artistic individuals have more than a little bit of the *puer* or *puella* in them. After all, it was the infant Hermes who invented the lyre.

Mercury with his healing rod, the caduceus, and his winged helmet, about to take flight

There are other factors which go into the creation of the *puer* or *puella*. In addition to the Mercurial factors we have cited, the astrologer should look for a relationship between this planet and the

Mercury as messenger of the gods, illustrated by Gustave Doré

Sun, Moon, or Saturn, because the Peter Pan syndrome always implies some parental difficulty. Liz Greene believes that we should also look for a strong Uranus, and this makes a great deal of sense. Uranus is the archetype of the inventor, the bohemian, the rebellious spirit—and it is also, according to esoteric astrology, the "higher octave" of Mercury. There is, indeed, a strong link between these two planets, and any aspect or relationship between the two is extremely important in a birth chart, especially as regards the individual's attitude towards traditional patterns of thought. The Mercury-Uranus type is excited by state-of-the-art technology and seeks to forge new pathways of thought, having shattered all barriers to mental growth.

Another theme of the *Homeric Hymn to Hermes* is the inter-relationship between Apollo and Hermes, i.e., between the Sun and Mercury. Again, we find that the intellect must be linked with a sense of direction or will. One of the rules of horary astrology, established long ago, is that when Mercury lies within one degree of the Sun, it is said to be "combust"—burned out by the intense solar radiation. However, in an individual's birth chart, this situation often produces precisely the opposite effect—the conscious will (Sun) and the rational mind (Mercury) become united in an extremely intense and highly focused way. If the Sun and Mercury are in this type of configuration, one must examine the sign and house placement to determine what the precise focus is, and next examine the aspect patterns from other planets in order to determine whether the individual is supported in achieving his or her aim.

Mercury possessed the caduceus, or healing rod, and we are reminded of his role in the healing process, the medical "arts"—though today art has been replaced with science altogether. Certainly, modern medical science gives us incredible information about the human body and its functions, but its total reliance on intrusive technology and external remedies applied while the patient is numbed, medicated, and totally excluded from the proceedings serves to remove the individual from his or her own healing process. This is counter to how that process actually works, thus further severing the connection and producing a greater duality between patient and healer. This is reminiscent of the relationship we spoke of earlier, that between the Sun and Mercury in a birth chart. If Mercury (the mind) exists in complete isolation from the Sun (conscious will) and in turn from the Earth (physical body), the wholeness of the individual begins to break down. When this fragmentation occurs, and when we are no longer empowered and irradiated by our internal fire or life-giving qualities, our immune systems become weakened and we are unable to resist invading armies. This disintegration of mind, will, and body is what produces disease as we know it. Similarly, it is the *union* of these three aspects of consciousness that unites and heals the disease. More than one healer has emphasized the relationship between the body and mind in assisting the healing process. An emerging field in the healing arts today known as psycho-neuro-immunology is precisely this, and is based upon the premise that the organism's thought-system contains within it the same ability to resist or combat disease as it did to accept it in the first place. The mind is a powerful thing and, when turned against the will or the body as a result of past or current abuses inflicted upon the individual, it further fragments the individual's internal defenses and induces the spread of infection or disease.

The Egyptians saw Mercury as Thoth—transporter of souls. The Greeks and Romans saw him as Hermes and Mercury—the messenger of the gods. Certainly, movement and travel have been a large part of the Mercury archetype and remain so today in astrology. The fact that Mercury is also the closest planet to the Sun and thus completes its revolution most speedily (88 days) has also contributed to the "here today, gone tomorrow" attribute we associate with this planet. The ancients rarely saw Mercury in the sky, and when they did it was for scant precious time, a fact which has also contributed to the perception of this deity as hidden or unreliable. Since Mercury can never be more than twenty-eight degrees from the sun, it is only when it is farthest from the sun that it can be seen for short periods just before or after sunset.

A printer's ornament depicting Mercury and his association with travel

Though we regard Mercury, Mercury-related objects, and thought in general as "mercurial" or speedy, it is not always so. When Mercury is traveling at its fastest rate, it moves in excess of three degrees per day (three times faster than the sun), but when it is traveling at its slowest, it is hardly moving at all. This phenomenon, known as a station, occurs just before and after a planet goes retrograde—that is, before it appears to move backwards in its orbit, due to our earth-centered perception of its slow rate of speed. Astrologers have always looked at the speed of Mercury to determine the quickness or agility of a person's mind or thought patterns. The slow-moving, stationary, or retrograde Mercury describes individuals who take time to answer or come up with solutions to problems, working things out carefully before committing themselves. Those with a fast-moving Mercury are quick to answer and possess minds that move at break-neck speeds, way out in front of everyone else, able to complete your sentences for you before you even know what you're going to say. This process also has to do with the distance between Mercury, the sun and the earth. Because when the Sun/Earth polarity (see Gaia) is united with Mercury by sign, house, or close degree, there is a better relationship between mind and body, producing a mind that is more grounded, more carefully guided to produce its answers.

Hermes, or Mercury

When Mercury is distanced from the will and body (Sun/Earth), it operates on a whole different plane (i.e., people who have "minds of their own"), and though the mind may be brilliant, it may take more work to integrate that mind with the rest of the system. And even though all planets but the Sun and Moon will go retrograde for a period of time, it is Mercury's retrogradation, three times a year for approximately three weeks at a time, that has earned a reputation as the time when everything goes crazy. If Mercury is indeed the messenger, the traveler, the connector of one world to the next, the mover of information and commerce, then its stationary or retrograde motion will seem to affect all these operations—especially today, in a world where computers, air travel, fax machines, telephones, ticker-tape, wire services and the like are what really seem to keep the world operating smoothly. While Mercury is not really *responsible* for the break-down of these operations, there is a widespread notion that these breakdowns most often happen when Mercury is retrograde.

In the body, Mercury rules the nervous system and lungs. The breathing apparatus is an integral part of Mercury's process, because if *prana* or breath is the link to the life force, then Mercury's relationship to the Sun is a key to how well one expresses one's will and purpose. For instance, a person with a Pisces Sun and Mercury in Aries might have a mind which rushes into new areas, forges new roads, and goes out on a limb for risky notions before the Pisces Sun will be even vaguely aware of what is taking place, or while it is still too fearful to act upon these new ideas. This type of individual may say yes to the adventurer and explorer within (Mercury in Aries) while his or her Piscean sense of purpose is still getting used to the fact that it has to take action at all! A solution to this dilemma can be seen by the progressed aspects of the Sun. At some point in one's life, the Sun will progress to a conjunction with Mercury or Mercury to the Sun, and at such times a more unified field of consciousness can arise.

We have already observed that Mercury operates in *relationship* to its surroundings, stimulated by sign and house, or by aspects from other planets. Not that Mercury doesn't act on its own—but seldom if ever does any planet operate purely independently. Perhaps if a planet were totally unaspected and in its own house and sign it would operate almost like a "pure" archetype, but it would still be somewhat conditioned by its surroundings, just as a child may think and act for himself but also quickly learns that the more he acts in accordance with "acceptable" or "normal" behavior, the less he will be cruelly mocked by other children. A good example of this is the character Data on *Star Trek: The Next Generation*. Data is not human; he is an android. Like an almost-pure Mercury, Data can perform thousands of calculations per second and is rarely, if ever, in error. However, he lacks human feelings (Moon), and strives toward developing some emotion in order to be more like his human brothers and sisters. Data doesn't need emotions; he works perfectly well without them—but he is colored by his environment in such a way that he *thinks* he needs them in order to fit in with his crewmates. Mercury also strives to think and behave in accordance with its aspects to other planets, its brothers and sisters. Whatever Mercury is "plugged into" is what drives it to action. The more we are aware of and in control of this process, the more we can consciously reach our desired destination without too many detours or mechanical failures.

But there is a more subtle, metaphysical aspect to Mercury which is too often ignored. Note that Apollo made Hermes the psychopomp, the conductor of souls between this world and the next. The god Hermes could move freely between the underworld, the earth, and Mt. Olympus. No other deity could come and go from the underworld as Hermes could—once one entered the realm of Hades, there one remained, unless one had been granted special dispensation from Hades himself. Thus it is with the human mind and its capacity to "travel" anywhere, its limits being entirely of its own making.

A Gnostic emblem showing Hermes leading the Soul

In medieval times, Mercury was also known as Mercurius, the god of the alchemists (see Virgo). Mercurius is "the alchemical androgyne,"[8] and there is an astrological tradition that the planet Mercury is androgynous, neither male nor female, but both. In Greek myth, the union of Hermes and Aphrodite produced the being known as the hermaphrodite, who was both male and female. In

Tantric Yoga, a unified field of consciousness is attained by awakening the kundalini energy, which, traveling up the central column associated with the spine, dissolves the two channels of male and female polarity which are entwined around that column. This image of psychic channels wound around a central column is reminiscent of the caduceus, the rod entwined with serpents which was in the possession of Hermes and which has become the icon of the healing professions. The dissolution of male and female polarities reminds us that in alchemy it was the death of the mythical king and queen at the moment of sexual union which produced the alchemical androgyne, the unified field of consciousness which arises when polarities cease to exist.[9]

It is the refined intellect, the mind transformed from cognizer to consciousness, which leads the soul from one realm to the next. The mind itself is beyond polarities—it is neither male nor female, good nor evil, *yin* nor *yang*. The purely rational or analytical aspect of mind may have a very masculine character, it is true, for the left and right hemispheres of the brain are said to have a male (left) and female (right) quality. But the entire spectrum of mind is a different creature altogether: it is the instrument which leads us to alchemical transmutation, and to true unity.

In some Tarot decks, the Magician card is depicted as Hermes or Thoth. He stands above the symbols of the four elements which represent the four functions of the human psyche—intuition, feeling, thinking, and sensation. Mercury, the alchemist, has the ability to unite the elements into a single whole.

A nineteenth-century engraving of the Venus de Milo after the original in the Louvre, Paris, France

VENUS

CHAPTER FOUR

*... When his love he doth espy,
Let her shine as gloriously
As Venus of the sky.*

—*Shakespeare,* A Midsummer-Night's Dream, III, II

In the beginning the world was ruled by Uranus, the Sky Father, and Gaia, the Earth Mother, the primordial pair. Uranus became a tyrant and was overthrown by his son Saturn (Cronus), who lay in wait for his father then leapt up and castrated him with a sickle. The creative seed of the primal sky god was scattered throughout heaven and earth. Some of it fell into the ocean and gave birth to Venus, whom the Greeks knew as Aphrodite, the goddess of love. She rose full-grown from the sea-foam, billowed up by the waves and riding on a sea shell. When she stepped ashore on the island of Cyprus, grass and flowers sprang up at her feet, and the Seasons, daughters of Themis, clothed her nakedness.

The poet Hesiod tells the story of Aphrodite's birth in the *Theogony,*[1] and the Renaissance painter Botticelli created a *Birth of Venus* which stands as one of the most famous works of art in the

Western world. Venus was always one of the most popular of all goddesses, worshipped throughout the ancient Mediterranean. Even in medieval Europe, when Christianity had officially banished the ancient gods and goddesses, she lived on in the poetry of the Troubadours and wandering scholars.

She enjoyed a variety of names and titles. The name Aphrodite itself means "born from the sea-foam." Often, she was known as Aphrodite Anadyomene, the "foam-born one emerging from the sea."[2] Her bird was the dove, known for its lascivious nature; her tree was the myrtle; and her sacred place was the island of Cyprus. She was called "the golden," and the classical poets imagined her as appearing to her lovers bathed in a golden light. She was "smiling Aphrodite" as well, the bringer of all delights, all sensual joys.

The planet Venus is said to be exalted in Pisces, and Pisces is a symbol of the great ocean. In classical Greece, many of the names of this goddess were associated with the sea. She was born from the sea-foam and she emerged from the waves. The cockle-shell was one of her symbols, and she was sometimes called Aphrodite Pelagia, "she of the ocean." Sea gods and goddesses are usually shape-shifters, like old Proteus in the *Odyssey*, and in Sparta the goddess of love was called Aphrodite Morpho, "she of the various shapes."[3]

The shape-shifting goddess of Sparta was often depicted as bound in chains. This talent for metamorphosis combined with the imagery of chains suggests that she was a form of the primordial Great Goddess. Robert Graves has attempted to reconstruct the myth which the Pelasgians (sea people), the neolithic or pre-Hellenic inhabitants of Greece, must have told about her.

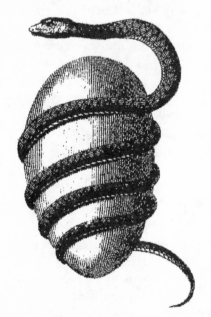

According to Graves, the goddess was worshipped by the name Eurynome, which means the "wide-wandering one" (i.e., the Moon). Born from primal Chaos, she danced upon the ocean waters, as Venus later rose dancing from the waves. Eurynome transformed the north wind into a serpent, called Ophion. The serpent coiled around her—hence the image of the goddess in chains. He impregnated her and she gave birth to the cosmic egg. Ophion wrapped himself seven times round the egg, until it split in two and hatched out all creation.[4]

This reconstruction of the primal creation myth is not pure speculation; archaeologist Marija Gimbutas finds evidence of a similar myth among the neolithic cultures of Balkan Europe.[5] The symbols which make up this ancient story survived, in some form, until com-

Ophion wrapping himself around the egg born of Eurynome

A nineteenth-century drawing by Paquier from a photograph of the Borghese Venus

paratively recent times. In the figure of the "lady soul" or *anima mundi* (see The Fixed Signs) who dances encircled by a wreath on the World card of the Tarot we may recognize Eurynome dancing on the waves, encircled by Ophion. And the alchemical symbol of the Ouroboros, the serpent biting its own tale, is reminiscent of Ophion wrapped around the cosmic egg—especially since the alchemists also regarded the egg as a symbol of original unity. In the Old Testament, the primal serpent may be both the tempter and, in Kabbalistic thought, the redeemer. Ophion wrapped himself seven times around the cosmic egg, and the number seven is as important in the *Book of Revelations* as it is in older pagan mythologies.

Psychologically, we may say that the desire for love, sex, and relationship is one of the first human functions—or perhaps *the* first—to emerge from that ocean of unconsciousness symbolized by Pisces. It is Venus, the goddess of love, who dances on the waters of the collective mind or world soul. She emerges from that ocean still clothed in golden light, smiling with the knowledge of other realms; she is a mediatrix or guide to the deepest layers of the unconscious. It is with that otherworldly glow that she appeared to her lover Anchises. As she approached him in his humble herdsman's hut, she was followed by wolves, lions, bears, leopards, and humming bees. She stood before him, all golden, clothed in red and anointed with oil. But if she embodied, for Anchises, all the power of the deep unconscious, she also embodied its treacherous watery underside—she lied to him, telling him she was only a mortal maiden.[6]

As the goddess of love and beauty, Venus quite logically became the planet of relationship, and since she is the traditional ruler of Libra, the marriage sign, this is fitting. But Venus isn't so much the planet of *relationship* as she is the goddess of *love*. It's important to differentiate between these two concepts, because marriage is not always about love. As we shall learn, marriage came under the domain of Juno (Hera).

In examining the mythology of Venus, we find that she was indeed married, but to what extent she acknowledged or honored her marriage is very questionable. We know that she rejected her lame husband, Vulcan (Hephaestus), the god of the forge, in favor of Mars, the god of war, with whom she enjoyed a long love affair and whose children she bore. And yet it seems that Venus' husband Vulcan was himself partly responsible for Venus' infidelities. Vulcan, the skilled artisan and craftsman, was married to his work, and did not possess much of a capacity for intimacy or relationship—something that a Venus needs.[7] On the other hand, Venus was adored by her lover Mars, though they experienced much turbulence in their relationship together. One of the best known stories involving Mars and Venus concerns the response of Vulcan when he learned that his wife was involved in a love affair with the god of war. It was Vulcan's fate always to be betrayed by his beautiful wife, but this time he was angry. He forged chains of gold, which he cunningly hid in the rafters of his palace on Olympus. Then he told Venus he would be taking a vacation to his sacred island of Lemnos.

A nineteenth-century drawing after the Venus of Cnidos

As Vulcan had anticipated, Venus invited Mars to join her in the palace. But Vulcan was hiding nearby; just as Mars and Venus were in the clinch, down came the magic net and trapped them in bed. Angrily, Vulcan called upon all the deities of Mt. Olympus to witness his wife's shame. The goddesses—who quite naturally supported the woman's point of view—refused to have any part in the affair, but the gods went to gawk. Mercury told Apollo that he would gladly change places with Mars—anything to get the goddess of love into bed. (Mercury had his chance later on; the

*The Soul of the World combines the symbolism of the goddess in chains and the goddess upon
the waves, from Robert Fludd's* Utriusque Cosmi Historia, *Oppenheim, 1617*

result was the hermaphrodite, a creature with both male and female organs.) Finally, at the insistence of Neptune, Mars and Venus were released from the chains of love.[8]

It is these two planets, Venus and Mars, that many astrologers still use to assess an individual's relationship needs in chart analysis. However, it should be noted that the love affair between Mars and Venus has nothing to do with stability or commitment—it is, in fact, an extra-marital relationship. The relationship between the two planets shows sexual or romantic attraction, certainly. It may, in fact, indicate a wild or ungovernable passion, and in India it is said that people with a conjunction of Mars and Venus in the birth chart are passionate and sensual to a fault. But Mars and Venus alone do not indicate the kind of long-term compatibility that is necessary for a marriage. The traditional factors which establish that kind of long-term union are the Sun and Moon, and the interaction between the horizon lines of the partners. As we shall see, the asteroid Juno is also very helpful in assessing relationship needs. Venus is interested only in the romance, the glory, and the passion of the moment. But certainly if Venus and Mars are interactive between two charts, it will add a spicy love life to whatever else the pair has going for it.

Venus rules Taurus and Libra, and in classical Greece she ruled Taurus in the ancient Olympian system as well. As the goddess of that sign she exudes raw sensuality, representing the aspect of the goddess whose sole purpose it is to enjoy the abundant earthiness of the physical world represented by nature and the body. Thus the goddess was sometimes known as Aphrodite Pandemos, patroness of "common love." Prostitutes worshipped her as one of themselves under the name Aphrodite Porne or Aphrodite Hetaira; she was even known occasionally as Aphrodite Kallipygos, "she of the beautiful buttocks."[9]

In Libra, however, she is more concerned with the interplay of opposites that exists in relationships. Venus is a docile and lovely goddess attracted to relationships with men of the wild—warriors and hunters such as Ares, god of war, and Adonis, the hunter of wild beasts. Polarities of this type are frequently encountered in Libra, the astrological significator of relationship. It is in Libra that these opposites are met and brought into harmony. Opposite elements are often at work in relationships, the first and foremost being that we are typically dealing with male and female counterparts. We are often magnetized by precisely those qualities that we ourselves lack, and we choose to incorporate those absent qualities into ourselves by becoming immersed in them through the medium of a partner who embodies them. Unfortunately, all too many individuals forget why they chose such a partner, and quickly attempt to transform him or her into an exact clone of themselves. Wildly differing temperaments, economic backgrounds, religious beliefs, and so on are often at work in these partnerships. Venus' role here is that of harmonizer, bringing opposites together in some workable fashion. The ability to "tame" these wild elements (a Mars or an Adonis) through the act of love-making (Venus) is another aspect of this polarity relationship. And finally, the introduction of strife and turbulence in love is characteristic of many relationships, and may serve as a commentary on the nature of love itself.

As astrological ruler of both Taurus and Libra, Venus embodies two other principles in the horoscope—self-worth in Taurus (what "I" alone possess) and how much value others place on that worth in Libra (do I please you, what do you think of me?).

Venus *is* beautiful and lovely, easily the most beautiful of the goddesses, but that isn't enough. She has to be constantly validated by others to know that this is so. When other beautiful women were lurking nearby, she was easily threatened by their appearance and presence, and at those times she revealed her jealous, angry side. Psyche was condemned to death by Aphrodite, whose personal dignity was insulted when mortals began speaking of a woman whose beauty rivaled that of the goddess of love herself. This is often the sad story of a woman— or man, for that matter—with a strongly placed Venus in her or his chart. For years such a person may be the golden child, the beautiful one that everyone else needs only to gaze upon to fall in love with. Then, when the Venusian begins to age and to see that beauty is ephemeral, she or he begins to "lose it." This is similar to the Snow White story with its clas-

Aphrodite, after the original in the Capitol at Rome

sic refrain, "Mirror, mirror on the wall, who's the fairest of them all?" (The glyph for Venus, it has been suggested, resembles a hand-mirror.) One day the mirror began to answer the aging queen, "It is Snow White." Outraged, the queen condemned Snow White to death, for she could not tolerate another in the kingdom more beautiful than herself. Snow White was saved from imminent death by the handsome young prince, the symbolic son of the queen, just as Psyche was rescued from death by Aphrodite's son, Eros. Both sons married the maidens they rescued and we are led to believe that they lived happily ever after. These two stories—one a Greek myth, the other a fairytale—closely resemble each other. It is a story that has been lived out through the ages, and one that continues to threaten those who

Personification of Venus from an engraving by Lucas Cranach the Elder, Wittenberg, 1506

get old and lose what they have always deemed their worth—their beauty and youth. (The beauty industry, a multi-billion dollar per year concern, attests to this.) The story also reflects the son's abandonment of the mother as his most loved and adored feminine relationship, and the transference of that adoration onto his new young bride.

Generally, then, Venus is that factor in the horoscope that addresses issues of self-worth and how that self-worth holds up or interacts in relationships. Venus had the power to make anyone, god or mortal, fall in love instantly. Thus we can analyze what makes people fall in love by observing their Venus positions, and also what kind of validation they need from others to bring about their own inner love. Recalling her love life on Olympus, we can see that Venus was not the most faithful or obedient of lovers. She delighted in her many sexual exploits and, as goddess of love, enjoyed the *act* of falling in love rather than the *task* of contributing to the maintenance of a relationship once the initial spark had dimmed. Such impatience is often the case for a Venus in Aries, Gemini, Sagittarius, or Aquarius. It is the beginning, when love is fresh and lively, that Aphrodite finds so exhilarating, not love as duty and certainly not the ethic which demands that one should "love, honor and obey till death do us part"—that is Juno's domain. Which is again why, when using Venus as the sole or primary point of comparison in relationship or marriage analysis, the result can be disappointment or separation. Because in the beginning, when the relationship is fresh and new, one experiences Venus' best input. But, as time goes by, Venus needs to be assured that the object of her or his desire is still stimulating and exciting.

It has often been said that Venus represents a woman's image of herself (the hand-mirror), while to a man Venus, a feminine archetype, is something which is typically projected onto the women he encounters. While not always true, this reflects how *most* individuals operate, particularly in adolescent romances which occur before one has reached the level of maturity or self-awareness that brings a person to a more balanced inner center.

We might find someone with Venus in Leo or Venus in the First House looking in the mirror quite often and asking the question "Am I still the most beautiful?"— and working very hard throughout life to ensure that the mirror is still answering affirmatively. Venus in Virgo or Venus conjunct Saturn may also frequently examine the mirror, but these are the women one often encounters in public restrooms who look in the mirror and tell themselves how fat or ugly they look, though to an observer there is nothing fat or ugly about them. This kind of self-criticism and/or perfection-seeking affects the type of relationship one draws to oneself—i.e., the partner will continually reinforce the Saturn/Venus or Venus in Virgo's negative self-image. Thus, even if a man were to come along and tell such a woman how lovely she is, she would have difficulty believing it, and her rejection of him and his attitude would mirror her own self-rejection. If we examine the Vulcan/Venus relationship, we may note that Vulcan was rejected in childhood, not once but twice, by both parents, and thus he came to feel and believe in his own inadequacies. When the goddess of love and beauty came along, something in his inner make-up could not allow her into his life. Inside him was the shame inflicted upon him by his family situation and which he carried throughout life. Ultimately he was able to transform his shame by pouring intense amounts of energy into his work and creating beautiful objects, worthy of the goddess of love and beauty—and reflecting the beauty that was truly within him.[10] Such is often the case when Venus in the chart makes strong natal contacts to Pluto, Saturn, or Neptune. The beauty and love is truly within, but buried under layers and layers of shame, guilt, insecurity, doubt and fear. It only comes forth slowly, bit by bit through one's life when one has made the conscious decision to go down and rescue it. Perhaps it is a concept tossed around too frequently these days that we cannot receive love from another until we truly love ourselves, but there is truth in this statement, and the astrological examination of the planet Venus in one's chart is the best mirror for this truth.

Another important story which concerns the goddess of love is that of Venus and Adonis. When the wife of King Cinyras of Cyprus bragged that her daughter Smyrna was more beautiful than Venus, the goddess took her revenge. She put a spell on Smyrna, who fell in love with her father, climbed into his bed while he was in a drunken stupor, and became pregnant by him. When Cinyras discovered what had happened, he pursued Smyrna with a sword. Venus transformed the girl into a myrrh tree; the sword split the tree and out tumbled the child Adonis.

Aphrodite—Venus

Adonis was brought up by Persephone, the Queen of the Dead, who soon fell in love with him. This provoked an argument between Persephone and Venus, both of whom now desired the young man. The matter was given over for judgment to the Muses, who decreed that Adonis would spend a third of the year with Venus, a third with Persephone, and a third by himself, hunting on the hilltops.

But Venus was a greedy goddess, and she used the arts of love to make sure that Adonis would disregard the sacred agreement and spend all his time with her. This made Persephone furious. She told Mars, Venus' lover, that he had a serious rival in Adonis. Mars transformed himself into a boar; he challenged the young hunter on the slopes of Mount Lebanon and gored him to death while Venus watched. Anemones sprang from his blood. Venus was still unwilling to relinquish Adonis to the Queen of Hades. She appealed to Jupiter, who granted Adonis equal time above and below the earth.

This story is similar to that of Persephone herself (see Ceres). It is also similar to the Babylonian myth of Ishtar's Descent, which was originally a Sumerian tale, and hence one of the oldest stories in the world. We shall deal with this story at more length later on (see Pluto), but the bare outlines are as follows:

The goddess Ishtar, Queen of Love, descends into the underworld to seek the soul of her dead lover Tammuz. On the way, she is ritually stripped of all her glory by the guardians of Hell. When she at last confronts the Queen of the Dead, she is hung on a meat-hook, as if she herself had been slain. Rescued at last by the will of the gods, she is restored to glory, this time as the Queen of Heaven.

The myth has a great deal to do with the cycle of the planet Venus. When that planet is still running *ahead* of the sun (i.e., when it is in an earlier degree of zodiacal longitude), it will appear in the sky as the Morning Star. Then, as it approaches superior conjunction with the sun, it will be invisible for a time—the goddess will descend into the underworld. Finally, the planet will reappear as the Evening Star, the Queen of Heaven, occupying a later degree of zodiacal longitude than the sun.

The myth of Venus and Adonis, or Ishtar's Descent, is important because it points to a psychological process of relationship. The goddess of love, when still untamed, is primal, sexual, and instinctual. As we have seen, she is more concerned with *love* than *relationship*. Dane Rudhyar theorized that individuals born with Venus as the Morning Star tend to be more impulsive in their relationships; they fall in love quickly and without a great deal of reflection. But after the goddess has served her time in the underworld, she becomes the Queen of Heaven rather than simply the goddess of love. There is a greater maturity in her gift of love, a greater concern with relationship as opposed to pure romance. Those born with Venus as the Evening Star may not always have more successful relationships, but they are more reflective, more cautious, and their attitude towards relationship brings Venus a bit closer to Juno. They also seem to be aware of love as a deeply transformative process.

The story of Ishtar's Descent, as we shall see, applies to all aspects of human consciousness—not just love. But in terms of relationship, this ancient drama implies that we must suffer through a period of painful growth before our primal instinct for love can be transformed into compassionate relating. After all, Venus is exalted in Pisces.

The cult of Isis, one of the personifications of the Great Mother, was widespread throughout western Asia and Europe and finally merged with early Christianity. Many of Mary's attributes were borrowed from Isis. Isis is shown here on a page from Athanasius Kircher's Oedipus Aegyptiacus, Rome, 1652

GAIA (EARTH)

CHAPTER FIVE

*I shall sing of well-formed Earth, mother of all
and oldest of all, who nourishes all things living on land.
Her beauty nurtures all creatures that walk upon the land,
and all that move in the deep or fly in the air.*

—*Homeric Hymn,* To Earth, Mother of All

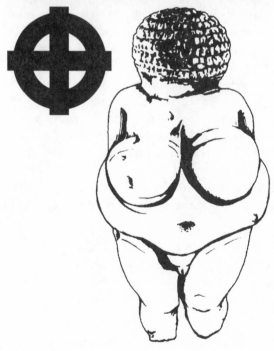

The earliest stories of creation in Greek myth tell of how Gaia was created out of the void. Gaia is *earth*, Mother Earth. Gaia was fruitful and gave birth to the mountains, the sea, and the sky. The sky god Ouranos (Uranus) became her husband and they became parents of the Titans, a pre-Olympian race who ruled Greece in the early days. These Titans were much more primitive than their descendants, but among them was one named Cronus (Saturn) who would eventually succeed his father. As we have seen, Ouranos had become a tyrant. He terrorized the Cyclopes, monstrous offspring of his union with Gaia. The Earth Mother could not bear to see her children abused in such a way and implored Cronus to help her put a stop to Ouranos' tyranny. Cronus, armed with a sickle, cut off Ouranos' genitals and tossed them in the sea, thus removing any further generative power from

Cronus devouring his children

Ouranos. He was cheered by his brothers and sisters and became the new ruler. Cronus slipped easily into rulership and ruled, many say, for a thousand years, marrying his sister Rhea. One day it was prophesied that Cronus would be overthrown by one of his own offspring just as he had overthrown his father before him. Gripped with fear, and to prevent this occurrence, he began to swallow every child born to him by Rhea. Rhea, like Gaia, was outraged that her children were being taken from her and, also like Gaia, devised a plan through which she could put an end to this misery. When Zeus (Jupiter) was born, he was quickly whisked away to a cave on Mt. Ida, and replaced by a rock. When presented with the newborn in his blankets, Cronus quickly swallowed it, unaware that it was a stone and not a baby. Zeus was raised in peace and prosperity and eventually overthrew Cronus. The same prophecy was eventually given to Zeus that a son he would father would someday overthrow him in his turn.

This lineage of fathers overtaken by their sons is a basic model of civilization as it has existed on earth for thousands of years. One dynasty or nation rules—perhaps for centuries—until the tides change and new rulers invade and a new order takes over. Usually it happens by means of war—who has the most weapons, the biggest armies, the largest treasuries, i.e., the most power. And the beat goes on.

But what if Gaia, the Earth, were to rise up again and say to her children, as she did to the Cyclopes, "I'm tired of seeing the way you're being treated, my children.

Can you please help me do something about this?" This is precisely what she has been saying for the past twenty-five years, in these closing years of the millennium which precede the Age of Aquarius, or, as some have prophesied, the two thousand years of peace.

Let's not forget that Gaia and Ouranos (Earth Mother and Sky Father) were originally partners. Uranus is the planet we associate with Aquarius—and Gaia has recently sprung back to life, fueled by the theory known as the Gaia Hypothesis. This hypothesis, developed by biologist James Lovelock, maintains that our planet is a living, breathing organism, and that each individual act upon the earth is linked to and has direct consequences for every other part of the planet.[1] This biologist, one of Gaia's children, speaks in her behalf to her other children of the need for their own preservation. Interestingly enough, the physical sciences are ruled by Saturn (biologists like Lovelock), who are sons of our industrial world (Uranus). It was the birth of the Industrial Revolution which coincided with the discovery of the planet Uranus (1781) and which led us into the age of technology and industry which has characterized our life on earth for these past two hundred years. While it has given us some tremendous breakthroughs in medicine, food production, communications, and travel, it has also been the culprit which has *caused* so much disease, toxicity, putrefaction of our rivers, streams, oceans, forests, and wildlife. What goes around comes around, and perhaps Saturn (science), the son of Uranus, can once again construct a marvelous plan (short of castration—although severe birth control and zero population growth have been suggested as potential remedies) to save Gaia and her children from extinction so that we may once again enter a Golden Age (see Saturn) and live in peace and health for two thousand years.

Before the Mycenaean Greeks established a system of creation and rulership which reflected their patriarchal social structure, the Great Goddess, in her many emanations, was the chief deity of Anatolia, the Aegean, and Southeastern Europe. She presided over earth, sky, moon, planets, stars, oceans and even the underworld. The Indo-European Greeks and Hittites who entered these regions from 3,000 to 1,000 BC made their compromise with the older faith by ritually "marrying" their masculine deities to the various forms of the Earth Goddess. This overtaking of matriarchal values by patriarchal gods developed slowly in Mycenean times, reached its peak in classical Greece, and by the height of the Roman Empire was even more powerfully in force. The Christian Church which conquered Rome adopted the Judaic concept of God the Father, though the medieval church honored Mary as the Holy Virgin Mother and began to place a great emphasis on the Mother of God about 1,000 AD, when the Piscean Age reached its midpoint and shifted from the Pisces polarity (the Dying Son) to the Virgonian or opposite mode (the Divine Mother).[2] Many Jungians view this Marian cult as simply the most recent incarnation of the goddess worship of old.

In Egypt there was a greater balance between the male and female deities who presided over the kingdom, but the Babylonians were decidedly patriarchal, as evidenced by Nergal's fiery descent to the underworld to usurp the queen's dark realm (see Mars and Pluto). The story of *Genesis* gives us a father-god who cast the blame for the fall of man onto a woman and a serpent, who were mythically linked together in rituals of life, healing, death, and rebirth. Though the older matriarchal concept has always remained intact as a kind of underground stream—the serpent plays the role of redeemer in Gnosticism and the Kabbalah—the ancient goddess, Mother Earth, has been buried deep in that element for which she is named. This is Gaia, the Earth.

We have little information about how the world was governed during the era of the Goddess, and there is still much to learn about this epoch in human history on our planet. Some scholars have assumed that sacred kings representing the son and lover of the Goddess were sacrificed during agricultural festivals, while other historians cite archaeological evidence that weapons which exist only for the sake of killing did not exist, whereas objects depicting an agrarian, peaceful society did.[3] Many objects of neolithic art are round little figurines with full breasts and bellies— pregnant women—celebrating and honoring the miracle of life.[4]

Cernunnos, after an image on the Gundestrup bowl, Gundestrup, Denmark

We, the inhabitants of a patriarchal era, perceive the sky as masculine and the earth as a mother. But the people of the neolithic, worshippers of Mother Earth, might have been just as likely to see the Great Mother in the sky, personified as the Moon. The earliest peoples of Europe recognized a male-female duality as the governing power of the universe. The Great Goddess and the Antlered God were the only true deities. This antlered god survived into Celtic times as Cernunnos, denigrated by Christians as the "witch-god." The important thing about Cernunnos is that he symbolizes oneness with all nature. The Lord of the Woods and Mother Earth are necessary for *grounding*. Gaia is about oneness with all nature. And if there is a sign that honors Gaia in its most glorious form, it would be Taurus, a suggested rulership.

The natural polarity of Uranus, Father Sky, is his mother and lover Gaia, the Earth. Sky and Earth form one of the most basic of all dualities—the *I Ching* begins with Chien, Heaven, and K'un, the Earth. As a sky god, Uranus is naturally concerned with intellectual, cerebral knowledge—hence this planet's connection with scientific invention and technology. But Uranus is also a planet of inspiration. Even scientists rely on that magical moment when an idea simply *emerges*, without any logic to support it. Uranus can only bring this kind of inspiration when it is deeply linked to an intuitive, feminine polarity. Science cannot function properly without feeling-values to control it. Without Gaia, the much heralded Aquarian Age, ruled by Uranus, could become a cold, cerebral exercise in technology, portrayed in many futuristic films as a world focused in a treeless, natureless laboratory. We are already too aware of this possibility; it looms like an unpleasant specter over the future of humanity. Is it any wonder, then, that the Gaia Hypothesis has emerged *now*, when we have such great need of it? Only through a consciousness of Gaia can Aquarian science heal, rather than destroy, the planet. From a mythic perspective, Gaia is the natural (and necessary) feminine pole of the coming age.

Earth plaque from the Max Adler Planetarium, Chicago, Illinois. Photograph by Ariel Guttman

It seems that the move is on to bring life on earth back into balance, but, as with the birth of any new order, there is always some last minute resistance—a final attempt to hang onto old concepts. It is not about going back to the way things were. We've certainly come too far for that. It's not about women having sovereignty over men, or men being supreme rulers of women. Gaia created *with* Ouranos, and Hopi legends of creation also postulate a creative unity of Earth and Sky. That is how regeneration has always occurred on this planet—through male and female in union—although we now have to deal with phenomena such as test-tube babies and we should not be surprised if new methods continue to be developed. Even so, unless the human gene pool has become badly infected with disease due to the results of living in the environments we have created (as depicted in Margaret Atwood's *The Handmaid's Tale*), the old-fashioned way will still be favored.

Many esoteric teachings contain a belief or assumption that at one time beings came from the sky in space crafts, mated with the primates that inhabited the earth, and subsequently gave birth to the race we now know as human beings (the Fifth Root-race of Theosophy). Thus, Darwin would be half-correct. We may be descended from apes, but we may also be descended from "gods" or aliens. Some of the earliest prehistoric artifacts that have emerged from underground caves in France and Spain depict images of a pregnant goddess, some with human heads, some headless, and some with heads of birds. Rather than assume that the goddesses were literally impregnated by birds, we might conclude that the bird image symbolized that procreative acts were initiated by beings who appeared to fly like birds or appeared in flying machines. Many tribes, both ancient and modern, have used birds as symbols of heavenly attainment.

If we think of Gaia as the embodiment of the Earth Mother, and Uranus as the embodiment of aliens and/or alien technologies (Sky Father), then the present human race is really a composite of both. Many people are unaware of the link between their bodies and minds; if allowed to exist in such a disconnected fashion, they also forget that all life-forms on this planet are similarly related. Thus, if we were to ascribe a meaning to Earth as a planetary archetype in the sky and in our horoscopes, we might sum it up as follows: the collection of veins, arteries, muscles, neuro-indicators, limbs, nerves and cells which make up the human body, and which all work together as a team to create a healthy, vital organism; or, in the macrocosm, the oceans, forests, deserts, mountains, rivers, and glaciers which make up our world, as well as the numerous species which inhabit the earth, allowing these parts to all work together to create a healthy, vital planet.

When the Earth is placed in a horoscope, its position is always located precisely 180 degrees from the Sun; thus an Aries Sun will always have a Libra Earth. Many astrologers believe that this polarity point is our "missing half." The six polarities of the astrological wheel constitute a whole; any sign is like one side of a coin, with its flip side or opposite sign creating the totality of being. Thus, an Aries is not only *attracted* to Libra, but *needs* what Libra has to offer in order to achieve wholeness. It might also be remembered that the Sun and Uranus, Gaia's two polarity planets, are considered polarity planets with each other in the astrological *mandala* by virtue of their rulerships over the opposites Leo and Aquarius respectively. And since Earth and the Sun are located in opposite places, both points are crucial to the integration of the self. Finally, in the esoteric system of astrology,[5] Sagittarius is ruled by the Earth. If we can get to heaven, we need earth to do it.

The Hopi Indian earth-woman, Hahaiwugti, mother goddess of growing who bore Man, conceived through the creator-father Sky

We have seen how the Sun is vital to the healing process, i.e., how Apollo was gifted in the arts of medicine and healing. And certainly the Sun as an indicator of vitality and energy has much to do with the health and well-being of an individual. But that is only part of the picture. When taken as a polarity, the Sun-Earth team and the aspects they form to the other planets can identify very specific areas of healthiness or disease in a system. If the planet Saturn in the chart is opposite the Sun, we tend to think of Saturn's melancholy, coldness and hardness impeding the Sun's natural abilities to shine. But what we might also think of is Saturn's conjunction to the planet Earth, and how using that conjunction effectively can actually aid in the healing process.

An image of the earth as the medium between light and darkness, from Maier's Scrutinium Chymicum, *Frankfort, 1687*

Let us see how this Sun-Earth polarity might operate in actual chart interpretation. We shall use the Taurus-Scorpio polarity as an example. Both of these signs have to do with resources and sexuality. Opposite signs are always concerned with the same issues. The polarity factor comes from the following difference in tone: Taurus is part of the spring quadrant of the *mandala*, hence concerned with individuality and emergence, while Scorpio is part of the autumn quadrant, and thus concerned with relationship. Taurus focuses on its own resources, while Scorpio focuses on the resources of others. For Taurus, sex is primarily a biological phenomenon, while for Scorpio it is a social (i.e., relationship-oriented) function.

The Sun, at its best, brings a person into balance and harmony. But it can only achieve this harmony through incorporating its opposite factor, represented by the Earth. A strong Sun without a consciousness of Gaia is divorced from nature rather than at one with it. When we develop a conscious sense of direction and purpose, we exalt our individuality over the collective power of nature. Taurus Suns may define their individuality through their possessions, and this is part of their destiny. But they can also isolate themselves from others by too great a reliance on those possessions, and become like the dragon sleeping on its golden hoard. It is only by incorporating the Scorpio polarity (i.e., by learning to *share*) that they can become one with the collective, earth-centered life all around them. Similarly, they may regard sex as a personal possession, and especially their children, the biological fruits of sex. Only when they learn to relate to others sexually, or to lose the ego through total union with another, will they connect with the Gaia force that links them to every other life-form on the planet.

Now let's try it in reverse. Scorpio Suns may be expert at understanding, using, or (at worst) manipulating the value systems or resources of others. They may never acquire a sense of their *own* values until they stop to define them in the same individualistic way that Taurus does—and until they do this, they will never be quite grounded. Similarly, Scorpios may define themselves by way of their sexual relationships. Only when they stop regarding sex as a social endeavor, and experience its earthy, biological power, will they really connect with the Gaia component. (It might even require the birth of a child to get them to do this.)

Strong links by planetary aspect to the Sun/Earth polarity will be critical in helping to define the energy one is working with in life. This is especially true of the square. For instance, if a planet is square the Sun in a horoscope, it will also be square the Earth. Thus, it will be the focal point of an astrological formation known as the T-square, a highly sensitive placement. Learning to understand this planet's nature, its problems, its paradoxes and its highest qualities of expression will help a person achieve the focused consciousness (Sun) that many are striving for here on earth, thus uniting spirit and body.

Among planets, the Moon and Ceres represent two different kinds of mothering. The signs Cancer and Virgo, associated with these planets, also represent different modes of the mothering instinct. But there is one more form of mother operating innately in our beings. That is Gaia—the polarity to the Sun. Just as the Sun in our charts is one form of father (the radiant, creative, spiritual father), Earth as its polarity would address the radiant, inner, spiritual mother. If there is to be an astrological "rulership" for the Earth, the suggestion here would be a Taurus rulership and a Capricorn exaltation. The Taurus rulership is obvious, but why Capricorn as the exaltation? Because Capricorn, the sign ruled by Saturn, is the sign associated with earth *management*. Let's not forget that Cronus (Saturn), Gaia's son, saved her children from Ouranos' tyranny. And finally, in 1988, when Saturn and Uranus made their conjunction at 0 degrees Capricorn, the world was focused on the emerging Gaia Hypothesis, and the race to save the planet from our own shortsightedness was in full acceleration. That same year, for the first time ever, *Time* magazine's Person of the Year was not a person at all, but Planet Earth.

In the introduction to this section on the planets, we talked about the willingness and eagerness of Westerners to explore new fields. It is in that spirit that we offer Gaia, the Earth, as a necessary archetype for personal and planetary healing at this time. Hopefully, astrologers will begin placing the Earth in charts, thereby making people more aware of how they are connected to the Earth in real life.

MOON

*You took the moon at full, but now she's changed.
Yet still she is the moon...*

—*Shakespeare*, Love's Labour's Lost, V, II

Lucius Apuleius, a Roman writer of the 2nd century AD, has left us a peculiar and exotic fantasy novel entitled *The Golden Ass*. Despite the fact that Christianity was rapidly taking over the Roman Empire at that time, Apuleius remained an unregenerate old pagan. His novel contains a lovely invocation to the Moon:

> *...you who wander through many sacred groves and are propitiated with many different rites—you whose womanly light illumines the walls of every city, whose misty radiance nurses the happy seeds under the soil, you who control the wandering course of the sun and the very power of his rays—I beseech you, by whatever name, in whatever aspect, with whatever ceremonies you deign to be invoked...grant me repose and peace...*[1]

Few people who are acquainted with astrology will be surprised to hear Apuleius speak of the Moon's "womanly light," for most of us know that the Moon is the quintessential feminine archetype, the visible symbol of the Great Goddess; and the reference to nursing the seeds beneath the soil fits in very nicely with the Moon's maternal role as the nurturer of all life. Some, however, may find it strange to read that the Moon controls "the wandering course of the sun and the very power of his rays."

The fact is: throughout most of human history, the moon has been of more symbolic importance than the sun. This is hard for us to credit in an age of "sun-sign" astrology, but in India it is still the Moon which plays the larger role in chart interpretation. And as recently as 1899, folklorist Charles Leland published a volume of tales gleaned from his researches among Italian witches which harks back to the ancient days when the lunar goddess reigned supreme. Entitled *Aradia: The Gospel of the Witches*, the story tells of how there were originally two principles in nature: the female principle or Moon, called Tana (Diana), and the male principle or Sun, called Lucifer.[2] Tana pursued Lucifer across the sky until she caught him, seduced him, and became pregnant. The daughter of this union was Aradia, the patroness of the witches. Note that it is the female principle which plays the aggressive role; the Moon pursues the Sun. And indeed, it appears that way in the sky, the moon on a constantly moving quest to catch up to the sun. Some scholars believe that in neolithic times, priestesses armed with stone sickles (symbolic of the crescent moon) pursued men through the sacred groves—sometimes to make love to them, sometimes to sacrifice them. Something of this archetypal pursuit survives in the British folk ballad called *The Coal Black Smith*—though the patriarchal Celts or Saxons have changed the story so that the male now pursues the female.[3]

A Gnostic emblem showing the moon goddess—Luna Regia—from Jacob Bryant's "Analysis of Antient (sic) Mythology"

Beliefs such as these go back ultimately to Paleolithic times, when the Great Goddess and the Antlered God (lord of the woods and the earth) were the only deities known. In those days, time itself was reckoned by the moon. Lunar calendars are always older than solar calendars; it takes a fair amount of mathematical observation to note the solstices and equinoxes, but a calendar based on the cycle of the moon is relatively easy to keep. Antlers and bones dating from the Ice Age are often carved with notches which run in series of twenty-eight to thirty, a mean lunar month.

In neolithic times, the moon was worshipped as the Great Goddess of Life and Death, and the waxing and waning of the moon was a symbol of the cycle of all earthly life. The cross of the four directions, a symbol of wholeness, frequently represented the moon. Another lunar symbol which goes back to the neolithic era is the bull, whose horns resemble a crescent moon and whose sexual vitality is emblematic of the life force.[4] (To this very day, the Moon is said to be exalted in Taurus.)

The most important single fact about the moon is that it goes through phases. Because water is symbolic of the feeling function, and because the moon has a strong influence over the tides, it is natural to associate the Moon with feelings; this in itself places the Moon primarily in a feminine mode. The mean period of the moon's revolution is twenty-eight-and-a-half days, which closely links it with the menstrual cycle. Thus, in ancient times, the Great Goddess herself was perceived in terms of phases; despite her many names, she had

Diana Triformis, illustrated by Diane Smirnow

three principal aspects.[5] In the beginning, she was the nymph or maiden, corresponding to the crescent moon. As the full moon, the Goddess manifested as the mother, her belly as round as the moon at full. The so-called "fat goddesses" of the neolithic illustrate this fertile, fecund aspect of the moon. As the waning moon, the Goddess manifested as the crone or wise old woman.

As Apuleius tells us, the Moon was worshipped under a multiplicity of names, and there is scarcely a goddess in the entire pantheon of the Greeks or Celts who does not possess a lunar aspect or manifestation of some kind. However, it is difficult to find any one goddess who represents the entire range of lunar symbolism. The so-called moon goddess of the Greeks, Selene, seldom appears in myth. The witch goddess Hecate is, as we shall see, a symbol of the waning moon. The classical goddess most often associated with the Moon is Artemis. However, the Greeks regarded her primarily as the Lady of Wild Beasts (see Sagittarius) rather than the Moon, and it was the Romans who made this deity, under her Latin name Diana, an essentially lunar goddess. But Artemis-Diana, in any event, represents the nymph or maiden phase of the lunar cycle: she is a young woman's goddess, not yet a mother, and her bow is a symbol of the crescent moon.

A particularly dynamic moon goddess is Arianrhod, who appears in the Welsh *Mabinogion* and who is called "The Lady of the Silver Wheel."[6] The king sends for her because she is alleged to be a virgin (the crescent moon), and hence a candidate for the office of the king's foot-bearer. But Arianrhod is already a mother (full moon), and suddenly births two children on the floor of the palace before running away. The first child is called Dylan; he is a god of the sea, which is fitting because of the moon's influence upon the tides. Nor is that the only link between Arianrhod and the ocean, for she dwells in a castle by the sea.

It is to this castle that Gwydion, magician and bard, brings Arianrhod's second child, still nameless. But now Arianrhod becomes the cruel mother (waning moon), refusing to acknowledge the child by giving him a name or the weapons of a warrior. Gwydion uses magic to trick her into giving the boy both gifts; the name she gives him is Llew Llaw Gyffes, the Bright-Shining Skillful Handed One. The Welsh Llew is surely the same as the Irish hero Lugh Samildanach, the Man of Many Gifts, who was originally a sun god. Here once again the Moon is exalted above the Sun, for she gives birth to him.

In an astrological chart, the Moon functions primarily as a receptacle—like the cauldron of the Goddess which became, in medieval legend, the Holy Grail (see the Four Elements, especially Water). Everything we experience is funneled into the womb of the Moon. Is it any wonder, then, that the Moon has traditionally been associated with memory? Everything we remember, everything we have experienced, is stored in the cauldron of the Goddess. Thus the Moon represents our feelings, our habit patterns; in short, the personal unconscious. Some esoteric astrologers call the Moon the planet of past karma—which is another way of saying that the Moon represents that limitless well of feeling patterns which, for the most part, unconsciously directs our actions in the present. Among the feeling relationships in our lives, none is more important than that with the mother, which is also symbolized by the Moon. The way in which we have been nurtured in early life (not to mention in the womb), the love that we receive (or fail to receive) plays a major role in forming the unconscious instincts that govern our behavior.

It is easy to see why ancient astrologers placed so much emphasis on the Moon. For to a great degree, we are directed by that network of unconscious feelings which the Moon represents. Many astrologers, however, seek to relate the Moon to the earlier portion of our lives, and claim that we journey figuratively toward the symbolism of our sun signs as we grow older. This is another way of saying that we must detach ourselves from purely instinctual reactions, and that maturity consists of linking ourselves more directly with a conscious purpose or sense of destiny (the Sun). This, however, is only a rule of thumb. In individual chartwork, it might happen that what is portrayed by the Sun is a warped or weak sense of will or purpose, while the Moon is beautifully aspected. Such an individual, as a positive lunar type, may find it preferable to trust her or his instincts, to value tradition or the past, and not to rock the boat. Such an individual may well find purpose in tranquility! According to Hindu astrologers, this is in fact one of the best of all possible fates.

This illustrates a difference in how East and West interpret life. If we accept the Moon as the archetypal feminine or *yin* symbol in astrology, then its receptive, tranquil, and highly intuitive mode fulfills an ideal model of Eastern thought. But in the West, where action, achievement, ambition and goals are priority modes of behavior, leaning towards one's Moon may be regarded as a static, non-productive form

Diana as moon goddess from Jost Amman's Kunstbüchlin, *published by*
Johann Feyerabend, Frankfurt, 1599

of behavior. It is a well-known concept in the astrological world that the Moon represents negative emotional patterning from the past that must be overcome or transcended in order to fulfill one's solar destiny. This sometimes results in a belief that the Moon *itself* is negative while the Sun is positive and must be developed at the expense of the Moon. This kind of one-sided emphasis tends to devalue the feminine. Such negative labeling of the Moon reflects a deep-seated fear of the unconscious or feminine principle characteristic of solar or patriarchal societies. Donna Cunningham in *Being a Lunar Type in a Solar World* gives some excellent material on what results for societies (and individuals) when lunar needs are either downplayed or totally ignored.[7]

The earliest calendars were lunar, and in fact there are thirteen lunar months in a solar year—a fact which may have something to do with the number thirteen attaining "unlucky" status in Christian eyes. It was the number thirteen that was linked with the Goddess as the number of full moons each year. Had the lunar calendar remained in effect, we would have thirteen months of 28.5 days each. Strangely enough, the only culture in the modern world to retain a lunar calendar is the most seemingly patriarchal of all—Islam, which is symbolized by the crescent moon.

Astronomers tell us that the moon is a barren, dry and rocky planet, a dead satellite of the earth, with no life-giving qualities of its own. How is it then, that the moon can symbolize all the life-giving qualities of the Goddess herself? And how can it be interpreted as a "watery" planet? As we have noted, the moon has a direct influence over oceanic tides. And when Galileo first observed the moon through a telescope he named the many craters *mares* or seas, implying water. The Apollo astronauts who landed on the moon in 1969 collected samples which, scientists later surmised, posed more questions about the moon's origins than they answered. Those who returned from that mission spoke of a profoundly spiritual experience which ultimately changed many of their life directions. What do we really know? The moon remains shrouded in mystery, as perhaps it should be, a keeper of the sacred mysteries.

Some books call the Moon "personality." Others say it is the "ego." Still others call it the "soul." The present authors have already given several other interpretations here. The truth is, there is no universal agreement amongst astrologers about the Moon in terms of its affect on the individual's character. One thing is

One of the earliest topographic views of the moon, from Johann Hevelius' Selenographia, *Danzig, 1647*

pretty universally agreed upon, however. It symbolizes "mother" and it symbolizes "feelings." *And* it is a very important factor in the chart to consider when dealing with the basic motivating factors by which people tend to live their lives.

Let's examine the mother first. In terms of zodiacal signs, we may recognize four emanations of the Goddess: Taurus, Cancer, Virgo and Scorpio. Taurus is associated with the fertility goddess; Cancer with the pregnant goddess about to give or just having given birth and the beautiful relationship that exists between mother and infant; Virgo is Demeter (Ceres), the earth goddess who seeds the earth with fruit, flowers and grain to feed the hungry earth-children, and who mourns for the separation of mother and daughter when she loses Persephone to the underworld; and finally, Scorpio, the goddess of snakes, is the

The Moon's Phases, designed by Hans Holbein II, from Sebastian Münster's Canones super novum instrumentum luminarium, *printed by Andreas Cratander, Basel, 1534*

underworld or wisdom aspect of the goddess as crone and wise old woman. It is these four phases of the goddess as symbolized by the signs of the zodiac that seem to correlate to the four phases of the moon. Ancient religion recognized three phases or faces of the moon—waxing, full, and waning. In our modern calendars, a lunar month is divided into four phases: first, second, third, and fourth quarters. Dane Rudhyar divides each phase into two and thus assigns eight phases to the moon in his classic work *The Lunation Cycle,* and correlates these cycles with the phases of human life.[8] We shall correlate the lunar phases with the emanations of the Goddess.

In her new or crescent phase, she is essentially a young woman running free across the mountaintops, at one with all nature. Full of vigor and life, she dances through the fields, sporting with animals and flowers. She even appears to be smiling at us from the sky when she is in this phase. She is complete unto herself, and stands apart from committed relationships. She may be sexually active (the nymph) or virginal (the maiden), but in either case she is still pure, innocent, hopeful. Artemis or Diana is the best-known representative of this type. In the second phase, she is totally absorbed in relationship, whether to her mate or, more importantly, to her child. Like Mary, she gives birth to her own holy infant. Her smile has become a radiant white light, the light which illuminates all those who are "in love." And it is this phase, as the moon waxes towards full, that lovers and honey-"mooners" find so beguiling. In the third phase, the moon begins to lose the fullness of her light.

The brightness that surrounded the mother with her child begins to wane as she is forced to sacrifice her child—like Mary or Demeter—so that the child can fulfill its own destiny. In this phase, there is a sadness to her as she mourns her loss. And finally, during the last quarter of the waning cycle, she hurries towards invisibility. Like Ishtar, she stands naked before the goddess of the underworld, discovers herself, and finds her way to the light (the Sun), or, like Persephone mating with Hades in the depths of the underworld, she gains the wisdom to begin the whole cycle over again. It is during this final waning phase that the Goddess manifests as the crone or wise old woman. Hecate, the so-called goddess of the witches, represents this phase. She had knowledge of herbs and magic elixirs, folk healing and the control of weather. She also had her familiar, for the image of a dog howling at the moon was associated with Hecate. This "moon-dog" is of great antiquity, for it is found on Balkan pottery going back to 5,000 BC.[9] Hecate was also the goddess of the crossroads (where witches were believed to perform their rituals), and this is reminiscent of the neolithic, for the cross of the four directions was a lunar symbol in those days.

The moon and moon-dogs, from a nineteenth-century Tarot deck

Let's also remember the moon's symbiotic relationship with earth. The earth, too, has four distinct phases, similar to the moon, literally demonstrated by the seasons. At the start of the year, the earth is barren, but just below the surface, incredible activity is taking place to prepare the earth for phase two, the spring, when seedlings and buds sprout everywhere. By the height of summer, the fullness of the flowers, fruit, and even weeds gives way to autumn when the lessening of the light prepares the earth for its journey underground. The symmetry of these four seasons of the earth and the four phases of the moon constitutes an integral part of life for us and keeps our world balanced and harmonious. While this cycle takes one month for the moon and one year for the earth (sun), in the astrological framework where one day equals one year by progression, the lunar phase takes 27 years. It is this 27-year period which, if examined carefully and broken into four sub-phases of almost seven years each, constitutes the same four phases which define our life's "seasons." An average human life span will consist of three complete phases (81 years), which again gives us the three emanations of the moon as portrayed by the triple moon goddess. Astrologers will also recognize this cycle as very close to the Saturn cycle of 28 years, which breaks down into the same formula.

In terms of the Moon's relationship to the mother, we have seen that the Moon, when full, symbolizes motherhood at its most glorified. But not everyone feels such a relationship with the mother. The key to the mother/infant relationship as suggested by the astrological chart probably has to do with the position of the Moon by sign, house, and aspects. Perhaps, too, the phase of the Moon at birth may describe the early years of the individual. A waning Moon might describe a child who felt some abandonment or isolation in the early years of life, and could similarly point to an "old" or very mature soul. Full Moon babies might feel the magnetic pull of the mother influencing them throughout their lives, even when it is time for them to release the tie

Diana, or Artemis, the maiden aspect of the moon

and establish autonomy. A New Moon child might always feel like a "babe in the woods" and may always be regarded as such by his or her family, even after maturity. An examination of the lunar phase at birth as well as the continuing progressed lunar phases will shed significant light upon life's seasons.

Besides the Moon, we suggest that there are other astrological references to the mother in the chart, including Earth and Ceres. The Moon contains the key to *emotional* security and love as represented early in life by the mother's love and the amount of security she felt and was able to pass on to the child. The mothering represented by Ceres is the physical act of providing that security and the tools given by the mother to assist the individual in making his or her own way in the world. In other words, if the mother as represented by Ceres squares or afflicts the Moon in a significant way, there are problems integrating the *forms* that the mother attempted to pass on. If, however, the Moon harmonizes nicely with Ceres, there would be an ease in expressing and dealing with the feminine in one's life. Of course, these aspects occur for both men and women, but it is often said that a woman becomes the embodiment of her own Moon much more easily than a man, who, experiencing the Moon (as primary archetype of the feminine) as a polar opposite, tends to find it outside of himself in his relationships with women in general or with the primary female in his life. This is not always the case, but often. Similarly, a woman may gravitate towards men who embody the characteristics of her own sun sign, "projecting" her Sun in the same way that a man is likely to project his Moon.

Full moon-rise over Joshua Tree, California. Photograph by Ariel Guttman

The Earth's position in the chart, a third form of mother, as polarity to the Sun, may reflect the *spiritual* connections to mother as symbolic of "The Great Mother" and also point to the forms our feminine procreativity will take.

Finally, there's "feelings." The Moon, as an ever-changing celestial body, reflects the ever-changing feelings and moods within us. When the negative aspects of the Moon are being expressed, we have no control over our moods or emotional outbursts. We are subject to whatever comes at us and have only our instinctual feelings with which to respond to that outer stimuli. This kind of lunar behavior, at its most extreme, leads to madness—or "lunacy," as the ancients referred to it. Of course, that's no fun. But the solution to this is not to completely avoid, ignore or deny our feelings, either. The interplay between the Moon and the Sun constitutes a harmonious relationship that strengthens both heart and mind, rather than attempting to be all solar (head) or all lunar (emotion).

NODES

The Moon's Nodes

To the ancients, an eclipse was one of the most awesome events in the celestial sphere. Seemingly without warning, the sun or moon would begin to disappear, as if it were being consumed by some invisible entity. Because villagers and townsfolk were so terrified by eclipses, a knowledge of such events put the knower in a position of power. Thus priests, astrologers, and shamans—religious specialists of all kinds—studied the secrets of the eclipse cycle. Some researchers believe that ancient monuments such as Stonehenge contain simple but effective indicators to measure that cycle.[1]

Throughout medieval and Renaissance times, astrologers continued to regard eclipses with great trepidation, predicting drastic changes in the weather or in political affairs as a result. Modern astrologers, however, pay little heed to eclipses—except for some specialists, most of whom are likely to disagree with each other.

The sun and moon in an early twentieth-century Italian book ornament

Considering the powerful effect that eclipses have always had on human consciousness, it seems clear that they must be important from a mythological point of view. But few people realize that a mythology of eclipses exists, or that the eclipse cycle can be easily noted in the birth chart by examining the Moon's Nodes.

Like the sun and the other planets, the moon travels across a band of sky called the ecliptic—i.e., the apparent path of the sun. But the moon may sometimes cross the band of the ecliptic, to the north and to the south. In fact, it does this every thirteen days—first to the north, then to the south, and so on. These two points of intersection, north and south, always lie directly opposite each other by sign and house and are called the Moon's Nodes. Each time the moon crosses the ecliptic, it does so at a slightly earlier degree of longitude. Hence the Moon's Nodes appear to move or "travel" in backwards motion, i.e., in retrograde.

It is an astronomical fact that a solar or lunar eclipse can only occur when the sun or moon is conjunct one of the Nodes. The Moon's Nodes, therefore, are the indicators of the eclipse cycle. In fact, ancient people probably became aware of the progress of the Nodes by attempting to predict eclipses.

The Nodes may not be actual planets or heavenly bodies, but they do appear in the mythology of Indo-European-speaking peoples. The Vikings conceived of the sun and moon as two chariots being driven across the sky—a concept shared by most Indo-European myth systems. But the Norse also conceived of two fierce wolves who pursued the solar and lunar chariots through the heavens. Every once in a while, one of the wolves would catch up to one of the chariots, which would begin to disappear inside the hungry jaws of the wolf. This was an eclipse. Ultimately, however, the luminaries always escaped being swallowed up forever.[2]

The most fully developed version of this myth comes from India. In fact, we may well have derived our own astrological tradition about the Nodes from Hindu sources, for the Nodes were being observed in India as long ago as the time of the *Rig Veda* (Hindu traditionalists place this work at about 3,000 BC, though conventional scholars argue that it is no earlier than 1,500 BC).[3] The Hindus conceived of the Nodes as a vast cosmic dragon. In the Western world, medieval astrologers called the North and South Nodes the Dragon's Head and Dragon's Tail respectively, which suggests that ultimately they gained their concept of the Nodes through contact with India. Such contact may well have occurred during the first few centuries before Christ, when Alexander the Great's empire stretched from the Aegean to the borders of India and provided numerous opportunities for cultural transmission.

The Hindu story goes like this. Both the gods and their primal enemies, the demons, needed the marvelous drink *amrita* to maintain their immortality and eternal youth. This *amrita* is, of course, the same word as the Greek ambrosia and it means the same thing—the magical liquid of the gods. In the Hindu story, this *amrita* had grown scarce. Everyone knew that it could be found deep within the Cosmic Ocean, but neither the gods nor the demons by themselves could extract it from such a depth. They needed to cooperate. So the two opposing groups of deities got together to seek the *amrita* they both needed. They turned the world mountain upside down, placing its sharp peak in the Cosmic Ocean. They wrapped Vishnu's great serpent around the mountain and began a tug of war with it. The world mountain was driven deep into the ocean floor, as if the gods and demons were churning butter in some gigantic churn. Many things emerged from that great ocean, including the legendary treasures of Hindu myth. Even Lakshmi, the goddess of love, was born from the waters in that churning (like Venus, also born of the sea-foam and the ocean waves).

At last the *amrita* was discovered. The demons scrambled to retrieve it, but a beautiful woman called Mohini suddenly appeared. Holding the nectar in a cup, she called upon gods and demons each to form a line and receive the divine substance.

The Alchemic Sky Dragon *linking the sun and the moon, engraved by V. Feil, from Hanns Singriener's* Vögelin Praktik, *Vienna, 1534*

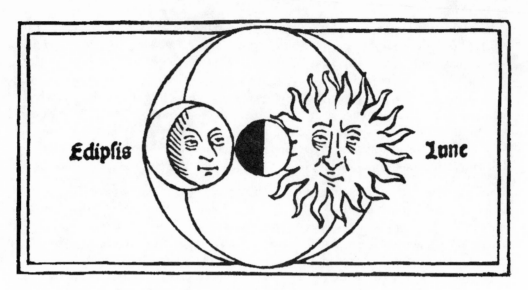

Lunar eclipse, from Johannes de Sacrobusco's Opus Sphaericum, *printed by Erhard Ratdolt, Venice, 1482*

As the gods were receiving *amrita*, a clever demon called Svarbhanu—a dragon-like creature with four arms and a tail—slipped into the line between the sun god and the moon god. Greedily, he slurped at the *amrita*. The Sun and Moon cried out, and the god Vishnu came to the rescue, slicing the demon in half. The beautiful Mohini continued down the line, but when she reached the end of the company of gods she vanished. She had been yet another aspect of Vishnu. The demons were cheated of the drink of immortality.

All of them, that is, except Svarbhanu. Though he had been sliced in half, he could not die, for he had tasted of *amrita*. He was now two beings, a dragon's head called Rahu and a dragon's tail named Ketu. Rahu and Ketu remained angry with the Sun and Moon for having cried out; hence they chased the two luminaries through the sky eternally, and, upon occasion, swallowed them.[4]

Hindu astrology gives each node a separate and distinct role or personality. Rahu, the North Node, is the demon's head, longing to consume the luminaries in its gaping jaws. Rahu represents our fiercest desires, the compulsions which control us to such a degree that they may even swallow our essential self—i.e., our Sun and Moon functions. Generally, the consuming desires represented by Rahu are said to be sensual or materialistic (depending on the house). Ketu, the South Node, is the tail of the dragon. It doesn't have a head, i.e., any particular volition of its own. It is a kind of receptacle. It swallows things into a black hole. It swallows up phobias, compulsions, hallucinations, illness. A person who is strongly under the influence of Ketu is generally subject to all kinds of unreasonable fears, nightmares, and mysterious ailments. Ketu is as psychological as Rahu is material. But for precisely this reason—i.e., because it deals with the power of the unconscious—Ketu is also a significator of wisdom and enlightenment. The material which forms our fears and dark visions is the same unconscious material which, when transformed, leads us to enlightenment. Western astrologers may think of Ketu as being a bit like Neptune—though Hindus themselves link it with Mars. If we think of it as being somewhat like a Mars-Neptune conjunction, we won't be far off. Rahu and Ketu both represent unconscious compulsions, but Rahu leans toward the worldly sphere while Ketu deals directly with the unconscious.

In Hindu astrology, any planet which is conjunct or in aspect to the Nodes is believed to be "swallowed up" or "eclipsed" by them. A planet may be eclipsed by Rahu, in which case its energies will be unconsciously directed towards material or sensual gratification. It may be eclipsed by Ketu, in which case that planet will veer away from outward expression and become linked with the unconscious—a situation which may result either in psychological turmoil, a quest for enlightenment, or both. This situation is especially powerful when the Nodes contact either the Sun or Moon.[5]

In the West, there is a great deal of variety as regards the interpretation of the Moon's Nodes. Much of the lore and speculation regarding these two points is decidedly esoteric. However, the most widely accepted interpretation is that the South Node represents habits, attitudes and behaviors which are "easy" for us, deeply ingrained, and which therefore represent the path of least resistance. But the path of least resistance is not the most positive or growth-oriented path upon which to walk. It is to our greater benefit to take "the road less traveled," to nurture and build up the qualities and behaviors which are precisely the opposite of our old patterns. This means putting forth definite (and sometimes painful) effort towards building up new behaviors that correspond to the house and sign position of the North Node.

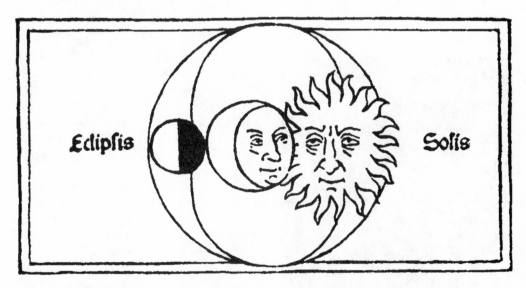

Solar eclipse, from Johannes de Sacrobusco's Opus Sphaericum, *printed by Erhard Ratdolt, Venice, 1482*

Though this interpretation sounds quite psychological, it has proven to work well from an esoteric point of view. Many astrologers regard the South Node patterns as part of our karmic inheritance, an imprint from past lives which must be overcome in order to keep growing. We overcome these patterns, or, to put it another way, we create "good karma," by developing the qualities symbolized by the North Node.

A strong theme that has emerged from interpretation of the nodal axis is that the Nodes are a path that the soul is following, a road, separate from the needs, desires and stimuli of the physical body and world. Thus the nodal axis, as a unit, relates to the soul's journey, with the South Node representing the direction from which one is coming and the North Node representing the direction toward which one is heading—the "tail" and "head" respectively. If this is so, it is no wonder that the interpretation of the South Node is somewhat negative, as if those who are really fulfilling their South Node are somehow resting on their "tail" instead of "heading" in a forward direction. And, as we have seen, the North Node, to the Hindus, represents a more material direction, while the South Node emphasizes the unconscious. The bias toward the North Node, in Western astrology, is not unlike the Westerner's propensity for accomplishment in the material world. The problem with this kind of interpretation—i.e., that one Node is "good" and the other Node is "bad"—reflects the kind of black-and-white interpretations that astrology has always been subject to and has fought hard to overcome, for any planet or sign can be good or bad, depending on how an individual uses its energy. It is, after all, energy, and affords us the opportunity to make conscious choices as to how we will use it. Obviously, when we're unconsciously motivated by desires over which we seem to have no control, then we are probably expressing the negative aspects of the South or North Nodes, but once we learn what motivates us and what effect such unconscious desires have upon us, then we can choose our expression more carefully. Still, both Nodes have value for us, and because they represent one of astrology's polarities, we are likely to bounce back and forth between the two extremes before we attain harmony and integration in the middle. Looking at the Nodes this way, we can see that addressing both the positive and negative manifestations of each Node can have some learning value for us.

The emphasis on one node as superior to the other reflects some of the misguided interpretation we encountered in relation to the Moon itself. Many astrologers feel we should direct our energy in a "solar" way and leave behind our "lunar" habits. The fact that the

Total solar eclipse. Photograph from NASA

Nodes are linked to the Moon may be responsible for some of this interpretative bias. We may lean strongly towards one Node, typically the south, because it involves memory patterns of the way we were for much of our youth, and then reach in the opposite direction, toward the other Node. Eventually the Nodes may be balanced, once both sides have been experienced and we have had the opportunity to see how both ends serve us in our life's development. Many talented individuals have birth planets conjunct the South Node, a signature that often indicates strong soul memory, reawakened quickly in a particular area of life. Thus some people's strength might lie in what they are bringing with them from the past. But if this becomes their total focus in life, then they are not balancing the Nodes, and perhaps not growing—stretching, as it were, to their North Node.

For instance, Ronald Reagan has Jupiter precisely conjunct his South Node in Scorpio and the Moon precisely conjunct his North Node in Taurus, and he very easily attained the status of a Jupiter even before becoming President of the United States. As a former governor of California, Hollywood actor, and President of the Screen Actors' Guild, this Zeus commanded respect in many circles. Jupiter conjunct the South Node suggests this quality had already been well developed prior to this life, and the conjunction in Scorpio adds to the power he was able to project. The conjunction in Taurus of the Moon with its own North Node challenges him to be personable, acquire substance, develop sensitivity to financial issues, appeal to the masses (the Moon), and to intuitively know when to act and when not to. Whether he has successfully met the challenges suggested by his North Node will be left to historians to decide, but it is certainly no accident that the Moon and Jupiter play such an important role in this charismatic figure's life. The Reagan administration was symbolically characterized by Jupiter opposite the Moon in these money signs—the rich became even richer, polarized by the poor, who became increasingly more destitute. Homelessness (the Moon) in the United States, a Jupiterian country of abundance and wealth, reached an all-time high, as did the national debt. In contrast, Lyndon Johnson's chart shows the nodal axis connected with Pluto in Cancer (North Node) and Uranus in Capricorn (South Node). Not only was his administration earmarked by these two rebellious planets, but the middle 1960s saw a conjunction of Pluto and Uranus which instituted massive unrest throughout the country and the world. Uranus and Pluto in conjunction were a sign of the times, and the man chosen to represent the nation during this time had the imprint of pre-birth eclipses spotlighting those two planets, and which were actualized as he fulfilled his life's destiny. His predecessor, John F. Kennedy, had the South Node conjunct Pluto. Remember, the demon who drank the drink of immortality was split into the two Nodes—thus both Nodes contain memory of past and future, beyond the body's physical-plane awareness, and therefore both Nodes must be reconciled in order to deal effectively with the totality of the soul's path.

Eclipses carried a negative connotation for a very long time, because the ancients were not aware of the astronomical reasons behind this temporary "swallowing up" of the moon and the sun. Even today, eclipses inspire fear and, more importantly, awe among certain people. This is true in chart interpretation as well. When an eclipse pattern brings a planet into its aura, the nature of that planet is highly emphasized. In mundane or political astrology, that planet's function is often played out in extreme ways, on the world's political stage and also through natural phenomena such as earthquakes, volcanic eruptions, etc. A recent case in point is the lunar eclipse of August, 1990. Involved within the orbit of that eclipse across the fixed signs of Aquarius and Leo were the squares of both Mars and Pluto in Taurus and Scorpio respectively. The entire fixed-cross pattern that this created sat squarely across the angles of Iraq's chart. At that moment, Iraq's leader, Saddam Hussein, invaded Kuwait, an incident which was to elicit a very strong counter-attack and reaction (Mars, Pluto) from the rest of the world. The next solar eclipse, which occurred on January 15, 1991, fell on the exact date that the United Nations sanctioned the use of force to remove Iraqi soldiers from Kuwait if they did not leave of their own accord. This eclipse brought transiting Saturn directly into its rays, and the entire pattern conjuncted the United States' Pluto exactly. Again, a strong reaction was elicited, and, with Plutonian power and force, the enemy was forced out. This is but one example of how eclipses, together with transits, can shape world events—but history is full of such examples. The path the eclipse etches across the earth's surface will typically point to the countries or areas of the globe where major change is due to occur.

Similarly, when an eclipse pattern figures prominently in the natal chart by transit, there is a significant change or stimulation occurring for the individual based on the nature of the planet being eclipsed. This is not necessarily to be seen as a negative influence. For instance, many people will have an eclipse occur directly on their Sun, and this will reflect a period in their life when their vitality, creative urges, and self-expression are at their peak—a time when they feel god-like (sun-centered) and bright. An eclipse to natal Saturn might help people identify their weaknesses, their bodies' physical limitations, and their own mortality. An eclipse to Venus might bring the love goddess into high focus in one's life, and many an eclipse to Juno can be an indicator of marriage.

The eclipse cycle as identified by the transiting Nodes takes approximately eighteen years to complete. Thus at nine years when the opposition occurs, and then again at eighteen when the cycle is complete, individual awareness may be at an all-time high and messages from the soul concerning its current phase may be influencing us.

MARS

CHAPTER EIGHT

"Monsieur Parolles, you were born under a charitable star."
"Under Mars, I."
"I especially think, under Mars."
"Why under Mars?"
"The wars have so kept you under that you must needs be born under Mars."
"When he was predominant."
"When he was retrograde, I think, rather."
"Why think you so?"
"You go so much backward when you fight."

　　　　　　　　—Shakespeare, All's Well that Ends Well, I, II

Astrologers of medieval and Renaissance times watched the progress of the red planet with some trepidation, for it portended war, fever, and plague. The Greeks looked with equal reservation upon the god Ares, whose domain was war. He was the legitimate son of Zeus (Jupiter) and Hera (Juno), though it is said that both parents hated him. He delighted in battle and violence for its own sake; and if heroes worshipped him or sought to develop some of his "martial" qualities, they also feared him. Even Homer, whose *Iliad* glorifies the arts of war, has little good to say of the god who ruled those deadly arts: he is called "murderous Ares," "violent Ares," and even "Ares, blood-stained man-killer and stormer of cities." His own sister Athene calls him "a thing of rage, made of evil, a two-faced liar." And when the god of war is wounded in battle by the hero Diomedes, he flies angrily back to Mt. Olympus to complain

Ares, or Mars, god of war

to his father. But Zeus tells him: "Don't whine at me, you two-faced liar. To me you are the most hateful of all the gods on Olympus. Wars, quarrels and fights are dear to your heart."[1] Ares had a twin sister named Eris (Discord), who accompanied him on the battlefield and who loved to stir up animosity by spreading false rumors and jealousy. His two attendants were Fear and Panic. His animal was the dog, his bird the vulture, and he was associated with the land of Thrace, a region to the north of Greece which was usually regarded as "barbaric" (despite the fact that Orpheus the poet was also a Thracian). There were no temples to the god of war, nor any sacred places,[2] though it might be said that his sacred places were the battlefields. He is seldom mentioned in any of the myths. Except for Aphrodite, who adored his passionate love-making, and Hades, who enjoyed recruiting the war dead to his underworld domain, Ares gained little favor or admiration on Mt. Olympus. His father, Zeus, had little respect for his warring, quarrelsome ways, preferring the clear-headed, rational approach of Athene. In battle, Ares was not the cool, commanding strategist that Athene was. He was continually losing his temper, rushing into battle hotheadedly, and at the wrong time. His passions not only drove him to battle, but provided the motivation for all his actions. He can thus be related quite easily to the "red" planet, since red is the color that appears when tempers rise to the boiling point—as well as being the color of blood.

But if Ares was seldom honored in Greece, in his incarnation as Roman Mars he was second only to Jupiter in rank. He was considered the patriarch of Rome, having given birth to Romulus and Remus, the founders of the city. To the Romans, who glorified war heroes and "martial" arts, Mars was a heroic god, his name invoked on battlefields. The month of March is named for Mars, for it was the time when spring weather allowed the troops to mobilize once again. In the birth chart, Mars is the warrior. He is also considered the motivating force or energetic level through which one is impelled to act. Judging from his mythology, we can deduce that Mars operates independently and quickly—when the urge strikes, nothing stops him. And that is the danger of an uncontrolled Mars in the chart. Of course, any planet operating independently and uncontrollably is dangerous, but Mars is particularly so. And how these urges manifest in an individual can be determined by examining the astrological Mars.

Head of Ares on a bronze coin of the Mamertinoi, Oscan mercenaries residing in Messina, Sicily, 220–200 BC. From the Michael A. Sikora collection

The Babylonians called the planet Mars Nergal, and, as with the Greeks, it symbolized the god of war. But Nergal was more than just a god of battles: he was the noonday sun that scorched the earth and burned the skin; he was a god of plague and epidemics; of every conceivable disaster. It is written that Nergal stormed into the land of the dead, deposed the dark queen who ruled there, and set himself up as king of the underworld. From other sources, however, it would appear that some sort of compromise was struck, and that Nergal ruled alongside of Ereshkigal, so that the land of the dead had both a king and queen, like the Greek Hades and Persephone.[3]

In any event, we can see that Nergal was associated with both the sun (the heat of noonday) and with the darkness (the underworld). This is significant, for it means that Mars is symbolically linked with the Sun and Pluto, and that he has been connected with these two archetypes since Babylonian times, perhaps even since the dawn of civilization in ancient Sumer. This connection is clearly represented in the astrological *mandala*, for the Sun is exalted in Aries, a sign ruled by Mars, and Pluto, discovered in 1930, was given rulership over Scorpio, a sign previously under the lordship of Mars.

If we think of Mars as forceful action, we can see that it has affinities with the Sun. And if we think of Mars as the god of war and destruction, we can understand its affinities with Pluto. But what is the precise psychological process symbolized by Mars, and how does it differ from those of Pluto and the Sun?

In this context, it is helpful to consider a Hindu myth. In India, Mars is associated with the god Kartikeya. This deity came into being out of necessity; the gods were being terrorized by a demon who, according to prophecy, could only be slain by a "seven-day-old son of Shiva." The gods created a beautiful illusion, the form of a woman so enticing that even Shiva, the great ascetic, was forced to ejaculate at the sight of her. His fiery sperm fell into the ocean and was nourished by the Pleiades, wives of the seven rishis (who are, in fact, the stars of the Big Dipper). They made a womb of earth and water for the unborn child, and in seven days Kartikeya, the god of war, burst forth to slay the demon.[4]

Mars, therefore, is about the power and purpose we need to slay our own inner demons. Even as Nergal descended *into* the underworld, the Mars force emerges *out* of our own personal underworld (Pluto). The sheer power of our psychological complexes, our fears and phobias, churns in our inner darkness until it finally explodes (Mars rules explosions) to the surface. No wonder Mars can be such a destructive force! It emerges into consciousness carrying with it all the negative energy of our inner demons. Naturally, this can cause quarrels, strife, outright warfare between ourselves and others. But the same energy which explodes so violently into our awareness can also be turned to good account, for it is this same powerful energy which can be used to combat our inner demons, to make war upon them. The power of Mars, when it first emerges from the Plutonian world of the unconscious, is an intensely sexual force—which is fitting, for it is linked with psychological complexes in the personal unconscious. This sexual element of Mars has always been recognized in myth; Ares was the lover of Aphrodite, and Kartikeya was born of Shiva's fiery sperm. In Mars, we see the connection between sex and aggression, between desire and action.

But what shall we do with this sexual force when it erupts out of the Plutonian realm to trouble our waking hours? Mars is an energy which, in its primal state, is without a sense of direction—but when linked with a strong sense of purpose, it can accomplish all things. Thus the planet of purposeful direction (the Sun) is exalted in a sign ruled by Mars, while Mars itself is exalted in Capricorn, a sign ruled by Saturn, symbol of discipline. When the raw energy of Mars is controlled by a conscious purpose, i.e., when it is subject to the Sun, symbol of the Self, balance and personal power are both possible. And when it is directed by Saturnian discipline, the explosive power of Mars can move mountains.

Mars corresponds to the "inner warrior," one of the most important of all male archetypes. But, as poet Robert Bly points out, most men in America today have grown up with extremely negative examples of the warrior archetype.[5] The "American warrior" fights for the maintenance of empire, or because he is ordered

Allegoric representation of the Life of the Children of the planet Mars, from an Italian engraving by Gabriele Giolita de Ferrari, 1533

to fight (typically for a cause not his own), or, like Rambo, simply for the love of killing. Bly goes on to say that the true warrior takes his directives from the "inner king."[6] In astrological terminology, we would say that Mars must take its direction from the Sun. It must fight for the cause of consciousness. The inner king, as we have seen, was symbolically identified in alchemy with the solar force—the "inner Sun" and the "inner king" were one and the same. Similarly, the alchemists regarded the Sun or King as the vital power underlying the Self, that multi-dimensional, God-centered individuality which is the goal of all spiritual work.[7] When the Self directs the Warrior, great things are possible: the Warrior's power is dedicated to personal growth, or, as the Hindus might say, to conquering our inner demons. As defender and protector of his family, Mars deserves some praise and recognition. It is true that stalwart defenders and protectors of any given cause are mobilized into action when Mars is dominant in the chart. It is this type of quick reaction—from the gut, not the head—that Mars represents.

The mythology of Mars may have provided the basis for our original thoughts about his behavior in a birth chart, but there is more to it than that. The most highly

acclaimed and recognized statistical research in the field of astrology is credited to the Gauquelins, who spent years studying the charts of famous individuals in order to confirm planetary significance. What they found surprised even them. A prominent Mars, for example, produced individuals who excelled at science, medicine, military, and business careers. Conversely, Mars was *least* apparent for writers, artists, and musicians.[8] And further studies concluded that Mars is prominent in the births of "iron-willed" sports champions in a very high statistical sequence.[9] While this may not surprise many astrologers who have always believed that Mars' nature excelled at military engagements and in sports, the surprise was the *area* of the chart that Mars occupied, the sectors known to astrologers as the Ninth and Twelfth Houses. These are the areas where the planet in question has just risen (Twelfth) or culminated (Ninth). Thus, the strength of the planet depends not upon the *sign* in which it is placed at birth, nor even the planetary aspects involved, but the sector of the chart in which it appears. Contrary

A nineteenth-century engraving of Ares from the original, in Villa Ludovisi, Rome

to popular belief, Mars in the Twelfth House is far from lethargic and apathetic; indeed, its presence there strengthens its nature. Since *all* planets found to be powerful in various professions turned up in these same sectors, we may also conclude that these two houses (the Ninth and the Twelfth, which are the natural placements of Sagittarius and Pisces, co-ruled by Jupiter) represent an individual's most deeply felt beliefs and convictions. These are then spurred to action by the presence of certain planetary energies, notably Mars.

In seven out of ten charts of U.S. Presidents, an angular placement of Mars appears in locations throughout the world where open acts of aggression existed between that nation and the United States, and where the President wound up sending military units to the scene.[10] Of course, with Mars angular in the U.S. chart (whether one uses the Gemini rising chart or the more popular Sagittarius rising chart), the propensity to "shoot from the hip" and fervently promote fighting and dying for one's country may be a natural response for the whole nation. But as the Gauquelin data showed, competitive sports is also governed by Mars, and has

Ares, or Mars, god of war

provided a useful outlet for the inner fire and passion that Mars innately symbolizes. When sports fans in a crowd are engaged in something like a World Series or Super Bowl, the expression of raw emotion and passion is appropriate and even encouraged. People who engage in sports are themselves fueled by Mars and hence are more successful in competition than those who do not have Mars prominent in their make-up. In fact, people who have a strong Mars should be encouraged to participate in sports, or at least perform routine physical exercise in order to blow off the tremendous amount of steam that can build up within them. When not allowed to do this, or when the Mars function is repressed in an individual, the amount of pent-up feelings held within typically results in blow-ups, explosions of violence, and abusive types of behavior that can result in serious consequences. This same pent-up feeling can also manifest as disease (especially inflammation or fever) within the organism if held in for too long.

Venus handing Mars a cup, from Jost Amman's Kunstbüchlin, *published by Johann Feyerabend, Frankfurt, 1599*

Another symbol for Mars, based on his amorous affairs with Venus and others, is that of the lover or Don Juan. Cultures strongly influenced by "machismo" may well be collectively embodying the Mars archetype. This brings up an important point. In the astrological scheme, Mars is always thought of as a "masculine" archetype, and its glyph (♂) is used in medicine to identify the male species. Yet everyone (male and female alike) is possessed of a Mars. Society encourages men to "own" their Mars and display it in prominence, but when boys show little interest in identifying with their Mars archetype, they are often berated, especially by other children. When they are uncomfortable with sports or other "macho" activities, they are regarded as effeminate. This leaves scars that sometimes wound more deeply than the ones encountered in actual battle.

On the other hand, women are strongly discouraged from developing the inner Mars that could become a highly motivating force in their own make-up. To display any kind of fighting anger or aggression is taboo for women, especially women who grow up in conservative or traditional settings, such as the American South, where women are supposed to smile, look pretty, and quench any natural high-spirited behavior. This is why Scarlett O'Hara has been a popular cultural archetype—she broke all the rules by displaying her strong Mars in a world where Mars was almost entirely repressed in women.

It is these two groups—the females that have been taught to repress their Mars, and the males who have been victimized as a result of a naturally "soft" Mars—for whom an afflicted Mars in the birth chart can pose serious consequences. Many women at mid-life reveal a sudden tendency to feel uncontrollable anger and hostility over seemingly small occurrences. This is often noted by the astrologer as a significant transit or progression to natal Mars, a planet which heretofore had been entirely repressed or ignored, and which now seeks an outlet. It's important to realize that, in such cases, the anger may take some time to work itself out, since it's been locked up for so long. Similarly, when men reach the mid-life crisis after years of castigating themselves for their apparent lack of Martian fervor, they must learn that they *do* have a crusading spirit—although theirs is a spirit which may be best employed in some social or spiritual cause rather than in the gladiatorial arena of business and sports.

When awareness is achieved—with *any* aspect—blind spots are alleviated and we become truly in charge of our lives. And that is the real beauty of understanding the astrological archetypes and how they operate in our charts—they provide a mirror for us to see visually what we otherwise can only feel or guess, thus making conscious what would otherwise be unconscious.

Ceres, from Jost Amman's Kunstbüchlin, *published by*
Johann Feyerabend, Frankfurt, 1599

CERES

*Of Demeter, the lovely-haired and august goddess,
and of her daughter, the fair Persephone, I begin to sing.
Hail, O goddess! Keep this city safe, and guide my song.*

Homeric Hymn to Demeter

Beginning in the late 18th century, discoveries occurred on earth and in the sky that would change the course of history forever. Uranus appeared in 1781 and Neptune surfaced in 1846. In 1802 there was another, lesser-known but equally important, occurrence — the discovery of Ceres, Pallas, Juno, and Vesta, the four major bodies in the asteroid belt. And while these new bodies were not considered true planets, Ceres sat precisely where one should be, according to Bode's Law — in the center of the solar system, between Mars and Jupiter. Classified as minor planets, these asteroids resemble their big brothers in terms of orbital characteristics; they are just a great deal smaller in size. In fact, the numerous bodies that make up the asteroid belt have orbits quite similar to the smallest planets in our solar system — Mercury, the closest planet to the sun, and Pluto, the farthest (at present).

Eleanor Bach pioneered the research on the asteroid goddesses and their astrological significance, inspiring many astrologers to place them in horoscopes.[1] Zip
Dobyns,[2] Demetra George,[3] and the late Tony Joseph[4] have continued and
expanded on this work, and the prevailing theories now are that Ceres and Vesta
(the "working" goddesses) belong to Virgo, while Pallas Athene and Juno (the
"relationship" goddesses) belong to Libra. One astronomical theory concerning the
asteroid belt (and there are many, because scientists, too, must speculate until their
theories are time-tested) is that the thousands of chunks of asteroids floating adrift
in a cosmic sea between Mars and Jupiter were once a whole planet. Because
Jupiter is so large and its gravitational pull so strong, this planet was pulled into
Jupiter's mass and exploded. Some esoteric theorists (including the authors)
believe that this planet represented an archetypal system of feminine wholeness—or
at least a significant portion of the feminine—which, like the Goddess culture of
old, was overtaken by masculine sky-gods such as Jupiter. These floating pieces
constitute the various fragments of the feminine which are seeking reunification.
We believe the asteroids as a whole represent Virgo, a sign whose natives sometimes get lost in the fragments, but always strive to pull the bits and pieces together
to make a whole.

It is fitting that these four asteroids lie near the planet Jupiter, for in myth each
of these goddesses was part of Jupiter's "family." Ceres (Demeter), Juno (Hera),
and Vesta (Hestia) were sisters of Zeus, and, like their brother, had major roles in
the Greek pantheon. Ceres was the earth goddess in charge of the agricultural
cycle. Vesta, the temple goddess, was in charge of mankind's spiritual center. The
other two—Juno and Pallas Athene—were Jupiter's wife and favorite daughter
respectively. Juno shared with her husband Jupiter
the rulership of the heavens and also presided over
the institution of marriage. Athene, Jupiter's
daughter, sprang from his brow and was truly her
father's daughter.

The introduction and subsequent incorporation
of these four asteroids into the zodiacal rulership
scheme (see The Zodiac) has eliminated some of
the outworn themes of astrology. The names these
four asteroids were given may seem coincidental to
some, but there is significance to the names, based
on their mythology. Each of the four goddesses for
whom the original four asteroids were named was
one of the twelve Olympians that were honored
and revered throughout the ancient world. Their
inclusion into the astrological system of rulership
restores balance and symmetry to a zodiac that has
long been deficient in feminine representation. And
in keeping with changing laws and changing roles

Ceres, or Demeter

in society, especially regarding women, the inclusion of these goddesses is timely. Unfortunately, there are many astrologers who are confused by the inclusion of these asteroids and still refuse to acknowledge them as part of the astrological framework.

Ceres, or, in Greek, Demeter, is associated above all things with the mysteries of Eleusis. Even today, it is not possible to be certain about what went on in the *telesterion*, the Eleusinian shrine. The initiates were sworn to secrecy. Human nature being what it is, we would logically expect that someone, sooner or later, would have spilled the beans. But

Demeter on a bronze coin of Petelia, Italy, 280–216 BC. From the Michael A. Sikora collection

despite the fact that the mysteries of Eleusis persisted for a thousand years, no one ever gave away the secret. Various ancient writers dropped a few hints, and scholars have used these hints to construct theories about the mysteries—some fairly logical, others quite far-fetched. But they are only theories. In the end, we do not know. When we consider the thousands of people who must have been initiated into the cult of Demeter over so many centuries, we gain a feeling for how compelling the experience must have been—so compelling that all the participants kept silence.

According to the story, Kore was the maiden daughter of Demeter (Ceres), goddess of the earth and the harvest. As she was picking flowers in a field near Eleusis, the earth opened up before her. With a rumble, a dark chariot emerged from the depths, driven by a dark rider. It was Hades (Pluto), lord of the underworld; he seized Kore and bore her unwilling into the land of the dead. For nine days Demeter wandered sorrowing, seeking her lost child. On the tenth day she came to Eleusis, and there she sat down to rest. The daughters of King Celeus found her there as they came to draw water from the well. The goddess was disguised as an old woman, and invented a story of hardship and deprivation which she told to the king's daughters. The girls decided that the old woman would make an excellent nurse for their young brother Demophoon. Carrying their water jars, they took Demeter to the palace of King Celeus and Queen Metaneira. The queen offered Demeter food and wine, but she consented only to take a cup of barley water.

Demeter became nurse to young Demophoon. Every night, when the parents were asleep, she placed the infant in the fireplace, so as to confer upon him the gift of immortality. But one night Queen Metaneira was wakeful. She walked into the room where the old nurse was standing over Demophoon, who lay in the blazing fire. Metaneira went into a panic. Demeter withdrew the child from the fire. Then she transformed herself from an old crone into the shining figure of the goddess. She was angry. By interrupting Demeter's magic, Metaneira had made it certain that Demophoon could never become immortal.

Triptolemus, the son of the Eleusinian king, had been herding his father's cattle when Kore's abduction took place; he had seen the whole thing, and now told Demeter what had happened. The earth mother began her mourning in earnest. She demanded that King Celeus build for her a temple in Eleusis. There she sat, forbidding the earth to bear fruit. The leaves withered and turned sere; the earth itself froze, and the world was in the grips of the first winter.

At last humanity stood in danger of extinction. Moved by the prayers of mortals, Zeus sent the messenger of the gods, Hermes, into the underworld to beg for Kore's release. Hades consented to give up the girl on one condition; that she had not yet tasted of the food of the dead. Kore had indeed been so sorrowful that she had refused to eat; thus she made ready to follow Hermes back to the world of light. But then one of the dark lord's gardeners stepped forward to reveal that Kore had, in fact, eaten seven pomegranate seeds. A compromise had to be reached. It was ordained that Kore would spend three months out of every year in the underworld, and nine upon earth. During her absence, the cold of winter would reign, but while she was above ground, the long Mediterranean spring and summer would flourish. Nevertheless, she was still the dark lord's queen, and thus her name would no longer be Kore, the maiden, but Persephone, "she who is to be feared."

After Persephone was restored to her mother, Demeter rejoiced. She taught the mysteries of earth and the harvest to Triptolemus, who was the mythic founder of the Eleusinian cult. It will be seen that the story of Demeter's doings in Eleusis runs like a secondary theme or counterpoint to the main story, i.e., the search for the missing Kore. And yet this tale of Eleusis played a large role in the Mysteries themselves—perhaps as large a role as the more familiar story of Persephone's abduction.

The initiates of Eleusis identified themselves not with Persephone but with Demeter herself. Thus the Roman emperor Gallienus, an initiate, sometimes called himself Galliena Augusta, a feminine form of his name. The candidates fasted, even as Demeter refused food and wine from Metaneira. Before they began their procession to Eleusis, they covered their faces and bathed in

Triptolemus, mythic founder of the Eleusinian Mysteries

*The road from Athens to Eleusis, along which initiates in the cult of Eleusis walked
with torches as part of the rites of their Mysteries*

the ocean. This combination of water and darkness suggests that the road to Eleusis
was also the road to the underworld. Water and darkness remind us of Persephone
as the underworld goddess—but they might equally remind us of Hecate, another
goddess with these attributes. In the *Homeric Hymn to Demeter*, Hecate appears, torch
in hand, and like Triptolemus she helps Demeter solve the mystery of where
Persephone has gone.

After the purification, the initiates walked to Eleusis, carrying torches. The
torches again remind us of Hecate, but also of Demophoon in the fire, for the *Hymn*
actually describes him as a torch or burning brand. At Eleusis, the initiates drank a
concoction of barley water, even as Demeter herself did. This concoction may have
been hallucinatory, perhaps containing the fly-agaric mushroom—the food of
Dionysus, the ambrosia (Sanskrit *amrita*) of the gods. There was a dance which followed. What happened afterwards was never revealed. Hints dropped by classical
writers allow us at least to speculate about what *might* have taken place. The torches
were dowsed, and a "divine marriage" celebrated between the male hierophant and
the priestess of Demeter. After that, Persephone was restored to her mother.

Finally, a single stalk of grain was revealed in a winnowing basket, and it was announced that the goddess had given birth—Brimo had given birth to Brimos.

It is Demeter as Brimo, rather than Persephone, who gives birth. In Arcadia, the most primitive part of Greece, legends were preserved which tell us how Poseidon (Neptune), in the form of a stallion, pursued Demeter in the form of a mare, and raped her. The result was a child known mysteriously as "the Mistress"— another name for Persephone as queen of the underworld.

When we discussed the Moon, we learned that there is widespread acknowledgement of a pursuit story in which the goddess pursues the god, or, in later times, the god pursues the goddess. In the story of Poseidon and Demeter we see another variation of this ancient story. The Arcadians also worshiped a "Black Demeter," i.e., a chthonic Demeter who was herself queen of the dead. Therefore, in all these stories, we are talking about *one* goddess who has three aspects—maiden (Persephone as Kore), mother (Demeter), and crone (Hecate, Demeter as the elderly nurse, and Persephone as Queen of Hades).

And who is the child Brimos? In the *Homeric Hymn*, Demophoon, the child in the fire, plays the role of Brimos. But the name Brimos means terrifying or wrathful. Hence the dark mother (Brimo), in rage over being raped, gives birth to a dark child. The Eleusinian hero Triptolemus is yet another name for this divine child, for later myths affirm that he traveled the world in a chariot drawn by serpents in order to teach agriculture and the Eleusinian Mysteries to mankind. But there is yet another interpretation: the divine child is Dionysus, god of wine and ecstasy. In fact, Dionysus was said, by the members of the Orphic cult, to be the child of either Demeter or Persephone. The most familiar story involving Dionysus makes him the son of Zeus and Semele. He is rescued from an inferno when Semele burns up, consumed by the sight of Zeus in the full aspect of his godhood. Like Demophoon, the divine child Dionysus is born in a blaze of fire. Like Triptolemus, he is a child of earth. Like Persephone, he makes an underworld journey—i.e., he is torn to pieces by women, only to rise again as the intoxicating vine. And like Brimos, he can be terrifying, for Dionysian ecstasy can lead to madness. Dionysus, like Christ, is the child of the divine mother, dying and reborn. This associates him with the Piscean archetype. The opposite polarity of Pisces is, of course, Virgo, the sign of Ceres-Demeter.

The process attached to Ceres as mother is to lose her child, Persephone, and then to regain her. Most of us do indeed "lose" our children—they grow up and move away. We feel the pain of separation. But our children do not return to us *literally*. The myth hints at a more symbolic "return." Note also that Demeter herself suffers rape; that she rages (Brimo) at her loss and violation. But the child of this loss, pain, rape, and frustration paradoxically brings ecstasy. The aspect of human consciousness which was so deeply experienced at Eleusis was one of sorrow and pain over the loss of innocence and the breaking of the bond between mother and child, followed by a rebirth into spiritual ecstasy—the Dionysian freedom of the Self. Ceres' position in the horoscope obviously involves her role as mother, and for that reason she can be associated with and is perhaps exalted in the sign Cancer. For centuries astrologers have associated the Moon, as ruler of Cancer, with the mothering principle, but it is not incorrect to link Ceres with that sign as well. The emotional, psychological, and biological connection between mother and chid as a unit is discussed in Cancer—and the Moon plays a large role in the birth chart as the primary agent of that association. But what of the "earth mother," who carefully and lovingly gives her child its first book to read at bedtime, who teaches the child to lace its shoes, and who provides the framework for the child to make its way in the world? This is what Ceres governs in the horoscope. Those with Ceres in prominent positions will identify strongly with their inner earth mother, or, in the charts of men, with their ability to play the role of "caretaker," and if Ceres is involved with the Moon there may be a strong emotional dependency between mother and child, such as Kore and Demeter shared with one another. Persephone, or Kore, was everything to her mother, and when her child became separated from her it was as if a part of her were lost and she could no longer function in the physical world performing her work—Ceres' other primary interest.

It should be no surprise that Ceres' position in the horoscope has a strong connection with food and eating habits, based on her role as grain goddess. An afflicted Ceres will usually result in one kind of eating disorder or another, a problem that afflicts too many people in the modern, industrial world. This may be a symbolic way of saying that since agricultural concerns have been taken over by industrialists who are more concerned with the quantity, rather than the quality, of the food produced, and who show little concern for the earth itself, there is consequently little nourishment which can come out of our modern food. In such a situation, even if the soil producing such food were healthy and clean and pesticides and chemicals weren't running rampant on our grocery shelves, would Ceres, symbol of Mother Earth, be happy?

Ceres' position in the horoscope can significantly affect one's ability to create and maintain a healthy working relationship with oneself. Ceres is happiest, of course, when Kore, her daughter, is with her for two-thirds of the year. This is the point in the cycle of nature when she flowers and greens the earth in magnificent splendor. When people are emotionally content (as with primary relationships) they are capable of producing their most splendid masterpieces—and think nothing of working over-time if they have to in order to get the job done.

Ceres' glyph (⚳), it has been noted, is Saturn's glyph turned upside down and reversed (see Saturn). The earth father Cronus and the earth mother Ceres appear to have a lot in common. In fact, Ceres *was* one of Saturn's children and was eaten by him; she also suffered her own child being "eaten" or swallowed up by the underworld. Saturn ate his children because he feared they would surpass him. Ceres couldn't eat without her child. Both planets have to do with parenting and both can potentially develop possessive, overbearing, or strangulating relationships with their children. And, naturally, both planets, poorly integrated in the chart, can experience eating disorders as well.

One might guess that the link between Ceres and Pluto is of significance as well, based on their mythological rivalry. It has been noted in a number of charts that a natally tense relationship between these two planets can produce a type of loss or sacrifice similar to the one Ceres suffered with Persephone. Additionally, transits to Ceres from Pluto may often pinpoint a period in a person's life when he or she is required to give up something of this magnitude.

The former Soviet Union adopted the sickle as its symbol. This was a country whose sprawling size challenged it greatly to simply provide enough to eat for its masses. The work force, or labor party, is associated with Ceres, and the birth chart for the Soviet Union (the 1917 revolution) contained a Scorpio Sun tightly conjunct the asteroid Ceres at 14 degrees Scorpio. Since both Scorpio the sign and Ceres the asteroid mythically symbolize time spent in the underworld and deal with themes of loss and grief followed by regeneration, it is no wonder that the people of this nation experienced 75 years "behind the iron curtain"—in the underworld, as it were. In this horoscope, both Pluto and Ceres would be considered strong—Pluto by virtue of its rulership over Scorpio and Ceres because of its close conjunction with the Sun, the life force of the chart. Thus, tight controls by the Soviet government have always been maintained on their citizens, whose only choice was silent complicity or defection. Pluto transiting through Scorpio (1984–1996) targeted the Soviet Sun-Ceres conjunction during 1988 and 1989, with a resulting death and rebirth, Scorpio style, of the Soviet Union. We can draw a parallel here to people's personal lives. Those who are parented by or in relationship with people containing strong Ceres-Pluto aspects may experience similar suffocation or strangulation until they eventually break free, but freedom often does not occur without a significant power struggle.

Ceres' relationship to the grieving process is perhaps one of her most important functions. Her grief was all-consuming. The Eleusinian Mysteries were concerned with important rites of passage honoring death and loss—an experience every human being must face at one time or another. The horoscope of Elisabeth Kubler-Ross contains an angular Ceres—in its rulership sign Virgo, on the Seventh House cusp. Kubler-Ross is the acknowledged pioneer of "death and dying with dignity," and has helped educate millions to allow the grief process to occur.

Often, Ceres in the horoscope will manifest as the area in which one can become fiercely protective and mothering, or adopt the "caretaker" role, aspects of life with which most Virgos and Cancers are all too familiar.

PALLAS

CHAPTER TEN

I begin to sing of Pallas Athena, the glorious goddess,
gray-eyed, resourceful, of implacable heart.
This bashful maiden is a mighty defender of cities,
the Tritogeneia, whom Zeus the counselor himself
bore from his august head, clad with golden and resplendent
warlike armor, as awe lay hold of all the immortal onlookers.

Homeric Hymn to Athena

Perhaps the most remarkable myth about Pallas Athene is the story of her birth. It is said that Zeus pursued the Titaness Metis, and made love to her. This Metis was the original guardian of the planet Mercury, and her name meant "counsel." She became pregnant as a result of the affair. At that point, Gaia announced to her grandson Zeus that the first child of Metis would be a girl, but if the Titaness were allowed to survive she would in time give birth to a male child who would supplant Zeus. Like his father Cronus before him, Zeus took action and swallowed Metis— though she continued forever after to give "counsel" from within his stomach. Later, as Zeus was walking along the shores of Lake Triton in Libya, he was seized with a raging headache. His son Hephaestus relieved his pain by the somewhat unusual expedient of splitting his head open. Out leapt gray-eyed Pallas Athene, daughter of Metis, clothed in armor and giving a great shout.

As a child of the father's brain, it was natural to associate Athene with the human intellect. But her roots go much deeper and extend far back into antiquity. One of her principal attributes is the shield she carries, emblazoned with the image of the Gorgon Medusa, a fierce female demon with snakes writhing from her head. According to legend, it was Perseus, who slew Medusa with Athene's help, that gave this trophy to Athene. Mythologists see an identity between Athene and this fearsome Lady of the Snakes. Taking his cue from the fact that she emerged at Lake Triton in Libya, Robert Graves believed Athene to be a Greek incarnation of the Libyan snake goddess Neith, and most feminist historians of mythology have followed this interpretation.[1] But it is possible that Athene's real origins lie in even more remote times. Many scholars believe that the famous Lady of the Snakes from the Cretan palace of Knossos is not a priestess but a goddess, and that this goddess is an early, Minoan form of Athene. Archaeologist Marija Gimbutas has argued that the Minoan culture of Crete was itself the last survival and highest development of the old neolithic culture of southeastern Europe. She goes on to say that one of the principal goddesses in this neolithic culture (c. 6,000–3,500 BC) was a Mistress of Waters whose epiphany or physical form was embodied in the snake, and that this is the "original" Athene, who was thus a kind of fertility goddess, bringer of the life-giving rain.[2] But if she was celestial, she was also chthonic, a creature of the under-world, and—from an astrological point of view—there are strong links between Pallas Athene and the archetype of Pluto.

Snakes played an important role in the secret teachings and mysteries surrounding life, death, and immortality (Scorpio) and Athene was, to the Greeks, the goddess of wisdom. Thus, we may conclude that Athene possessed the wisdom not merely of the intellect, but the instinctual feminine wisdom sacred to the Goddess. Something of this more primal Athene has survived in the attribution of the owl to this goddess as her sacred bird. The owl has always been known as a bird of "wisdom"—and yet we typically understand this to signify a deep inner knowing or understanding rather than wisdom of a purely intellectual type. That the Greeks made her the goddess of intellectual wisdom is not so much a statement about Athene as it is about the Greeks, who glorified the intellectual process. Athene's knowledge, however, was never purely cerebral: it was *useful*. It is said that Poseidon and Athene took part in a competition to determine which one would become the patron

Head of Athene wearing a crested helmet ornamented with a griffin, on a didrachm of Velia, Italy, 400–350 BC. From the Michael A. Sikora collection

deity of Athens. Poseidon created the horse; Athene produced the olive tree. Because the olive was considered of even greater utility than the horse, Athene won the contest—and, of course, the city of Athens retains her name to this very day. She was also the goddess who was said to have invented weaving, cooking, pottery, mathematics, the plough, the chariot, and ship-building—all the "useful" arts. Among the warlike Romans, Athene was said to be exalted in the arena of battle. Her Latin name was Minerva and she was renowned for her strategic skills on the battlefield. As a warrior, however, Athene was a strategist and thinker rather than a butcher. She always preferred diplomacy and negotiation to outright conflict.

The picture that has been painted of Pallas Athene, even in contemporary feminist literature, focuses on her role as a daughter of the patriarchy, i.e., Zeus' daughter.[3] And astronomically it is true that Pallas Athene comes closer to Jupiter than

Minerva (Pallas Athene) with an owl and Medusa shield, from Jost Amman's Kunstbüchlin, *published by Johann Feyerabend, Frankfurt, 1599*

any other of the "Big Four" asteroids. It is not entirely incorrect to regard her as being within Jupiter's shadow. It is also true that Athene cast the deciding vote in the trial of Orestes—a case involving the question of mother-right versus father-right. Athene's vote, against the mother, has been interpreted as patriarchal bias on her part. But this patriarchal bias was not so much a characteristic of Athene as it was a sign of the times. Athene is the upholder of laws and justice, and, as the agent of such, reflects the laws currently governing the land.

Thus we can observe that Pallas Athene's evolution from the primal Snake Goddess, possessor and protector of feminine wisdom, to the Greek "daughter of the patriarchy," to the Roman goddess of war parallels the path for women through the centuries. Up until the late 19th century women were powerless to develop their own intellectual skills, and indeed were punished, condemned, or burned at the stake if they dared display any knowledge of healing or magic. As times change and feminine wisdom is once again restored to its former status, Pallas Athene's wisdom will again be honored and celebrated in its many forms.

Unlike many of the gods and goddesses of Olympus, who preferred to lie around consuming nectar and ambrosia, this goddess was far from idle. In fact, a person with a strong Pallas Athene signature in the birth chart may have no idea how to relax. Athene was a highly skilled, intelligent, courageous, inventive, and industrious goddess. We can identify Pallas Athene's most important function in the birth chart—her strategy, judgment, and wisdom—by assessing her house and sign position.

One can see whether it is Athene the skilled artisan, Athene the strategist, Athene the warrior, Athene the intellectual, Athene the inventor, Athene the indus-

Archaic head of Athene and an owl, on a fifth-century BC tetradrachm piece depicted on contemporary (1944) Greek currency. From the Michael A. Sikora collection

trialist, or Athene the knower of life's mysteries which gets the individual's best attention. For example, in the United States chart Athene is in Aquarius conjunct the Moon, a signature that surely relates to the inventive and highly skilled use of technology that this country has pursued in its ongoing development. It also suggests our open and candid glorification of the skilled technicians who break new ground in a country which strives to maintain a competitive leadership role among industrialized nations. Athene conjunct the Moon would also lend support to the idea that women's opportunities in management and even leadership positions are available in a country where all it takes to get ahead is pure ambition and "getting the job done." China has Athene in Virgo and, while this is the chart for their most recent government (the 1949 revolution), this position of Athene reflects the world's perception of the Chinese workforce and its ability to create, laboriously but efficiently, miniature handicrafts and machinery parts in thousands of factories.

It is no secret that Zeus' favorite child was Athene, and the Greeks reflected their chief god's opinion by honoring her second only to Zeus. Thus, the father-daughter bond is established here, just as the mother-daughter bond is paramount

A nineteenth-century engraving of Pallas Athene, after the statue by Phidias

The Tholos at Delphi, Greece, is one of a number of buildings standing in a precinct dedicated to Athene. Beginning of the fourth century BC. Photograph by Ariel Guttman

with Demeter and Persephone. Athene's paradoxical relationship with her father—and by extension with the prevailing world-view symbolized by the king of the gods—has been responsible for the most popular image of the goddess in our modern world. Whether seen from the vantage point of astrology[4] or Jungian psychology,[5] the Athene-type woman is readily recognized as an archetype—perhaps even as a stereotype. Heavily armored behind her emotional defenses, disdaining relationships by choice, she charges ahead into the world armed with her briefcase and dressed in a gray suit sporting outsized shoulder-pads. As a businesswoman, she plays hardball with more force than the men, whom she delights in overpowering (Margaret Thatcher fits this archetype). Toni Wolff and Linda Schierse Leonard have named this Athene type the "armored Amazon."[6] But this is only one aspect of Athene, and not necessarily her most healthy manifestation. It is true that most Amazons tend to be Athenes; but most Athenes are not Amazons. In order to genuinely realize the potential embodied in this goddess or asteroid, it is necessary to incorporate some of her deeper, owlish, serpentine wisdom.

In identifying Athene's specific mode of wisdom in any given birth chart, one must first determine how she relates to the signs and planets that represent the father symbolism in the chart. When Athene is dominant in a chart there is often a strong projection onto the child in early life by the father. Whether accepting the father's projection, which an Athene would most likely do, or rejecting it, which might be symbolized by an early transit of something like Uranus to Athene, the ultimate goal is to break through the shield and armor and get in touch with one's own personal wisdom. It often comes as a shock to those who have been living in the father's shadow or projection all their lives to have to come to terms with the fact that this no longer works for them. It is then up to these people to get in touch with their own sense of inner wisdom by breaking out of the suit of armor they have worn for so long.

It is in the arena of love that Athene seems to have been at her weakest, and her armor is symbolic of the difficulty she had in establishing any kind of close relationship. Many gods and Titans offered themselves to her in marriage, but she rejected them all. Often, she failed even to understand the sexual implications of relationship. For instance, she once asked Hephaestus to forge for her a suit of armor. Hephaestus replied that he would do it "for love." Athene naively thought that the celestial smith intended to work for her out of the goodness of his heart, but Hephaestus, who was accustomed to being paid for his work, meant something quite different by the word "love." When he tried to have his way with her, she resisted. Hephaestus ejaculated on her thigh. In disgust, she wiped his seed away with a piece of wool and threw it down to earth. From this unlikely source was born Erichthonius, child of Athene. He was part man and part serpent, hence a representative of the older, chthonic Athene, the Lady of the Snakes; but he was also the first to institute "father-right" in ancient Greece and to reckon bloodlines through the father's side. But if Athene shunned relationships, she was not as brutal as Artemis, who had Actaeon torn to bits for gazing upon her nakedness. Tiresias caught a simi-

The judgment of Paris, from a Greek vase of the third century BC

lar glimpse of Athene; in punishment, she made him blind, but she softened the sentence by giving him inner vision, the power of prophecy. And she *did* care to have her gray-eyed beauty acknowledged; along with Hera and Aphrodite, she took part in the famous Judgment of Paris, wherein the Trojan prince was asked to judge which of the goddesses was most beautiful (he chose Aphrodite). It is worth noting, however, that when each of the goddesses tried to bribe Paris by offering him certain favors, Pallas Athene offered him something eminently practical and patriarchal: she said that she would give him victory in battle.

When one must compete skillfully and successfully in a "man's world," there is often no time or place for developing emotional sensitivity, or so one might believe. And yet just the opposite is true—the ultimate winning edge is achieved when feminine elements of feeling, compassion, and sensitivity are added to already well-endowed faculties of ingenuity and industriousness, especially since compassion is likely to be something the opponent lacks. In fact, as more and more female leaders enter the world of politics, business, medicine, and law, the extra ingredient seems to be that she can and does do it all! This is the archetype of the super-woman that emerged in the 1980s—the woman who could take care of home and family, oversee professional concerns, handle the budget, maintain social relationships, and solve the problems of everyone around her—in short, the personification of Pallas Athene.

For the past twenty years or so, Pallas Athene has been one of the most dramatically visible archetypes emerging into Western consciousness. But the asteroid, of course, has a role in the horoscopes of men as well. And if Pallas Athene frequently sharpens the intellectual skills of women, or thrusts them into the patriarchal world with great force, it is likely to do the opposite in the charts of men. It has a softening effect; when Pallas Athene is strong in a man's chart, he is more likely to be able to temper his rational, scientific slant on reality with a bit of compassion or sensitivity—with the deep wisdom symbolized by the owl and the serpent which renders knowledge "useful."

Pallas Athene lies between Mars and Jupiter, its orbital revolution taking approximately five years. Thus, every five years or so one will get a Pallas return, a transit that can be thought of as a time to get renewed by or in touch with one's inner wisdom and skill, a time when, in any competitive event, the individual will have increased chances of being victorious. It may also point to periods when the individual is pursuing a path of intensely focused study, studies which will ultimately result in feelings of superiority, enhancement, or enlightenment.

Head of Juno, after the Ludovisi Juno, Ludovisi Museum, Rome

JUNO

Wedding is great Juno's crown:
O blessed bond of board and bed!

—*Shakespeare*, As You Like It, V, IV

Like other goddesses of Greek myth, Juno's (Hera's) story (her-story) is one of the conquest and subjugation of the Goddess of Heaven. Homer often describes Hera as "white-armed Hera," and the color white, along with Hera's status as a goddess of relationships, has led some mythologists to suspect that she was originally the Goddess in her full-moon aspect. Her totem bird was the peacock; her sacred animal was the cow. She was associated with the city of Argos, and it was near there that she was said to take her annual bath in a sacred spring, a rite which renewed her virginity. Another place sacred to her was the Aegean island of Samos, where she spent her wedding night with Zeus—a night which lasted three hundred years.

When Zeus (Jupiter) claimed Hera as his wife, he was not simply taking a marriage partner, but incorporating within his ruling domain the entire matriarchal world, previously headed by his new bride. When the invading Indo-Europeans entered Greece, they found it necessary to incorporate many of the previously existing religious customs and rituals into the new system, so that the indigenous populace would put up less resistance. According to classical scholar Jane Ellen Harrison, many of the gods of the Greeks were ritually married to one or another aspect of the Goddess, in order to merge the two systems.[1] Thus Hera was merged with the new ruler of the gods, Zeus. In the human social sphere, this corresponds to the custom of arranged marriages, marriages of convenience in which two powerful families, nations, or political opponents agree to a political or social alliance by merging their families and future heirs, a tradition that has been repeated for centuries, especially among royalty and powerful families, as a way to increase their power and holdings.

In pre-Grecian times, Hera was the name by which the Great Goddess was known in the region of Argos. Her marriage to Zeus gave her a special status as one of the Olympians; in addition to being Zeus' wife, she was also his sister, one of the children of Rhea who was swallowed by Cronus. Astrological historian Rupert Gleadow reports that she had rulership over the sign Aquarius in early times, placing her opposite Zeus himself as the ancient ruler of Leo.[2] But asteroid specialists Zipporah Dobyns and Demetra George suggest a Libra rulership for Juno.[3] Libra, like Aquarius, is an air sign but it is concerned with equality and primary one-to-one relationships rather than the relationship to the community at large that Aquarius signifies.

Juno, or Hera

Libra does seem a fitting sign for Juno's rulership; her name was given to the month of June, a month still chosen above all others as the most desirable month for marriage. She presided over marriage as an institution and was always invoked at wedding ceremonies in ancient times.

In Rome, the word *juno* for females corresponded to the word *genius* for males; these terms implied the soul, or, more precisely, the vital indwelling spirit or animating principle. Each woman carried part of the Goddess with her as part of her soul. Later the word *juno* fell out of use, but *genius* remained common, perhaps giving the Church Fathers of the early Middle Ages the idea that women were soulless.[4] It was Juno's distinction to be one of only two goddesses (along with the goddess of love, Aphrodite) on Olympus who were legally married. Her marriage to Jupiter was stormy and turbulent, and Greek myth is filled with stories of their quarrelsome interludes: his frequent infidelities, her jealous rages, and their mutual attempts (often successful) to revenge themselves upon one another. One may wonder why Jupiter, who could have any woman in the world or goddess in the heavens, would continue this kind of relationship. But were he not married to Juno, Jupiter would not have been himself, for Juno is the embodiment of Jupiter's female polarity as Jupiter is the embodiment of Juno's male side. Her strength and temperament empowered him and vice versa. Their relationship is a prototype for the importance that marriage, no matter how turbulent, plays for a highly visible political leader or monarch.

Zeus and Hera on an ancient Greek coin, a detail from contemporary (1944) Greek currency. From the Michael A. Sikora collection

Their marriage was not always stormy. In the beginning Jupiter courted and seduced Juno, pursuing her quite passionately. She at first resisted, then finally succumbed to his advances. But she was not happy being someone's wife, even Jupiter's. She preferred to live as women had once lived, in the Goddess era, free and independent, openly pursuing relationships on her own terms. Early in her marriage she got tired of Zeus' arrogance, his lordly ways. She gathered all the other Olympians around her in a conspiracy—the only one who did not join in was Hestia (Vesta), the mystical and reclusive goddess of the hearth. Zeus was tied up while he slept. Hera took over Mt. Olympus; there was a queen of the gods rather than a king. But Thetis, the goddess of the sea, had pity on Zeus. She called the hundred-armed giant Briareos to set him free. Enraged at Hera's treachery, Zeus hung her from the sky, her wrists bound with gold. The other gods were embarrassed to see her like that, hanging from the vault of heaven, squirming and squawking; but they were afraid to speak out against an angry Zeus. It was Hephaestus, Hera's rejected son, who finally prevailed upon Zeus to set his mother free. Zeus kept her as his wife, but placed her under tighter lock and key.[5]

It has been suggested that Juno's position in the horoscope is related to an individual's marriage potential. A study conducted on long-term marriages revealed that one partner's Juno aspecting the other person's Ascendant/Descendant (the axis in astrology relating to relationships and marriage) was the most frequently occurring aspect in these married couples' charts.[6] But no matter what position she holds in an individual chart, it must be admitted that Juno's marriage to Jupiter was usually stormy. Still, because she represents the institution of marriage and was always called upon to bless the newlyweds, her position should always be taken into consideration when studying the charts of those who desire to be married, along with her position on the intended date. Harmonious aspects to Juno from other principal planets help to seal a positive outcome for the couple.

Juno's jealousy and vindictiveness towards Jupiter was not based simply upon his frequent extramarital affairs. It also had to do with the fact that he continually *lied* to her about his escapades. As a lover, he dressed himself up in many disguises, thinking that he was fooling everyone. Juno's humiliation increased with each new affair, after which Jupiter would return home and beg her forgiveness, only to repeat his infidelities again and again. Perhaps, in the beginning, Juno could have forgiven one or two violations of the sacred vow of marriage, but when the contract was knowingly violated time and time again, there was no more acceptance or forgiveness. Similar patterns among modern individuals may reach the point where anger turns to rage, rage turns to disease, and one is eventually consumed and sometimes kills because of it or is even killed by it. The frequency of crimes of passion in the present day may indicate a collective dysfunction of Juno.

In one myth, the wrath of Hera is made visible in a very graphic way. Some stories name the monster Typhon or Typhaon as a child of Gaia, slain in combat with Zeus. But another version of the tale makes the monstrous serpent or dragon a child of Hera. Fuming with jealousy because Zeus had brought forth Pallas Athene from his own head, she herself gave birth, without male intervention, to Typhon. This serpent is male, but in myth is associated—or perhaps confused—with the Python, the female serpent of Delphi. Hence in some versions of the Delphi story, Apollo, the favorite child of Zeus and patriarchal hero, slays a monster born of the Queen of Heaven's jealousy and rage.

Thus, Juno's appearance in a chart may not be related strictly to marriage; she also represents the internal emotional rage which develops and combusts when a loved one has deceived, betrayed, or misused his or her vows of loyalty and devotion. It is something that occurs frequently in the love and marriage game. No matter how much love may have departed from the relationship over the years, when one partner leaves for another person (whether for one night or permanently), the wrath of Juno can be felt.

Another dynamic of the marriage between Juno and Jupiter illustrates the notorious double standard, still in evidence today. It was fine for Jupiter to have as many sexual liaisons as he wished, but not for Juno. The Junos of modern times who sit around pining over a spouse's infidelities but refuse to do anything about it, or who inflict their anger on the spouse's lover rather than the spouse, are examples of a dysfunctional Juno principle at work in the chart.

There is a great deal of sexual repression in the Juno nature. Though one story claims that the prophet Tiresias was struck blind by Pallas Athene, another story lays the blame on Hera. It is said that Zeus and Hera were once engaged in a debate as to who got more pleasure out of sex—men or women. Zeus, the eternal playboy, claimed that women received far more joy from the act than men did. Hera insisted that men simply had their way with women and left them with nothing. The

debate became an argument. The quarrelsome pair called upon Tiresias to settle
the dispute, because he had lived as both
a male and a female. Tiresias answered,
without hesitation, that women received
nine times more pleasure than men. Hera,
still refusing to admit that she enjoyed
sex, struck him blind.

It is interesting to note that the marriage between Jupiter and Juno produced very little in the way of offspring,
and that their children, especially Mars,
embodied the stormy and tormented
aspects of their parents' relationship —
except for Hebe, who may once have
been Hera's maiden aspect, and who
became cupbearer to the gods. Jupiter's
most interesting and powerful children
were fathered upon other goddesses or
upon mortal women. Juno gave birth to
Mars and Vulcan (Hephaestus), and had
no particular affinity for either of them;
thus her role in the horoscope may be
that of someone more concerned with
peer relationships than with parent/child
relationships.

Hebe

In fact, Juno's relationships with her children, and especially with the talented
Vulcan, point out one of the complexes most frequently associated with this archetype. Juno is, after all, a queen—and Hera's golden throne was one of the goddess'
principal symbols. And a queen must have something over which to rule.

Although Juno tends to be a problematical planet or archetype, it is nevertheless a common theme. It is sometimes the "society wife" or husband who assesses
life according to the status she or he achieves. Such people build for themselves a
little queendom or kingdom in their own community, and *must* let everyone know
they are seated upon a throne of gold. For a woman of this type, marriage to a doctor or a lawyer equals success, while marriage to a mechanic or a janitor equals failure. It doesn't matter if the doctor is an alcoholic or the lawyer an abuser. It doesn't
matter if the mechanic is the kindest of men or the janitor a promising poet. A man
with this kind of Juno complex may choose the archetypal cheerleader or society
girl, neglecting his real emotional needs for the sake of a partner who will look and
act correctly in the social sphere. The relationship, its success or failure, is defined
purely in terms of status.

This focus upon social approval is frequently extended to the Juno individual's children. When Hephaestus was born, his mother Hera was shocked to see him misshapen, deformed, unlovely. She cast him away from her in disgust. He fell from heaven and landed in the sea. There the ancient sea goddesses Thetis and Eurynome found him, loved him, nurtured him. They gave him a cavern in the ocean depths, and it was here that his artistic brilliance first flourished; he took jewels from the bottom of the sea and set them in gold and silver brooches. Thetis wore one of those beautiful pieces of jewelry on a visit to Mt. Olympus, some nine years later. Hera was fascinated by the workmanship, and forced Thetis to reveal who had made it. Then she called up her rejected son from the bottom of the sea and gave him a fabulous smithy on Mt. Olympus itself—on the tacit understanding that he would make jewelry for his mother.

The Juno person's love for his or her children is very conditional—they have to meet her social expectations in order to be worthy of parental affection. Hephaestus was ugly, and not at all godlike—hence, Hera cast him out. When the Juno person's little boy becomes the star athlete or class valedictorian, when he appears to be on the way to law school (like his father), the parent just beams. Such parents may ignore the boy or show their venom if he is slow in school or inept at sports, or even if he would prefer to be a gardener rather than a doctor. Juno will adore the beautiful daughter who heads the cheerleading squad and seems ripe for a high status marriage—then cast her out with great suddenness if she should become pregnant before she graduates from high school.

Hephaestus, son of Hera

But in the end it is Juno who suffers. These people seek love, whether from their spouses or their children, but their love is conditional upon status and success—how much loyalty can they really expect? Hephaestus, upon arriving at Olympus, hated his mother so deeply that he chained her to her golden throne. He refused to let her go until Zeus promised him Aphrodite in marriage. The loser, the rejected one, made good in the end. But in order to do so, he was obliged to rebel against the woman who made him, quite literally, an outcast. When Juno people focus all their attention on what they want their children to be or achieve, and consequently neglect the issue of who these little strangers really *are*, they will almost certainly incur the resentment of their children, who will strike out angrily against the status and social respectability

The marriage of Jupiter and Juno

which mean so much to Juno. The angry drifter, the hoodlum, the high school tramp—as well as the artist, the rock star, the poet—all of them probably have a Juno for a parent.

For a long time, Venus has been erroneously associated with marriage in the horoscope. This may be due to the fact that for centuries she and the Moon were the only female planets in the chart. But with the addition of the four major asteroids, the proper functions can be restored to the proper goddesses. While Venus has associations to love and romance, she is *not* at all fond of marriage. Based upon the stories of her relationship with Jupiter it would seem that Juno has just as little reason to favor married life, but mythologically she is the one who properly rules that institution. Typically, Juno in the birth chart will represent the type of partner or the type of marriage desired. If there are dignity and exaltation signs for Juno, they would probably be Libra and Scorpio, the signs most closely associated with pair-bonding.

If Juno in the horoscope is in a "weak" position, perhaps afflicted by power planets such as Jupiter, Saturn, Pluto, or even the Sun or Mars, one might experience a relationship or relationships filled with disgrace and humiliation; one may be subject to victimization at the hands of a spouse who is too powerful or too threatening to challenge. Of course, it is possible that men, too, might find themselves in this predicament. Up until recently, these negative Jupiter/Juno roles were typically played out by a man who was dominant in the professional or political world (Jupiter), married to a woman who lived in his shadow (Juno). But recently it has become just as likely that the woman will play Jupiter, possessing a powerful and dynamic career and wielding power of a threatening nature over a male spouse who feels inadequate or powerless. It is also true that many women with a strong Juno archetype live in their husband's shadows, and are gloriously content with such a position.[7] Others stay in the relationship out of fear, shame, or guilt, feeling they have no alternative.

It has frequently been found in chart comparison that Juno contacts from one chart to another "bind" a couple together in unexplainable ways. It is definitely meaningful to check these Juno contacts when examining the astrological significance of a relationship. Juno's aspects to planets, other asteroids, and particularly the angles of a potential mate's chart will give clues as to what is expected in the marriage and how it will work out.

Juno was a powerful head of state, Queen of Olympus by virtue of being the first of Rhea's daughters to emerge from the jaws of Saturn. There are many Juno individuals who, for one reason or another, decide to "marry" themselves to their positions in life rather than to another individual. Juno's chosen positions, no matter in what field, will typically involve power. Thus power struggles, similar to those that were played out between Juno and Jupiter, may also involve parents, authority figures on the job, or even sibling and peer relationships. That is not to say that Juno will always be the one in power, but when Juno is dominant in a person's chart he or she will be likely to experience both sides of the power game—as one who is initially abused by the system (perhaps due to sexual, racial, or other discrimination), but one who has the strength, will, and determination (and sometimes the spirit of revenge) to fight back and eventually overtake a system that formerly subjugated him or her.

Thus Juno in the birth chart describes, at worst, feelings of victimization or jealousy in relationships due to an overwhelming surrender of one's power for the sake of the relationship, and, at best, a power truly centered in oneself, revealing charisma and magnetism that emanates out to all who come into contact with it.

VESTA

CHAPTER TWELVE

Hestia, in the lofty dwellings of all,
both of immortal gods and of men who walk on the earth,
you have attained an eternal abode and the highest honor,
together with a fair and honorific prize: for without you
there can be no feasts for mortals, if at the beginning
yours is not the first and last libation of honey-sweet wine.

Homeric Hymn to Hestia

Like the other goddesses for whom the asteroids were named, Vesta has undergone some very radical changes during her long history. She is one of the oldest and most revered of goddesses, and what she represents is still regarded as sacred.

Almost all tribal peoples regard the center of the village, or the center of the home, as the symbolic center of the universe as well. This kind of thinking is based on the notion that humankind is a microcosm of the universe; we are all the cosmos in miniature. A Lakota shaman, for instance, travels to the other world by ascending the column of smoke which rises through the central hole in the teepee. Why? Because the fire and the column of smoke are symbolic of the tree at the center of the world, the tree that shamans climb to reach the world of the gods.[1] The fire which burns at the hearth of every village household is the visible center of

🌿 115 🌿

the family universe. Vesta's Greek name, Hestia, literally means "hearth." The hearth-fire, as the central point, was also symbolic of the life-giving aspect of the Goddess, the focus of domestic life. The fire of the hearth was never allowed to be extinguished, and was always a source of inspiration and renewal.

There are very few personifications of Vesta in the ancient world. Perhaps this is because she represents an indwelling spirit, which is hard to personify. In the modern world it is difficult to imagine what gathering around the family hearth is like, allowing Vesta's presence to capture our spirits. Today, the family sits around the TV/VCR and it is a totally different experience. But all those who have sat outdoors at a campfire or beside their own fireplaces indoors have felt the magic that the fire works upon them. When one stares into a fire, an alteration of energy occurs. At most, one may find oneself entering a trance-like state, or at least slightly shifting his or her sensory input patterns to where the mind becomes more relaxed and calm. Thus, Vesta's invisible presence as the *spirit* of fire still allows us to shift our focus out of the left brain and into the right. Anyone who has ever participated in a group campfire can attest to the fire's ability to purify thoughts, bring unity to the circle, exert a calming influence over everyone present, and "divinize" the air. In the Old Testament, God appeared to Moses on Mt. Sinai in the form of a burning bush. He also led the Israelites into the Promised Land, guided by a pillar of fire and clouds. In the Kabbalah, this fire is regarded as the Shekinah, the indwelling feminine presence of God—to the Greeks, Hestia. Its purpose is to focus, strengthen, spiritualize, and divinize. Therefore we may associate Vesta with that inner motivation which gets our best, most focused attention.

Just as there are few images of Hestia, there are also very few myths about her, although the meager references which exist are extremely revealing. She was the

first-born child of Cronus and Rhea, thus the first to be swallowed up by her father. First to be born, she was the last to emerge from the jaws of Cronus when the divine children were disgorged back into the world. Thus Vesta is alpha and omega, the beginning and the end, the first and the last. She vowed to remain eternally virgin, and, true to her meditative nature, stayed apart from the quarrels of the gods. When Dionysus became one of the Olympian gods, it was necessary that another deity should quit Olympus, for there could be only twelve Olympians. It was Hestia who offered to resign; her worship was so deeply established among the people that nothing could shake it, and besides, she was

Fire is an appropriate symbol for Vesta

weary of the petty jealousies of the
Olympians.

It is from ancient Rome, rather than
from Greece, that most of our clues
about Vesta are derived. It is a common
belief that the Romans simply adopted
their gods wholesale from the Greeks,
but this is not *quite* true. Deities named
Jupiter, Juno, Diana, Saturn, Vesta and
so on were worshipped in ancient Italy
long before the Latin-speaking peoples
received any significant cultural influence from Greece.[2] But when the
Romans did begin to take over the Greek
city-states, they developed a kind of infe-
riority complex about their own lack of
cultural sophistication. They willingly
and gratefully assimilated the more highly developed mythology of the Greeks,
matching Greek tales with their own,
more rustic deities. However, the worship of the primitive Italic gods was
never really set aside, and the Italian war
god Mars was reverenced more deeply
by the Romans than Ares ever was by
the Greeks. A similar situation pertains
in regards to Vesta, the ancient Roman

Vesta, or Hestia

goddess of the hearth who was assimilated to the Greek Hestia. For in Rome,
Vesta's priestesses, the Vestal Virgins, enjoyed a status which was unique in the
ancient world.

But in order to understand more clearly what the Vestal Virgins represented, let
us return to the idea that man is the microcosm and the universe is the macrocosm.
The vital power which informs the center of the universe not only has its analogue
in the worldly home and hearth, it also has its correspondence in the human body—
the most significant microcosm of all. This vital power is customarily imaged as a
fire or serpent—it is the shakti or kundalini of the Hindus, the Shekinah or
indwelling presence of God reverenced by Kabbalistic Jews. The Vestal Virgins not
only tended the actual fire which was the symbolic center of the Roman Empire;
they also tended the inner fire which was the vital spirit of the people. They were
vowed to celibacy; at the core of their order was the most direct connection to
divinity that mortals could experience. The Vestals were those who reflected the
light of the sacred. They enjoyed the most extraordinary privileges of any religious
order in the Roman Empire. If a Vestal encountered a prisoner on his way to execu-

tion, she could set him free. It was the Vestals who were the keepers of important wills and public documents; Mark Antony had to secure Julius Caesar's will from the Vestals before he could read it aloud in his famous oration over Caesar's corpse. But if the Vestals were regarded as especially sacrosanct, they were also subject to the most bizarre of penalties. A Vestal Virgin found guilty of breaking her vow of chastity could be buried alive.

Despite the fact that the Christian Church was deeply threatened by the political power of the Vestal Virgins, the most vital remaining devotees of the Goddess, the early Church Fathers failed to eradicate the worship of Vesta until the 3rd or 4th century AD. The Vestals were among the last pagans to give way to Christianity, and they had a peculiar afterlife in the Church itself. The nuns of the Christian Church, like the Vestals, are virgins consecrated to a marriage with God.[3]

Vesta is the brightest of the asteroids,[4] and that is fitting, for she was the keeper of the sacred fire. Prometheus may have stolen that fire from the gods to give to mankind (see Uranus), but it was Vesta who kept it alive. Astrologers Demetra George and Zip Dobyns suggest a Virgo rulership for Vesta,[5] and long before the asteroid was discovered the Greeks associated the goddess Hestia with Capricorn.[6] Because of her rulership over sacred or spiritual fire she could also be logically associated with Sagittarius or Scorpio (the kundalini fire itself). In fact, she seems to partake of all these signs; her fire is an *inner* fire, the fire which ultimately motivates us to live out our passions or, as Joseph Campbell said, to "follow our bliss."

Examine the chart of any individual—or, for that matter, of any nation—and the position of Vesta will most likely reveal the object of most singular focus. The

School of the Vestal Virgins, a nineteenth-century engraving after the painting by Le Roux

U.S. birth chart, for instance, has Vesta in Taurus, which seems fitting for a nation of people pretty singularly focused on leading the world in GNP. Britain's Vesta in Capricorn gives us a clue as to how that country honors tradition, "proper" behavior, and the class system. France's Vesta in Leo reminds us that in that country, love, art, beauty, and pleasure in all their magnificent splendor are reverenced above all (who else could have focused so much energy on the Palace of Versailles, and dedicated the fruits of that focus to the "Sun King," the embodiment of Leo?). Dane Rudhyar, whose Vesta was in Aquarius, pioneered the concept and coined the phrase "humanistic astrology" in our own century.

If a healthy Vesta in the birth chart corresponds to an individual's ability to focus and direct his or her inner fire towards a specific cause, project, ideal, or spirituality, then a dysfunctional Vesta will result in a complete lack of focus or direction. People who lack Vesta qualities or whose Vestas are afflicted will tend to be directionless, unable to define or forge a path for themselves. This can result in a lack of boundaries—people with a weak Vesta have no ability to stand apart from the crowd, or from people who might take advantage of them. Similarly, a weak Vesta can result in a weak immune system. The body is helpless to fight off invading armies of micro-organisms just as the individual is helpless to fight off those who would invade him or her psychically, physically, or emotionally. Sexually abused individuals often have Vesta in strong aspect to Mars, Jupiter, or Pluto, three planets known for their dominating sexual attitude, and who

The Vestal Tuccia was accused of breaking her vows but, as a sign of her purity, was given power to carry water in a sieve from the Tiber to the temple. From a nineteenth-century illustration after the painting by Le Roux

affirm "I'll take what is mine" regardless of the response. Vesta-Saturn contacts often show up as a domineering father who may very easily "swallow up" the child, who subsequently lives in fear of him, as the mythology of this father-daughter pair makes clear. Victims of child abuse and, later, beatings by a spouse, may be individuals with a dominant but afflicted Vesta. Vesta will not readily fight back. These people are used to living in the shadow of someone who may be monstrous and terrifying. But eventually they strengthen themselves through the discipline they exert over the development of their own spiritual devotion and inner fire, so that they may eventually free themselves from these tyrants.

Vesta, the asteroid whose orbital position is nearest to Mars, is especially linked with this red planet. Both represent the polarity of sexuality, and both are prone to problems in that area. Vesta's matriarchal rulership over the kundalini fire is reminiscent of the temple prostitutes of the ancient Near East, while her Graeco-Roman and post-Christian symbolism is identified with chastity and virginity. Thus she represents a polarity that has characterized the feminine mystique for well over a thousand years—the "Madonna-Whore" complex which has been a common male image of women throughout the Christian centuries. To some men, a woman who does not embody virginal chastity is automatically a whore—in medieval terms, a consort of the devil. Though this radical dualism has been absent from our media and literature for the last three or four decades, it is still a tacit assumption among men (and women!) whose feminine polarity is deeply disturbed. And there are entire cultures—notably the Islamic Near East—which still take this dualism all too seriously.

Demetra George discusses this polarity of Vesta in assigning her a dual rulership.[7] The rulership proposed is Virgo and Scorpio, two signs whose glyphs resemble each other, save for the fact that Virgo's glyph turns inward, representing the ascetic or virginal polarity, while Scorpio's glyph turns outward, which correlates with the outward expression of one's sexuality.

For those who are deeply aware of the serpent power or kundalini within themselves, there are two basic responses, two ways to manage this force which is, at the same time, both sexual and spiritual. In the Virgo mode, the Vesta individual may choose to *control* the sexual force. At its best, this choice creates the yogi, the technician of the sacred who channels the vital power into a path of conscious spiritual evolution. To our contemporary way of thinking, it may seem anomalous to regard an individual who is dedicated to spiritual principles or practices as one who also possesses a strong sexuality, yet this is precisely the state one finds oneself in when Vesta is strongly emphasized in the birth chart. To manage this power with confidence, to stoke the inner hearth-fire like an alchemist stoking the fire in his crucible, is an exceedingly difficult task, and too often the Vesta person's desire for spirituality winds up simply as sexual repression. Like Pallas Athene, who lived in her father's shadow for years, the Vesta individual may find himself or herself living in the shadow of religious or cultural ethics, behaving "correctly" and sublimating his or her sexual nature in order to gain God's or society's approval. But the Vesta person is also capable of extreme abandon. Remember that Hestia relinquished her Olympian status to Dionysus, the god of ecstasy and intoxication. Hestia and Dionysus are both emblematic of the creative sexual force; both are motivated by the kundalini fire. But where Hestia preserved and controlled that force, Dionysus gave himself up to it altogether in orgiastic delight. Those who follow the Scorpio polarity of Vesta may experience problems with promiscuity (the whore part of the Vesta duality) when the psycho-sexual force or kundalini is unleashed. Either way, the proper management of an extremely vital sexuality is implicit in the Vesta personality—we might even call it the essential Vesta dilemma.

We are reminded of another similarity between Virgo and Scorpio by way of Ceres' rulership over Virgo and Pluto's over Scorpio. They both endure suffering for the loss of Persephone when she is with the other one. They both symbolize the individual's need to acknowledge the sensitivity and attachment we all have to these primary relationships with child or mate, and both signs possess the ability for incredible inner focus. In this last respect, they both share Vesta's talent for concentrated purpose.

In chart analysis, Vesta will reflect an individual's sense of spiritual direction. Whether people consciously follow a spiritual path or simply follow their heart's desire or their natural urgings, Vesta helps define and focus their intention. Like Pallas Athene, the embodiment of creative intelligence whose skills lie in many areas, Vesta too is emphasized in several domains. She is capable of feeling great passion as keeper of the inner fire, but over the years her function has been to tame, control, or hold such passion in reserve. When women were stripped of their power in matters of church and state the spirit of the Vestals went underground, resulting for many in an even greater determination to keep the fire burning and dedicate themselves to devotion and prayer in quiet, unassuming ways. During the ensuing centuries it has been the woman who, operating from hearth and home and family, has quietly influenced her family's spiritual direction and choices to such an extent that those who are influenced by her are often motivated to follow pathways that reflect their initial experience of early family gatherings around the symbolic fire. Thus Vesta has operated in unseen ways. Presently, however, we may see Vesta operating more publicly, in an era where the spirit of the Vestals infuses men and women who have chosen to dedicate their lives to the spiritual unfoldment of themselves and others, or who have elected to act as spiritual representatives for large groups of people. This process may unfold quietly and unassumingly, as in the case of Mother Teresa, or through writings and lecturing, as with Lynn Andrews and Shirley McLaine, all of whom embody a strong Vesta.

Jupiter and his eagle, from Jost Amman's Kunstbüchlin, *published by*
Johann Feyerabend, Frankfurt, 1599

JUPITER

CHAPTER THIRTEEN

*And in the temple of great Jupiter
Our peace we'll ratify; seal it with feasts.*

—*Shakespeare*, Cymbeline, V, V

To the Babylonians, the planet Jupiter was known as Marduk, who, like Greek Zeus and Roman Jupiter, was the king of the gods. His story is told in the *Enuma Elish*, the Babylonian epic of creation. In this ancient poem, a primordial sea monster or sea serpent called Tiamat rouses her chthonic armies to revolt against the heavenly gods. The gods choose, as their champion, young Marduk, son of the heavenly king. Marduk rides forth in his chariot, defeats the armies of darkness, and destroys Tiamat. He fashions earth and sky from the remains of her gigantic corpse. He sets the stars in their courses and establishes the calendar.[1]

The reader will remember that this was also the main theme in the story of Apollo and the Python, which we discussed in the chapter on the Sun. And indeed, we are dealing with precisely the same myth. Marduk (or Zeus or Jupiter) is the king of the gods.

Apollo is the Sun, and the Sun was the "king" of the planets. The Sun and Jupiter both exercise the kingly function of bringing order into chaos, of harnessing vital energies for the purpose of conscious achievement. And indeed, both planets participate in the masculine archetype which Robert Bly calls the inner king.

In astrology, however, the Sun and Jupiter are quite different planets. It is up to the astrologer to define the difference between these two kingly archetypes. Jupiter has often been described as a social planet, whereas the Sun is termed a personal planet—perhaps the *most* personal of planets. The Sun can bring each individual's vital force under his or her personal control, and this focusing of power gives us a sense of direction. It can orientate us towards business, learning, relationships, or spirituality—any number of possible goals. But how do we extend that energy into the world? How does our directed energy function in the social sphere? Answering these questions is Jupiter's role. With Jupiter, our directed will is focused on particular social goals, and learns to embody particular social attitudes.

As king of the gods, Jupiter was the administrator of the classical cosmos. People with strong or elevated Jupiters tend to be administrators of their own cosmos, and while a prominent Jupiter in a horoscope is traditionally associated with professions like law, big business, or higher education, Jupiterians may engage in any enterprise, as long as they know they are on the upper rungs of the social ladder and under no one's laws but their own. The important questions are: what kind of attitude do we bring to the achievement of our goals? What kind of spirit do we embody during our quest for success?

The Babylonian god Marduk, associated with the planet Jupiter

Exploring Jupiter's role in myth, we can form a picture of the positive or well-adapted Jupiter attitude. A great deal of emphasis must be placed on the fact that Jupiter was the *king*. To the ancient Greeks, the king was essentially a father-figure, a caretaker of the people. Homer's *Iliad* gives us a remarkable group of kings—Agamemnon, Odysseus, Menelaus, Ajax, and so on—all gathered before the walls of Troy. These kings are a remarkably diverse lot; Ajax is all brawn while Odysseus is all brain, and Agamemnon gravitates between extremes of nobility and cruelty. But they all have one thing in common: they regard themselves as protectors of their people. Jupiter has been described (especially in esoteric astrology) as the protector or "inner guide" of the horoscope. A Sixth House Jupiter may protect our health, while a Twelfth House Jupiter may give us spiritual protection. To make our way in the world by following Jupiter's path may not always lead us to our bliss, but it will certainly lead us to a kind of success—and by very easy stages.

Jupiter bringing order into chaos by defeating the giants

Another feature of the Homeric kings is that they were all "givers of gifts." When a bard sang or when a champion won a contest, the king was expected to bestow gold arm-rings, or cattle, or beautiful women. Jupiter in a horoscope may bestow gifts upon us; it also represents our own capacity for generosity.

Let us remember Zeus' role in bestowing immortality upon those whom he deemed worthy. Chiron was freed from his suffering and placed in the heavens as Sagittarius as a reward for his services to mankind, though Prometheus was condemned to a rock by Zeus for another charitable act. Hercules was given immortality for his courageous acts and Zeus set Callisto's image among the stars. Hephaestus was given Aphrodite's hand in marriage. Zeus' word eventually freed Persephone from Hades (although he had originally sanctioned the act of abduction that sealed her fate in the first place). Cronus, too, was banished to Tartarus by Zeus for his unkindly acts. Asclepius was struck by one of Zeus' thunderbolts for raising the dead. In other words, Zeus had the power and authority, as sovereign ruler, to reward one and bestow immortality upon another, or condemn them to terrible fates, based on his judgment of those acts. It should not be forgotten that Jupiter is a planet associated with lawyers and judges, and Jupiter's transits can bring people the euphoric elevation to stardom or golden opportunity of a lifetime. It can similarly pass judgment resulting in banishment or complete immobility.

The inner king (Sun and Jupiter) organizes and focuses the entire range of our psycho-spiritual energy and directs it towards a specific purpose, while the warrior (Mars) does the actual work. The Sun may be regarded as the essential core of our being which directs us towards our true spiritual goal. But it is only through Jupiter that we make that goal *real*, in a worldly sense. This kingly planet impels us to walk in the world with generosity and a benevolent spirit. It protects certain paths and avenues of our lives, so that we may find an appropriate road to success. To follow Jupiter's road to abundance enables us to maintain a spirit of generosity and good fellowship.

But Jupiter has its drawbacks. There is such a thing as too much abundance. One example, very well known to astrologers, concerns the physical body. If Jupiter is in one of the houses that pertains to the physical body (First or Sixth), or when it transits those houses, we may experience physical abundance—that is to say, we may eat too much and put on a great deal of weight! Similarly, Jupiter may lead us to over-confidence, to a certain arrogance or smugness, or to a condition of static complacency. In combination with Venus and/or Neptune, it may increase indulgence in sex, drugs, food, and drink.

We can resolve these negative Jupiter issues by taking a wider view of things. Zeus had a special throne atop Mt. Olympus; seated there, he could look out over everything taking place on earth below. Similarly, the Norse god Odin sat on his throne in Asgard, the divine world, and gazed upon the human world below. On Zeus' shoulders perched two ravens, Thought and Memory, his constant advisors. (The theme of the mountaintop throne will be familiar to readers of *The Lord of The Rings*.) Jupiter rules the sign Sagittarius, the sign associated with philosophy, which is known for its ability to take a broad (and therefore tolerant) view of all human

activity, and to synthesize different branches of knowledge into a vital, philosophical whole. This synthesis is a very Jupiterian trait, though it should also be remembered that it is difficult to notice small details from a great height. In order to acquire the practicality which brings grand dreams into manifestation, Jupiter needs the help of Mercury, that master of detail.

We have seen Jupiter as the divine warrior who becomes the king, as the apostle of consciousness who slays the dragon, and as the philosopher on the mountaintop. But what about Jupiter the lover? In Greek myth, it often seems as if Zeus' entire function is to impregnate goddesses, demi-goddesses, and mortal maidens, thus to produce heroes. And yet astrologers have always looked upon Jupiter as an asexual planet without any particular role in the relationship game. The signs that are ruled by

The Norse god Odin on his throne in Asgard, the divine world

Jupiter have powerful sexual connotations: Pisces derives mystical ecstasy from the act of love, while Sagittarius manifests a frisky but totally uncommitted sexuality worthy of Zeus himself. But the real clue to Jupiter's role in the sexual process lies in the fact that the most ancient Greek astrologers associated this god with Leo.[2] Leo, of course, is the sign which symbolizes children; astrologers read a person's relationships to his/her children from a consideration of Leo or the Fifth House. In Vedic astrology, Jupiter is still regarded as a significator of children, as well as of the Fifth House.[3] Another meaning for the Fifth House is *creativity*.

Jupiter, or Zeus

This, then, is the rationale which lies behind Jupiter's prolific fertilization of women and goddesses. It was not an oversexed nature or even a desire to become involved in a relationship; it was the express desire of the sky god to be the progenitor of a new race of people. The stories do not focus on Jupiter's love-making abilities as, for instance, they often do on those of Mars. Instead, they depict the act of mating as specifically directed towards the prolific production of offspring. Never is it said that Jupiter and his chosen lover are infertile; always a child, and sometimes several, are produced from these unions. Jupiter's actions bear fruit. And, more than anything else, he was the king of the gods, and when he spotted a particularly beautiful female, whether goddess or mortal, married or single, willing or unwilling, he felt he was entitled to have her. Let us not forget that the female archetypes with whom Jupiter mated were once powerful goddesses, holders and carriers of feminine wisdom. To "mate" with them allowed Jupiter to acquire some of their knowledge, and also to give birth to children who would hopefully embody the best of the genetic components of each of their parents.

Jupiter's many mythological children, therefore, may be taken as metaphors of his prolific creativity rather than as indications of an overly active sexual nature. Jupiter is abundance personified, and his abundant nature is as likely to express itself in the production of progeny as in anything else. A narrow-minded Jupiterian may, however, regard his or her children as possessions, contributions to one's social position. This tendency to regard children as status objects is notable in the case of Juno as well, and Juno, of course, was Jupiter's bride, his feminine polarity.

As a social planet, Jupiter is not expected to have much of an in-depth personal relationship with the other people in his life. Thus, strong Jupiter types will seem to have many relationships with many different people, but they are all *purposeful*, like his relationships with the goddesses and women who bore his children. He did not spend time getting to know these women very well, nor did he need to. Similarly, his children were virtual strangers to him (with the exception of Athene, his favorite). He was proud of them or annoyed with them according to their deeds and reputations. Such is the Jupiter type of parent—unwilling to spend quality time with the family, but aware of their actions from afar. It is this farsightedness that resulted in his knowing whether to deliver a thunderbolt or a jewel—did the actions of his offspring please or displease him? It is true that Jupiter is exalted in Cancer, the sign of family. Thus it can be said that even if a strongly dominant Jupiter does not seem to be in charge of the world, he or she can certainly be regarded as the family patriarch or matriarch.

The same is true of relationships with friends. Jupiter's friends, in such a context, are likely to be his peers—rulers of other kingdoms, heads of other companies, socially prominent and highly visible career people, philanthropists, or society's demigods. While friendships do occur between these people, they are not the *motivating* force behind Jupiterian activity. Jupiter didn't "need" friends, but he did need to have the respect and admiration of his subjects. He took people and used them as he pleased—and still, his actions were regarded as acceptable for the king. His interests were supposedly for the good of the kingdom, not for personal gain. A judge (a Jupiterian profession) who must pronounce sentence on a criminal and determine if this person should be incarcerated or if he is free to go hopefully bases his decision on the impact it will have for society at large, not on whether he likes or dislikes the person. Similarly, Jupiter's favors or lack of them supposedly have nothing to do with personal like or dislike, but are motivated by how favorable one's interaction with society has been. On the other hand, we have the archetype of Jupiter the father-god who very clearly showed his wrath and displeasure with his children when they didn't meet his expectations for proper and dignified behavior. The astrological Jupiter often shows what we think we should do in order to accommodate ourselves to social standards and "get ahead" in the system. And the more we accommodate, the more we do get ahead. As previously observed, Jupiter may not lead us to follow our bliss, but we can certainly feel blessed by the gods in having attained society's affirmative nod when Jupiter is well integrated. And because Jupiter represents righteousness and philosophical dominion, we may elect to do what we believe to be right action and thus feel spiritually rewarded by Jupiter as well.

Astrologically, Jupiter has always been the significator of good fortune and good fellowship; another name for the god in Latin was Jove, from whence derives our word "jovial." It is true that the Greek Zeus could be terrifying at times. He was the god of thunder, wielder of the lightning bolt. Like Pallas Athene, he wore the terrible face of Medusa as part of his armor, and his bird was the noble but predatory eagle. His sacred tree was the oak, symbol of kingship (the oak is king of the forest), and at Dodona the priests of Zeus divined the future by listening to the rustling of the wind through a grove of oak trees. But after the worship of the gods was no longer taken seriously, Jupiter was perceived in a somewhat different light. Humanists of the late Middle Ages and early Renaissance looked back to Graeco-

Chryselephantine statue of Zeus Olympios, restored—a nineteenth-century illustration

Roman times as a kind of golden age, mellowed by time and distance (similarly the Greeks looked back to the neolithic as a golden age, and forgave Cronus or Saturn his tyranny for the sake of his rulership over a wondrous era). These Renaissance scholars remembered Jupiter's kingly glory, forgot his rage, and created for themselves a picture of classical times that resembled a vast garden party, with nymphs, wine, and the singing of the breeze in the olive trees. And it is this time-mellowed Jupiter that has passed into astrological tradition. Sagittarius, ruled by Jupiter, falls in the part of the year between Thanksgiving and Christmas. The spirit of the season, hectic and stressful as it often is, is imbued with the Jupiterian activities of exchanging gifts and offerings, producing huge spreads of food and beverage and gathering together our numerous offspring, no matter how far and wide they may have wandered. Family members who normally have nothing to do with each other for most of the year are supposed to put aside their differences and act like they are all happy and well-connected with each other. Even the archetype of Santa Claus is confused by many astrologers with the archetype of Jupiter—he knows and sees all of his children throughout the year, and the number of gifts you can expect under the tree corresponds directly to how naughty or nice you've been. Many astrologers feel that Jupiter's transit through a sign (which lasts a year, since Jupiter circles the zodiac every twelve years) will reward us with fabulous gifts that are appropriate to the sign or house in question. For instance, Jupiter's transit over the Midheaven would reward or advance the native in career matters, Jupiter's transit over one's Fourth House cusp might bring a bigger and better living situation, Jupiter's transit to the Seventh House might bring a wonderful partner, etc. The results of Jupiter's activity by transit may not always be quite this tangible, but it always brings the *opportunity* for growth and abundance, inwardly or outwardly.

SATURN

CHAPTER Fourteen

*Very often, therefore, in human affairs we are subject
to Saturn, through idleness, solitude, or strength,
through Theology and more secret philosophy, through
superstition, Magic, agriculture, and through sadness.*

—Marsilio Ficinco (1433-1499), The Book of Life

Saturn constitutes one of the most
complex archetypes in the astrological *mandala*. Most of the other
planets reveal their problematical
side when combined with Saturn—
and indeed, Saturn is the archetypal taskmaster among the planets.
Darkness, doom, disease, and delay
are all laid upon Saturn's shoulders. But Saturn was also the ruler
of the mythological Golden Age,
the mellow springtime of humanity. And it is part and parcel of
astrological tradition that Saturn's
benefits may be greater—or at
least more substantial—than those
of any other planet. Of course, it is
human nature to put all the blame
on one side of the fence while
simultaneously placing all the credit somewhere else, and in astrology
these polarized roles have been
foisted upon Saturn and Jupiter
respectively. But there are always
two sides to everything in nature
(and in astrology), and as we have
seen that Jupiter has his down
side, we must also observe Saturn's
more positive characteristics.

Let us explore Saturn's dark side first. The Greeks knew him as Cronus, one of the seven Titans. The ancient Greek writers derived the name Cronus from *chronos*, meaning Time. Cronus was a child of Ouranos (Father Sky) and Gaia (Mother Earth). When Ouranos became tyrannical and despotic, Gaia persuaded Cronus to overthrow his father. Cronus lay in wait for Ouranos and castrated him with a sickle; thus he became king of the gods. He married his sister Rhea, and, like his father, became a despot after his own fashion. He came to believe that his children would try to overthrow him, even as he overthrew his own father. As soon as Rhea gave birth, Cronus swallowed her children, consuming his own offspring. First Hestia, then Demeter, Hera, Hades, and Poseidon disappeared inside Cronus' belly. But when Zeus was born, Rhea wrapped a stone in swaddling clothes, and it was this stone which Cronus unwittingly swallowed. Zeus was kept safe; when he grew up, he hired himself out as cupbearer to old Cronus, and fed him a potion which caused him to vomit up all his children. Supported by his brothers and sisters, Zeus took up arms against Cronus and the other Titans. After ten years of war the new gods, the Olympians, reigned supreme. Cronus and his brethren were imprisoned in Tartarus, a dark and gloomy region at the ends of the earth.[1]

The astrological Saturn has always been associated with the letter of the law rather than the spirit: the Gnostics and early Kabbalists identified Saturn with the god of the Old Testament, whom they regarded as a tyrannical father, obsessed with the rigid enforcement of the law. And indeed, there may be a very ancient symbolic link between Saturn and Yahweh, for Yahweh's Sabbath or holy day is Saturday—Saturn's day.

In fact, there is an association between the male trinity of father-gods represented by Jupiter, Saturn, and Uranus that may symbolically represent patriarchal religious and political thought through the ages. Ouranos, the original father, was the Greek version of Varuna, the Vedic creator god. He ruled before Saturn. Then along came Saturn, armed with a sickle, who overthrew Ouranos by castrating him, thus ending his generative power. Then came Jupiter, who, like the "Son of God" Jesus, was perceived as a savior of future generations who would no longer be ruled by a tyrannical father-god who swallowed his children. The associations between Jupiter's rulership and Christianity fit the astrological signs that Jupiter rules—Pisces, the sign associated with Christianity, and Sagittarius, the sign associated with philosophical belief systems and the awareness of a higher force governing nature. Thus, it is not so much the father overthrowing the son who in turn overthrows another son that is important here as the tendency of any order to progressively give way to a new one. While Judaism never overthrew pagan religious thought, it certainly paved the way for a whole new system of beliefs to take hold. Similarly, Christianity did not overthrow Judaism, but its influence has formed Western culture for the past two thousand years, and the pendulum of Western history has swung in a new direction. It would seem, then, that the trinity of Uranus, Saturn, and Jupiter represent three father-gods who enforce their own laws in keeping with their own peculiar natures, and it is these laws or dictums that one

Saturn about to devour one of his children, from Jost Amman's
Kunstbüchlin, *published by Johann Feyerabend, Frankfurt, 1599*

must address in reading their symbolism in the astrological framework.

Saturn often appears as a significator of the father in astrology, as does the Sun, but in Saturn's case the connection to the father often symbolizes problems with him. A child with a tyrannical Saturnian father may easily be "swallowed up" by his or her overbearing parent. A domineering Saturn in a natal horoscope may thus indicate the all-consuming father who seeks to mold his children in his own image and force them to live according to his standards. One of the sad consequences of such a situation is that the child will often become a tyrannical parent in his or her turn! Such a child may *wish* to break away from the controlling parent role, but will have trouble doing so—for the simple reason that he or she doesn't know any other way to do it. After all, we learn how to parent from experiencing our own parents. Mythologically, Cronus was himself the son of a domineering father; he became domineering in his turn. Zeus overthrew Cronus, but, like his father, worried that one of his children might try to unseat him. As modern psychology tells us, a dysfunctional family is a self-perpetuating institution. In order to break free of the pattern, one must develop one of the more positive aspects of Saturn—the mentor or ruler of the Golden Age. Such a task requires commitment, devotion, and a lifetime of hard work. Saturn, when it manifests as a psychological complex, holds on more tightly than any other planet (with the possible exception of Pluto). To attempt to transform Saturn into the inner teacher is a difficult task because it forces us to deal with some of Saturn's other problematical aspects as well.

Cronus ended his career as a prisoner in Tartarus. The planet Saturn may literally place us in our own personal Tartarus, locking us in chains of isolation so heavy that we may feel as if we are indeed in a dark hole at the ends of the earth. What may intensify the pain of this type of predicament (or karma, which is one of Saturn's esoteric associations) is that Saturn has already been all the way to the top and then fallen into that dark and lonely pit. He was once the ruler of an entire kingdom and then suffered banishment and loss of power. This "isolationist" Saturn as well as the "fallen" Saturn are characteristics which affect even our modern interpretations of the planet, although more recently the psychologically oriented astrologer, such as Liz Greene, has taught us to illuminate his bright side once his darkness has been unearthed.[2] But our astrological inheritance from most of the early Roman and medieval texts, and even until the era of humanistic astrology, has tended to portray Saturn solely as the miserable, miserly fallen angel rather than the ruler of the Golden Age. And indeed, when we have experienced a visitation from Saturn resulting in a pit of despair and darkness, we may feel so ashamed, so afraid that we will never again rise out of that darkness that we keep ourselves psychologically locked in Tartarus for a long, long time. It is the *fear* of never rising up again to amount to anything, the *guilt* of having done something terrible in the past which must subsequently be punished, and the *humiliation* of having been on top of the mountain before we fell, that many Saturn complexes are about. Once we recognize these energies, whether imposed from the outside or self-imposed, we learn that the only way up and out is through the taking of personal responsibility for the predica-

Saturn's rings, which represent limitations and boundaries in our lives. Photograph from NASA

ment at hand. Many sufferers of Saturn problems remain in their isolation chambers for years because they have not yet taken personal responsibility for the situation in the first place, preferring to blame parents, society, the boss, or outside circumstances for their continuing misfortune.

Saturn, therefore, represents our limitations and these limits are symbolized in various ways. First, Saturn's time on the throne as omnipotent ruler, which at first seemed limitless, eventually came to its end. Second, there are the limitations and boundaries represented by Saturn's imprisonment in Tartarus, a dark and lonely existence. Third and perhaps most symbolic of all, to the ancients this planet was the most distant member of the solar system, and hence represented the limit or boundary of the sphere of the planets. Symbolism is not confined to ancient times; we create our own symbols to this very day. Probes sent to the planet Saturn have convinced scientists that this planet has the most complex set of rings in existence. The force field of these rings may be responsible for Saturn's gravitational field. Gravity, staying within boundaries, and setting limits are all areas where Saturn rules. When we attempt to transform Saturn from tyrant to mentor, we encounter all our limitations, both material and psychological. Our repressed instincts, our dark recesses of the soul, all come up for review. Saturn subjects us to restrictions and delays on the material plane as well. Leaky roofs, cars that don't work, unpaid bills, and the agony of standing in line to fill out forms in triplicate—all these things are part of Saturn's domain. Saturn may induce in us a state of depression—a state of mind in which we feel truly confined in endless darkness.

Medieval and Renaissance scholars associated Saturn with one of the four humors of ancient medicine and, not surprisingly, it was the melancholic humor which Saturn ruled.[3] This is as good a metaphor as any for Saturn's depressive influence. Marsilio Ficino warned his fellow Renaissance magi of Saturn's gloomy power over philosophers and scholars. According to Ficino, men of learning were more likely than other mortals to suffer from Saturnian afflictions.[4] And to the Gauquelins, men of learning do indeed come under the influence of Saturn's rays, as it was scientists' and physicians' birth charts that showed overwhelming placements of Saturn in the "Gauquelin sectors" when examined statistically.[5] But if scholarly gloom was associated with Saturn, so was scholarly wisdom. Father Time brings serenity as well as anxiety. And his wisdom is the wisdom of the earth itself.

Hesiod speaks of five ages of mankind: Gold, Silver, two ages of Bronze, and an Age of Iron. As gold is the purest of the metals, the Golden Age was the purest age of mankind. Silver, Bronze, and Iron represent a degeneration in human consciousness.[6] Hesiod's Golden Age seems, in many ways, to hark back to a prehistoric wonderland: no one worked, the weather was eternally pleasant, the fruit fell from the trees of its own accord, and sheep and goats were abundant. The happy mortals of the Golden Age spent their days dancing and praising the gods, and death was to them as friendly as sleep. It was Cronus who ruled over this Golden Age. This, plus his sickle (the instrument with which he castrated Ouranos), suggests that he was in one sense or another an agricultural deity. If we examine the earliest religion of

A more contemporary version of Saturn devouring one of his children, after Goya's Saturno, *c. 1820*

Italy, this surmise is borne out, for Saturnus was originally a god of fields and harvests.[7] (The glyph for Ceres, the female goddess of grain, is another form of Saturn's sickle, but facing in the opposite direction.) Saturn's winter festival, the Saturnalia, was a time when all license was permitted, when staid Roman warriors and matrons frolicked like the carefree children of the Golden Age; a time when current reality was turned upside down, and masters waited upon their servants. And there is another, less pleasant, feature of this time of year which also suggests the symbolism of Saturn. The completion of the year at the winter solstice marked the time when the tax collectors appeared. All monies owing to the government, landlords or debtors had to be accounted for and paid. This is another face of Saturn and its ruling sign, Capricorn: accounts must be settled. Even today this inspires fear or avoidance at tax time for those who cannot pay their taxes or settle their accounts. When people are gripped by the fear of losing their belongings due to not being able to pay their bills, they are usually humming the tune of Saturn's less glamorous side.

In Babylon, the planet Saturn was called Ninib, and this Ninib, like the Italic Saturnus, was an agricultural deity. Saturn's correlation with agriculture suggests the nature of time itself. Fruits can come to harvest only at the proper season or time, once the groundwork has been completed. There is no forcing fruit to bear before its time. Similarly, those with well-placed Saturns have a sense of "good timing." They lay their groundwork carefully, planting seeds at the right time, then patiently water and feed their plants, awaiting harvest. They impress others with their organizational ability, even though they may be somewhat overbearing or authoritarian about how things should be done.

Saturn's proverbial wisdom is that of the earth itself. It is no accident that contemporary Americans refer to the retirement years as the "golden years;" Saturn rules old age, and even today we seek to make of this time a golden age—albeit with erratic success. Those who persevere, who learn to confront their limitations, their tyrannies, and their own darkness; who bend themselves slowly, over time, towards gentle and tolerant acceptance of the world around them and of themselves—these are the individuals who experience Saturn as the ruler of an internal golden age. They age with dignity and wisdom, enjoying their golden years.

Saturn is the inner teacher. This teacher may turn into a tyrant, a grim patriarch obsessed with laws and restrictions, or it may become a true mentor. As Robert Bly puts it, American men (and presumably American women as well) desperately lack true mentors.[8]

The concept of the mentor is itself drawn from classical mythology. Mentor, a character in Homer's *Odyssey*, is the elderly advisor of Telemachus, Odysseus' youthful heir. While Telemachus sought in vain for his absent father, it was Mentor who guided his actions with sage counsel. At any rate, it *appeared* to be Mentor. In fact, Pallas Athene was speaking to Telemachus, using Mentor as her vehicle.[9]

The relationship between Mentor and Telemachus brings out several important points. First of all, the advisor, Mentor, is not the young man's father. As Bly has pointed out, a young man cannot be initiated into the mysteries of life by his father. Their bond is much too close, and qualitatively different. The mentor needs a certain amount of detachment from his protege.[10]

Unfortunately, our society does not recognize the spiritual need for a mentor figure, at least not in the present day. In days of old, a man served alongside his teacher as apprentice, especially in the age of fine craftsmen. This relationship has all but vanished in our fast-paced technological age. It is still possible, especially in the cloistered walls of a university or monastic setting, to develop and maintain this type of relationship. But when the father figure tries to play the mentor's role he usually winds up becoming a tyrannical Cronus in the process. Very few of us have the opportunity to be initiated into the mysteries of life (and especially the "myster-ies" of career, a true Saturnian domain) by a genuine mentor figure. Most of us have to cultivate an inner mentor, or choose a figure from history. (Bly himself chose William Butler Yeats.) Saturn in the horoscope is the planet most suited to play the role of inner mentor—but we must free Saturn from the stigma of the tyrannical parent before it can play this role in earnest. As long as we remain sad-dled with limiting attitudes, Saturn cannot function at its best. It may make tycoons out of us, but it won't make us happy. We need the earth wisdom of Saturn in order for this planet to show us its best side, and earth wisdom is a feminine wisdom. It is significant that the *Odyssey* tells us that Pallas Athene was speaking through Mentor, for this suggests that the inner teacher needs a balance of masculine and feminine polarities in order to be truly effective. Astrologically, Saturn is exalted in Libra, a sign which is traditionally ruled by Venus and has also been associated with the asteroid Pallas Athene, thus uniting the patriarchal symbolism of Cronus with

Saturn, or Cronus

feminine elements. Perhaps the most complete symbol for Saturn is one which comes from popular folklore—Father Time. This allegorical figure is clearly derived from Saturn. Cronus means "time," and Father Time makes his appearance on New Year's Eve, which occurs during Saturn's astrological month, Capricorn. Father Time carries a sickle in one hand—the sickle which marks Saturn's status as a harvest god, or the sickle with which Cronus castrated Ouranos. At the turning of the year, old Father Time magically disappears, replaced by the New Year's babe. Even though most of us watch this drama to the strains of a Guy Lombardo-style orchestra, it is pure myth. For it is the Divine Child who is born at the winter solstice.

Saturn may present us with limita-tions and restrictions. It may mature us by forcing us to work within these boundaries. Saturn may hold over us the shadow of a tyrannical parent, a shadow from which we must learn to emerge. All these works are accomplished only through time, but their accomplishment leads to a rebirth, a golden age of the spirit which may occur at any time, not only in our later years. The most typical periods for this accomplishment to manifest come during the "Saturn returns," something most astrologers and their clients are familiar with. At age twenty-nine, fifty-eight, and eighty-seven this occurs, a time when individuals are tested by this planet in many different disciplines. The first return, at twenty-nine, usually implies a sobering period—the individual accepts that maturity and responsibility must now replace youthful abandon. The second Saturn return at fifty-eight can be one of the most glorious Saturn experiences, if the individual has truly achieved the wisdom that Saturn is seeking. It can also be experienced as one of the most difficult of times, especially if an individual is not inspired by his or her work and sees life as a continuing drudgery. Few people make it to the third Saturn return, but coming on the heels of the Uranus return (see Uranus) it can undoubtedly be profound.

Chiron and his students

CHIRON

CHAPTER FIFTEEN

I could wish that Chiron, Philyra's son...
the departed, were living yet,
child wide-minded of Uranian Kronos, and ruled
the Pelian glades, that beast of the hills
with the heart kindly to men, as of old when he
reared the gentle smith of pain's ease to heal bodies,
Asklepios, the hero who warded sickness of every kind.

—*Pindar,* Third Pythian Ode *(trans. Richard Lattimore)*

The "planetoid" Chiron was discovered in 1977 and was named, as
is the custom, by the astronomer
who discovered it—in this case
Charles Kowal. The chart for the
discovery suggests that we are
encountering something incredibly
profound: the Ascendant corresponds to the center of the galaxy
(26 degrees Sagittarius), while
Pluto sits on the Midheaven and
Chiron himself is a hemispheric
singleton, retrograde, and grounded in the Fourth House in Taurus.
Every other planet is above the
horizon.[1]

Astrologers were quick to use
Chiron from the moment his presence was announced. Following
the publication of early Chiron
material by researchers such as
Zane Stein,[2] astrologers began
placing this odd creature in charts
and observing his behavior by
transit. Since his discovery a mere
fifteen years ago, he has become
quite a hit.

Astronomers, on the other hand, are not quite sure what to do with him, but several theories have emerged; those which depict him as an outsider who has been captured by our solar system seem to be the most common. He somewhat resembles the asteroids, those chunks of rock floating between Mars and Jupiter, but Chiron, though similar in appearance to an asteroid, is located far away from the asteroid belt. In fact, his orbit, between Saturn and Uranus, constitutes something of an anomaly, being extremely elliptical. He has been called a planetoid or minor planet. Recently, however, astronomers have suggested that Chiron is in fact a *comet*, or at least a "dirty snowball" which was in the process of becoming a comet before it was trapped into orbit around our sun.

Because of his small size and peculiar location, as well as his unusual orbital path, the word "maverick" began to be applied to Chiron by astrologers—a maverick being one who acts independently of any social group and refuses to conform to any particular tradition, who lives by his own rules. Zip Dobyns likens him to a Jupiter-Uranus combination, Zane Stein links him with Sagittarius, Barbara Hand Clow and Philip Sedgwick would proclaim him ruler of Virgo, Erminie Lantero and Tony Joseph suggest a Scorpio-Sagittarius blend (Ophiuchus, the giant Asclepius) and Al Morrison, a specialist in astrological oddities, insists that comets don't rule signs at all! Richard Nolle also feels rulership is, in general, unnecessary.

Most importantly to our present purpose, however, Chiron is one of the first planetary discoveries to be assessed in terms of its mythology from the very outset. Pioneering studies by Erminie Lantero and the late Tony Joseph approached Chiron as a true emerging archetype, drawing on mythic sources to determine what Chiron's astrological influence was likely to be.[3] This involved a fair amount of research, since Chiron's story is found in obscure classical works like the *Library* of Apollodorus and the *Argonautica* of Apollonius of Rhodes rather than in the more familiar Homeric poems, Hesiod, or Ovid's *Metamorphoses*.

A representation of Centaurus (Phyllirides—the poetic name for Chiron), from Hyginus' Astronomicon, *Venice, 1482*

Chiron, according to one account, was the child of Cronus or Saturn. The first father of the gods pursued and made love to a nymph named Philyra, but was surprised in his love nest by his outraged wife Rhea. At the moment of climax, Cronus turned himself into a stallion and fled Rhea's jealous wrath. But the mixture of horse and god had already been accomplished; Philyra gave birth to Chiron, half human and half horse, and from Chiron sprang the race of the centaurs.

In Greek myth generally, the centaurs were depicted as creatures of raw instinct, prone to drunkenness and uninhibited, sometimes violent, sensuality (much like the negative aspect of Taurus). Chiron, however, was an exception to the rule. The centaur king lived in meditative isolation in his cave on Mt. Pelion, a reclusive philosopher who occasionally emerged from his solitude to act as teacher to exceptional mortals. He possessed knowledge of celestial mechanics (i.e., astronomy and astrology), nature, medicine, and mathematics, and his expertise in these areas was respected even by the gods. Among his most famous mortal pupils were Actaeon, Aeneas, Achilles, and, most especially, Jason, whose relationship with Chiron is detailed in the *Argonautica* of Apollonius of Rhodes. Chiron trained all these men to become sacred warriors. He was also the teacher of Asclepius, child of Apollo

A typical centaur

and a mortal woman. Asclepius learned the art of medicine from Chiron—but being the son of a healing god (Apollo), he surpassed his tutor and became acknowledged as the patron deity of the healing arts. His symbol was a rod entwined by a serpent, similar to the caduceus of Hermes, although the caduceus features two serpents, while the symbol of Asclepius features only one. In either case, the symbolism seems to represent the passage of the *kundalini,* or serpent power, up the spinal column, which, in the case of Asclepius, suggests that it is this inner vital force which is the operative principle in all true healing. Asclepius was slain by one of Zeus' thunderbolts when he usurped the privilege of the gods and began to raise the dead back to life.[4]

Chiron met his own end in a most peculiar way. The hero Hercules, engaged upon his Twelve Labors, had stopped at Mt. Pelion to broach a cask of wine with the centaurs. The party turned into a drunken brawl, and Hercules began shooting at the centaurs with his poisoned arrows. The shouting and the sounds of battle disturbed Chiron in his cave. Wondering what was interrupting his meditations, he emerged—and was promptly hit in the heel (or, in some versions, the thigh) by one of the deadly arrows.

Though Hercules grieved over wounding his old friend, there was nothing to be done. The wound was a magical one, and not even Chiron, the great healer, could heal it. The centaur king was in such pain that he wearied of life. During his long and philosophical existence, death was the only thing he had never experienced, and even though he was born immortal he now longed to be mortal—to die. But even at the end, he struck a bargain with Olympus which proved to be of immense benefit to humanity. Prometheus, the rebellious Titan who befriended humankind against the gods, lay suffering on a mountaintop, chained to a rock by order of Zeus. It had been decreed that Prometheus could only be released if one of the immortal gods were to die and descend to Hades—an unlikely prospect at best. But now Chiron demanded that Prometheus should be released because the conditions of the decree had been met. Chiron walked willingly into the underworld, and Prometheus, savior of mankind, returned to earth.[5]

All the components of Chiron's mythic story have a strong relevance to the interpretation of Chiron in the birth chart, but it is his role as the healer which has been most remarked upon. The constellation Ophiuchus is said to represent Asclepius and is in the vicinity of Scorpio, which may account for Scorpio's traditional association with the medical arts. But we have no planet or major asteroid which represents this god of healing. Hence Chiron appears to have become the *carrier* for the Asclepius archetype, which is to say that people who are strongly under the influence of Chiron may also embody the archetypal characteristics of Asclepius. (This concept of "carrying" an archetype will become important in the next two essays, when we discuss Uranus as the carrier of the Prometheus archetype, and Neptune as the carrier of Dionysus.)

Chiron's methods of healing were based primarily upon diet—Achilles was fed upon honeycomb, bear's marrow, and the umbles of lions and wild boars. Asclepius, too, healed by techniques which we would nowadays associate with magic. The priests of the temples of Asclepius (two of which are still standing, one at Epidaurus and one on the isle of

Asclepius, student of Chiron and a renowned healer. Illustrated by Diane Smirnow

Cos) would enjoin fasting and meditation upon the prospective candidate for healing. When the candidate was thus prepared, he underwent a ritual cleansing by the priests, and was then sent to sleep within the precincts of the temple. The next morning, he related his dreams to the priests, who diagnosed and prescribed accordingly.

Chiron is connected with alternative rather than traditional methods of healing. At the time of Chiron's discovery, heart, liver, and kidney transplants had extended human life to such a degree that they appeared to offer a serious alternative to dying — Chiron's mythic confrontation with the lord of the underworld. But we had become dependent on technology for our very sur-

The centaur Nessos, true to the violent passions of his kind, was killed by Hercules when he attempted to ravish Hercules' wife, Deianeira. From an Attic amphora, seventh century BC

vival. At the same time, another interesting phenomenon was occurring in medicine—a strange new child called "holistic health care" was coming into prominence, and twentieth-century medicine was being significantly challenged for the first time. Thousands began turning to holistic medicine for answers to problems that modern science could not or would not address. During the first few years after Chiron's discovery in 1977, there was still only a handful of holistic practitioners. There were, of course, chiropractors—and the term "chiropractor" is linguistically related to Chiron. The name Chiron means "the hand," and the term "chiropractic" implies one who practices medicine with the hands. Interestingly enough, chiropractic was developed by Daniel Palmer when he was fifty-one-years old, i.e., when Chiron was returning to the place it occupied in his birth chart.[6] In the early 1980s, there was an upsurge of other holistic healers such as acupuncturists and naturopaths. An overwhelming number of such practitioners have very strong Chiron placements in their birth charts. In this new field, there has been a great deal of wild speculation, trial and error, and liberal exploration into ways totally unknown and untried. Prior to the 1970s, massage therapy (another eminently Chirotic art) was still associated

Asclepius and his daughter Hygeia who, as goddess of health, was closely associated with the cult of her father

with dark parlors in red light districts. Now, a mere decade and a half since Chiron's discovery, massage therapy has become a much sought-after healing discipline, along with sports massage, herbal remedies, cranio-sacral therapies, and a host of other arts. The field is a burgeoning, multi-million dollar per year industry, gaining thousands of new followers annually.

The significance of Chiron for medical astrology may well be quite major. People with life-threatening illnesses which go into remission are good examples of Chiron's power, and Chiron's placement in the birth chart may indicate not only the part of the body most open to affliction, but the inner source of the problem as well. For instance, Chiron in Cancer may indicate a sensitive stomach, but it should also draw our attention to imbalances in the emotional body or long-standing problems in the family situation which may have induced that sensitive stomach in the first place.

Not everyone with a prominent Chiron, however, will go into the healing arts. Chiron is just as much the teacher as the healer, and a large number of school teachers, especially at the high school level, seem to be powerfully under the influence of Chiron—like the high school science teacher in John Updike's *The Centaur*, who found himself living out Chiron's myth in his own mundane life, striving to heal the wounds in his soul.

The magical wound is perhaps the single most noticeable contribution of Chiron to the charts of ordinary men and women. Chiron was wounded in the heel or thigh, and only death could give him release from pain. The position of Chiron in a birth chart often points to a kind of inner wound in the native's psyche. The wound is often sexual because Chiron is said to have been wounded in the thigh. In any event, some part of us has to die in order to heal that inner wound. We must relinquish some old and outmoded portion of our beings, some karmic or childhood hurt—and when we have done so, we find that we have released our true creative potential. Prometheus has been unchained, and the inspiring power of Uranus is free to enter our lives. This, then, is the wound which can make us whole again, and that is why it is a "magical" wound.

For many modern Americans and Europeans, and most especially for men, the magical wound of Chiron involves the father. Saturn or Cronus was Chiron's father, and he fled the scene at the very moment of Chiron's conception, never to return. So, embedded in this archetype is the abandonment of the child by the father. From 1935–1939, and again from 1945–1952, Saturn and Chiron were in square to each other—which is to say they were at a 90 degree angle to each other, one of astrology's more difficult relationships. They were in opposition from 1986–1988. During these years, the strong, positive father was noticeably more absent in modern society. A separation between fathers and sons had been occurring since the middle of the 19th century. More and more, men no longer worked their own land or devoted themselves to skilled trades in their own shops. The advent of industrialization and the factory system separated men from their traditional way of life. It separated fathers and sons as well. Boys no longer participated with their fathers in the work of the fields, or in learning the family trade.

By the time Chiron and Saturn squared each other between 1945 and 1952, fatherly strength had fled from our world as swiftly as Cronus fled from the scene of Chiron's making. Almost all American or European men had become city-dwellers who drove to work in the morning, returning tired, grumpy, and distant in the evening. Children and wives experienced the father or husband primarily as a frustrated, isolated, unhappy creature. During this era, comic strips like *Blondie* or *Life With Father* made their appearance, portraying the father as a silly, foolish and lazy individual, cringing and fussing under the regimen of a powerful wife, and fleeing from her wrath as Cronus fled from the outraged Rhea. The archetype of the father had reached an all-time low. During the 1986–88 opposition of Saturn to Chiron, divorce had increased to the point where twenty-five to thirty percent of American children now grow up in homes without any father at all.[7]

But Chiron was also in opposition to Uranus between 1951 and 1989, a generational aspect which points the way to healing the father wound. Chiron set Prometheus free, and, as we shall see, Prometheus is vitally linked with the archetype of Uranus. In some sense, Uranus is a component of the Wild Man, the deep and creative masculine power—a power which is spiritual and life-giving. Wild, shaggy Uranus, the mad Trickster, is a level of masculinity which heals the father wound by connecting us with the earth itself. Chiron, too, is wild and shaggy, half animal. And he is a shaman.

Chiron corresponds to the archetype of the wounded healer, and the wounded healer is the shaman. Among Siberian and Native American tribes, it is often the cripple or the neurotic who is considered chosen by the gods to act as the shaman or medicine man, the healer of the tribe. In Siberia, especially, a lame leg (Chiron's wound) is regarded as a possible indicator that the child or adolescent is a shaman in the making. Among Native Americans, a terrible illness often serves as the experience which marks a person as a medicine man—the famous Lakota shaman Black Elk experienced his great medicine vision during an illness he suffered at ten years of age.[8] If we were to interpret this process psychologically in terms of Chiron's position in the birth chart, we would say that the task of healing Chiron's inner wound opens up our own potential to heal others.

Given his shamanic function, it is not surprising to find Chiron connected with Native American affairs. It was during the late 1970s—right after Chiron's discovery—that the Native American Religious Freedom Act was passed by Congress, thus allowing or encouraging medicine men to begin practicing in the mainstream world, and sparking the revival of interest in Native American shamanism which has become such a vital force today.

Chiron may also be connected—at least on an esoteric level—with the Mayan Calendar and its mysteries. The 260-day sacred calendar of the Aztecs and the Maya interpenetrates with the 365-day solar calendar in such a way as to create a complete cycle in just under 52 years. Chiron's orbital period is 51 years—an almost exact correlation. (Barbara Hand Clow believes that the correlation may once have been even more precise, but that changes in the Mayan Calendar over centuries are accountable for the difference.)[9]

The centaur Chiron on a bronze coin from Bithynia during the reign of Prusias II, 185–114 BC. From the Michael A. Sikora collection

Yet another interesting phenomenon occurring during the 1970s was the collective search for answers to questions which could no longer be approached through traditional means. It was the height of the age of the guru, when people all over the world, primarily the youthful, were collectively banding together in new types of religious movements. The guru represents the person with the answers, who can unlock your mysteries and bring you enlightenment—freedom from the confines of the physical realm. The deeper implications of this phenomenon may have been a generation collectively in search of someone that could help to heal the wounds of the absent father, to serve as mentor and guide, to make them whole once again.

Chiron's emergence during this social and spiritual movement may indicate that Chiron represents, at least in part, the light beyond the darkness of Saturn. Its glyph (⚷) resembles a key, which we may take to be the key which unlocks the mysteries of the universe. Chiron's orbital position between Saturn and Uranus gives us another clue to its significance. Before the discovery of Uranus in 1781, Saturn was the end of the line, the final boundary of the solar system. The last two hundred years may be characterized as Uranian in nature, focused upon the technological developments and advancements we have engineered. But we have also come to see the universe in terms of the spiritual creativity embodied by Uranus, as well as in terms of the other outer planets, Neptune and Pluto—i.e., we now see the universe as a largely untapped field of light and energy, as a possible source of immortality (or at least of rebirth) awaiting us. This awareness of the outer planets stands in direct contrast to the concept of Saturn as the final boundary, a concept which implies death, darkness, and the limitations of physical or worldly reality. Chiron's position makes of it a bridge between Saturn and the outer planets, a bridge between darkness and light.

This concept finds its source in Chiron's myth. The Titan Prometheus, the Wild Man or rebel, endowed humanity with creativity and enlightenment. He stole the sacred fire from heaven so that mortals need not live in darkness. As such, he represents the creative spirit which lies within all of us and which, astrologically, is symbolized by Uranus. But most of us are unable to tap our true potential or realize our own enlightenment because we remain trapped in our material or psychological boundaries. We are chained by Saturn's rings, just as Prometheus was chained to the mountaintop with chains of adamant. It was Chiron's death which released Prometheus. Similarly, it is our ability to heal our own inner wound—the magical or spiritual wound which lies at the heart of all our human pain—that enables us to set our Uranian creativity free, and thus surge forward to realize the power of the other outer planets.

The classification of Chiron as a comet also adds to the symbolism of this archetype. Chiron emerged from his cave to selflessly serve mankind and bring mortals to a new level of consciousness regarding life and death. When he was finished with his task, he returned to an even deeper cavern, that of the underworld. (In a sense, Chiron, like the Fisher King of the Grail Myth he so greatly resembles, is a Christ figure; he heals, then suffers, then dies so that we all may live.) Comets also come blazing into our awareness out of deep space and then, having imprinted their fire upon us, they depart. But if Chiron is indeed a captured comet, it is likely to be with us for a long time. We may suspect that the wounded healer is emerging into collective consciousness on a more permanent level—no longer as the saint or avatar who performs his mission and then is seen no more.

Chiron's cycle of fifty-one years implies a Chiron return at that age. Some people are not especially sensitive to this process (at least not yet). For others, it may be a critical turning point. We have already seen how Daniel Palmer developed the art of chiropractic during his own Chiron return. Another good example may be found in Elisabeth Kubler-Ross, who pioneered the concept of conscious dying in the West. (Chiron himself, in choosing death over a weary immortality, is an outstanding example of "conscious dying.") Kubler-Ross was born with Chiron in early Taurus; hence she experienced her Chiron return in the very year of Chiron's discovery, and this was the year her hospice work began in earnest.[10]

URANUS

From women's eyes this doctrine I derive:
They sparkle still the right Promethean fire;
They are the books, the arts, the academes,
That show, contain and nourish all the world:

—*Shakespeare,* Love's Labour's Lost, IV, III

The Hindu god
Varuna, akin to the
Greek Ouranos

Uranus constitutes one of the most confusing of all planetary archetypes—though perhaps even this confusion is appropriate to the planet that upset the ordered concepts of Ptolemaic astrology simply by virtue of its discovery.

Because Uranus was discovered during the American and French Revolutions in 1781, it has been correlated with freedom, independence, and a revolutionary or rebellious nature. And it is fitting that the planet just beyond Saturn should represent a break from tradition or a freedom from the ordered and structured world that Saturn represents. Uranus, "the planet different," orbits on its belly at a 90 degree angle from the way everything else in the solar system behaves. This should also give us a clue as to the nature of the Uranian mind: a good 90 degrees off from most everyone else!

The word "pioneer" has been applied to Uranus and indeed,

Ouranos was the original sky god, castrated by his son, Cronus. Illustrated by Diane Smirnow

those born with Uranus in prominence seem to possess an incredible pioneering spirit—Sigmund Freud, Carl Jung and Ram Dass (Sun conjunct Uranus); J. Krishnamurti (Sun opposite Uranus); Gandhi (Uranus conjunct Midheaven); and Albert Schweitzer (Saturn opposite Uranus), to name but a few.[1] And with this pioneering spirit and god-like consciousness has often come the sacrifice of a personal or earthly life among these individuals. But these Uranian/Promethean types have contributed significantly to the evolutionary process of life on earth. And no matter which chart you prefer for the United States (Gemini rising, Sagittarius rising, or Virgo rising), Uranus either rises, sets or culminates! This makes America and Americans for the most part highly identified with the planet Uranus as a national archetype, characterized by freedom, independence, iconoclastic behavior, the breaking of social, economic and racial barriers, technological craziness—and of course, the hubris or pride that results from being a super-power and feeling superior (god-like) in comparison to every other nation, whether justifiably or not.

Uranus is the iconoclast, the divine rebel; he is also the creative power of human will. It is as the creator rather than the rebel that he makes his first appearance. The Latin word Uranus is derived from the Greek Ouranos, which is in turn related to Sanskrit Varuna. The god Varuna, in the *Rig Veda*, is both the creator and the guardian of cosmic law. He creates the entire universe through the force of his *maya*—though here we should understand the word *maya* to mean "creative will" rather than the more familiar "illusion." Having created, he also maintains, for he is the judge and guardian of *rta*, the law, the moral order which governs the world. In a sense, his creation is a continual process; Varuna is lord of the "waters above heaven," the source of the life-giving rain.[2] In the 6th or 7th century before Christ, the Persian prophet Zarathustra (better known to us as Zoroaster) transformed this Vedic deity into Ahura Mazda, the Lord of Light, who was similarly the guardian of the cosmic law.[3]

In ancient Greece, Ouranos was the original sky father, the first child of Gaia or Mother Earth when she emerged from the primordial chaos. He gazed down upon his sleeping mother, and poured gentle rains upon her so that she would flourish with trees, flowers and grass. He also became her mate, and the two of them gave birth to a number of monstrous beings, including the race of one-eyed Cyclopes. Finally, they gave birth to the first family of gods which ruled over humankind, the seven Titans and their sister-spouses, the Titanesses. But Ouranos became a tyrant. He imprisoned the Cyclopes in Tartarus because they had attempted to rebel against him. Gaia was enraged and persuaded Cronus (Saturn), youngest of the Titans, to lie in wait for Ouranos, and castrate him with a sickle. The seed of the dying sky father spilled forth upon the earth; it produced the terrifying goddesses of vengeance called the Furies, but it also produced Aphrodite (Venus), the beautiful goddess of love.[4]

Uranus, then, is the essential force of creation. Twice in the Greek myth he rains his creative force down upon the earth, just as Varuna rained down his *maya* or creative will. Ouranos creates all the foliage and vegetation which blossoms upon the body of the Earth Mother; he also gives birth to such dichotomous concepts as love and vengeance. In each case, his power flows forth as a rain from the sky. In astrology, Uranus has been given rulership over Aquarius. As we shall see (in Aquarius) this sign has always been associated with the "waters of life" that are poured forth from heaven. Thus Aquarius is indeed a fitting symbol for this god of primal creativity. We are more inclined, in this technological era, to think of those Aquarian waters as electricity or cosmic energy, but the essential meaning of creative will (the *maya* of Varuna) remains unchanged.

The sheer power of Uranian creativity seldom reaches us in its pure, "cosmic" form. The first stirrings of creative power ordinarily cause turbulence in the psyches of most individuals; a turbulence which expresses itself as rebellion against the past. Thus Uranus is best known to most astrologers and to their clients as the Divine Rebel. As such, this planet becomes the *carrier* for an archetype which is quite different from that of the primal sky father, but which is even more important to our individualistic, turbulent society. Uranus has become the carrier for the archetype of Prometheus.

Prometheus was of the race of the Titans, son of Eurymedon, the Titan associated with the planet Jupiter. His twin brother was Epimetheus, and the name Prometheus means "foresight," while Epimetheus means "hindsight." And a prophetic or futuristic slant on reality was characteristic of Prometheus, who always befriended human beings, and defended them against the gods. Some versions of the myth give Prometheus a true Uranian function as creator spirit, for he is said to have fashioned the first humans of clay, and then to have breathed his vital spirit into them to make them live. Along with Hephaestus, Prometheus had helped to bring forth the goddess Athene from Zeus' forehead, and it was Athene who taught Prometheus the various arts and sciences, which he in turn passed on to mortals.

It was his love for humans which made of Prometheus the great rebel. The gods were accustomed to taking the better portion of each sacrificed bull, leaving men with the offal. But when the matter of the divine portion came up for review, Prometheus played a trick on the gods. He carefully disguised the carcass of the sacrificial bull so that when Zeus chose his own portion, he had in reality chosen the fat and bones, leaving the best meat for mankind. Zeus was not pleased. He ordained that the pathetic mortals should eat their meat raw; he withheld from them the gift of fire.

With Athene's help, Prometheus climbed to the top of Olympus. Holding a fennel stalk, he waited till the chariot of the sun, driven by the Titan Helios, came flashing by, striking sparks of divine fire from the rocky top of Olympus. Prometheus captured a spark of the divine fire with the fennel stalk, and gave it to humankind—a literal "enlightenment."

But Prometheus had twice rebelled against the dictates of the gods. Zeus ordained a terrible fate for him—he was to be chained to a mountaintop in the Caucasus, where an eagle would rip his liver out. But each day the divine rebel's liver would be renewed, and each day the eagle would come again, thus keeping Prometheus in a perpetual torment. This mythic fate was suffered by the Viking god Loki, another divine rebel who rejected the will of the gods.

But, as we have seen, the torment of Prometheus did not last forever. Humanity still had a few friends in the immortal world, and it was given to Chiron, the centaur king, to sacrifice himself so that Prometheus might be released.

Uranus in the birth chart has been equated with an individual's social rebelliousness. While this, to some degree, is true, it is equally true that the bohemianism of the last few decades is as much the product of Neptune as of Uranus. The planetary rebel has also been credited with a talent for scientific invention. We suspect that this is also true; after all, Uranus was discovered at the onset of the industrial revolution, and the Promethean spirit was one of inventiveness. It is this particular aspect of Uranus which astrologers fasten on when they envision the Aquarian Age as one of advanced technology—although now, as we become more and more aware of technology's dark side, it may behoove us to re-think or re-envision what Uranian creativity is really like.

The point is: all of the catchwords we have been accustomed to use for Uranus suggest only *part* of the archetype. Uranus may or may not be socially rebellious— his urge for freedom may be expressed on an internal level rather than through lifestyle. As a rebel, he is also the Wild Man or Wild Woman, the Trickster spirit that lives according to its own rules.

Uranus has the Promethean inventiveness, to be sure, but the tyrannical rule of the sky god Ouranos should warn us that science and technology can become tyrannical or restrictive forces—unless, like Prometheus, we are always conscious of our need to serve humanity through our inventiveness. But Prometheus, we must remember, was rewarded for his creativity by being chained to a mountaintop, and this is an aspect of Uranus or Aquarius that few astrologers, with the exception of Liz Greene, have noted: the incredible loneliness and isolation that overwhelms us when our Promethean spirit is at last fully awakened.

The loneliness and isolation experienced when we embody the Uranus archetype is similar to the isolation experienced through the Saturn archetype. Saturn experienced the fall from grace when his son Jupiter dethroned him and banished

Prometheus stealing the fire of the gods, illustrated by Diane Smirnow

him to Tartarus. Uranus, too, was dethroned by his son, Saturn, resulting in a scattering of his parts into the sea. Prometheus, whose spirit soared, was condemned to being chained to a rock, and it is these conditions of exhilaration and banishment that overwhelm a person when under the influence of Uranus by transit or progression. First, there is the unbridled need to create or generate. Like the progenitor of the first race of earthly gods, one responding to the Uranus archetype will feel omnipotent and, exhilarated by the feelings resulting from such a magnificent cocreation, induce more and more creation, without any forethought as to what the results will be or what effect these creations will have upon their creator or the world in which they emerge. In mythology the Earth Mother Gaia put a stop to it; time and distance brought some objectivity and perspective to the matter. Still, to Uranus it all happens explosively—the sudden awareness that one can create magnificent things, and the sudden ending or fall from the god-like state which results when one is thrust back into real time. Similarly, Promethean energy is a soaring spirit, flying high with the gods, aware of the universal order of the cosmos, but trapped in an earthly body in which we seem to be chained or severely restricted in movement. Thus, those Uranians who have not found a way to reconcile their creative dilemma suffer from a sense of frustration and, often, isolation. When one resides in the kingdom of the gods but is chained to the earth, the world can be a very lonely place. It can also induce fits of violence.

The seed of Ouranos gave birth to the goddess of love, Aphrodite. Almost all of us have experienced Uranian attraction and magnetism at work in matters of love. We have all too often heard, however, that love affairs begun under the influence of Uranus may end as abruptly and intensely as they began. Uranus, like the other outer planets, requires nine months to complete a transit over a particular planet or degree. What begins at the start of the Uranus transit may be finished by the time of its conclusion. Many people have experienced a sudden, overwhelming need to create a totally new lifestyle for themselves and break out of a routine or relationship. They become overwhelmingly attracted to someone's magnetic field or experience some other Uranian form of liberation during Uranus transits to natal planets. But often, by the time the Uranus transit is complete, the person is brought back down from the heavenly heights and must adjust to earthly reality once again. When one is experiencing a Uranus transit (especially to the Sun, Moon, or angles), he or she may seem very out of touch with the everyday concerns of life— mundane routine does not hold much interest during these times. These periods are often characterized by a feeling of being elevated to euphoric states usually reserved for the gods—like Prometheus stealing fire or Uranus involved in acts of magnificent creation. Electrical impulses buzz around us, we seem to be tied to giant computer networks which offer tons of new and exciting information, our nervous systems are highly stimulated—and we certainly have to concentrate in order to feel grounded. While these states may be experienced as highly fulfilling, the crash back to earth can seem very harsh once the phase is completed. But imagine living in this state all the time—it would require great skill to operate realistically and efficiently in a perpetual Uranian universe. Saturn is the earth god, and demands that we frequently abide by his laws. Uranian periods are meant to offer a welcome change from Saturn, giving us a chance to seize the freedom we need, break free of outworn modes of behavior, stay progressive, and keep our creative juices flowing. But there are people *born* with a highly emphasized Uranus factor in the chart and these people are extremely stimulated most of the time. Their awareness can certainly be god-like or otherworldly. They may frequently have visions of extra-terrestrials, as this would be a common Uranian/Promethean symbol—that of gods residing above us coming into our sphere to either help us with our evolutionary process (Prometheus/Chiron) or to inflict vengeance and punishment upon us, like Zeus in his fits

Lightning is associated with Uranus as well as with Jupiter. Photograph by Michael Guttman

of anger. Men have always told myths about how the gods are either angry or pleased with us, based on how we interact with nature. Lightning and thunderbolts (symbols of Uranus and Jupiter) are traditional symbols of those times when the gods are angry with us. And visitors from other planets are usually described as helpful to their less-evolved earth siblings or as wantonly destructive, seeking to conquer us.

There is perhaps no better way to assess the influence of Uranus on human affairs than to take note of the four Uranian stages in human life. Uranus takes eighty-four years to circle the zodiac; hence it will square its natal position when we are about twenty-one, oppose itself when we are forty-two, square itself again at about age sixty-three, and then return to its own place at eighty-four. These, then, are the four Uranian moments of a person's life, and we may borrow a phrase from psychologist Gail Sheehy by calling them "predictable crises of adult life."[6]

The first Uranian square takes place in our late teens or early twenties. Here we see the Uranian spirit of rebellion at its purest: this is the age when we embody the Wild Man or Wild Woman, dress like bohemians, repudiate the values of our parents or of society, live with people we never intend to marry, and finish it all up by running off to look for America on the back of a motorcycle. Of course, some people never go through such a phase of rebellion, though it might be healthier if they did so. These naturally Saturnian characters, having neglected to sow their wild oats, may find the *next* Uranian phase very difficult to deal with.

It is said that "life begins at forty," which is society's unconscious way of recognizing the Uranus opposition. Psychologists call it the "mid-life crisis." Conservative (Saturnian) astrologers—and there seem to be fewer of these all the time—may look at this period of life with great trepidation and characterize it as chaotic. But more Uranian astrologers regard it as potentially the best time of life. This is when we become aware that we are not yet old, but no longer young. We don't know everything, but we do know a lot. When Uranus first squared itself at age twenty we *thought* we knew it all; but by the time we reach the opposition we realize we don't know anything, and that realization brings on a certain kind of enlightenment which gives us a key to unlock the secret doors of the future. That, coupled with some Saturnian experience, outfits us in grand style for the next phase of life, where we begin to reap the harvest we have worked so hard to cultivate. We ask ourselves in this phase whether or not we have achieved our goals, realized our dreams. If we are wise, we realize that it is time to shift the focus of our attention from purely material or worldly concerns (Saturn) to more spiritual, creative, and individuated goals (Uranus). Those who are open to this Uranian moment will be ready to soar. They are old enough now to use the skills they have learned through dealing with Saturn's world—skills that can help them find the inner and outer freedom which was still so nebulous and hard to grasp when they were twenty. Those who cannot or will not listen to the voice of Uranus at this time may begin to do some very strange things. Mom smokes pot with her kids, visits an astrologer for the first time, or has an affair; Dad drives to the accounting office on a new Harley and pinches all the secretaries. Those who manage to keep both the creativity and the chaos out of their lives may run the risk of developing major illnesses—especially male executives who are unwilling to get out of the fast lane.

The final square occurs at approximately sixty-three. It is significant that our society has chosen this period as the age of retirement. We are finally being set free from Saturn's world. This is the phase when Mom and Dad sell the house, decorate the Winnebago with stickers which announce "We're spending our children's inheritance," and hit the road. Now, having finished the game, they may finally discover America after all—which is what they tried to do forty years ago!

Uranus returns to its own place when we are eighty-four. Most of us miss this one, for it is still beyond the average life expectancy of contemporary Americans—though it may not be for too much longer. Too often, we are tired, sick, or bed-ridden when we reach this phase. This tells us something about our society: we do not value or validate old age, and consequently we are not equipped to receive its blessing. Saturn, the symbol of old age, was cast into Tartarus to spend his final years. Similarly, we cast our elders into nursing homes or retirement centers to live out their old age. But these are the years when truly magical things can happen. If we were to take a cue from native tribes who honor and revere their elders and set them to teaching the youngsters, we would experience the ultimate Uranian enlightenment, because symbolically this final Uranian infusion suggests a spiritual rebirth, a willing acceptance to begin detaching ourselves from the world altogether, and to fix our gaze upon greener, "freer" pastures.

Some very profound occurrences take place when Uranus is orbiting in conjunction to another planet, especially the outer or trans-Saturnian planets. Uranus made its last conjunction with Saturn during 1988 in Saturn's sign, Capricorn. New political paradigms emerged and will continue to emerge until the outer planets Uranus and Neptune leave Capricorn in 1998. Uranus rendezvoused with Neptune during 1993 in the sign Capricorn. Because Capricorn is an earth sign, normally associated with management, government, and economy, the late 1980s and the entire decade of the 1990s can be characterized as a period of shifting political realities or, as the psychics call it, "earth changes"!

Uranus conjoined Pluto throughout the 1960s with the exact conjunction occurring in the middle of the decade, a case in point for the experience of unreality that can occur during a Uranus transit. Both these bodies in space symbolize *change* — with Uranus the changes are intended to improve, revolutionize or be progressive in some way; but with Pluto, who, like Shiva, is a god of destruction, change needs no rationale. Thus we witnessed a time period so out of the ordinary that historians are still trying to define what took place. Things were set into motion during that decade which will most likely take an entire cycle (eighty-four years) to make themselves fully manifest or be comprehended by us. That the two planets met in the astrological sign of the earth goddess (Demeter's Virgo) suggests that a new earth awareness (perhaps of a religious nature) was emerging that will begin to turn the tide on Uranus' previous technocratic ascension. A new wave of "earth cadets" emerged, advocating an exodus from our polluted cities and back to the land, a return to "natural living," and, most importantly, voicing a commitment to fight the pollution of the earth's forests, rivers, and oceans and to prevent any more species from becoming extinct. The trend continues some thirty years later, but the momentous uproar that citizens and politicians find themselves in at present will not have anywhere near the same fierce intensity that characterized the years of the conjunction — though we may well experience a deep spiritual intensity around these issues as a result of the Uranus-Neptune conjunction of 1993.

Neptune on a "seahorse" from Jost Amman's Kunstbüchlin, *published by Johann Feyerabend, Frankfurt, 1599*

NEPTUNE

CHAPTER SEVENTEEN

Ye elves of hills, brooks, standing lakes and groves,
And ye that on the sands with printless foot
Do chase the ebbing Neptune and do fly him
When he comes back...

— *Shakespeare*, The Tempest, V, I

From the watery realm of the oceans comes Poseidon, brother of Zeus. When Zeus became commander-in-chief of Mt. Olympus, he divided the rulership of the world with his two brothers, Poseidon and Hades. Hades was given the domain of the underworld while Poseidon was to oversee the oceans. Thus it is his oceanic form we are most familiar with, though Poseidon also governs horses and earthquakes.

Contact with the great ocean of the collective unconscious, that eternal storehouse of images and dreams, may bring forth psychic earthquakes and sweep us into the stormy realm of Poseidon. In general, however, astrologers perceive Neptune as a soft, almost feminine planet—and some would drop the word "almost." Neptune appears strongly in the horoscopes of idealists, musicians, painters, dancers (*especially* dancers), as well as among alcoholics, drug addicts, therapists, and those who follow a spiritual vocation. The typical Neptunian is otherworldly, his or her vision tuned to an inner reality which may create fantasy castles that delight the multitudes, or which may lead the native into a dark underworld of escapism and substance abuse.

This dreaminess should alert us to the fact that Neptune is acting as the carrier for an additional archetype, other than the stormy, wrathful sea-god Poseidon. And it is the spirit of Dionysus—so conspicuous in our modern culture but noticeably absent from the sky—that is embodied in the planetary Neptune. According to the Orphic version of the myth, Persephone, Queen of the Underworld, was the mother of Dionysus. And in the mysteries of Eleusis, it was Dionysus who was revealed as the miraculous child of Demeter. He was, in archaic times, the divine son of the Earth Mother, or even of the underworld mother. His origins come from deep in the unconscious. The most common story of his birth, however, makes him the son of Semele, a princess of Thebes; his father was Zeus. Jealous Hera tricked Semele into making a fatal request of her lover: she demanded that Zeus show himself to her in all his glory. Zeus granted the unfortunate boon, and Semele was consumed in fire at the sight. But her six-months' child, Dionysus, was sewn into the thigh of Zeus, so that he might be born in due time. Hidden from Hera, he was raised by a group of nymphs called the Hyades; they disguised him as a girl. We should not wonder, then, that Neptunians have a feminine softness, or that male Neptunians are the softest of men: Dionysus is the child of the Great Mother, and he was raised as an androgyne. The Neptunian male genuinely loves women; he even understands them.

When Dionysus became conscious of his godhood, he showed himself as more than just the mother's child; he also embodied the Wild Man. After introducing the cultivation of the vine to humanity, he traveled the world, spreading drunken ecstasy wherever he went. His devotees, the maenads, were inebriated women who danced with wild abandon, and, in their madness, tore men to pieces. Here we see two of Neptune's most popular attributes embodied: its connection with the art of dance, and its link with alcoholic or narcotic intoxication.

Dionysus is primarily a god of religious ecstasy. He may be one of the oldest gods we know. Robert Graves has drawn attention to a Stone Age painting in the cave of Cogul, which shows a man in the center of a group of wildly dancing women.[1] This, as well as his status as Demeter's earth-born child, suggests that it was originally Dionysus himself who was torn to pieces by the maenads. The Divine Mother's child becomes her lover and is ritually slain by her priestesses so

Dionysus on a bronze coin from Bithynia during the reign of Prusias II, 185–114 BC. From the Michael A. Sikora collection

A nineteenth-century engraving of the Bacchanal, the frenzied worship of the god Dionysus, or Bacchus, after the Borghese vase in the Louvre

that he may rise again. Marija Gimbutas has identified a deity of Old Europe (c. 5,000 BC) whom she calls the Sorrowful God, and whom she believes to be a precursor of Dionysus in his aspect of the sacrificial god.[2] The Divine Child, grown old, becomes the Sorrowful God. In the midst of the sacred dance, he is slain. But he rises again, personified as the vine—which is to say, his resurrection is ecstasy. Christianity embodies this same myth, slightly modified.

Ecstasy is both the gift and the fatal flaw of the Neptunian individual. Nowhere is this better illustrated than in our own recent cultural history, especially the 1960s. Astrologers often refer to this decade as a very Neptunian time—and indeed, the drugs, the love-ins, the idealism, the colorful bohemian garb all suggest Neptune very strongly. It was during this decade that Dionysus—long banished from sight in our puritanical culture—made his dramatic reappearance. The rock stars of that era (Dionysus and Neptune are both connected with music) were androgynous young men with long hair, sons of the mother. Like other men of that era, they looked to women rather than older men for initiation. Hence they gained a lunar spiritual insight but lacked solar strength. And whenever they performed, they risked being almost torn to pieces by crowds of female followers.

If they were never torn to pieces literally, they were certainly slain symbolically, and by the power of the collective unconscious. It is dangerous to be possessed by an archetype. The ordinary human ego can't quite handle it. When we begin to believe that we are godlike beings, above and beyond human laws and limitations, we risk being swallowed by the Earth Mother. The rock stars of the 1960s made that descent by way of sex and drugs—two of Dionysus' favorite tools. Jim Morrison of the Doors is a prime example. By some accounts, he consciously believed himself to be possessed by the spirit of Dionysus. Thus he surrendered too willingly to the Wild Man within, and it killed him.

"Ariadne Abandoned," who was rescued from the island of Naxos by Dionysus

The healthy shaman, he who heals the tribe, does not fall victim to the kind of archetypal possession that so easily afflicts the contemporary Neptunian. He dances his god-dance, then puts down his mask and returns to ordinary human consciousness. A similar process takes place in the theater, which makes an excellent analogy for two reasons: theater in the Western world arose from the festivals of Dionysus, and Neptunian individuals tend to do well in the performing arts. An actor, like a shaman, trains himself to take on another personality—in ancient times, this was always the personality of a god. He wears the mask, dances the dance, chants the sacred chant—and then he is done. The tribe has been healed. The sense of catharsis so important to the Greek dramatists has been achieved. Archetypal possession—the surrender to collective Neptunian illusion—takes place when we are incapable of removing the god-mask. Another example is Marilyn Monroe, who had Neptune rising (along with Venus at the Midheaven), and who descended into a world of drugs and alcohol because she was unable to lay down the mask of Aphrodite. The goddess consumed her.

How, then, shall we manage the force of ecstasy—the direct line to the world of the gods which seems to be the province of all Neptunians, for better or worse? How shall we teach ourselves to lay down the mask of the sacrificial god, or the Wild Man, or whatever mask we have chosen for ourselves? The myth of Dionysus suggests two answers. One answer is: a love relationship based on the highest

Neptunian ideals. During his wild journey around the world, Dionysus came at last to the island of Naxos. There he found Ariadne, princess of Crete, who had helped the hero Theseus slay the minotaur and topple her own father's kingdom. For her devotion to Theseus, she had been poorly rewarded: the conquering hero abandoned her on an island. Dionysus fell in love with her and married her, and it was shortly after this that he was admitted to the company of the Olympian gods. Through his marriage, he acquired maturity and balance. He took his place among the gods, and abandoned his wandering lifestyle. But note that Ariadne was a victim—one of love's walking wounded. The Neptunian is typically attracted to relationships that have a savior-victim quality, and this is often unhealthy. It is only by concentrating the focus of a relationship on transcendence—Dionysus went to Olympus while Ariadne was given a celestial home as the Corona Borealis—that the Neptunian heals his or her own inner longings and achieves maturity of soul. Neptune has been called the higher octave of Venus, and Venus is exalted in Neptune's ruling sign, Pisces. This suggests that Neptune's highest manifestation is universal, all-encompassing love and compassion.

But if the Neptunian relationship is potentially dangerous on account of its savior-victim tendencies, then the second solution to the Dionysian dilemma is even more fraught with peril. We are told that the god descended into the underworld, retrieved his mother Semele, and ascended with her to Olympus. A child of the Divine Mother, so close to the collective feminine that he may be torn to pieces by it, Dionysus faces up to the Mother directly. Similarly, the Neptunian can choose to make a descent into the unconscious, to face the world of dreams and images which make his or her life a joy and a torment. The Neptunian may choose to confront Pluto, the dark lord—or, in this case, the dark lady—of the underworld. After all, the Orphic version of the myth tells us that Persephone herself was Dionysus' mother! But the mother may eat her child if he ventures too deeply into her domain. For the Neptunian, a direct descent into the unconscious may prove fatal. But if there is sufficient courage, it may also lead to salvation.

Astrologers are prone to associate Neptune, including its artistry and spiritual dimension, with the dreaminess of the sea. Its rulership over Pisces conjures such images, but Neptune certainly has its dark side. Probably no planet has been more misunderstood and maligned in astrology texts than Neptune. Perhaps because this archetype rules the ocean (the collective unconscious) where logic and rational processes cease to exist, one must look with other eyes to "see" Neptune. In any case, seen or unseen, his power to shake up our everyday world has been amply demonstrated.

The planet named Neptune was discovered in 1846 while in the sign of Aquarius, and it seems it may have more of an Aquarian flavor than we have previously suspected. Fourteen years after its discovery, Aquarian Abraham Lincoln became President of the United States. This was a man whose principles were typically Aquarian (Promethean) and whose task it became to abolish slavery. Indeed, slavery and bondage seem to be one of the keynotes of Pisces, Neptune's ruling sign, while freedom is the issue Aquarius embodies. Its discovery in the latter sign points to a Promethean explosion: Neptune can no longer be shackled to chains and held in bondage against its will when in Aquarius (i.e., when Prometheus is nearby). Slavery is an issue which humanity has dealt with since its beginnings and an issue which continues to plague our world. We will once again witness the transit of Neptune through Aquarius, along with Uranus, beginning in 1998, its first return to that sign since its discovery. Once again, freeing those who are still shackled will no doubt be a keynote of the era.

The problem with slavery and bondage is that once we are freed, we are expected to make choices for ourselves, accept the responsibility for those choices, and then live by them. Unfortunately, even when we have the freedom to do this, it is seldom done. One of the most difficult things, it seems, is to wipe the sand out of our eyes, wake up and manifest our visions. Even when given opportunities to do that, many of us prefer to live life with eyes closed, blaming everyone else for our sorry lot. In psychological circles and in treatment centers all over the country, this process is called denial, and it is one which tears at the very fabric of the unification of body, mind, and spirit, the synthesizing process with which the sign Pisces and its ruling planet Neptune is most associated.

Denial literally means "to look away." Denial, as played out in our society for so long, is based on this principle—looking away from reality. When reality (Saturn) is ignored or denied, Neptune takes over with dreams, fantasies, addictions, free-floating anxiety, etc. And this is what plagues our society in the last part of this Piscean Age. Basically, addiction stems from co-dependence, co-dependence stems from feelings of unworthiness or shame, and shame begins with someone else (typically a parent) scapegoating themselves and placing the blame on us for their own unworthiness. It is played out in family systems over and over again, as John Bradshaw has pointed out most eloquently in his works.[3] Thus, the cycle keeps repeating itself until we finally open our eyes and dare to *see* ourselves in the mirror as we truly are, and not through the eyes of denial or through the fantasies we've created around ourselves for so long. Of course, this process takes a lot of courage and strength, and most people prefer the path of least resistance. In examining the astrological position of Neptune, one can usually pinpoint the areas most prone to denial and self-delusion.

Neptune in his wrathful aspect

Many astrology books give a very negative description of Neptune, especially if Neptune happens to be "afflicted." According to some texts, if Neptune is transiting something in

Amphitrite, wife of Poseidon

your chart, you may as well go to sleep, check yourself into the local treatment center, take a holiday, or go on a spiritual retreat for the next two years—forget about getting anything accomplished. In truth, this does not reflect reality, and if it did, our entire world would be dysfunctional most of the time, because in one way or another we're always getting a Neptune transit. This is a characteristic that Neptune shares with its brother Pluto, the two gods who were relegated to the underwater and the underworld realms. They reside in domains where it's easier to ignore or push under the carpet all the things we don't want to deal with directly—the domains of the personal (Pluto) and collective unconscious (Neptune). These two departments are very much "up" for humanity right now, as they are related to the two newest planets in our solar system.

Whether we observe Neptune's rulership over drugs and alcohol, the oil industry (our technological addiction), or even our addiction to spiritual attainment, everybody seems to be seeking some form of Neptune these days. In a way, it's like a glittering carrot that always seems to hang in front of us. We think we can almost touch it, but in reality it always stays just far enough away to keep us reaching. So what does happen to individuals who have transits of Neptune affecting them for a time? The same thing that happens to people who are *born* with prominent Neptunes, only the people born with this placement devote their entire lives to understanding its properties and making the necessary adjustments, while people experiencing it in a significant transit are only forced to come under its spell for a year or two.

Neptune (Poseidon) was not always a nice guy in mythology. In fact, he excelled at throwing storm clouds and nets in the way of his intended victims, making them lose their way at sea for long periods of time. The most famous story of his revenge and treacherous deeds is told in *The Odyssey*, detailing Odysseus' attempt to return home from the Trojan War. Many people feel that they can't *see* where they are going while under a transit of Neptune. Certainly, there is some truth to this, and yet the vision of the future comes in other ways when we are cut off from a purely physical sense of reality. Thus one of Neptune's jobs may be to encourage the opening of the third eye, to develop the trust and reliance on faith and a higher power that comes when an individual no longer is able to control his or her own course.

We have mentioned Neptune's association with vision twice. When given the opportunity to see the truth, people often don't take it, and second, when clear vision is taken away from them they insist on trying to see anyway. This is the tricky aspect of Neptune, which does indeed have influence over our ability to see. Most people whose vision is poor have Neptune in prominent aspect to the Sun or Moon, the traditional significators of vision and the eyes.

If we think of Neptune as an underwater god, rising from the vast sea of primordial consciousness, we get a picture of a deity or person who is much more centered in the chaotic feeling and instinctual process than in the ordered, disciplined and logical realm. Personal feelings to some extent govern the Neptunian type but, more than that, Neptune represents *universal* feelings—those that drift across the ocean containing a little bit of everything and everybody. With so much sensitivity and tenderness, most Neptunians don't survive very well in the outside world, unless they are gifted with a well-endowed Jupiter and/or Saturn to get them through. But in time they figure out that they are not of this world and, *most importantly*, that they don't have to act like they are or conform to anyone else's expectations. Their challenge in life is to keep in touch with their inner spiritual center while continuing to function on the material plane, a process similar to that of Pisces with its two fish swimming in opposite directions (see Pisces). Pisces and Neptune have the ability, beyond all other signs and planets, to absorb everything around them. Thus they also have the least amount of personal ego or boundaries. Poor boundaries are a watery or water-sign affliction generally, and are also characteristic of Vesta, but nowhere is the lack of boundaries more apparent than when there is a Pisces or Neptune affliction in the chart. When an individual is possessed of a strongly afflicted Neptune, he or she may lack a sense of per-

Neptune, or Poseidon

sonal definition or will or purpose or identification in the outer world, and the result can be so harmful that a strong solar or Saturnian force is necessary to bring the person back. The same lack of definition may even be true of one's inner world—if Neptune is not backed up by a strong Moon or Venus, there can be much doubt and confusion as to what one's inner beliefs really are. This is what people are so fearful about when Neptune transits occur—they no longer seem to function in the rational, linear world the way they once did. Their way of outer adaptation no longer works. Everything begins to crumble; nothing makes sense any more. The ego has to dissolve or step aside for awhile while Neptune throws its net over our charted course, thereby forcing us to learn to navigate by other means, i.e., by trusting our intuitive faculties or by learning to develop them if they don't already exist. When Poseidon threw storm clouds in Odysseus' way, the returning hero was forced to add insight to his intellect in order to keep going—and it still took him ten years to get home. Obviously, people who have existed solely in the rational world will have difficulty in suddenly trusting the realm of their instincts. Like the unwilling Odysseus, most people do not openly embrace transits of Neptune. These people may feel tidal waves of emotion flooding them at the very beginning of a Neptune experience, and this is often quite frightening.

But it is also a necessary process. The dissolution represented by Neptune is important at certain stages of life when we have become too full of ourselves or our attachments to material pursuits. Neptune can certainly inflate our sense of ego or importance (especially regarding spiritual life), but it can also act as a deflationary device. Even economic cycles are affected by this planet—when Neptune conjoins with Jupiter inflation is at its height; with Saturn, deflation, recession and economic fears predominate. With Uranus, all traditional forms and economic barometers are shattered. We are in the midst of a once-per-century conjunction of Uranus and Neptune, which prevails throughout 1993. Because the conjunction takes place in Capricorn, many astrologers speculate that a major reshaping of the political and economic realities that govern our planet are up for change. Since Neptune rules socialism in its purest sense, i.e., the giving up of personal values in favor of the masses, and since Uranus rules the democratic process, there is a possibility that these two systems may finally find a common ground and achieve a merger of some sort, one which will characterize the opening years of the 21st century. Certainly, there will be kinks to work out at first, but it is the right kind of planetary conjunction to institute a vision that many have already prophesied—that of a one-world government and a planetary coalition that works together to serve the world rather than divide it. We spoke of Uranus' attunement to extra-terrestrial beings, and Neptune has a similar sensitivity. However, Uranian visions look more like a science fiction movie, filled with beings who arrive in space-ships to save or help planet Earth and its inhabitants, while Neptunian visions look angelic and devic, straight from God. Still, whatever form our collective visions may take, there is likely to be a heightened sense of awareness of these forms—the feeling that something or someone outside of our physical realm is monitoring and influencing events on earth.

As a god of storms and earthquakes, Neptune was able to unleash his primal rage and emotional intensity upon the earth and sea at will. This aspect of Neptune is not well understood, but it is the ultimate result when emotions and instincts are not allowed to exist above ground or when they are not released at proper intervals. It is this kind of explosion which both Neptune and his brother Pluto can unleash. In mundane astrology Neptune governs earthquakes, hurricanes, and tidal waves (and, it seems, oil spills) while Pluto rules volcanic eruptions. These kinds of occurrences are quite beyond our control and can wipe out thousands of people at a time with no particular warning as to exactly when or where they will strike. This correlates to the kind of fear, trepidation, or out-of-control feeling one may experience during a transit of Neptune or Pluto—simply because one has no way of knowing what will be wiped out or why—and indeed, one has little to say about the matter anyway.

Neptune last rendezvoused with Pluto in 1892 in the sign Gemini, an era characterized by the quickening pace of air and land mobility, communications, and technological know-how, as well as by the beginnings of "New Age" consciousness among the early Theosophists, the artists and performers who made up the core of the Order of the Golden Dawn, and even among the millions of readers of Du Maurier's best-selling novel *Trilby*, in which the sinister hypnotist Svengali (Pluto) dominates a beautiful young singer (Neptune). Since 1945 and until 2000 Neptune and Pluto will be traveling at about the same speed and will remain in a sextile (60 degree) formation, an indication that powerful evolutionary processes for humankind can take place easily and naturally, and a time when racism, prejudice, war and injustice can have their best chance to be dissolved and overturned.

PLUTO

CHAPTER EIGHTEEN

But when a black-faced cloud the world doth threat,
In his dim mist the aspiring mountains hiding,
From earth's dark womb some gentle gust doth get,
Which blows these pitchy vapours from their biding...
And moody Pluto winks while Orpheus plays.

—*Shakespeare*, The Rape of Lucrece

When the planet discovered in 1930 was named Pluto, the world was embarking upon yet another crisis. This period of time was the darkest hour of the 20th century; indeed, of the whole post-industrial era. The United States was in the grips of a severe depression so great that people were jumping off buildings left and right because they had lost their fortunes. In Europe the age of the dictator was in full swing: Hitler, Mussolini and Franco and their dark armies evoked terror. Gangsterism in both America and Europe was on the rise and Mafia bosses were implementing their own brand of terrorism. In the scientific arena the atom bomb, made from plutonium, was in its early stages. The world was poised between two world wars; fear and darkness prevailed. And one more Plutonian element emerged from the depths of the underworld—depth psychology and the psychoanalytic process was in its heyday with

Freud (Plutonian sexuality), Adler (Plutonian power drive), and Jung (Plutonian transformation) as key spokesmen.

Pluto the planet was quickly assigned to the rulership of Scorpio since both planet and sign have underworld affinities. And as Pluto's astrological interpretation began sixty years ago, it was a synthesis of mythology, world events, and the meaning of the astrological sign Scorpio that initially formulated the planet's symbolism. Time has proven these meanings correct, for we have seen the dark world of Pluto emerge quite clearly in our century. The fear with which the aforementioned gangsterism, terrorism, dictatorship, nuclear waste, and economic depression were greeted during Pluto's discovery has now become a constant fear, and all one has to do is turn on the nightly news to see that such stories dominate. A new kind of enemy has emerged in the form of atomic energy as well—an enemy that could annihilate the world in a matter of minutes, especially in the wrong hands.

Thus Pluto, whom the Greeks called Hades, was reintroduced into our world. Like his brother Poseidon, Hades was given rulership over a region of the world less glorified than what brother Zeus commanded. Hades ruled the realm of darkness and dread—the world of the dead.

Pluto enthroned

Pluto, like his brother Zeus, was swallowed by their father Cronus. Once freed from Cronus' shadow he became ruler of the underworld. He always lived apart from the light of day, and metaphorically we can assume that this had an effect on his character. The planet Pluto, which is a tiny little planet, sits at the far reaches of the solar system, beyond the giants Jupiter, Saturn, Uranus, and Neptune. The sun cannot shine on Pluto.

Astrologers are sometimes confused by Pluto's symbolism in that the planet appears to be both masculine and feminine. The feminine counterpart of Hades is Persephone, and many women who have Pluto in high focus have experienced a strong resonance with Persephone and her story. She was abducted at a very young age by Hades, and though she ultimately came to enjoy her life as queen of the underworld, she too has always lived in shadow—in the shadow of her mother Demeter, whose possessiveness was extreme, and then at Hades's side.

The story of Hades' ascent into the upper world to abduct his bride Persephone has already been detailed here (see Ceres). Once Hades captured Persephone and made her his queen he presumably had no problems with her, but he may have *need-ed* her in order to truly be king of his dark domain. In pre-patriarchal societies, there was always a goddess in the underworld as in the upper world. And psycho-logically, the feminine instincts fare much better in the underworld regions of the unconscious than masculine aspects do. Thus the addition of Persephone to the underworld partly restored it to its original feminine rulership. While Zeus and Hera had many quarrels and power struggles on Mt. Olympus, there is no mention of such squabbles between Hades and Persephone. They ruled *together*, except for the months when Persephone was allowed to return to her mother, Demeter.

If some of Pluto's interpretation was derived from its association with Scorpio, then we must also look at Mars, the former ruler of Scorpio, and at the fact that Pluto is considered the higher octave of Mars in traditional astrology. There are defi-nitely correspondences between these two planets—for instance, they are both asso-ciated in some esoteric systems with the power-center chakras, the first and second, where instincts and survival are paramount. But there are some vital differences.

Mars was primarily a war god; he expresses energy at a very conscious, physical level. Pluto too has a warrior spirit, but it is embedded in the underworld or uncon-scious, and is therefore released sporadically and awkwardly at times when we are least able to control it. That, in a nutshell, is the key to Pluto. It defies control. It has a life of its own, and when one is involved in a Plutonian process, all one can do is wait until it clears before the rational mind can take hold again. Fittingly, Pluto is given dominion over the personal unconscious and psychotherapy in general. We were introduced to such states of "abnormal" behavior through both Uranus and Neptune, the other two higher octave planets. Uranus' outer limit suggested the pri-mordial chaos from which it first emerged, something akin to the realm of air, i.e., the higher octave of Mercury. Neptune's wild frenzies and deep meditations are born in the depths of the ocean—emotional chaos or transcendent ecstasy at its most intense. With Pluto we often unleash the underground turbulence of years of repressed feel-ings, and as Mars' higher octave, Plutonian feelings usually include rage and vio-lence that have been left to simmer far too long. Why so much anger? Was Hades an angry god? There is no mention of anger in his mythology, but we are told that his brother Zeus took heaven and earth to rule, while he was left with the kingdom of the dead—something that might well inspire jealousy and perhaps anger.[1]

Thus both sides of Pluto may represent repression and domination—typical childhood experiences of the Plutonian, who must eventually empower himself or herself to "take back" that lost power. This is how the wounded Pluto can accelerate its own healing process. However, there are many Plutonians who never quite get the process working in a sufficiently healthy way to do that. The Plutonians who are still raging over their abductions or dominations continue to live in darkness, or in the shadow of that experience or person. Usually they seek vengeance on their abusers, or, worse, turn into abusers themselves. Pluto healed may become

Hades, Persephone, Hermes, and souls entering the underworld

Persephone, who transforms her abduction experience into wisdom and empowers herself with the mysteries of life, death, and the spirit world. Persephone alternates between two worlds—the living and the dead, the light and the dark, the conscious and the unconscious—in order to bring balance and equilibrium into her being. Pluto unhealed remains trapped in Hades, in the dimly lit underworld, jealous of his brother Zeus, angry at his father Cronus, abducting all the Persephones he can sneak away with, and conversing only with the dead, lifeless forms that appear before him.

Because Pluto has dominion over the world of dead souls, one cannot escape the symbolism this presents to us in astrology. Many astrologers, such as Jeff Green, correlate his position with the journey of the soul.[2] Liz Greene correlates Pluto with the underground, instinctive rulership of the Moirai, the Fates whose law was final and absolute and could not be overturned, even by Zeus himself.[3] Once a soul was condemned to Hades' domain, there it remained. Obviously, Pluto deals with life and death issues, and many people tremble at the thought of a Pluto transit as if impending death were near. Death of some kind is indeed always near, but Pluto is not only (or even primarily) about *physical* death. There is usually some kind of psychological death or loss experienced during a Pluto transit. It can feel like one has been sucked into a black hole. When such periods arise, it is best to just let well enough alone and let it pass. Nothing can pull us out of that hole until we are ready to emerge.

Whether one views Persephone's return to the underworld as a yearly cycle representing the seasons, as a human cycle representing the losses and gains one experiences in life, or as the soul's journey to the underworld (afterlife) and back to the next body (reincarnation), her myth has become one of the most often enacted dramas regarding life and death.

Perhaps the most powerful of all Plutonian myths comes from ancient Mesopotamia rather than Greece. It involves the descent of the goddess Ishtar into the underworld. Ishtar, however, is a Babylonian name, and the same story was told of her Sumerian counterpart Inanna, making this one of the oldest myths on record.

Ishtar was in mourning over the death of her lover, Tammuz. She began her journey to the underworld in an attempt to bring him back. Successively, she passed each of the gates to the land of the dead. Each time she reached another gateway, the dark guardians who kept watch there demanded something of her. She gave up her crown, her jewelry. Finally she gave up her clothes. Hence the goddess of love was stark naked by the time she reached the throne of the underworld queen.

This underworld queen—the female incarnation of Pluto—was known as Ereshkigal in the Sumerian version of the story. She seems to be one of a kind with the Gorgon Medusa of Greek myth. Medusa had a mane of hair which was comprised of writhing serpents, while Ereshkigal, more primal yet, has hair of leeches. Her reception of Ishtar is far from favorable: the goddess of love is hanged from a meat-hook as if dead, a carcass mouldering in the bottom of hell.

But the gods cannot countenance a world in which there is no goddess of love. They send their messengers to the underworld, to demand of Ereshkigal the release of the goddess. So it is that Ishtar returns to the land of the living. Now, however, she is somewhat more than just the goddess of love. She is the Queen of Heaven.

The myth of Ishtar's Descent has a basis in actual astronomy. As we have observed (see Venus), it relates to the disappearance of Venus as the Morning Star and its reappearance as the Evening Star. But the psychological resonance of this myth is of even greater significance.

Note that Ishtar begins her journey because of an overwhelming sense of loss— her lover Tammuz is dead. When we are faced with a Plutonian experience, whether because of Pluto's position in the birth chart or because of a Pluto transit— we typically feel such a sense of loss. Sometimes we may find that something of great value is snatched away from us. This is not always the result of an actual encounter with physical death, as it was for Ishtar (though in fact it *may* be). Instead, we may experience the "death" of a relationship, the loss of a job, the necessity to sell a beloved home and move to a strange place. The variations are endless. But one way or another, we are forced to give up *something we thought we couldn't live without*. No wonder, then, that the Pluto experience can be so terrifying. No wonder we feel as if we are literally face to face with the lord or lady of the dead. For we are bereft of support, our security vanished into thin air.

But that is only the beginning. Whatever the initial experience of loss may be, it sends us spiraling down, deep into the unconscious where we come face to face with our own personal demons. And as we descend, we seem to lose more and more of those things which made us feel safe and secure. Like Ishtar, we are stripped of our robes of glory. These robes of glory might be material possessions, but more often they are attitudes, carefully cherished assumptions about life. Everything we took for granted begins to seem meaningless. We no longer have any sense of foundation, whether moral, emotional, or spiritual. At last, we face up to the ultimate darkness. Ereshkigal, the queen of the dead, with leeches in her hair, is the face we see in the mirror. Persephone's name means "she who is to be feared." And at the heart of a Pluto experience, we face our own worst fears. We seem to be nothing but raw emotion, or simply a collection of organs and feces tied up in a bag of skin. We have reached rock bottom; we're hanging on a meat-hook in the deepest part of hell. But that's when the other side of Pluto takes over. Some still small voice, like a messenger from the gods within us, begins to whisper words of solace, of hope. Something changes inside of us, something which, in the beginning, we may be unable to define. We begin to rise. The goddess of love is about to become the Queen of Heaven. We are reborn.

Psychologists and astrologers have both drawn attention to this drama of descent, and Liz Greene properly links Ishtar's Descent with the planet Pluto.[4] Jungian analyst Sylvia Brinton Perera calls it a "way of initiation for women."[5] And indeed, there is significance in the fact that it is typically a feminine archetype which makes this classic descent—Inanna, Ishtar, Kore-Persephone. The descent into the underworld represents the acquisition of the "serpent wisdom," which we have defined as an essentially feminine wisdom—after all, Medusa had serpents in her hair, and Scorpio, the sign traditionally associated with the serpent, is ruled by Pluto. Thus the process of initiation through pain, grief, darkness, and emotional resurrection is an essentially feminine process. Men don't do well with this particular journey. Orpheus descended into the underworld to reclaim his bride Eurydice, but failed to bring her back into the light. Theseus made an underworld journey, but got trapped there, frozen in a chair of stone. He was released by Hercules, one man who navigated Hades successfully—but only because he remained essentially untouched by the experience. Only Dionysus descended into the underworld with so much success that he brought his mother Semele back to the land of the living— and Dionysus was raised by women as a woman. Homer says of Dionysus: "a man, but as if a woman."[6] Hermes, too, could successfully come and go from Hades' domain, but he has also been assigned androgynous qualities. The Plutonian descent, while it may occasionally be experienced by men, is primarily a feminine path. For men, the path of initiation and descent is more properly indicated by Chiron's sacrifice and the liberation of Prometheus. Men experience the planet Pluto rather differently than women, yet there is no denying that men can feel as transformed by a Pluto transit as do women.

The Roman god Pluto was associated with wealth because the ancients measured earthly wealth in mineral (i.e., gold and silver) terms. They had no paper currency. Because minerals came from *beneath* the earth, they were part of Pluto's realm. Physical or material wealth may sometimes result from a prominent Pluto, but more important is the wealth that resides in the underworld of our unconscious, and the more we become acquainted with what takes place in that kingdom the wealthier we become spiritually. Yet there is no denying that Plutonian people can attain great material wealth as well. Our word "plutocrat," meaning one who rules through wealth, is derived from Pluto's name, and most corporate raiders, tycoons, and politicians (in America predominantly the rich run for office) have a strong or dominating Pluto in their charts. But it is just as likely that a Pluto transit will wipe out a family fortune rather than bring riches. When one's life is unbalanced and there is total and absolute focus on the attainment of material wealth without the development of the spiritual wealth inside, Pluto can have devastating effects on the tides of for-

Persephone on a bronze coin from Syracuse, Sicily, during the reign of Agathocles, 317–289 BC. From the Michael A. Sikora collection

tune. During the Great Depression (1929 and 1930, the year of Pluto's discovery) people killed themselves because they couldn't bear to exist without their money. Such a dependency and attachment upon materialism has affected our world ever since, and has resulted in a severe state of *koyanisqaatsi*, the Hopi word for "life out of balance." A strong Pluto typically shapes an intense, brooding kind of man, more often than not an introvert. Such an individual is likely to be focused on the things which constitute symbols of power in our culture—sex, money, and power itself. Politicians and financial moguls will generally have very strong Pluto positions in their birth charts—Richard Nixon's Pluto is at the Midheaven opposing Mars, and John DeLorean's Pluto is at the Nadir opposing his Sun. Such men may seem to the world to be ruthless, for they possess the volcanic quality of the true Plutonian—a force which erupts into the daylight world with all the power of an earthquake or an atom bomb.

But despite their worldliness and apparent ruthlessness, such men are motivated primarily by the unconscious, for that is Pluto's realm. Their intense need to manifest themselves in terms of a culture's symbols of power is a need which is founded in that world of complexes and insecurities we associate with Pluto. This, of course, implies that such individuals have a deep, powerful, forceful relationship with the unconscious. It is more often than not a tragedy for the man himself when he fails to recognize that his thirst for power is rooted in his own unconscious. By neglecting his psychological depths and projecting his Plutonian power into the outside world instead, he may engineer his own downfall—Nixon and DeLorean are both good examples. Pluto issues can only be settled by facing them at home, in the realm where they originated—the unconscious.

Carl Jung, with Pluto conjunct his natal Moon, turned his Plutonian power drive directly toward its source, and thereby opened the door to deep layers of the human psyche which were unknown territory for people of the early 20th century. And this is the true potential of the Plutonian personality—to open up hidden sources of knowledge and wisdom. Hence those who possess a strong Pluto can put it to work in a positive way as therapists, scientists, or researchers of any variety. If we look back to the years immediately preceding Pluto's discovery, we can see that Pluto was at work in the field of literature just as it was in psychology and economics. James Joyce's *Ulysses* appeared in 1922, and there is no character in all literature quite as Plutonian as Joyce's heroine Molly Bloom, who delivers her final soliloquy while menstruating on a chamber pot in the hours just before morning, remembering sexual experiences past and present.

The planet Pluto is often accused of possessing an overly-sexed nature. This is not entirely justifiable from a mythological point of view—outside of his abduction of Persephone, Hades' sexual urges are never mentioned. Presumably Hades and Persephone enjoyed a healthy sexual relationship. And other gods, notably Zeus, frequently abducted maidens and goddesses for sexual encounters. When Pluto is in a sign or in strong aspect to a planet associated with sex, it can definitely lead to obsessions with passion. For instance, Pluto with Venus or Mars will increase the lustiness of the individual's expression. Pluto with Jupiter can lead to prolific procreative drives, while Pluto with the Moon can result in a Demeter/Persephone/Hades type of relationship.

Pluto transits are long and slow. They represent significant periods of soul-growth and/or transformational experiences in a person's life. Usually these transformational experiences result first in the symbolic death process (going underground), feeling loss, sorrow, pain, separation, or grief of some kind (the experience of actually visiting Hades in his underworld domain). This may occur by way of entering the unconscious through a spiritual experience, therapy, dreams, regression, or psychic phenomena. Ultimately, these experiences result in clarity and evolutionary acceleration, and one can emerge into the light of day again feeling truly reborn. When we successfully emerge from such a process, we spiral up the evolutionary scale; we not only progress horizontally through time and space, but vertically as well. For those who do not have Pluto deeply embedded as a significant part of their life experience, this process is long and slow and may take lifetimes to complete. But those Plutonians who commit themselves to making their lifetime a significant one in the evolutionary cycle will undergo this process many times. Such a life becomes "out of the ordinary;" these people do not connect to the mainstream world very well, but they possess a richer storehouse of inner experience than other, more worldly mortals.

THE SIGNS

Representation of the horoscope with the seven planets, the twelve signs of the zodiac, and the twelve houses, engraved by Erhard Schön, from the title page of Leonhard Reymann's Nativitäts Kalender, *Nuremberg, 1515*

Armillary sphere with zodiac, from Johann de Sacrobusco's Textus de sphaera, *printed by Simon Colins, Paris, 1531*

THE ZODIAC

CHAPTER NINETEEN

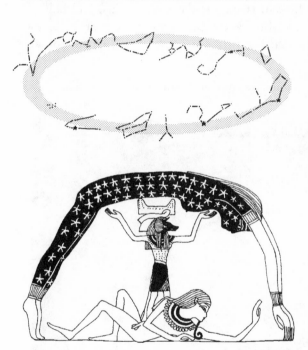

As they observed the night sky, the ancients noted that certain celestial bodies seemed to remain in the same position, whereas others moved along a specific path. These moving bodies were, of course, the planets, who were called "the wanderers." The Babylonians named the planets after their gods, and tried to chart their restless motion through the sky. They divided the heavens into three large strips which they called the paths of Anu, Enlil, and Ea (more of their gods). The Path of Anu lay in the middle and it was along this path that all the planets, as well as the Sun and Moon, perpetually moved. Today we know this band of sky as the ecliptic.[1]

The Babylonian astrologers needed a yardstick against which to chart the journey of the planets along the ecliptic. Thus they duly noted the starry constellations which lay along the Path of Anu, and gauged each planet's course according to which constellation it appeared to occupy—i.e., which constellation served as a backdrop for its motion.

But which of the many possible constellations should be used as measuring devices? It took many centuries for the twelve signs of our modern zodiac to be agreed upon. An early Babylonian document lists no less than eighteen constellations, or signs, along the Path of Anu.[2] Finally, however, the twelve signs we know today were established, and the 360-degree circle of the ecliptic divided (somewhat arbitrarily, it is true) into twelve segments of thirty degrees each. This worked out rather nicely as a calendar, for the sun would spend approximately one month in each of the twelve signs.

Precisely when and how the twelve zodiacal signs were chosen is unclear. Most scholars believe the zodiac to be an invention of the Babylonians, though Egyptian and even Greek influence has been postulated by others. The name itself is Greek, and probably means "the animal circle." The first syllable, *zo*, is a Greek word signifying animal or biological life, as in our words *zoo* and *zoology*. The identification of the zodiac as an animal circle is fairly obvious, for most of the signs are symbolized by animals.

Some of the signs, however, are human (Gemini, Virgo, Aquarius, and half of Sagittarius), so perhaps we should think of the zodiac in terms of the root word *zo*'s larger frame of reference, i.e., biological life forms in general. Thus the zodiac becomes *The Circle of Life*.

Though each sign has its own particular mythic resonance, the zodiac as a

The elaborate zodiac clock at Hampton Court shows the phases of the moon, the signs of the zodiac, and the twelve houses. Photograph by Ariel Guttman

whole constitutes one great proto-myth. The sun's journey through the year is a drama of birth (spring), activity (summer), death (autumn), and resurrection (winter). The four major turning points of the year are the equinoxes and solstices. At the spring equinox (Latin meaning "equal night") the days and nights are of equal length, though the days are growing longer as befits the season of vibrant, potent growth, whether of the earth or of human consciousness. The summer solstice (Latin for "stationary sun") marks the longest day of the year, and hence the season of liveliest, most abundant purpose. It is also the moment when the days begin to grow shorter, and this is why the harvest god, symbol of fertility and growth, was ritually slain upon that day. The days and nights are of equal length again at the autumn equinox, but now it is the nights which are becoming longer, and the world rushes towards its autumnal

Urania holding an armillary sphere with zodiac, from Johannes Stabius' Prognosticon *1503–1505, designed by Albrecht Dürer, Nuremberg, 1502*

death, just as the human spirit must occasionally experience psychological death, a journey to the wintry underworld. Finally, on the shortest and darkest day of the year, the sun turns round again and the days begin to grow longer. This is the winter solstice, when all gods of rebirth are symbolically born. This is the moment of the birth of the Higher Self.

Thus the zodiac signifies the whole process of the development of human consciousness—the cycle of death and rebirth common to all mythologies everywhere, and which constitutes the essential story or myth of the human soul. This journey of consciousness forms the basis of the myth of the hero, as Joseph Campbell has demonstrated in his famous book, *The Hero With A Thousand Faces*.[3] In mythology, and in "primitive" thinking generally, there is always a correspondence or element of synchronicity between what happens in the sky or the outer world and what happens inside the heart of humanity. This is a very important point—one which lies at the foundation of astrology and probably *why* it has existed and persisted for so many millennia. The sun's annual drama of death and rebirth reflects the same process taking place eternally within the individual. A number of myths seem to link the hero's journey with the sun's zodiacal journey in a very direct way—the

An illustration by Diane Smirnow of the zodiac from the temple at Denderah, Egypt

Babylonian epic of Gilgamesh and the Greek story of the twelve labors of Heracles being prime examples. In short, anywhere the number twelve appears—the Twelve Tribes, the Twelve Gates to Jerusalem, the twelve months of our calendar year—we are dealing with our journey through all the parts to arrive at the whole.

Dane Rudhyar identified the psychological process symbolized by the zodiac in his classic study, *The Pulse of Life*, first published in 1943.[4] Rudhyar saw this season-al cycle in terms of two opposing principles, the Dayforce (masculine or *yang*) and the Nightforce (feminine or *yin*). The Dayforce is essentially individualistic and rep-resents the growth of the ego, while the Nightforce is collective and measures our integration with larger social and spiritual units. Thus Rudhyar interpreted the childlike egotism of Aries as symbolic of the growing Dayforce, but, because the days and nights are still equal, Aries has one foot in the collective and may easily

The Zodiac, from Le grant kalendrier et compost des bergieres, *printed by*
Nicolas le Rouge, Troyes, 1496

embody collective roles and resonate to collective needs rather than to his or her
own individual desires. Libra's talent for relationships or, more accurately, for relating, has to do with the fact that the equal powers of the Dayforce and Nightforce
are now leaning towards the collective, towards the importance of the other. The
reputation of Sagittarius for far-reaching philosophical concerns arises from the fact
that it falls in the shortest days of the year, when the collective element has broad-
ened to include the cosmos, and when the individual can only immerse himself in
the needs of a greater whole.

In the chapters that follow we discuss the character and framework of the zodiac in terms of the seasonal round. It's important to note that we are speaking of the

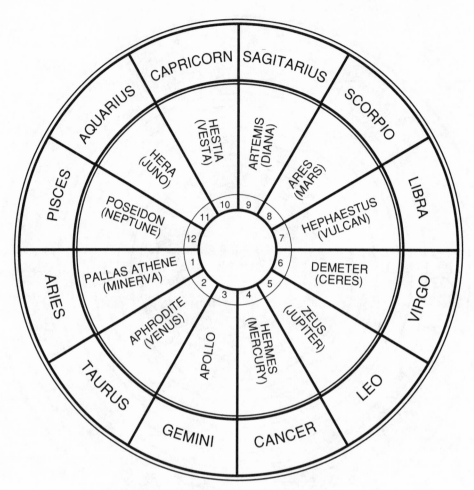

The Olympian rulerships

seasons in the *northern* hemisphere when we say that Aries represents a growing Dayforce. Let's not forget that in the early days, when the zodiac was being developed, religious ritual was strongly linked with nature, as survival was dependent upon it. Thus the gods (planets, signs) in the sky had a direct relationship to the earth and its activities. Since astrology comes from the temperate regions of the northern hemisphere, the character of each sign is in accordance with the seasons of the northern rather than the southern hemisphere—though the symbolism of the signs as we know them seems to work as well for Australians and Brazilians as anyone else.

Many astrology textbooks have divided the wheel of the zodiac or the wheel of the houses into quadrants and hemispheres, assessing many personality factors according to how many planets lie in which region. Following the theme of Dayforce and Nightforce, there are two types of people which are defined by the horizon line: those with the majority of planets above the horizon live in the daylight region while those below occupy the nightworld. Planets which lie above the horizon in the daylight sector of the wheel are generally solar-based, and can be viewed as "objective," having the rational and logical framework symbolized by the masculine or thinking mode prominent. Below the horizon, where there is no light, that which cannot be seen but which is intuited predominates. Thus the lower hemisphere embodies a lunar-based, more inner, subjective framework where intuition and instinct shine. These hemispheres are the product of the division of the wheel into twelve houses, based on the diurnal movement of the earth's rotation. While not strictly tied to the twelve signs, the houses (and planets, for that matter) have a resonance or symbolic tie-in to the signs of the zodiac. Another division of the wheel by hemisphere is east and west. This is the dividing line created by the I.C. (*imum coeli*—Fourth House cusp) and M.C. (*median coeli*—Midheaven) and which forms the meridian of the chart. Planets located in the eastern hemisphere are considered to be more self-reliant, while planets in the west are considered other-oriented. This correlates to the position of Aries at the eastern-most point of the natural wheel and Libra in the west.

Additionally, the wheel can be divided into four quadrants. We are told that the first quadrant (Aries, Taurus, Gemini) relates to individual and personal development. The second quadrant (Cancer, Leo, Virgo) relates to interpersonal relationships with family, children, etc. The third quadrant (Libra, Scorpio, Sagittarius) relates to relationships with people outside the family unit, while the fourth (Capricorn, Aquarius, and Pisces) relates to the development of transpersonal interests and activities which involve the community or world at large.

People often forget that all twelve signs are contained within each horoscope. They are prone to make comments like "I'm not a Cancer, so I'm not much of a homebody." But the sign Cancer, along with each of the other eleven, is a part of the integral wheel of life that makes up the framework upon which we are built and reflects everything contained within the organism. Our bodies are microcosms of this larger framework, and thus there are parts of the body which correlate to the twelve signs; these correspondences are quite useful in analyzing bodily strengths and weaknesses. Within this framework, then, there is no such thing as a "bad sign" or a "good sign." They are all integral to the whole functional operation of a being. Certainly some signs will contain no planetary emphasis while other signs may contain stelliums (large groupings of planets) indicating the particular focus or emphasis one might choose in a given incarnation. In analyzing the myths and origins of these signs, we hope to uncover more clues for the individual as to just what focus or emphasis he or she has chosen for a lifepath. Another important component of the zodiacal wheel is the system of planetary attributions, for in this way two of the primary factors of the astrological art (planets and signs) are woven together into a symbolic unity.

As we have remarked, the horoscope is a *mandala*. Throughout astrological history, the signs of the zodiac have been attributed to or symbolically linked with various planets and/or deities. These attributions form yet another component of the astrological *mandala*. What is not generally known, however, is that the planetary or

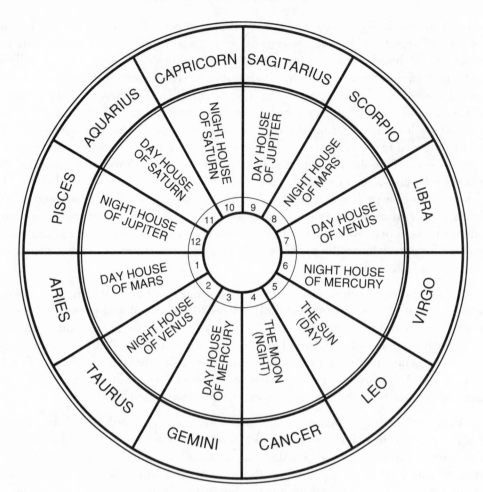

The Ptolemaic rulerships

deity attributions have changed from time to time. Astrological historian Rupert Gleadow must be credited with restoring the earliest such *mandala*, a system of correspondences which dates from Plato's time.[5] The signs were not yet ruled by planets: instead, they were ruled by the "twelve Olympians," the principal gods and goddesses of the Greek pantheon (see page 186).

Several important points emerge from a study of this ancient system. In the first place, we can see that the masculine and feminine elements are still in a state of perfect balance. There are six gods and six goddesses. If a particular sign is ruled by a god, its opposite sign will be ruled by a goddess. The concept of psychic opposites goes much farther than a mere division into male and female. For instance, Aries is ruled by Pallas Athene and its opposite sign, Libra, by Hephaestus. Both of these deities were born from a single parent, rather than through ordinary sexual union; female Athene was born of masculine Zeus, while male Hephaestus was born of female Hera. Apollo (Gemini) and Artemis (Sagittarius) were twins. Zeus (Leo) and Hera (Aquarius) were the king and queen of heaven respectively. Aphrodite

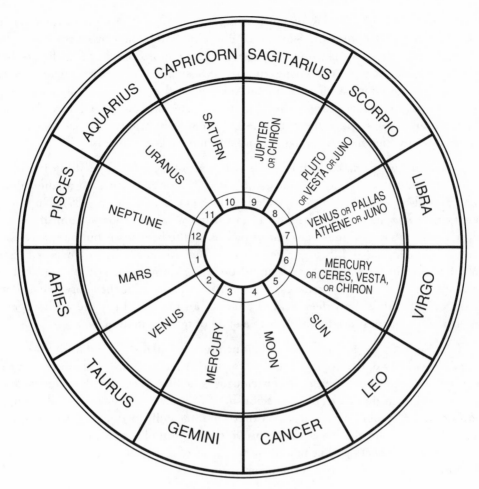

Contemporary rulerships

(Taurus) and Ares (Scorpio) were lovers. Some of these pairs of opposites are more difficult to understand, but we shall have occasion to discuss them later on.

In the time of Claudius Ptolemy, an astrologer of the late Roman period, a new system of attributions was established. In this *mandala*, the seven ancient planets were designated as the rulers of the signs. Beginning with the Sun (Leo) as a symbol of the archetypal masculine and the Moon (Cancer) as the archetypal feminine, the rulerships fanned out, in orbital order, on each side of this primal pair. Each planet ruled a "day house" (i.e., a masculine sign) and a "night house" (feminine sign). Due to this fan-shaped structure, Saturn, the most distant planet known to the ancients, ruled the two signs which oppose the Sun and Moon, while the other planets were also arranged in pairs of opposites—Mars with Venus and Mercury with Jupiter. This elegant *mandala* (see page 188) lasted from late antiquity until the discovery of Uranus in 1781.

Uranus has always been the iconoclast, the enemy of tradition. In keeping with its mythic role, Uranus brought an end to the traditional horoscopic *mandala*. A sign had to be found for the new planet to rule, and in time it was given to Aquarius. The discovery of Neptune in 1846 and of Pluto in 1930 further upset the classic balance. As the science of astrophysics becomes ever more precise, astrologers have been confronted with an increasing number of heavenly bodies which may have relevance to the mythic patterns of human life. Since the early 1970s alone, we have begun to give consideration to the four major asteroids and to Chiron. As if this were not enough, we have the option to use an almost infinite number of asteroids, thousands of which have been named and charted in recent history.

What are we to make of this embarrassment of riches? If we study the planetary attributions which are either established or under discussion at the present time, it will be seen that there is no longer any pattern (see page 189). No pattern means no *mandala*. It would be easy to take a negative or gloomy point of view on all this, and to say that the chaos in our picture of the heavens is but one more yardstick of our chaotic and disorganized society. But this is not by any means certain. What *is* certain is that we have a mind-boggling number of options and choices available to us which our predecessors never dreamed of. Furthermore, we are now in an era of radical and deep-seated change, an era in which the archetypes of human consciousness are themselves in a state of transformation.

This sort of change ought not to be unexpected when we stand at the transition point between two astrological ages, Pisces and Aquarius. After all, an astrological age implies a collective phase of consciousness lasting over two thousand years: a quantum shift in that collective consciousness will have some sort of visible impact on our inner, symbolic realities. Another *mandala* will, in time, emerge from the seeming chaos, and the ideas which provide such stimulus and inspiration to contemporary astrologers will in time form the basis of a new structure, a new *mandala* to represent a new phase of consciousness.

THE ELEMENTS

CHAPTER
TWENTY

The Four Elements:
Fire, Earth, Air, and Water

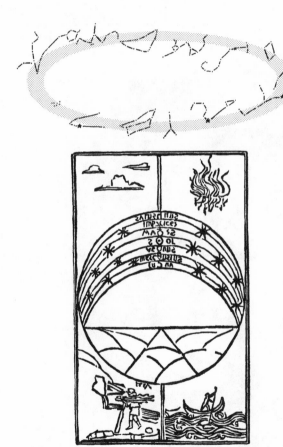

The four elements and the orbits of the planets, from Philippe de Mantegat's Judicium cum tractibus planetarii, *Milan, 1496*

Astrology divides its psychic reality into four "elements"—fire, earth, air, and water. Like so many other aspects of the astrological tradition, the four elements appear to have come to us from ancient Greece. Aristotle divided the physical world into these same four elements. Yet it is clear that the ancient astrologers were referring to a psychological set of elements rather than a physical one.

Indeed, if we examine mythology, we find that this same fourfold division of reality is common from Ireland all the way to India. In ancient Celtic mythology, it was said that the gods brought four treasures with them from their mystic homeland in the West: a sword, a spear, a cauldron of rebirth, and a stone that cried out whenever a king set foot upon it. These same mythic treasures of the ancient Celts appear in the medieval legend of the Holy Grail.[1] Perceval, the pure knight, finds himself in the magic castle of the Grail. As he sits with the castle's guardians at a feast, he watches a procession pass silently through the hall. The eerie figures who march so quietly through the castle are carrying four sacred objects: a sword, the spear that pierced Christ's side, a fish on a plate, and the Grail itself—the cup from which Christ drank at the Last Supper. These same four objects show up still later in the Tarot, where they form the suits of Wands (the spear), Cups (the Grail or cauldron), Swords, and Pentacles (the stone or dish).[2] Kabbalistic magicians and witches have always linked these four treasures with the four elements: the spear or wand symbolizes fire, the cup or cauldron represents water, the sword is air, and the pentacle, stone or dish is earth.[3]

Psychologist Carl Jung, a close student of the Western mystical tradition, believed that these four elements were symbolic of the four functions which govern the human psyche. These functions were intuition (fire), feeling (water), thinking (air), and sensation (earth). The four functions are comprised of two pairs of opposites: intuition and sensation, thinking and feeling. Intuition and sensation are ways of *perceiving*, while thinking and feeling are ways of *judging*. Each of us develops one of these four functions to a higher degree than the others; this is our *dominant* function. Its opposite automatically becomes our *inferior* function, representing a way of

The Chaos of the Elements, from Robert Fludd's Utriusque Cosmi Historia, *Oppenheim, 1617*

judging or perceiving which is our blind spot, part of our undeveloped self. Thus those who are dominated by their feelings may think in a scattered or illogical way, and those who are profoundly practical (sensation dominant) are usually skeptical or fearful of the inner world of dreams and visions (intuition). Each function may operate either in an *introverted* or *extraverted* manner. Jung believed that no human being could be completely balanced and whole unless he or she balanced these psychic functions. This, according to Jung, was why mystics such as the alchemists were always concerned with

Christ as the Primal Man with the four elements, Anthropos, *France, 1487*

transforming the square into a circle—because they recognized that true enlightenment consisted of shaping our fourfold inner nature into a harmonious whole.[4]

As we shall see when discussing each of the four elements separately, they serve unique and important purposes in the shaping of human consciousness, and ultimately, integration. Most of us will remember *The Wizard of Oz*, which tells of Dorothy's mythic journey to find her way back home. Before she could reach her ultimate destination, however, she was joined by some very curious characters (parts of herself). The Tin Man was searching for a heart (water); the Cowardly Lion was in pursuit of courage (fire); the scarecrow lacked a brain (air). When the magical ruby slippers were finally placed upon Dorothy's feet (earth), her wish was granted and she was quickly whisked back to her home. Her odyssey allowed her to integrate the four elements.

Though the astrological tradition is similar to Jung's typology of the psyche, it is not quite identical. Astrologers, for instance, would place an emphasis on the fact that two elements, fire and air, embody masculine, active, or *yang* qualities, while earth and water are feminine, receptive and *yin*. Another difference lies in the balance between the four inner elements. When a large number of planets occupy the fire signs in a birth chart, we would expect that the individual endowed would possess an extremely intuitive temperament, much like Jung's intuitive personality type. In the Jungian schema, such an individual would automatically be assumed to relate very poorly to worldly, tangible things, for she or he would have an inadequately developed sensation (earth) function. But from an astrological point of view, it is possible that a birth chart may include a great deal of fire (intuition) *and* earth (sensation), thus uniting precisely those elements or functions which Jung places in eternal opposition. The conflict within such an individual, pulled with equal force toward the opposite worlds of spirit (fire) and flesh (earth), may be quite intense, but such an individual also has an unusually high potential to unite the inner opposites and attain wholeness. Though the astrological system is indeed very closely related to Jung's, it is a little less structured and contains more variables.

FIRE

In Jung's typology, fire represents the intuitive function, although that word requires some explanation. As we have seen, fire is one of the masculine, creative, *yang* elements. But we are accustomed to thinking of intuition as something feminine—as in the phrase "woman's intuition." But what we call intuition is, in fact, a very high development of the feeling function. The faculty of intuition, as symbolized by the fiery element, actually describes something quite different.

Let's look at it from another perspective. Astrology textbooks often equate fire with "energy" or "spirit." It is the vital spirit which moves us, inspires us, which endows us with whatever quantum of energy we may possess. Horoscopes which are lacking in fire often show individuals who are listless, easily fatigued, and short of energy.

This connection between fire and spiritual energy or vitality is found often in Gnosticism and the Kabbalah. These systems of thought postulate an original spiritual unity from which all created things arise. But the more solid or earthly these created things become, the more they are divorced from the original spiritual oneness. The Gnostics believed that our world, the Earth, was a kind of prison, the ultimate development of materiality. But even here, on Earth, we still possess a portion of original divinity in our souls. That divinity is symbolized by fire—Gnostics and Kabbalists both refer to "the divine spark." They use the analogy of a bellows—undertaking any kind of spiritual practice will fan the spark, build it into a blaze, and thus reunite us with the source of all being.

The alchemists, who were spiritual descendants of the Gnostics, deeply concerned themselves with the four elements, for their goal was to fuse all of them and thus create something new, something complete, a quintessence. Psychologically, we may say that they were striving to unite all four psychic functions and give birth to the Self. They regarded fire as one of the agents of transformation. It was by means of a slow, regulated fire that one substance was transmuted into another, rising in the crucible through several stages of transformation. Researchers have seen in this a distinct parallel with Eastern disciplines such as yoga or Taoist meditation. The fire is the vital spirit within us, called *kundalini* by the Hindus and *ch'i* by the Chinese. By regulation of this fire—by control of our vital energies—we effect the transformation from ego to Self.

Seen in this light, intuition is that vital spark within us which simply *knows*. It is the source of our essential energy, that which gives light to our eyes and determines the strength of our presence. Intuition *knows* without needing to analyze. It *perceives*; it never judges. Those whose charts are rich with planets in fire signs have that vital energy, that intuitive knowing. From looking at the chart alone, it may be difficult or impossible to tell whether a person is an introvert or extravert. We might suspect that planets in the Eighth or Twelfth House, for instance, would denote an introverted temperament, though this is not always the case. (In fact, the Fourth House

A salamander alive in the flames, from Michael Maier's Scrutinium Chymicum,
Frankfurt, 1687

is a better indicator of introversion—as the present authors, both with Fourth House Suns, can attest.) But the balance of the elements *will* give us clues as to whether we are dealing with an intuitive, feeling, thinking, or sensing type.

Extraverted fire signs may be great entrepreneurs. They really know how to play a hunch. They tune in, with that inner knowingness, to events taking place in the outside world. But if they can make a fortune, they can also go broke, for they tend to overlook physical limitations. They likewise ignore their own health, for they often have a poor relationship with the earth element or sensation, which is their polar opposite (that is, unless their charts contain a good deal of earth for balance and contrast). They are often susceptible to "burn-out" as they get bored easily, seeking always to rekindle their flame. If they are great speculators, they may also be irresponsible adventurers.

Introverted fire sign types have the same highly developed perception of psychic reality which characterizes their extraverted cousins. But these people turn their awareness inward. They are more comfortable with their dreams and visions than with physical realities. If the car or the lawn-mower breaks down, they won't have the vaguest idea how to fix it; problems with money or machines may actually fill them with anxiety and dread. Jungian analyst Edward Whitmont says that these are the people who will boil their watch while looking at the egg to see what time it is![5] One of the present writers is an intuitive introvert, and must confess that this is *almost* literally true. Of course, it goes without saying that these introverted fire-sign types are also the great prophets, artists, and visionaries of this world. The vital spark of fire is fierce and flaming within them; despite their painful inwardness, they occasionally blaze forth and change the world with a book, sermon, or symphony which touches the spirit within all of us.

Fire may also be defined as the principle of spontaneous combustion. People possessing a great deal of the fire element—for instance, if the Sun, Moon, or Ascendant are in Aries, Leo, or Sagittarius, or if Mars, Sun, or Jupiter (rulers of these fire signs) are near the four angles of the horoscope in the First, Fourth, Seventh, or Tenth Houses—can relate completely to spontaneity and combustibility. Since Aries is the first, most primal form of the expression of fire, this sign is credited with (or accused of) more spontaneity or impulsiveness than any other sign. Because it is *cardinal* fire (see Chapter Twenty-one, "Modalities"), which in many ways acts as double *yang*, Aries seems to need no signal from outside before acting. It is truly an intuitive voice from within that sparks its flame. Because Aries is the

The elements of fire, earth, air, and water meet in volcanic activity, Big Island, Hawaii, 1989.
Photograph by Ariel Guttman

first of the fire signs, and also the first sign of the zodiac, childlike qualities and a self-centered concern with one's own personal needs are emphasized. So also is the purity of the fire element, since it is driven by the cardinal mode that inspires action — from the hot-headed, easily irritated impatience of unevolved Ariens (or, as John Bradshaw would call them, "rage-aholics"),[6] to the pioneering, fearless warriors, one-pointed and singularly focused on their path when more evolved.

In its fixed mode, fire operates through the solar-ruled blaze of Leo, and what fire is more *fixed* or contained than the Sun, Leo's ruler? Fixity in astrology expresses itself primarily in a *yin* way, thus Leo can easily embody fire's essential *yang* need to express its creative drives outwardly as well as the *yin* urge to attract, center, and contain some of its warmth and intuition within, giving nurturance to its offspring as Leo is prone to do. This light within is the power of magnetism and attraction which many Leos possess, a light that attracts others to them, a light so bright that they themselves can be seduced by what they perceive as their own greatness. With Leo's fire being contained and focused through the fixed mode, there is not as much spontaneity or constant motion as there is with Aries and Sagittarius; instead, Leo is content to express its creative fire through reproduction, either biological or artistic. And, like other fire signs, it needs space in its environment to do that.

In the third and final stage of fire, Sagittarius' *mutability* suggests a distribution or dissemination of the fiery, inner spiritual impulses. Thus, many Sagittarians need to spread the truth wherever they go and to whomever they meet, whatever that truth might be. Since mutability paradoxically gives both completion and changeability to the nature of things, Sagittarius' fire is always stirring the pot to see what images will emerge. As the third and final stage of fire, purification of the self is an issue with Sagittarians, and we usually find them at one extreme or the other — over-indulging excessively, even to the point of death (for example, Jimi Hendrix and Jim Morrison) — or polishing, cleansing and refining their earthly vehicles in preparation for their immanent reconnection to the Source.

The fire function plays an important role in the health and vitality of an individual. The earth's main source of natural fire is solar, the sun, which gives us heat, life, radiance, and warmth. As mentioned previously, people lacking in the fire element will seem to be without natural radiance and warmth, will feel uninspiring and seem unenergetic and listless. Often, too, they will complain of being cold, even when it is not. On the other hand, too much fire can cause excessive bodily heat, whereby the inner fire seems to rage uncontrollably. Fire people that have too much stress in their lives will feel spasms, muscle pains, or aches in parts of their body that are unable to assimilate or release the stress by any other means. Thus, release of this fire is important through physical expression — running, aerobics, sports, and games. A reminder of this fire principle is the Olympic torch-bearer who kindles the fire from Olympia's sacred hearth, relaying it to the site of the games. The mental expression of fire often results in creative genius when inspired, or anger and irritation when contrary. At the highest level, the evolved fire individual channels pure energy from the source, having overcome his or her need to be concerned with personal ego.

Of all the four elements, fire needs the most room to breathe. If asked to do a job with others, especially when someone in charge is breathing down their necks, fire signs can "set the place on fire" or explode with anger. Because of this difficulty in working with authority figures, fire signs are the first to recognize their need to be their own authority figures. Thus, many people with excessive fire will be free-lance, entrepreneurial types who run their own businesses and work their own schedules, leaving themselves free (even if it's only the illusion of freedom) to create when the impulse strikes, or directing their time into organizing the flow of energy around them. Earth and water types may simply fail to understand these fire-directed individuals whose greatest fear is living out their lives in an ordinary, predictable routine.

The fire signs typically have the ability to express their conscious purpose and will more energetically than others. Because their passions are expressed directly, one may feel overpowered by the presence of people whose fire element predominates, since their energy, enthusiasm, and motivation level are high. On the other hand, they have the capacity to bring energy "up" when it is "down" in others, as their capacity to channel energy from the source is often powerful and direct.

The fire signs (especially Aries and Leo or the First and Fifth Houses) often don't do well on cloudy days or handle depression easily. They need sunshine and invigorating stimulation to keep them motivated, happy, and productive.

Also, each of these signs maintains a primary relationship with something: in Aries with Self, in Leo with offspring or direct creations of the Self, and in Sagittarius with the "God-Self"; these three invisible partners are projected into a huge variety of life experiences by the fire signs.

EARTH

The earth signs would seem to be fortunate beings in many respects, as they possess an innate ability to master the things of this world. They live in the realm of the senses. Of course we all live in the realm of the senses, but some of us are not terribly comfortable with that fact. We wish that we were more practical, had more common sense, or more money. In other words, we wish we had a better relationship with what Jung would call the sensation function, or with what an astrologer would call the element of earth.

Those whose charts are heavy in earth signs (Taurus, Virgo, Capricorn) or who have earth planets emphasized (Saturn or Ceres) do have that special relationship with the physical. These people know how to make money and keep it. They can fix their cars, excel at home repair, and honestly enjoy the comforts of everyday life. They can do all those things that their opposites, the introverted fire types, find so difficult. They are the elemental types who are "most likely to succeed"—or at least to enjoy a high level of material status and prosperity.

There is, of course, a darker side to the earth element. The Gnostics and alchemists symbolized earth or matter as a mythical female figure called Physis (appropriately enough, for earth is a feminine or receptive element). In the mythic dreamtime before history, the Cosmic Man gazed upon the newly created world. He saw his reflection in the waters of the world, and became enamored of that reflection, like Narcissus in the earlier Greek myth. He swept down from heaven to earth, leaning over the waters for a better look. Physis, the feminine personification of earth, fell in love with the Cosmic Man; she reached up, caught him in her embrace, and pulled him into the depths of the earth. He remains trapped there to this day.[7]

These petroglyphs at Galisteo, NM, may represent the elements. Photograph by Ariel Guttman

We have already touched upon some of the meanings of this Gnostic myth when we examined the element of fire. The Cosmic Man represents the essentially spiritual mode of perception called intuition, which, as we have seen, is a creative or masculine function. When the myth says that the Cosmic Man is "trapped in the embrace of earth," it points to that divine spark of consciousness which is embedded in the material body. The myth symbolizes the trap or lure of the earth plane or material world, whereby the divinity that resides in us all is put aside or forgotten for the more pressing and immediate needs that the world demands from us and, oddly enough, rewards us with. The constant pursuit of these rewards—be they toys, gold coins, fruits, or real estate—can set in motion the vicious cycle whereby the more we attain, the more we desire, thus pulling us farther and farther away from the spark within, and trapping us in the earth plane for lifetime after lifetime. The Hindus call this the Wheel of Samsara, and the wheel can only be reversed by a diligent and consistent force, much like the energy it would take to reverse gravity, in order to free oneself from that entrapment.

While fire represents the spark, earth represents the body. Hence, earth signs are the people most likely to feel cut off or alienated from that divine inner spark. Just as the introverted fire type dreads bank accounts and V-8 engines, the extraverted earth type fears the psychic world. These are the people who loudly proclaim that they don't believe in magic or astrology, that the only things which are real are the things they can touch. These are the people who get nervous around artists and mystics, who fidget uncomfortably during any conversation that involves the world of intuition, dreams, or visions. In short, what they can't see or touch with their five senses is beyond their realm of comprehension, and to them it does not exist. Thus the earth type—especially the extravert—is the type most easily trapped in materiality, like the Cosmic Man in the embrace of Physis. Unless there is a substantial amount of fire in the chart, she or he may find it painfully difficult to awaken that spark of divinity through creativity, dreams, or meditation—all the avenues which the fiery types take for granted. The medieval alchemists recognized this problem when they spoke of "redeeming the spirit in matter." This, of course, means awakening the divine spark within. The alchemists phrased it in terms of extracting an essence (spirit) from the stone (matter) in order to create the Philosopher's Stone, a purified or perfected stone or body.[8] For most earth sign types, this process will involve beginning with the earth itself—i.e., with the physical body. These people will have to pursue paths such as yoga, exercise, and proper diet before they can float free. The earth element must be purified or—as the alchemists would have said—transmuted. This is an issue we shall take up again when we consider Virgo, the mutable earth sign.

Not all earth types are noisy, materialistic backslappers, however. There are a few who are reflective and introverted. The introverted earth type is likely to be a sculptor, a carpenter, or a painter—entirely absorbed with her or his inner sensations. These people are so detached they seem not to care about anything or anybody around them. They appear to be even "spacier" than the introverted fire types. But these earthy introverts are rare; one seldom encounters them. Earth sign types are overwhelmingly extraverted by nature.

Just as fire's overwhelming need is for the freedom and space to act upon its intuitive function, earth's primary need is security. To earth, security represents safety. There are no surprises, everything is in its place and you know what you have. Those who possess an excess of planets in earth signs may therefore be overly controlling, even (or especially) with small things. This is due to their excellence at functioning when they know where things are and they can count on them always to be there. Because of their relative ease at manipulating the material world, their greatest humiliation occurs when they go to do something and it doesn't work. So, to avoid future embarrassment, they set about their mechanically proficient repair work and set everything in place so that they can count on it to function properly the next time. This works well when the repairs involve computers, cars, appliances, or other machines—but earth types may try to eliminate surprises by sculpting, molding, or repairing people in the same way, with much more unfortunate results.

One of the greatest cosmic jokes must surely have to do with the fact that the earth element *always* follows fire on the astrological wheel. If, after reading the description of the fire sign types you wonder how on earth (no pun intended) they function on this planet, wonder no more. Every fire sign automatically progresses into an earth sign as his or her next phase of development, like it or not, as earth always follows fire in the astrological *mandala*. Thus, the opportunity to manifest *physically* the visionary, intuitively inspired wisdom gained in fire exists for all those who make such a progression. But this progression too often turns into yet another example of spirit trapped in a body. It is reminiscent of the game children some-times play of catching fireflies and trapping them in a jar. Shortly their light disap-pears, as inside the jar they have no ability to spark or fly. But soon they are released again to light up the skies, for the pain of watching their spark die out is a reminder to us all that letting our own spark die is a fate equal to death.

The entrapment has nothing to do with the earth being a negative element. Fire explodes while earth implodes. Fire is *yang*; earth is *yin*. Fire is intuitive; earth con-cerns itself with the world of sense orientation. In fact, studies show that 75% of the population of the United States fits Jung's sensing mode; only 25% is intuitive.[9] Everyone has the ability to be intuitive, so why is it not more like 50/50? Because the challenge lies in *trusting* intuition and *using* it, and that's the less secure path. In earth, as we have remarked, *security* has a lot to do with how one functions. Obviously, the individual whose chart contains a mixture of fire and earth *can* bring inspiration into the world of form. But pure earth—and we are generally speaking of the purity of an element when we describe its nature—doesn't always have the option of expressing its vision creatively. The individual endowed with a great deal of earth has often been put here to understand and master the elements of material existence. That mastery may begin with a sense of one's own physical body—including its basic survival needs like food and shelter. It may extend to the general maintenance and well-being of the body and then to ways which save the body time and energy by creating machinery to do the job for us while we oversee and manage the operation. We may recognize these three stages of adaptation as representative of the three earth signs, Taurus, Virgo, and Capricorn respectively.

No matter what the elemental breakdown of your individual chart may be, the fire element is likely to be most noticeable between puberty and the age of thirty, while earth reigns supreme from about thirty to sixty years of age. It is clear, then, that the earth element gets our best, most productive years. This is when we spend a great deal of our time drudging out a living, even working overtime to insure security, the earth element's hardest taskmaster, for ourselves and our offspring. This dedication to work is tolerable because we have convinced ourselves that the visionary, leisurely pursuits of life will be enjoyed in our golden years. Unfortunately, in those years many people discover that the body has worn out or that the issue of security is *still* primary, or that the tensions and stresses developed during the working years cannot be easily set aside so that leisure, recreation, and inspiration can take over. The biggest lesson for earth types, then, is to relax and enjoy the process of earthly attainment while still in the process. Earth signs enjoy *doing* rather than *being*. In the doing stage they are always aware of the world around them and what needs to be taken care of. Often they wind up doing every-one else's job because no one else can do it as well, yet they remain resentful because they are doing all the work. As a result of this and the seriousness with which they perform their tasks (except perhaps for Taurus, who knows how to take it easy), their limbs and joints often suffer. Overworking the body is like overwork-ing a horse or a car. Cars *must* get taken in for regular tune-ups or they will not function. The same is true of the human body. Heavily stressed earth types often suffer from back, neck, and shoulder pain (carrying the world on their shoulders), from loss of teeth or gums (gritting their teeth and carrying on, no matter what) or, in short, from stress in all the visibly apparent features of the body—hair, skin, nails, teeth, and bones.

What we may fittingly honor in the earth element is its ability to perform realistically, in an orderly and sensible fashion in the material world. That such a vast and potentially chaotic world can function with such astounding efficiency is due to the efforts of those earthy types who oversee the operation. In times of crisis, earth types are often responsible for getting the situation handled, coolly and rhythmically, without skipping a beat. And they are loyal. If they promise something, they usually deliver. And let's not forget that it is the earth types who have something to show for their efforts at the end of their lives.

AIR

The air may be as clear as crystal; we may gaze into a cloudless sky. But when the clouds do appear, the air, the very sky itself, may grow turbulent. It may howl and blow, or simply brood in shades of gray. And, though the air may be warmed now and then by the sun, it was classified by Aristotle as an essentially cold element.

The air is the mind or, as Jung would have it, the thinking function. As we have seen, intuition (fire) and sensation (earth) represent modes of *perception*. Thinking (air) and feeling (water) represent modes of *judgment*. Most of us lean heavily on two functions; one which enables us to perceive, and another which helps us to judge our perceptions. The extraverted air sign type is likely to make such judgments according to traditional rules. These people are the scientists, the objective thinkers who give form and structure to our society. Their cousins, the introverted thinkers or air sign types, tend to be more original. They may, in fact, be gifted theorists and philosophers, though their philosophy will tend to be at odds with the prevailing world view. Both types are likely to be teachers.

We live in a culture which worships reason, and has, in some sense, elevated it to a godlike status. But there is a serious drawback involved with such an attitude. In Eastern religions, the mind is recognized as an ambivalent thing, not entirely trustworthy. Dane Rudhyar observed that the mind makes an excellent servant, but a terrible master. An old theosophical aphorism says that the mind is "the slayer of the real" and that the true seeker must "slay the slayer." In other words, our minds can deceive us, and logic can alienate us from that intuitive divine spark which forms our real connection with the Higher Self. Hinduism, Buddhism, and other Eastern meditative disciplines have always striven to go *beyond* the intellect.

Note that in the Tarot, the thinking function is symbolized by the suit of Swords, and that the Swords cards tend to depict images of strife, challenge, or

Alchemical allegory: "The Wind hath carried It in his belly," from Michael Maier's
Scrutinium Chymicum, *Frankfurt, 1687*

conflict. The medieval heretics whose philosophy lies at the heart of the Tarot recognized the ambivalent nature of the mind. So did the authors of the Grail Legend, who also regarded thinking as a sword.

In the Grail Legend, the world has been turned into a barren wasteland because the Grail King is sick, wounded in the thigh or groin. This myth is of great symbolic significance for our own time. The image of the wasteland itself brings to mind our current ecological crisis. The thigh or groin represents the power of the primal instincts and of sexuality. The Grail King's instincts have been wounded by too great an application of intellect. Thus the Grail stories, written between 1150 and 1200 AD, curiously foreshadow our own era. Our civilization has become too dependent on the thinking function, which has set us at odds with our instincts and our feelings. Because we are alienated from our feelings, we have allowed our civilization to develop in an unbalanced manner, with too great an emphasis on logic and technology. In so doing, we have created a literal wasteland.

Athene, the Greek goddess of wisdom and knowledge, is always depicted with a helmet and a sword. While many interpret the sword as part of her battle dress, for she had powerful dominion in that field, it more probably refers to the sword of the mind and correlates to the sharpness and strategy which was her principal gift. The "brainchild" of her father Zeus, Athene's wisdom and intellect, along with her armored dress, kept her distinctly separated from the world of feeling and emotion. (We explore more of this symbolism in Chapter Ten, "Pallas Athene.") Air, the element of the mind, and water, the element of feelings, have an extremely difficult time integrating with one another, as do fire and earth.

Those whose horoscopes contain a powerful emphasis on air signs (the Sun, Moon, or Ascendant in Gemini, Libra, or Aquarius, or angular placements of Uranus, Mercury, or Pallas Athene) are likely to have difficulty contacting their feelings. They may appear cold and ruthless, incapable of touching others through the heart. They *think* they have an answer for everything, and that logic can supply that answer. When their emotions do emerge, they often do so in bizarre ways, so that the thinking or air types (especially the introverts) may indulge in some very peculiar emotional reactions. If one were to express the personification of air in cartoon form, one might see a picture of a hot air balloon as the head and two little sticks as the body. Air, more than any other element, is often "up in it," or, metaphorically speaking, in their heads, and distinctly not in their bodies.

But enough has been said about the negative qualities of the air sign types. If we sometimes see them as responsible for all our ills, that is only because our civilization stands at a crisis point as regards thinking and feeling. Air sign types, of course, have just as much heart and soul as anybody else. It's just that they have more difficulty in reaching that level. It is their task to wield the sword of the intellect and

Lightning storms activate all four elements. Photograph by Michael Guttman

"slay the slayer" of the real. This is the same as saying that they must use the mind to go beyond the mind—a paradoxical statement and a difficult task, but true.

The best thing we can do for these people is to listen to them when they make that rare show of feeling, rather than criticizing them for their lack of emotion. (After all, that only drives them more deeply into their rigidly entrenched positions.) And we may also do well to remember that without their clear, precise reasoning, we would not enjoy the comforts or technological luxuries that we possess today. Your compact disc, your new car, your precious VCR and your computer—you owe all these things to the logical and penetrating minds of the air sign types.

It's easy to see how Gemini, Libra, and Aquarius make up the air triplicity of the astrological wheel. Like the mind, all three of these signs have dual aspects as symbolized in their actual glyphs, and as represented by their function in the zodiac. The entire circle of the zodiac is represented by animals, except for one set: the air signs, which have more "human" symbols. In anthropology we learn that the distinguishing factor between man and his mammalian brothers and sisters has to do with the fact that man can think. Man has a mind and intellect, and therefore can reason. The animal world outside of man relies predominantly upon instinct.

The image that defines the first of the air signs, Gemini, is a set of male twins (Castor and Pollux, or other mythological twins whom we will discuss under Gemini). In this first air sign, the mind is still in a childlike state, crawling everywhere, curious to know and learn about everything it encounters. For this reason, there is an ability to learn many things simultaneously and quickly, just as the young, energetic child learns to mimic his environment. In Gemini, the duality of the mind is expressed at its most extreme: the two children not only have separate bodies and goals, but the mythical rivalry between them symbolizes the dialogue and argument the mind experiences when many inner voices are speaking but none of them are sufficiently developed to actually respond to the demands of the moment.

For Libra, the symbol is a set of scales, sometimes held by a woman, sometimes not. The scales are symbolic of the stage we reach with the second air sign—that of balance. In Libra the duality factor is less pronounced than in Gemini, as it is *one* person in possession of a *pair* of scales. Still, the pair is seeking a balance of opposites, and Libra is forever concerned with justice or fairness. In fact, the scales of Libra have been adopted by the legal field as a reminder that there, too, justice and fairness must rule. Libra's position on the astrological wheel gives it a unique role, in that it is situated at the midpoint of all the signs, and therefore is said to have the greatest objectivity or ability to see all sides of a question equally. Whether or not this is entirely true, most Libras will tell you that their life-path always involves some variation of this balancing act.

If Gemini represents the individual grappling with the duality of his or her own mind, and Libra balances self with another, it is Aquarius, the third and final stage of air in the astrological *mandala*, that shoulders the task of using the air quality to detach itself from personal issues and extend a helping hand to humanity at large.

In fact, the common complaint about Aquarians on a personal or relationship level is that they're too detached and not sensitive enough to personal needs. This is quite true, since Aquarius (like the Vulcan Spock, on the *Star Trek* TV series) is often concerned with the good of the many over the good of the one.

The impression often given is that Aquarians always make the *right* decisions, and this is not necessarily the case. Aquarius, like Gemini and Libra, is driven by the mind, and, as a result, can put blinders on other areas of human concern, making for a cool-as-steel, rather dry approach to life. When planets occupy air signs, conscious purpose and directed willpower are aimed at the "airy" pursuits, the world of ideas, concepts, and problem-solving. Relationships with people who can act as receivers through which to "air" these concepts and ideas become the goal for the air sign type.

In matters of health, the air triplicity deals with the ability to circulate blood through the pathways of the body, the arteries and veins. When air is poorly represented in the chart, circulation will be poor. When air is overly emphasized, dryness of skin, hair, and temperament will be apparent. Techniques of breathing are extremely important to air signs, and the yogis recognize the vital breath or *prana* as the connecting link between the body and the self. All air types, and especially Gemini, which rules the lungs, could benefit from routine breathing exercises and often need to live in places where the air is clean and pure. They often need to be elevated as well, in high altitudes. While a dry climate goes well with their temperaments, it will also exacerbate the dry conditions which may result in their bodies if the air element is excessive. In such cases, lubricants and natural oils will assist.

WATER

The element of water symbolizes the flow of human feelings, and it is no wonder that the Moon, that great significator of emotion, finds its home in a water sign, Cancer. A horoscope heavily endowed with planets in the water signs shows an individual who trusts her or his feelings, an individual who is emotional rather than mental.

If extraverted, these people are exemplars of all the social graces, for they are attuned to the feelings of others. The introverts are the people we typically call "still waters that run deep," those brooding, sensitive, inarticulate souls who remain locked in an internal cocoon, like Laura in Tennessee Williams' play *The Glass Menagerie*. Because they live by their feelings, the water-sign types (unless they also have a great many planets in air signs) will neglect thinking values altogether. The extraverts in particular will accept the judgment of society without question, and all the "pure" water types, whether introverted or extraverted, tend to have opinions rather than ideas.

Feeling values may be expressed in any number of ways. In Cancer, water is in its cardinal mode of expression. The feelings are active. They make things happen.

Cardinal water is like a rushing stream in the full flood of early summer, charting a course toward its ultimate destination, the sea. In Scorpio, water operates through the fixed mode of expression, like a quiet pond or a lake frozen over in winter. Thus it is said that Scorpio people are very tenacious, or even downright retentive, when it comes to their emotions. Once they have invested their emotional energy in anything—be it a marriage or a socio-political cause—they simply don't give up. They're locked in, like the frozen lake. It is as difficult to see beneath the surface of Scorpio as it is to see the bottom of a lake. The true emotional core, the power of water, lies hidden beneath the placid, somewhat clouded exterior. In Pisces, water occupies a mutable sign. Here, the shifts and variations upon the emotional theme become endless. There is no bottom to the deep feelings contained within Pisces, for Pisces is the ocean itself, endless in its variety and infinite in its changes. And, like the ocean, Pisces is ultimately unknowable.

Waterfall on the Big Island, Hawaii.
Photograph by Ariel Guttman

We have seen how the four elements make their appearance in mythology as the four treasures of the Grail. The role played by water in this particular myth has a powerful meaning for our civilization as a whole. Jung claimed that medieval myth in general, and the Grail Myth in particular, raised all the issues which now confront our civilization.[10] Western Civilization, born in the upheaval created by an emerging Christianity and a dying Graeco-Roman civilization, first took shape during what we call the Middle Ages. So it is during the Middle Ages, according to Jung, that the principal myths of Western Civilization also took shape. In the Grail story, the knight Perceval is seeking the cup from which Christ drank at the Last Supper. Until the Grail is found, the world will be a wasteland. The inner meaning of the story is clear. It is the quality of *feeling*—symbolized by the watery element and the magic cup—which is most sadly lacking in Western Civilization. The authors of the Grail Legend had already realized, back in the Middle Ages, that our culture was leaning too strongly in the direction of science, of the rational intellect. A repression of the feminine principle (the symbolic Grail) has crippled the inner king, and now the world is a wasteland—a curious anticipation of the current eco-crisis to which our scientific orientation has led us. According to the myth, healing for the culture can only come through the medium of the *feelings*. The Grail is the symbolic descendant of the cauldron of rebirth in Celtic mythology, so we should not be surprised to discover that the Grail, the sacred vessel, is in itself a feminine symbol, nor should we be surprised to note that the cupbearer in the Grail Castle is a woman whose name means "Chosen Response." It is only through greater reliance upon and union with the element of water, the feminine faculty of feeling, that our civilization can heal itself.

The Sun represents the ego, and the ego's ability to transmit the intentions of the personality, coupled with its ability to filter outer stimuli, is perhaps unique. The Sun's powerful rays of light, when in strong aspect to other planets, enhance or magnify its intentions and purpose. But let's suppose we have an overcast day outside. We say the sun isn't out, but that's not true. The sun is always out during daylight hours. On a cloudy day we still see where we are going without the use of artificial light, but we are not necessarily aware of the sun's presence. So it is with many whose Suns are placed in the element of water. There are veils and many layers of psychic and/or emotional material between those whose Sun occupies a water sign and the object of their attention or interaction. You won't get sunburned by these types, but you will get a sense that there is more going on underneath the surface than there is above. Water puts out fire, so when the watery nature is strong, those whose Suns are placed in water signs won't express themselves as powerfully on the outside as the fiery Sun people do. But their inner lives are a different story! Behind the clouds and fog are many kinds of experiences, both inspirational and turbulent. And it is by wrestling with these extremes that enlightenment comes for such individuals. When the Sun, a fire planet, is placed in a water sign, the fire/water theme may be strongly apparent elsewhere in the chart. Both elements have to be honored. Because water signs absorb feeling and sensation, and because the Sun symbolizes how we express that which is part of our inner being, it is the water Sun's task to externalize those watery depths in whatever way it can.

In a birth chart, when we see an abundance of the element water, we immediately see that the individual has a great capacity to feel. If the planets that are placed in water signs are nicely aspected and free to "flow," they often indicate people who will use these gifts in a caring and sensitive way. They may become connected to the healing professions or helping professions, using their psychic and psychological awareness in a way that keeps the principle active for themselves, and also circulates the knowledge to those with whom they are connected. They may be artists or musicians, mystics or poets, teachers or group leaders who, by virtue of their ability to tap into their feelings, inspire others to do so. This process, however, does not always come easily.

Water, as mentioned previously, is probably the most repressed of the four elements in our culture. The last two hundred years have focused our attention on industrialization and high technology. So much more reason, then, for feeling and sensitivity, which water represents, to be present in our lives. However, this has not been the case. We have gone to an extreme to incorporate technology and science into our lives, developing mega-minds and corporate wizards who live in a gray

Water and earth meet at the coast

chrome and glass world of robotized think-tanks, wear gray suits, and whiz through airports looking like a maze of mechanical briefcases, and who respond, on command, to their computer-like programming. These, too, are the scenes that flash before our children in the multitude of videos that are penetrating their very open, psychic, and impressionable young minds. Meanwhile they are told that the expression of feeling is not allowed. Girls get to express it a little longer (at least through their teenage years), but boys are told at a very young age not to cry, as that is a sign of weakness and not very manly. But soon girls, too, are mocked when the natural expression of tears overflows.

Many of the diseases of today can be linked to principles of limiting feeling or repressing the water principle in our lives. When we observe a dam built to contain or hold back the natural flow of water, we note that a tremendous amount of manmade force must be employed to halt that natural flow. Imagine what we do to our bodies by obstructing the free flow of the water process. It takes a lot of strength and resistance to keep the feelings—or natural flow of emotional responses—back. Our bodies have a natural way of releasing water or expressing feelings locked inside—tears. Yet many feel silly or stupid or even guilty when they let the tears flow. Think also how healing it feels to have a good cry. It's similar to a refreshing morning shower, the shower having taken place internally.

When the water function is blocked in a person's life, it may show up in the chart as a lack of planets in water signs. It may also be symbolized by planets in water signs that are highly stressed or challenged by planets in air or fire signs or by planets of an airy or fiery nature. In these cases, the person has often been blocked from expressing the natural flow of his or her feelings or made to feel the need to repress them for fear that if they were let out they would explode. The combination of water with fire, for instance, is quite volcanic. The hot fiery emotions mix with the water and steam in a cauldron several levels below consciousness, until a transit, eclipse, lunation, or progression sets them off and creates a highly volcanic eruption. This is often true when Scorpio is involved, since Scorpio is the sign of fixed water, water that stays contained beneath the surface, sustaining the feelings before they can be processed. When positively integrated and expressed, the combination of water and fire creates people who are passionate, sensitive, fiery, and warm, encouraging their feelings to flow freely and spontaneously.

The mixture of water with air is very Pisces-like, creating clouds of rain which are sometimes turbulent, like thunder and lightning over the ocean, at other times soft and soothing, like a summer shower. When properly expressed, the water/air mixture can create the verbalization or vocalization of feeling—writers, musicians, songwriters, poets, etc. One of the most productive mixtures of air and water in recent times was the Beatles, which featured two creative intellects (John and Paul) with their Suns in air signs (Libra and Gemini respectively) supported by two musicians (George and Ringo) with their Suns in water signs (Pisces and Cancer). Singer-songwriter team Paul Simon (Libra: air) and Art Garfunkel (Scorpio: water) also created beautiful harmonies together, but it is well-known that they preferred working independently. Both groups gave us stimulation on both the verbal (air) and musical (water) levels.

As we have seen, the air principle is connected to the thinking function, while the water principle is connected to the feeling function. When air and water are in competition with each other they are not always easy to reconcile. The mind tells the emotions to control themselves, while the emotions have no parameters for control—they are responding to pure feeling. When the air principle is too strongly dominant and controls the water principle, the outward manifestation is often like the thunderstorm—a critical, caustic, overly judgmental response to a situation that hardly seemed worthy of such a display.

Earth with water can usually create a harmonious flow. Earth needs water to grow and survive. Water can use a container such as earth (similar to Cancer) to keep from spilling out and running rampant, potentially destroying everything in its path. When earth and water are too dominant in a birth chart without the addition of the other two elements, "mud" is created, or a sense of stasis and complacency with the current situation; motivation is lacking.

We can see from this, then, that the water function in the chart will help to lubricate the psychic joints and offer a connective element to keep the feelings and emotional responses flowing freely, and that when we block such a function we can do great damage to ourselves and others. We can also see that the balance of the four elements is necessary for wholeness and integration.

MODALITIES

The Three Modalities:
Cardinal, Fixed, and Mutable

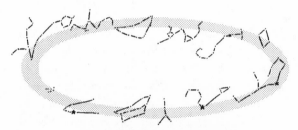

*The fixed signs are shown in the corners of this
nineteenth-century French Tarot deck*

The scheme of the four elements is
one way of categorizing astrology's
psychic reality; the scheme of the
three modalities is another. These
two systems intertwine in the
astrological *mandala*; and, as we
shall see, they add layers of meaning to the zodiacal signs.

Just as each sign may be classified according to its element, it
may also be classified according to
its mode. Four elements times
three modes equals twelve signs.
Thus we have one cardinal air sign
(Libra), one fixed earth sign
(Taurus), one mutable water sign
(Pisces), and so on. Each sign is a
unique blend of element and mode;
no one sign has precisely the same
constitution as another.

According to Jung[1] and to
Vedic astrologers,[2] odd numbers
are masculine. The number three
is an especially strong example of
this, for Christianity itself con-
ceives of God as a trinity; hence
our Christian civilization is founded on the masculine principle as

represented by the number three. Even numbers are feminine, and the number four in particular appears again and again in mythology and in non-Western religions. Jung observed that the structure of the human psyche appears in dreams as a fourfold entity; thus one is brought to the conclusion that the human soul is essentially feminine.[3]

The astrological *mandala* unites the numbers three and four. It unites masculine and feminine energy, *yin* and *yang*, into one reconciling symbol, the horoscopic circle. Within this union of *yin* and *yang*, there are subtler shades, for the elements themselves can be divided into masculine (fire and air) or feminine (earth and water) components. Astrology partakes of the ancient wisdom inasmuch as it unites masculine and feminine symbols in an archetype of wholeness. This wholeness was lost long ago in the Western world. Even before the advent of Judaism and Christianity with their strong patriarchal biases, the analytical minds of the Greek thinkers were already bending our civilization towards its present masculine or scientific course. The horoscope, however, resonates to an older, more balanced world-view.

If we ask ourselves where or how these modalities came to be, there is no clear answer. Certainly the modes have been part of astrological theory since Ptolemy of Alexandria, though they seem not to have been known to the Babylonians; in fact, the whole system of elements and modes appears to be of Greek origin. Whatever their origin, the modalities are a very ancient concept. One may find many similarities between the three modes of Western astrology and the three *gunas* or attributes of classic Hindu philosophy.[4] The three *gunas*, which we shall explore in some depth with the individual modes, are *rajas* (activity), *tamas* (inertia), and *sattva* (spirit or harmony). They correspond fairly well to the cardinal, fixed, and mutable modes respectively.[5] Classical Hindu medicine, or Ayurveda, also recognizes a similar division of three "humors" (doshas) or physical types: *vata* (*sattva*, mutable, air); *pitta* (*rajas*, cardinal, fire); and *kapha* (*tamas*, fixed, earth/water).

Should we, therefore, assume that Greek astrology was influenced by Hinduism? Such an influence is certainly not impossible. Practitioners of the Vedic system which includes astrology claim that it is at least 5,000 years old. Alexander the Great, a Greek conqueror, had Hindu yogis in his entourage and conversed with them frequently on philosophical matters. His military exploits gave birth to a civilization which was part Greek and part Asian, and which stretched from the European mainland to the borders of India. Many ideas flowed back and forth across the Near Eastern caravan routes in those days. Sanskrit, the language of classical Hinduism, is related to Greek. Both are classified as Indo-European languages, implying that at some distant point in time they had a common ancestor. Most scholars now believe that the search for this common ancestry leads back to the fourth millennium before Christ, and to the southern part of the former Soviet Union.[6] Here, on the great steppes, lived a number of warrior tribes — sword-wielding patriarchs and masters of horsemanship. Everything we know about these early Indo-Europeans suggests that the number three was of vital importance to

The four signs of the fixed cross are represented on this cathedral window as: Aquarius—the man (St. Matthew); Leo—the lion (St. Mark); Scorpio—the eagle (St. John); and Taurus—the bull (St. Luke). Photograph by Ariel Guttman

their religion. These nomads traveled west from their original homeland and invaded Europe. They make their appearance in the Balkans about 3,500 BC. Archaeologist Marija Gimbutas has argued that the Balkans were the seat of a very early proto-civilization which she calls "Old Europe."[7] The culture of Old Europe was based upon the worship of the Great Goddess; it was a world of peaceful farming villages, a true matriarchy. Not surprisingly, its religious artifacts suggest that the feminine number four was of prime importance. But in the middle of the fourth millennium BC, Old Europe was invaded by nomads who carried bronze swords and who carved horse heads on their burial artifacts. These invaders, argues Gimbutas, were the Indo-Europeans. She goes on to say that the same story of conquest is repeated later on, when the patriarchal Mycenaean Greeks invaded the goddess-worshipping civilization of Minoan Crete (according to Gimbutas, there are strong reasons to believe that Old Europe and Minoan Crete were branches of the same matriarchal civilization).

Here, for the first time, we see the conflict and eventual union between the patriarchal religion based on three and the matriarchal world-view based on four. In Greece, especially, the two world-views achieved an uneasy but workable synthesis. The Indo-Europeans brought their war-like gods—Zeus the Sky Father, Ares the Warrior, and others—into a Greece which still worshipped the Great Mother. The invaders and the original inhabitants hammered out an uneasy compromise in which the new gods became sons or consorts of the Great Mother[8]—as when Zeus is depicted as the child of the Cretan goddess Rhea, or the husband of Hera, the name under which the Great Goddess was worshipped in Argos. Gaia, the earth mother, gave birth to Ouranos, the sky god. And Gaia was also worshipped at Delphi long before Apollo appeared and claimed that spot as his home.

The astrological *mandala* of elements and modalities may well be part of the symbolic legacy of that synthesis. If the four elements represent a survival of the matriarchal world-view, then the three modes may represent the concepts of the Indo-European invaders who brought an end to Old Europe.

In summary, then, we see that three, the number of modes in astrology, symbolizes a masculine, sky-based father principle while four, the number of the elements, relates to the earth-based mother-goddess worship. The astrological wheel of four times three balances masculine and feminine, or *yin* and *yang*, in a circle of wholeness. After all, while some may argue that God is male and some claim she is female, life on this planet has no possibility of emergence save by a union of both. And we are told that beyond this earth plane there is no necessity for male *or* female differentiation; that we are merged beings. But on that plane there is no need for classifications such as cardinal-fixed-mutable or fire-earth-air-water, either. *Everything* merges and becomes one.

CARDINAL

The cardinal signs *initiate* energy. Theirs is the driving power, the will to action. They may be motivated by a vision, or purely by the obsession to perform some kind (*any* kind) of action—but they *will* act. Sometimes they seem like a whirlwind or, better still, a bulldozer. They charge ahead, and all that anyone can do is to get out of their way.

Among the three Hindu *gunas*, the cardinal mode corresponds to *rajas*. *Rajas* is from the same root word as *rajah* or *maharajah*, meaning king. This same word appears in European languages as *rex* (Latin) or *roi* (French), not to mention *regal* and *royal*. In ancient India, kings were warriors; it was their path to take up arms and conquer on the battlefield, just as it was the duty of a *brahmin* to meditate and study the scriptures. Similarly, those whose horoscopes contain an emphasis on cardinal signs are on the path of action. They need a cause, a battle, a field of activity. Without it, they tend to be frustrated bundles of nervous energy.

Turning once again to classical Hindu philosophy, we find that *rajaguna* has one outstanding failing: anger. Cardinal people have a volatile, fiery temperament and may easily explode unless they have an outlet for their abundant energy. Cardinal signs like to *start* things. When we study the *mandala* of the zodiac a bit more closely, this will become apparent, for the cardinal signs correspond to the four primary angles of the birth chart and to the beginning of the four seasons as well (i.e., the equinoxes and solstices). And not only do they *start* things, but it seems that things get started *for* them. It frequently occurs among multi-cardinal individuals that their lives take off and get moving before they really know what they're doing or why. This energy that some attribute to "beginner's luck" may not last forever, but with cardinal signs, that's usually fine—because by the time things get to the point where conscious planning and routine sets in, the cardinal types are already looking for a way out of the old and into something new.

Aries manifests its cardinality in a more obvious way than the other signs. Aries people create activity purely for the hell of it. They need to be doing something, even if it is only ramming their heads against a wall, fighting for a lost cause, or beating a dead horse. They don't really care, just so long as it gives them something to *do*. Capricorn, the cardinal earth sign, is a bit quieter, but more relentless. Capricorn will plod rather than rush towards a particular goal, but, like any cardinal sign, it will never be deflected from its purpose. It is the cardinality of Capricorn which endows it with the strength of purpose necessary to reach the top of the corporate or political heap—or the inner strength to manifest its winter solstice myth and relentlessly search for the inner light.

Some students of astrology have found it a little less easy to identify the cardinal qualities of Libra and Cancer. And indeed, if we think of Libra solely as the relationship sign, we will have a hard time spotting its essentially cardinal nature. But, as Dane Rudhyar pointed out in *The Pulse of Life*, Libra represents the autumnal equinox, when the power of collective humanity begins to overshadow the power of the individual ego.[9] We have to think of relationships in this broader context. A Libran who channels all of his or her relating power into a marriage or other intimate relationship may not be expressing the full range of Libran cardinality: that wider spectrum of relationship is manifested by those Librans who have envisioned a new humanity based upon what the American Indians or the Buddhists would call right relationship. Mahatma Gandhi is an outstanding example of this type of Libran.

The cardinal nature of Cancer may also seem a little hard to spot. This is because Cancer's field of activity is the human heart. Cancer is the time of the summer solstice, when the days are longest and the sun shines brightly. This may seem a bit confusing to some, since the Sun is usually regarded as a masculine planet and Cancer is a quintessentially feminine sign. But as we shall see (in Cancer), Cancer unites solar and lunar energy in a very important way—and if we apply Joseph Campbell's outline of the hero's myth to the passage of the sun through the zodiac, Cancer represents the mystic marriage, the union of male and female energies.[10]

The signs of the cardinal cross, illustrated by Diane Smirnow

The cardinal energy of Cancer is expended in building a solid foundation for the solar ego, so that it may better express its purpose. This foundation may be a real home and family, or it may be the inner center of one's being (which is why we think of Cancer as psychic).

Cardinal signs are like the first-born of a family—driven to achieve or pursue a vision which is nearly out of reach. Therefore, there is constant motion and activity, never a state of perfect restfulness; it is as if a carrot were dangling in front of them, urging them to go just one more mile until it is theirs. Exhausting though it may seem, those who possess a strong cardinal modality prefer it that way. Resting does not come easy for these types, unless they drop from sheer energy depletion.

The drive that each of the cardinal signs possesses operates in a different way and corresponds roughly to the element in question. For instance, Aries cardinality will express itself through fire, Cancer through water, Libra through air, and Capricorn through earth. Aries, the *fire* sign, is driven to achieve some sort of personal victory—to be the first, the fastest, or the best at something. Cancer's *water* flows constantly like a river in search of its ultimate home, or whatever will make Cancer feel secure and safe. Libra, the cardinal *air* sign, is driven by its need for constant balance and harmony in a world that seems bent on keeping things in a state of imbalance most of the time. Capricorn, the cardinal *earth* sign, is driven by its desire for mastery over the physical world, whether perched atop Mt. Everest, on the top rung of the corporate ladder, or, in keeping with its winter solstice symbolism, striving to keep that inner light aglow.

The incarnational cycle of the cardinal mode is that of productivity and action. No wonder we are so content to rest and stay put by the time we reach the fixed mode! The same process holds true for our experience of the world at large when many planets are transiting through cardinal signs. For instance, during the late 1980s and early 1990s, three or four of the outer (weightier) planets have transited cardinal signs—Saturn, Uranus, and Neptune all in Capricorn, with Chiron simultaneously in cardinal Cancer. Such a line-up in the sky forces a great deal of activity on earth, and we have observed "earthquakes" being experienced both geologically and geopolitically—earth movement and political movement. This is how excessive amounts of cardinality tend to operate, both individually and collectively. There seems to be this sense of urgency with cardinal signs—if we don't do it now, we'll miss our time slot. For this reason, a person with strong cardinality is likely to experience impatience with people or situations that seem stagnant, and can easily experience boredom even with their own projects, because the act of initiating or creating is itself the stimulant and that moment of genesis is now past. Once the new and different becomes the routine and needs daily maintenance, cardinal people can become rather disenchanted.

It's no accident that the yearly seasonal cycles begin in the cardinal signs. The first days of spring, summer, fall, and winter correspond precisely to the first degrees of Aries, Cancer, Libra, and Capricorn respectively. We know these as the equinoxes and solstices, the four times in the year when the earth and sun are poised at precise angles of increased magnetic potency. Perhaps this has some effect on the biochemical components of the multi-cardinal individual. One thing is for certain with cardinal signs—life should not be without drama.

Complex and potentially stressful life situations arise for individuals who are born with many different planets in cardinal signs. When planets occupy three of the cardinal signs within a close orb so as to form 90 degree angles to one another, astrologers call the configuration a cardinal T-square. When all four cardinal signs contain planets, the configuration produced is called a grand cross—or, more specifically, a cardinal cross. Such configurations point to an individual's need to express all situations *simultaneously*, even when there seems to be competition between the various situations and each voice cries out to be addressed separately. In cases like this there is no either/or. *Everything* needs to be taken care of or the various situations will peck relentlessly at one's brain until they are given what they want. And what do they want? When three are present, as in the T-square, the resolution is often in the missing leg—which makes sense, as that sign is the polarity of the sign situated at the focal point of the T, the sign receiving the most stress. Polarity therapy operates along the same principle, in that it relieves the stress of one point in the body by addressing a corresponding opposite. So if the T-square involves planets in Cancer, Libra, and Capricorn, Libra is the most stressed and finds its release in Aries. When all four signs are tightly configured in the grand cross, the individual must maintain a steady and focused flow to each of the four—individual needs (Aries) must balance and harmonize with partners' needs (Libra); family or personal concerns (Cancer) need to be given as much attention as worldly or professional concerns (Capricorn). While this may sound incredibly stressful, people seem to handle the four-pointed cross much more easily than the T-square, wherein individuals are struggling with only three of the four elements. Perhaps this is so because, as we observed earlier, four is a number that rests upon a secure foundation, originating from the feminine source of life-giving power, and offers more stability and security than three, a number which is in constant motion.

FIXED

If the cardinal signs engage in activity purely for activity's sake, the fixed signs act only when absolutely necessary. Cardinal energy is like a hurricane, raging along on its path. The fixed signs capture that hurricane in their strong hands, and root it— or, more precisely, *fix* it—to one spot. They turn the power of the wind into windmills so that it will produce something tangible.

Among the three *gunas*, it is *tamas* which corresponds to the fixed signs. The basic meaning of *tamas* in Sanskrit is "inertia;" of all the three *gunas*, *tamas* has the most negative connotation. It is associated with sloth, materiality, and the darkening of the mind through immersion in sensual things. And it is all too easy to see the tendency of the fixed signs to get stuck in ruts. Taurus, as a fixed earth sign, gets stuck in things of the physical world, money or sensuality; Leo, as fixed fire, in self-indulgence, the famous Leonine egotism. Scorpio, the fixed water sign, becomes overly attached to its emotional desires, and Aquarius, the fixed air sign, can easily become stuck in rigid thought patterns or fanatical adherence to an idea.

But such an interpretation concentrates purely on the failings of the fixed signs. In fact, the power of each of the four elements becomes *concentrated* in the fixed signs, and thus may achieve its most potent form of expression. There is an astrological tradition that the central point of each fixed sign (i.e., the 15th degree of each sign) represents this maximum focus of power. We have observed this in recent history. When Pluto reached the 15th degree of Scorpio for the first time in November, 1989, the Berlin Wall came down, an event that had incredible implications for Eastern Europe and the world. When Pluto reached the 15th degree of

Scorpio for its third and final pass in August, 1990, Iraq invaded Kuwait, beginning a series of chain reactions that the world will be dealing with for quite some time.

Such an emphasis on the power of the fixed signs is reflected in mythology. Ezekiel's vision of the fiery chariot (*Ezekiel* 1:4–24) is perhaps the most famous example:

> *I saw a storm wind coming from the north, a vast cloud with flashes of fire and brilliant light about it; and within was a radiance like brass, glowing in the heart of the flames. In the fire was the semblance of four living creatures in human form. Their faces were like this: all four had the face of a man and the face of a lion on the right, on the left the face of an ox and the face of an eagle.*

Here we see the four fixed signs: Aquarius the man, Leo the lion, Taurus the ox, and Scorpio the eagle. In early and medieval Christianity, the authors of the four gospels became associated with the four fixed signs. Matthew was represented as a man, Mark as a lion (hence the Lion of St. Mark, the emblem of the city of Venice), Luke as an ox, and John as an eagle. (Note that the most esoteric gospel, that of John, is attributed to Scorpio.)[11] In Kabbalistic magic, the four elements are frequently symbolized by the fixed signs, and they appear yet again on the World card in the Tarot, where they show that the four functions of the psyche have been harmonized into a unity or wholeness—a *mandalic* circle inside which a female figure, the *anima mundi* or world-soul of the alchemists, is dancing.[12]

The positive side of the fixed signs is *stability*. They are the builders, whether of earthly things (Taurus), artistic creations (Leo), occult powers (Scorpio), or world-changing visions and ideas (Aquarius).

In most respects, it is easy to see the "fixed" aspect of these signs. Taurus in particular has a talent for taking raw energy and fashioning it into something useful. It is also Taurus which has the reputation for indolence, laziness, and all the qualities of inertia which the Hindus would attribute to *tamas*. Leo's fixity of purpose lies in its focus upon itself. We may think of this as a very negative quality, and yet such self-absorption is often necessary for the artist to transform his or her feelings into some tangible product or result. Scorpios specialize in "fixed feelings." They can nurse a grudge for years, or show the greatest possible commitment to a relationship—they may even hold on long after it is time to go. This concentration of feeling upon a single object or obsession has its uses. Scorpios make the best occultists; they have a talent for transforming raw emotion and feeling into spiritual or magical power.

It is often difficult for people to conceive of Aquarius as a fixed sign. Isn't Aquarius supposed to be free and easy, a wild-eyed dreamer romping through the tulips of life? But Aquarians may become fixed upon a single ideal—despite abundant evidence from the world around them that the ideal just won't work. Abraham Lincoln may be a case in point. Like many Aquarians, his ideals have taken in excess of a hundred years to manifest.

Fixity is the modality which allows us to hold onto or preserve what we began in cardinal and what will be dispersed in mutable. It is, therefore, a very important function in astrology. There would be no sense of what came before without the fixed mode. Individuals born into families with cultures which are strongly rooted in traditions and customs dating back hundreds of years typically have important points (especially the Moon) in fixed signs. For them there is an innate sense of maintaining the custom and passing the tradition down to the next generation. In fact, offspring and progeny, typically associated with Leo, the fixed fire sign, can be related to fixity in general, based upon the fixed individual's need to reproduce itself or maintain and carry on the line.

Fixed types have greater endurance than others. Perhaps because they are often from families or geographical regions with a long history, they are content to keep things secure and wait for just the right moment to make a move. This drives their cardinal associates (who are already driven) a bit crazy. They are almost opposites, with cardinal seeking a battle or cause to conquer and fixed expending the majority of its energy holding on to what it has.

It's not that fixed signs aren't active—far from it. It's just that they very seldom adjust to *change* or adapt to new input. This is where their insistence on maintaining the status quo can have dire consequences for them. As times change, economic trends change. We live by cycles that are ever-changing waves of continuous ebb and flow. Changing with the times or learning new and modern methods are often required just to keep up. Fixed sign energies often proclaim that "it worked for my father and for his father, and by God, it's going to work for me!" when in fact, it is already obsolete. Yet the fixed signs know when to play a hunch and often strike it rich due to their keen talent for "knowing when to hold and knowing when to fold." And if they don't strike it rich, it's probably due to sheer stubbornness and refusal to let go.

While the cardinal T-square signifies too much activity, the fixed T-square is likely to exemplify too much inertia. It's interesting to note that the planets which produce the most severe life-altering changes are Uranus and Pluto, planets that are rulers of two fixed signs, Aquarius and Scorpio. It's no surprise that it takes so much force to move the fixed signs.

The fixed T-square and grand cross occur for individuals who have developed such a strong inheritance of fixity that it has become a crisis and must now be handled. Such people are often grappling with decisions as to which values are true and lasting, and which are only ephemeral. Fixed T-square individuals experience most dramatically the cycles of "feast or famine." There are times in their lives when they gather things in, collecting and nurturing them. Often, tests of the right use of power then occur for these individuals. When they have it, how much do they share? How willing are they to yield to another's point of view or compromise their positions to help others in need? Is their concern only for personal gain, or for planetary well-being? Have their methods, ideas and practices become dogma, wherein

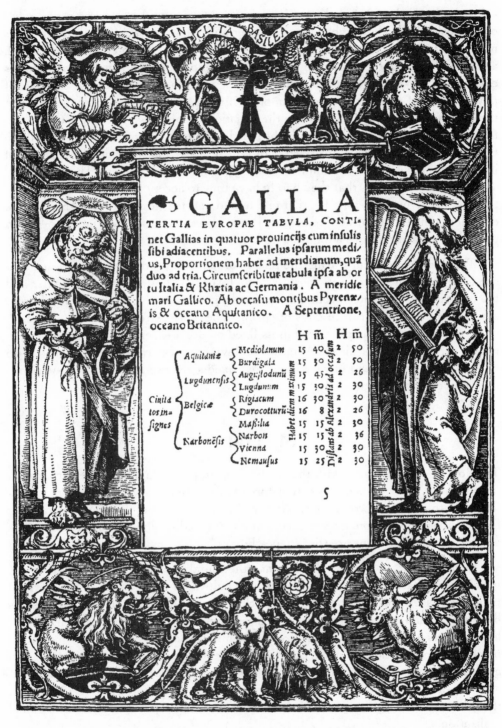

GALLIA

TERTIA EVROPAE TABVLA, CONTI-
net Gallias in quatuor prouincijs cum infulis
fibi adiacentibus.   Parallelus ipfarum medi-
us, Proportionem habet ad meridianum, quâ
duo ad tria. Circumfcribitur tabula ipfa ab or
tu Italia & Rhætia ac Germania. A meridie
mari Gallico. Ab occafu montibus Pyrenæ-
is & oceano Aquitanico.   A Septentrione,
oceano Britannico.

		H m̃	H m̃
Aquitaniæ	Mediolanum	15 40	2 50
	Burdigala	15 30	2 50
Lugdunenfis	Augujtodunū	15 45	2 26
	Lugdunum	15 30	2 30
Belgicæ	Rigiacum	16 30	2 30
	Durocotturū	16 8	2 26
	Maßilia	15 15	2 30
Narbonēfis	Narbon	15 15	2 36
	Vienna	15 30	2 30
	Nemaufus	15 25	2 30

Ciuita
tos in-
ſignes

S

*A title page by Hans Holbein the Younger showing the four fixed signs of the zodiac, from the
print shop of Adam Petri, Basle, c. 1524*

rules cannot be bent? Are they mechanically programmed beings who no longer consciously think about what they're doing and what consequences their actions may have for others? Issues of power are big tests for the fixed cross types as well, as the ability to gather during gathering time and release during release time is experienced. When they have outlasted their usefulness regarding a position of power, mode of thought, relationship, or as "guardian of the castle," they are given the opportunity to let go and release the situation of their own accord. If the invitation is refused (and it often is with the fixed modality), Pluto and Uranus will be there to catapult the reluctant fixed sign into the next phase, which of course will initially seem like a time of "famine" to the typical fixed personality. This is all such a shock to their systems that they barely have time to accept their fate and get "into" the new phase until it's time for that one to end and the next one to begin. Change does not come easily to the fixed signs. But it is necessary, as their next move is to mutable, and that requires a lot of flexibility.

The fixed signs occur during the phases of nature's yearly cycle when each season is being experienced in its most extreme form. The hottest days of summer and the coldest days of winter occur during fixed signs, as do the most colorful days of autumn and the most fruitful days of spring. The most extreme expression of each of the four elements is experienced in its fixed mode: fire's most extreme expression is Leo, earth's is Taurus, air's is Aquarius and water's is Scorpio. That, too, has to do with the containment and inward focus that fixed signs need in order to experience their process most dramatically.

MUTABLE

The flow of energy begins with the cardinal signs; power, unleashed, emerges with driving force. In the fixed signs, that force is captured, rooted to one spot, transformed into a base of productivity. And in the mutable signs, the power spirals out from its fixed foundation, growing, communicating, educating, taking varied shapes and forms. Mutable signs are the "shape-shifters."

In the system of the the three *gunas*, the mutable signs correspond to *sattva*, which means harmony. *Sattva* is the attribute cultivated by devotees of the spiritual path, for it seeks balance rather than worldly accomplishment. The mutable signs have always had a reputation for seeking wisdom and knowledge; they make excellent teachers and communicators as well. Gemini is the master of words and of the names of things, hence the magician. Virgo is the devotee, purifying his or her energies through a process of alchemical transmutation. Sagittarius is the spiritual seeker *par excellence*, mastering wisdom in the quest for the Self. And Pisces is the mystic, the visionary who fights against the ghosts of the karmic past in order to win final realization.

But if the mutable signs possess a natural spiritual bent and represent energy spiraling upward, back to its source, they also experience difficulties in dealing with

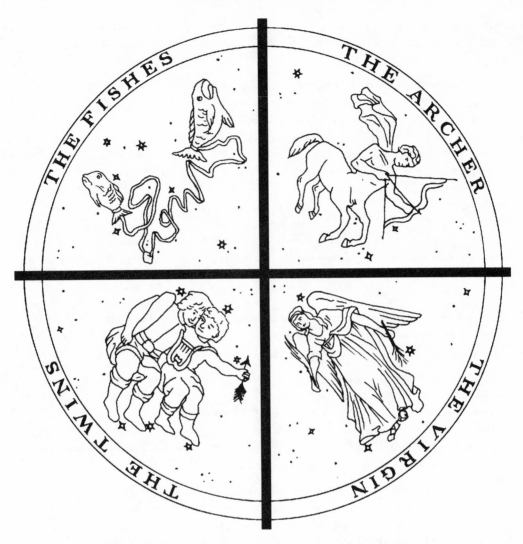

The signs of the mutable cross, illustrated by Diane Smirnow

the material world, for the diffuse and variable nature of their energy often makes it hard for them to focus their attention on the here and now. Unless the spiral is consciously directed towards a spiritual purpose, it may wander at random, disconnected and nervous. Mutable signs are usually aware that they are seeking *something*—but they don't always know they are seeking liberation. Even when they *do* become conscious of the nature of their search, they may have trouble focusing on a particular path. Far more than other signs, they are likely to indulge in what has been called "spiritual promiscuity"—drifting restlessly from one religion or New Age group to another, always finding something slightly amiss with each new vision of the path, always hungering for something *more*. This is particularly noticeable with the two Mercury signs, Gemini and Virgo, for Gemini is easily distracted by the flow of thoughts, ideas, and images, while Virgo finds that everything human falls short of the spiritual perfection it seeks. Sagittarians and Pisceans, on the other hand, are frequently impelled to absorb *all* paths and wisdom traditions without discrimination.

Mutable signs also manifest a great deal of confusion when it comes to emotional matters in general and relationships in particular. Their talents lie in the sphere of mental and/or spiritual action, not in relatedness. The two Mercury signs, Gemini and Virgo, are often accused of being cold. Gemini may, in fact, be more concerned with its internal mental chatter than with other human beings, though Virgo can manifest a very beautiful sense of relatedness. Sagittarius, like Gemini, is more likely to be concerned with goals than with relating, while Pisces, like Virgo, may be too painfully empathic to navigate through the tangled world of real human emotions. Mutable signs also tend to live by their own individual morality—a morality which may have more to do with their unique spiral of perception than it does with any form of social mores. Hence the mutables have a reputation for experimenting with alternative forms of relationships.

Nervous, mental, glittering with charm, the mutable signs are also distant, detached, lost in worlds of their own imagining. Combining the energies of the cardinal and fixed modes, they embody a paradox, a union of opposites. This union of opposites lies at the heart of their changeable and frequently bewildering behavior.

A species' ability to mutate keeps it current with the evolutionary demands of its era. Likewise, the mutable mode's overriding concern is that of adapting, changing, and mutating to the current demands of its world. The trouble is that the world, as the mutable signs see it, is always changing. "The only thing constant is change" is a vision of reality which was given expression in the *Metamorphoses* of the Roman poet Ovid, who had the Sun in mutable Pisces.

The four mutable signs occur during nature's yearly cycle at the four times of the year when the season is about to change. The anticipation of impending change is probably the psychological force behind mutable's reluctance to stay put externally or centered internally. And in fact, it is this internal dialogue or drama that keeps mutable-mode individuals continually stirred up.

When major transits (outer planet transits to one's Sun, Moon, or angles, or outer planetary returns) occur to or in mutable signs, it is usually a time of great dispersal in life. One phase of life is ending and, as with the impending change of seasons which occurs during mutable signs, a new phase is about to begin.

While the fixed mode's survival depends upon control, organization, and focus, the mutable world is a world of limitless possibilities. Like water, mutable has a very poor sense of boundaries, except perhaps for Virgo, whose compartmentalization process can be endless. This lack of boundaries can create an isolation similar to the void experienced by a space traveler. Mutables are often the ones who are starkly aware of all the grains of sand on a beach which is only one of millions of beaches on a planet that is only one of millions of bodies floating through space, *ad infinitum*. So getting down to practical considerations can be a real challenge for mutable types.

If you examine each of the four mutable signs you will find that they are easily lost in that kind of process. Gemini collects voluminous tidbits of information but still has no real explanation of life. Virgo views life so as to find meaning in all the parts while remaining totally unaware of the whole. Sagittarius' view through a telephoto lens is always in search of the intangible, and Pisces' multi-colored lenses and filters are all too aware of everything out there but of nothing which lies right in front of them. (Pisces, in contrast to Virgo, is aware of the forest, but keeps stumbling over the trees.)

With all these deep issues to ponder, it is a wonder that the mutables ever get anything accomplished. Yet their perceptual states of mind, their expanded or altered states of awareness all have one ultimate goal—to keep the mutable individual striving towards the deeper meanings of life, towards philosophical or psychological parameters of existence.

Those whose charts contain mutable T-squares have a very different dilemma than their fixed friends. Since mutable is already innately dispersing and disrupting, those whose mutable energies are further diffused by having multiple choices are often driven nearly insane by the internal pressure to keep exploring new realms, to keep "mutating." Perhaps the best advice these people can keep in mind is: yes, you'll get to experience it all, but quit trying to experience it all *at once*.

Amun, the ram-headed Egyptian god

ARIES

ARIES, *The Ram*

SIGN: *Aries, the 1st Zodiacal Sign*

MODE: *Cardinal* ✣ ELEMENT: *Fire* ✣ RULER: *Mars*

ADDITIONAL MYTHIC ARCHETYPES: *Athene* ✣ *Phrixus and Helle* ✣ *Jason* ✣ *Luke Skywalker*

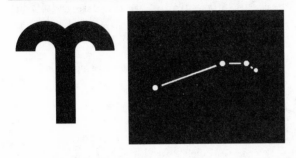

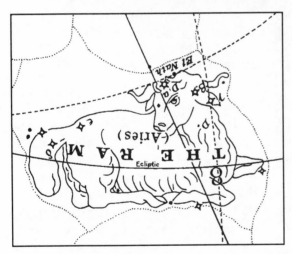

The earliest lists of zodiacal constellations come from Babylon. One may search in vain for any mention of Aries in these early zodiacs, for the sign with which we now begin the astrological year was unknown to the Babylonians. In its place stood a constellation they called the Hireling and which symbolized a farm worker or other manual laborer. It is to the Egyptians that we owe the sign of Aries, although in the beginning it was called the sheep as often as the ram.[1]

The *rising* of a particular sign is linked, in the minds of modern astrologers, with the *heliacal* rising, which means "rising with the sun." This, of course, always occurs at sunrise. But in ancient Egypt, it was the *evening* rising which was deemed of greatest importance. The evening rising of Aries would, of course, have occurred during the month of Libra. This was the month of the flooding of the Nile, and the month when farmers led their flocks away from the rising waters and separated the rams from the ewes.[2] But as well as playing a role in the seasonal calendar of the Egyptians, the ram had a spiritual or religious function as well, for it was sacred to Amon-Ra, who was associated with the Sun. And the Sun is said to be exalted—i.e., to reach its peak of power and effectiveness—in Aries. One of Christianity's most celebrated events is Easter, which honors the resurrection of the soul after death, the ultimate victory of the spirit over the body. It is always celebrated on the first Sunday following the first full moon of the spring season.[3] In recognizing that the astrological wheel and the seasonal year begin at this time with Aries, which represents new life, birth, and beginnings, we see a natural harmony in celebrating this event at this time of year. Among the twelve Olympian gods, Aries fell under the protection of Athene, for several reasons. Athene was the patroness of the art of weaving, and the ram or sheep gave abundant wool, the material of weaving *par excellence*. More importantly, Athene was born full-grown from the *head* of her father Zeus (Jupiter), and Aries rules the head in medical astrology. This focus on the head denotes a very mental or intellectual emphasis, whether linked with Athene, the goddess of wisdom, or with the sign Aries.[4] We do not ordinarily think of Aries as an exceptionally mental sign, but when Mercury, Uranus, or the asteroid Pallas Athene are placed in Aries in a horoscope, there is usually a powerful, perhaps overbearing intellect.

An early twentieth-century Italian illustration of Athene

The Aries intellect is purposeful and volatile as well, and this relates to the rulership of Mars. Among the planets it is Mars, the god of war, which rules Aries. (The Greek name for Mars was, of course, Ares, but this word is quite unrelated to the word Aries, signifying ram.) It is from the rulership of Mars that Aries acquires much of its reputation for aggressiveness.

Much, but not all. For the essential meaning of the sign is embodied in its position in the yearly cycle. On the vernal equinox or first day of spring, the days and nights are of equal length. In Rudhyar's terminology, this means that the power of the individual (Dayforce) and the power of the collective (Nightforce) are equal as well. Why, then, do we think of Aries as an essentially individualistic, perhaps even egotistical sign? Because at the vernal equinox it is the Dayforce of individuality which is growing stronger, for the days are getting longer. Thus Aries represents the power of the individual ego *emerging* from the collective ocean. Aries must fight against the pull of that collective past in order to assert its individuality. Like a newborn child, it shouts to announce its arrival in the world.[5] The full force of the Martian spirit is employed in the battle to *be*. This is why Aries is always at the beginning of things—just like a child. Everything is perpetually new.

It is no wonder that Aries is the archetype of the pioneer, the explorer of new lands. Nowhere is this pioneering or adventuring aspect of Aries better expressed than in the myth of the Golden Fleece, the tale which the Greeks associated, beyond all others, with the sign Aries.

Mars, ruler of Aries

The story begins with Phrixus and Helle, the children of King Athamas. Phrixus and Helle were about to be sacrificed on a mountaintop by their father to appease the gods. However, it was not the gods who demanded the sacrifice of these young children, but rather their stepmother, so that her own children would be heirs to the throne. As they were about to be killed, a winged ram with a golden fleece (one of Zeus' totems) magically appeared, told them to quickly jump on his back, and they began to fly to a distant land called Colchis, safe from the wrath of their parents. Helle, the girl, lost her hold and fell into the sea, but Phrixus safely arrived in Colchis and sacrificed the ram to Zeus. The magical golden fleece of the ram was given to the King of Colchis for safekeeping. This part of the story may have had its origins in the spring equinox custom of the annual sacrifice of the king or the king's son, who would dress in a ram's fleece. The celebration took place in April when Aries was conjunct the vernal point. Later a ram was substituted for the man.[6]

The task of recovering the fleece and bringing it home from Colchis, which lay at the far edge of the Black Sea in the Caucasus Mountains, fell to Jason. The son of a king whose throne had been usurped, Jason had been raised in seclusion in the wilderness, brought up by the wise centaur Chiron.

When Jason emerged from the mountains into the world below, the usurper of the throne, Pelias, felt threatened by his very existence and thus sent Jason upon a seemingly impossible quest. Jason, who possessed the true Arien gift for leadership, was able to gather together all the heroes of ancient Greece and enlist their aid to build a ship called the Argo. Leading this able-bodied crew, Jason set sail for Colchis. Encountering many dangerous adventures along the way, he and his many companions ultimately reached their destination. However, it was only with the help of Medea, daughter of the King of Colchis, that he was finally able to capture the fleece. Thus Jason sailed home in triumph, having become the hero—a role

Phrixus and Helle

which all Ariens strive to play. Once home, however, he abandoned his wife Medea and, tiring of the old in typical Aries fashion, set his sights on new adventures, including a new woman. Medea, perhaps a Scorpio archetype, was a powerful sorceress, and not at all amused by this turn of events. Eventually, in a fit of rage, she murdered Jason's new bride and her own children by Jason.

It is clear from the myth that Jason embodies the Arien archetype of the pioneer, the explorer, the adventurer. But there are other, more meaningful levels at work. As Liz Greene has pointed out, there are two negative father figures in the story, the usurper Pelias and the evil King of Colchis; and it is one of these father figures, the usurper, who sends Jason on his quest.[7] The negative father image appears again and again in the lives of Aries people, whether male or female. Often the personal restlessness and willful activity of the Aries type can be understood as a quest to throw off the father's yoke. This can never be accomplished simply by cursing the father and turning one's back. The Arien, like Luke Skywalker in the *Star Wars* films, must look behind the dark mask of Darth Vader to see the fragile human being underneath—the father whose inner wound has torn a gap in his own soul and the soul of the child.

Note also that Jason's chosen bride turns out to be a "dangerous sorceress." The archetype of the sorceress often appears as an image of the "woman within," the *anima* or feminine component of a man's soul. The myth of Tristan and Iseult is a good example, for Iseult is the daughter of a sorceress. The passion of a Jason or a Tristan for such a "dangerous" female figure shows that these heroic men have not recognized their own feminine sides; their feminine nature has become hidden, hence dangerous. And indeed, Arien men do seem to have difficulty recognizing and honoring the eternal feminine. Obsessed with outward achievement, they fail to see "the woman within," and, consequently, they have a hard time relating to women in their lives. Venus in Aries, for instance, often appears in the charts of men who fall in love with women simply because they're beautiful. These Venus in Aries types seldom take the time or trouble to know the real person behind the bewitching mask.

But what of the Aries woman? She, too, is likely to be fueled by issues involving the father, for her father is likely to have suffered some deep and abiding wound. Her archetypal pattern is more often than not modeled after Athene, the father's daughter, and her battle is often with the mother. Because she perceives women as weak and vulnerable and respects the authority and power given to men, she can easily lose touch with her own femininity and become the warlike Amazon ruled by Mars in her search for power, money, or authority. In this context we might remember that the Golden Fleece was sacred to Zeus, and that the goddess Athene sprang full-grown from his head. Athene, as we have seen, was associated with the sign Aries in early times. Athene defends the cosmic law of her father Zeus—just as Arien women, in their quest to succeed in the outer world, are likely to buy into the values of our masculine society. As we have remarked, though, most Athene types are not Amazons, but many Amazons are Athenes. The same may be said of women who possess an abundance of the Arien archetype, and for whom the masculine role models they have observed will stimulate their desire for action, achievement, and heroism far more than the underplayed, often victimized roles that women have

The building of the Argo, the ship that would take Jason and his Argonauts in search of the Golden Fleece

been forced into since the patriarchal system began. Times do change, however. In classical times Athene defended the patriarchy, but today we often observe Athene women using their inexhaustible Arien energy supply empowering themselves and the feminine movement in general.

Two Arien women come to mind in analyzing this dynamic—feminist Gloria Steinem, with Sun, Mars, and Uranus in Aries (and Pallas Athene close by, although in Pisces), and Anita Bryant, with Sun, Jupiter, and Juno in Aries. Both women began their careers portraying an idealized feminine goddess image— Steinem worked as a Playboy Bunny and Bryant a beauty contest winner, a Miss America contender. Steinem's short-lived career as a "bunny" was instituted as a research project to experience first-hand the sexual harassment and victimization women are subjected to in such a role. Her four planets in Aries endowed her with the strength, courage, and leadership to fight for women's rights and to bring to public attention unjust laws regarding women. She inspired millions of women to stand up for themselves, their values, and their families. Bryant, on the other hand, used her public voice to decry "unfeminine" women, including "feminine" men. Anti-gay and anti-feminist, Bryant maintained that a woman's place is beside her man. Here we see two Aries women powerfully influenced by the patriarchy—and who expressed that influence through opposite polarities.

Three of our Aries characters (Athene, Jason, and Mars) are brave and fearless warriors. All three of these figures have strong masculine role models or fathers. Phrixus, another Aries character, not only has an overbearing father who is willing to let him die, but a wicked stepmother at the heart of it all. It is not uncommon for Aries to deal with strong parental figures or older siblings in their developmental years. These figures help to shape the Aries character, for if Aries is bold and assertive on its own, a domineering parent or an interfering family member encour- ages even more assertion—and often becomes the dragon that Aries must slay.

Aries is about emergence and assertion of the individual ego, and often that includes doing battle with anyone who stands in the way of attaining that goal. Even in childhood, Athene and Mars did battle with whoever would accept their challenge or seemed to threaten their personal authority or autonomy. We find with many Ariens the need to do battle, even when there is no real threat. But often these battles, for Aries, represent something more than simply looking for a fight. Observe small children playing together who boldly display their untamed, if yet undeveloped, assertions of personal power. Often there is a playfulness, a desire for a sparring partner (as we will also see in Gemini) that gives fuel to Aries' fire. Ariens live their lives looking for drama, adventure and, most of all, fresh begin- nings. The cardinal and fiery nature of Aries gives very little rest to these individu- als. They are in constant motion, and when their lives get too quiet, or things start running too smoothly, they are ready, like Mars, for a battlefield or, like Jason, for a hero's quest.

The characters in the Aries myths seem to possess a highly developed relation- ship with the physical vehicle, and it is true that Ariens feel best when vigorously

A ram, symbol of the sign Aries, from Edward Topsell's The History of
Four-footed Beasts and Serpents, *1607*

exercising their physical bodies. But, as previously noted, some Ariens, like Athene, channel their ceaseless energy into their intellect and display an incredible wisdom and strategy which revolves around ground-breaking areas of new thought. Pioneers of the intellect and spirit such as Ariens Dane Rudhyar and Joseph Campbell are two such examples: their vigorous, untiring energy and passions were poured into their work. Other Ariens like Jason pour their passions into causes, and these individuals are able, like young Jason, to enlist the aid of important people in carrying out their work. We have noted that Aries rules the head in medical astrology, and Ariens are just as likely to be mental over-achievers (again like Athene) as they are to suffer from headaches and Mars-influenced fevers.

The association of Aries with the head in medical astrology reflects its two rulers, Mars and Athene. When a prophecy was made to Zeus that a child born from his union with Metis would one day supplant him, he quickly decided to put an end to Metis and her pregnant child, and therefore swallowed them both. One day he was consumed by a raging headache so great that he asked Hephaestus, the smith god, to use his hammer and split open his head. At that instant, out popped Pallas Athene, fully grown, dressed in armor, helmet, and sword. (Thus, Hephaestus became the midwife for Athene). Such headaches occur for people who are about to give birth to some enormous idea, event, person, or experience in their life. The creativity may be swelling inside of them, bursting at the seams, and they may have no apparent way to release it.

The other kind of headache is reflective of Mars, the warrior. As ruler of Aries, Mars possesses a fearless, courageous, and aggressive nature, always ready to do battle. The negative expression of Mars, therefore, can be related to fearfulness, lack of courage and non-assertive behavior, but more importantly, to his raging temper. Mars was possessed of much anger and a bad temper, which totally displeased his father. We are told as children that it is improper to show anger or display bad tempers. When enough bad tempers have no outlet for release, we rage with headaches.

The craftsmanship aspect of Athene's weaving skills often figures prominently in the Aries' life. Competitive, yes — she delighted in contests, and of course in winning. But that, too, spurs Aries forward. There are many Ariens who are similarly delighted by exercising their creative skill and craftsmanship. This will be especially true of those who have Venus, Ceres, Pallas, or the Moon in Aries.

Planets in Aries in a horoscope will typically express themselves by leading rather than following. They are individuals first, true unto themselves. This is especially true of an individual with Sun, Moon, or Ascendant in Aries. These individuals will be very personally connected to their own process of development, their impulse to let nothing stand in the way of attaining self-knowledge or personal fulfillment. Those with the Sun in Aries are particularly focused on expressing their "beingness" in its purest form. Moon in Aries people need always to be emotionally stimulated, which may result in constantly changing relationships or activities. Additionally, the excitement of new creation gets them out of their heads and makes them feel alive. Sun and Moon in Aries alike may favor driving at high speeds with the car radio blasting, or, better still, playing drums or rock and roll. Mercury in Aries fuels the competitive spirit; these people may feel intellectually superior and lead in reading or writing skills. At its worst, Mercury in Aries or the First House (or negatively related to Mars or Pallas Athene) can result in sibling rivalry such as

Ram-headed statues at the Temple of Karnak, Luxor, Egypt. Photograph by Diane Smirnow

both Hermes and Ares experienced with their elder siblings, Apollo and Athene, who were highly favored by father Zeus. It may also induce the continual motivation to try and outwit these siblings (or anyone in life that represents them), to demonstrate one-upmanship and strike back at anyone who has incurred the notorious Martian jealousy.

Venus in Aries provides a Venus-Mars interplay which can obviously enhance one's love nature, and anything from writing erotic poetry to engaging in numerous affairs can dominate one's attention. These people may hunger for fulfillment from their mates, yet be essentially unsatisfied due to their need to seek some new adventure lurking over the horizon. Mars in its own sign or house expresses itself through leadership in sports, battles, body-building or sexual conquests.

Ceres in Aries functions as an independent agent, favoring exploration and new adventures. There is not much emotional bonding with the mother or with women; instead, there may be competition with her and with others who seem to represent her. Pallas Athene would seem to be exalted in Aries, based on her association with this sign, and hence to embody the full range of her strategy, intellectual, and artistic skills. Juno in Aries may be very independent in relationships, but strongly desirous of a partner anyway. Vesta, whose spiritual qualities enhance any sign, may seem to be somewhat of a loner in Aries, perhaps self-conscious and awkward in social situations, but very singularly focused on personal inner development and sexually permissive when pursuing intimate relationships.

Jupiter in Aries or the First House may produce a strong leader, especially of a political or religious nature, who will be able to shape society's laws or influence the way in which they are carried out. Saturn is in its "fall" in Aries, which can make this a very difficult placement. These people may take longer to realize their ultimate goals, and their difficulties are often blamed on society (or father) who seem to be continually blocking or thwarting their efforts. At their best, however, these people possess a leadership ability similar to that of Jupiter in Aries, and may also become the master craftsmen, builders and architects of the world once they see how truly talented they can be.

The outer planets, Uranus, Neptune and Pluto, work on a collective rather than an individual level. In other words, Uranus in Aries is not so much a personal characteristic as it is one that influences the whole group of people born in the seven-year period during which Uranus transits the sign Aries. The last occurrence of this transit was in 1928-35, when powerful leaders such as Stalin, Hitler, Mussolini, and Franco arose. Hitler's following, in fact, supported his idea of a pure "Aryan" race. All were tormented souls, but powerful charismatic leaders whose love of battle and showmanship eventually resulted in their downfall. Groundbreaking technologies also occurred during this period—ideas whose time had come, including the New Deal, Roosevelt's answer to the financial crisis wrought by the Depression. These outer planets may still have an Arien tone in the charts of individuals, however, if they happen to occupy the First House or make strong aspects to Mars or Athene.

Chiron, the wounded healer, is likely to apply much of his learning to self-study and healing when in the First House, and may also be fond of the teacher-student relationship that Chiron developed with Jason and others. Uranus in this pioneering house can exhibit brilliance both mentally and physically, as one's entire system is imbued with the catalyzing force of creation. These people can be highly individualistic, going against the grain of the system and setting up their own rules. For Neptune, this is a difficult position; its watery, ego-dissolving nature works against the fiery Martian ("I AM") spirit of Aries and the First House, creating a steamy and troubled emotional environment. The Martian capacity for action may seem to be weakened, though *reaction* is strong. People with this placement may find great success when they carefully and deliberately examine the deeper feelings that lie at the root of their emotions and set to work understanding them. Depression is also common with this aspect, as depression is often the result of repressed anger. Spiritual or artistic leadership is, however, highly possible with this combination. Pluto in the First House or Aries stresses the archetypal connection between Mars and Pluto (Nergal's conquest of the underworld). This position can intensify one's passions as they pertain to both fighting and sexuality. It can also serve as a powerful force in releasing one's inner demons, and shows up strongly among both psychologists and their patients.

Aries is the *first* sign on the zodiacal wheel, and while there is no real beginning or end to a circle, its function is symbolized as the *first* in human evolution. Emerging from the stars and returning to the stars is an important theme in Aries. We come into Aries from Pisces, the primordial womb of the cosmos, and in the quest for the Golden Fleece or the gold that the alchemists sought, we come into communion with our own divinity. In Aries we discover that our battles force us to deal with the world of externals, but in the end bring us closer to an understanding of ourselves and the gift of consciousness with which we have been endowed.

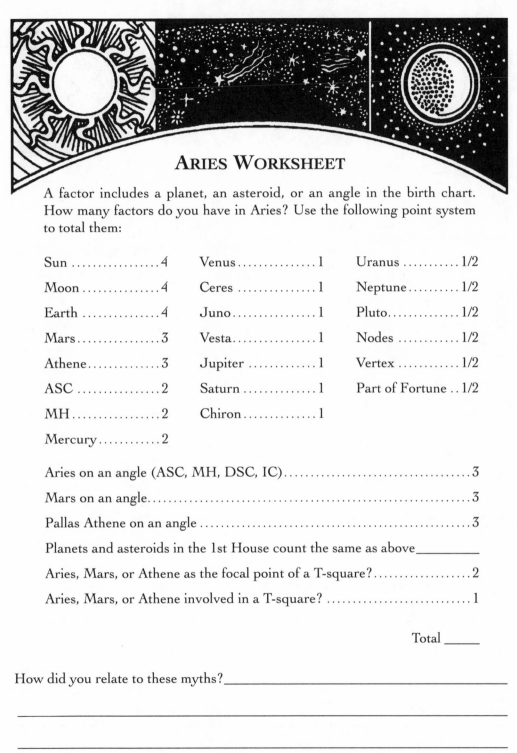

ARIES WORKSHEET

A factor includes a planet, an asteroid, or an angle in the birth chart. How many factors do you have in Aries? Use the following point system to total them:

Sun 4	Venus 1	Uranus 1/2
Moon 4	Ceres 1	Neptune 1/2
Earth 4	Juno 1	Pluto 1/2
Mars 3	Vesta 1	Nodes 1/2
Athene 3	Jupiter 1	Vertex 1/2
ASC 2	Saturn 1	Part of Fortune . . 1/2
MH 2	Chiron 1	
Mercury 2		

Aries on an angle (ASC, MH, DSC, IC) 3

Mars on an angle 3

Pallas Athene on an angle 3

Planets and asteroids in the 1st House count the same as above_____

Aries, Mars, or Athene as the focal point of a T-square? 2

Aries, Mars, or Athene involved in a T-square? 1

Total _____

How did you relate to these myths?_____

_____

_____

_____

What house does Aries occupy in your chart?

_____

10th   House — mother   1st   House — self

4th   House — father   11th   House — friends

7th   House — mate   5th   House — children, lovers

3rd   House — sibling

Keeping in mind that these houses represent these relationships, how has Aries energy expressed itself through others in your life? _____

_____

_____

_____

What house does Mars occupy and how is it expressed? _____

_____

_____

What house does Pallas Athene occupy and how is it expressed? _____

_____

_____

Insights: _____

_____

_____

_____

TAURUS

TAURUS, *The Bull*

SIGN: *Taurus, the 2nd Zodiacal Sign*

MODE: *Fixed* ❧ ELEMENT: *Earth* ❧ RULER: *Venus*

ADDITIONAL MYTHIC ARCHETYPES: *The Moon and all Moon Goddesses* ❧ *Europa* ❧ *King Minos and the Minotaur* ❧ *Ishtar* ❧ *Ariadne and Theseus* ❧ *Pasiphae* ❧ *Dionysus (Bacchus)* ❧ *King Midas* ❧ *Daedalus* ❧ *Hephaestus (Vulcan)*

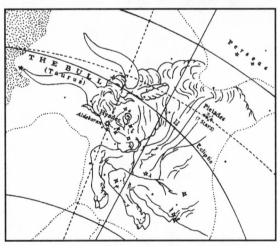

Like Aries, Taurus was important in the Egyptian seasonal calendar. It was during the evening rising of Taurus (i.e., during the month of Scorpio) that cattle were coupled and oxen yoked for plowing. More importantly, however, Taurus was once the beginning of the zodiac, and Aries rather than Pisces the final sign. The star Aldebaran, in the middle of Taurus, was called "the bull's eye," and was instrumental in fixing the starting point of the zodiacal circle.[1]

This indicates that the zodiac, and perhaps astrology itself, went through its formative period when the vernal equinox was in Taurus. This era, which we call the Age of Taurus, extended from about 4,000 to 2,000 BC. It was during this period that Sumerian and Egyptian civilization began to take shape in the Near East; during this period, also, that the Minoan Civilization of Crete reached its first peak and Stonehenge was being built in England. The Taurean Age has been characterized as a matriarchal era in which the worship of the bull was paramount, but this is an oversimplification. The matriarchal period of Western Civilization had its origins much earlier (in the Age of Cancer, not surprisingly), but by the Age of Taurus the simple farming villages of the Cancerian Age (8,000 BC) had been transformed into the sophisticated civilizations mentioned above. The glyph or symbol that astrologers use to denote Taurus is a bull's head with the horns prominently displayed. The bull's horns were analogous to the crescent moon, and represented the principle of growth and generation.[2] (Both Taurus and the Moon are associated with that principle to this very day.) Since the Great Goddess was the source of all growth, all generation, the fertile bull was imaged as her consort, the male principle necessary for the cycle of birth and growth to continue.[3] Goddess, moon, and bull—these were inseparable symbols of the seasonal round. It is no wonder that the month of Taurus falls during the most abundant and fertile period of spring. And though we now think of Taurus as ruling the neck or throat in medical astrology, the ancient Egyptians linked that sign with the genitals.[4] It was not the bull *per se* that was worshipped during the Age of Taurus, but the eternal round of the seasons, the cycle of growth inherent in nature and in humankind.

All over Crete one finds stone images of the bull's horns, called *bucrania*. Cult statues and figurines from the Balkans have been discovered which combine the symbols of the bull and the waxing moon in a way which leaves no doubt as to the identity of the two concepts. These items date from about 4,000 BC, and were created by the farming peoples of the neolithic era.[5] The moon, of course, is the Great Goddess, in her waxing phase associated with fertility and growth. Folk wisdom still tells us that it is better to plant during a waxing moon, and any good magician knows that spells for abundance and increase should always be performed during a

The "Horns of Consecration" from the Palace at Knossos, Crete. Photograph by Ariel Guttman

Egyptian sacred bull, illustrated by Diane Smirnow

waxing moon. Taurus, therefore, is associated with the Moon just as much as with Venus, its planetary ruler. In astrological tradition, the Moon is said to be exalted in Taurus; this tradition is part of a mythologem which extends all the way back to the neolithic.

The exaltation of the Moon in Taurus, however, has another significance. In Hindu tradition, the Moon is said to be exalted precisely on the degree of the Pleiades—which, in our present-day tropical zodiac, is located at 29 degrees Taurus. To the Hindus, the Pleiades were the wives of the seven celestial wise men, who were themselves the stars of the Big Dipper. The Pleiades are famed in Hindu myth for nurturing the war-god Mars when he was a child. In Greek myth, the Pleiades are the daughters of the Titan Atlas, who carries the world on his back. All these myths affirm the Taurean (or lunar) qualities of nurturing or sustaining.

Taurus was ruled by Venus (Aphrodite) in the Olympian system, and it maintained that rulership when the planetary deities were assigned their zodiacal signs. The mythic link between the love goddess and the bull is very ancient indeed. The Babylonian *Epic of Gilgamesh*—which probably had its origins in Sumer—tells how

Europa abducted by Zeus in the form of a bull, illustrated by Diane Smirnow after the early fifth century BC painting from the Archeological Museum, Tarquinia

Ishtar, goddess of love and battle, sent a bull against Gilgamesh, who, as a champion of the patriarchal order, was the enemy of the Great Goddess.[6] Greek myth also links the Great Goddess with the bull. One of the most famous of Zeus' love affairs was his abduction of the maiden Europa, daughter of the King of Phoenicia. In the shape of a bull, Zeus carried Europa across the Mediterranean to the island of Crete, where he mated with her and fathered the Cretan royal house. Since the word "Europe" derives from Europa, it is clear that Europa is the goddess mother of the peoples of Europe, borne out of Asia on the back of her sacred animal, the great bull. It is also significant that Zeus and Europa came to land on Crete, for Crete appears to have been a predominantly matriarchal society where the Great Goddess was worshipped as the supreme deity.[7] The frescoes from the Cretan palace of Knossos depict women who are lively, smiling, bare-breasted. Their arms entwined with snakes, they often give the impression of being priestesses. The worship of the bull, as we have seen, was also highly developed on Crete. (The two animals indicated, the serpent and the bull, may remind us of Taurus and its opposite sign, Scorpio.)

The bull that carried Europa to Crete was not the only bull to figure in the mythology of that mysterious and important island. Even more famous is the Minotaur, the man with the head of a bull. According to myth, the god Poseidon (Neptune) brought forth a bull from the sea, and sent it to King Minos of Crete, who was told to sacrifice the bull. But Minos refused to obey the divine command; he kept the magic animal. This angered the gods. They drove Minos' wife,

The Minotaur, from a Corinthian amphora, fifth century BC

Queen Pasiphae, mad with lust. She mated with the bull of Poseidon and gave birth to a monster, half-man, half-bull, the Minotaur. Hidden in a labyrinth beneath the palace, the Minotaur was a fearsome beast who demanded human sacrifice. Unwilling captives were brought from the mainland of Greece to be offered to the Minotaur. It was one of these captives, Theseus, who gained the confidence of Minos' daughter Ariadne and enlisted her help in slaying the Minotaur. She gave him a magic thread with which to chart his way through the labyrinth. Theseus descended into the darkness, found the Minotaur, and killed him. In her well-known novel, *The King Must Die*, Mary Renault linked the story of Theseus and Ariadne with the ancient Cretan sport of bull-leaping, in which young men and women literally somersaulted over the backs of bulls in the arena.[8] She also associated this myth with the take-over of the old Cretan civilization by patriarchal Mycenaean Greeks—a surmise which is well supported by archaeology.

In all of these stories, the bull is linked with a female figure, and we may suspect that in every case this female figure was once the Great Goddess. Ishtar, mistress of the bull who fought Gilgamesh, was the Babylonian equivalent of Venus, the ruler of Taurus. Europa was the eponymous mother of her people. The name "Ariadne" means "the pure one."[9] She too is another incarnation of the goddess of all things, and it is likely that even the unfortunate Pasiphae was, in some earlier myth, the Great Goddess.[10] The goddess, of course, has many aspects: she is mother, wife, lover, witch, wise old crone, and medium. But in the case of Taurus, she is primarily the goddess of growth, fertility, and sex, as is fitting for a sign which occurs during the springtime, when all things are in their most abundant state of growth.

"Sustaining" is the principle with which Taurus is strongly connected. Astrology considers Taurus, the sign of fixed earth, to be the most fertile, fruitful, and constant sign. While some might complain of Taurus' slowness to act or its intolerable stub-bornness, Taurus, like the bull, steadies and roots itself in one place until ready to move. Then, as if a red flag were waved in its path, it becomes a locomotive. But this process occurs for Taurus only when it is ready, not necessarily when everyone else expects it to be so. This makes the Taurean temperament unique; its fixed, sustain-ing power from within likens it to the archetypal feminine principle of the Goddess.

Modern astrology equates Taurus with fixity, fertility, fruitfulness, and securi-ty—all energies that relate in some way to things that grow in the earth. While not every Taurus is a gardener, it is true that their lives closely parallel the cycles of nature. In the Taurean's spring cycle, it is important which seeds are planted, as well as making sure that the right thing is planted at the right time. One cannot plant flowers in the dead of winter. The seedlings must be watered properly and given the right amount of light, food, and nurturing. Such tasks are required of Taureans, and during this spring cycle their proficiency at sustaining the young plant, waiting, and watching its growth patiently, is more important than the expec-tation of instant results. The summer cycle is associated with an ease of existence which many Taureans try to extend beyond its normal time frame—that of sitting back and basking in the richness of the beauty around them, observing the vibrancy of color and the abundance with which nature has rewarded them for their careful planting and nurturing. They pluck the delicious fruit surrounding them. But this too must pass, and with the approach of autumn comes harvesting and storing for the winter, as well as marketing the richness of what they have grown. Meanwhile, they prepare for the cycle of growth to wane. During these times, Taureans must build their stores for the winter that is surely approaching, carefully pre-serving their wealth and allocating its distribution wisely in anticipation of the cold ahead. During the winter they may not be actively bringing in new capital, but they are inwardly focused on the barrenness of the trees which require pruning, the soil resting beneath the ice. In time they will emerge again with spring.

Theseus and the Minotaur

When Taurus lives its life in accordance with the four seasons, it lives in harmony with its nature. Because Taurus is a fixed sign and doesn't always flow easily with the tides of the changing seasons, it often gets stuck in life. To be intolerant because fruit is not blooming in winter will not make fruit appear at that time of year. Patience and the inner knowledge that "to everything there is a season" is Taurus' greatest gift, and the Taurean ability to either fill up or let go when necessary is an equally valuable asset.

While planetary rulerships are used in astrology to link a planet with a sign, they are by no means carved in granite, and there are many mythological figures which can be associated with this sign; indeed, Taurus has a richness of mythic associations which is unsurpassed in the zodiac. The ruler of Taurus is

Butting bull on a bronze litra of the Campanian Mercenaries in Sicily, 344–336 BC. From the Michael A. Sikora collection

Venus because of Venus' association with love and fertility, and the worship of the Great Goddess during the Taurean epoch. Venus relates to the artistic abilities with which so many Taureans are gifted. Astrologers are so fond of characterizing Taureans as plodding and materialistic that they often forget to note the artistic achievements of this sign, especially noteworthy in the field of music and specifically in singing. (Taurus rules the throat, and many opera singers have a Taurus Sun or Ascendant.) Shakespeare was a Taurus, and no writer in any language glorified nature more than he did—every tree, bush, bird, animal, and weather pattern of the English countryside is lovingly described in his plays. As the love goddess, Venus can embody many different aspects of relatedness. And Gaia, the symbol for Earth, has already been discussed as a fitting Taurean archetype.

Here, in Taurus, we might also consider the two female figures in the Theseus myth: Pasiphae and Ariadne. Pasiphae was driven mad by lust, and overpowering sexual urges are just as characteristic of Taurus as they are of its opposite sign, Scorpio. Ariadne held the thread which allowed Theseus to make his way safely into the labyrinth by torchlight—a beautiful image, inasmuch as psychologist Irene Claremont de Castillejo tells us that the inner man or *animus* of many women often appears in dreams as a torchbearer.[11] Indeed, female Taureans who are strongly under the influence of Venus can make any man a torchbearer, for they have the ability to guide the man they love into a personal labyrinth where the demons are met and conquered. These Ariadne types, above all other women, are inspirers of men, awakeners of the hero within. But women who rely on their beauty or their intimate relationships to define themselves may wind up in a dilemma similar to that of Ariadne, whom Theseus cruelly abandoned on the isle of Naxos when he was finished with her. But Ariadne found a way to wholeness through spiritual and creative ecstasy, for she became the bride of Dionysus. Dionysus is himself connected with the Taurean archetype, and some astrologers hypothesize a planet called Transpluto or Bacchus (the Latin name for Dionysus), which they associate with Taurus.[12] King Midas may well symbolize some of the more extreme aspects of Taurus. He was the pleasure-loving King of Phrygia whose sole ambition in life was to attain gold. When his wish was granted, it became a curse. *Everything* he touched, including his food, clothing, and even his daughter, turned into gold.

The archetype of the master craftsman is also quintessentially Taurean. Some esoteric astrologers link Taurus with the invisible (hypothetical) planet Vulcan, named for the clever blacksmith of the gods (Greek: Hephaestus) who was the husband of Venus. Another Taurean craftsman is Daedalus, the gifted architect who built the labyrinth for King Minos of Crete—then became trapped in it, as so many Taureans become trapped in their worldly possessions or achievements. Myths have a way of mingling and merging with each other—it will be recalled that Zeus, in the form of a bull, was the progenitor of the Cretan dynasty, and that a bull-headed beast, the Minotaur, lived in the Cretan labyrinth constructed by Daedalus.

Minos himself may symbolize the father-figure whose need for control and emotional repression creates the opposite effect, i.e., chaos. A wild, emotionally untamed beast is born into Minos' family, and he is so horrified by it that he locks it in the basement. Although Taurus is often attracted to its polarity Scorpio, it is also frightened by its fierce instinctuality, and may attempt to keep it well hidden, forbidden to enter the rational, controlled, day-world Taurus typically maintains. Thus the beast remains banished to the underworld, in exchange for human sacrifice which it demands and receives. Here we can certainly observe the extremes of the Taurus/Scorpio polarity when family dysfunction becomes pathological.

Planets in Taurus operate in a very "earthy" manner. The planets' natures will either be harmonized by their attunement to the natural rhythms of the earth, or else impeded by these same cycles. The Sun may focus its attention on the physical aspects of Taurean fixed earth: stability, security, fertility, and whatever is required to achieve those aims. These people may also be gifted in creative and procreative abilities. They need to be careful, though, of parching the earth with too much solar fire (i.e., too much intensity, over-working the soil, expecting too much too soon from what they have to work with). The Moon and Earth are at their happiest here, and its natives go through their own natural rhythm of four distinct phases (the Moon each month and the Earth each season), closely resembling nature's cycles. Moon in Taurus people need to spend time in the garden, getting the dirt underneath their fingernails—or, in the absence of a garden, to experience soft, relaxed, earthly pleasures. Herbs, incense, massage, music, food and wine, or a walk in nature will do.

*King Midas of Phrygia, Apollo, and Pan, principal characters in the story of
King Midas' golden touch*

Mercury in Taurus or in the Second House can be grounded, mechanically proficient, and somewhat cautious, though its free-floating nature may be somewhat mired by earthy Taurean concerns. The link between Mercury and Taurus' ruler Venus may compensate for the drudgery by bestowing a flirtatious and/or artistic nature. Venus herself in Taurus is free to address her needs for prosperity, sex, and love quite liberally when in her own sign, and is tremendously nurturing and sustaining. Mars adds a sense of motivation and energetic application to the Taurean need for building and sustaining the future, though the parched-earth syndrome is even more of a danger here than with the Sun.

Ceres in Taurus has a need to establish material security and be a good provider. As with the lunar types, these people flourish in the garden or kitchen. Pallas Athene sometimes seems to be riding a wheelchair in Taurus. Her nature is more suited to flying free (like Mercury) through the airwaves, accessing information in a split second. In Taurus, she is expected to elucidate her concepts carefully, patiently, clearly, and in a no-nonsense way. At best, her terrific ideas and inventions could be applied to the earth itself, as when Athene suddenly produced the olive tree for the Athenians. Juno in Taurus values partnership and these people will work diligently at maintaining monogamous relationships, having difficulty letting go of them if such a need arises. Vesta in Taurus may be singularly focused on developing personal resources that are highly valued in the marketplace.

People with Jupiter in Taurus or the Second House may find that they have the natural "midas touch" but must be careful that their assets don't consume them as Midas' did. Here too, there may be a conflict between earth (Taurus) and fire (Sagittarius) and care must be taken to insure that one's vital energy or spirit is left with enough inspiration to pursue the loftier realms rather than getting stuck in producing only material goods. Daedalus is a good example of this, for he was able to build himself the tools that would allow him to escape from his material entrapments. Saturn in Taurus may work hard for whatever gains are made, but you can be sure those gains will eventually be forthcoming with Saturn's penchant for management and authority over the earthly realm. When Chiron is in the Second House, there is often a deep conflict centering around what should be valued—and if the wounded healer is very strong in the natal chart, one may discover that value in a healing or helping profession. Uranus lends Promethean fire to all issues of money or personal resources, but natives with this placement are just as likely to have an erratic employment history as they are to make their living in an unusual or exciting way.

Neptune and Pluto's behavior in Taurus may be more difficult to assess, since these slow-moving outer planets connect primarily with collective patterns of cultural significance in a certain time frame. Pluto was last in Taurus during the Victorian Era (1852–1884), and Neptune during the same period (1874–1888). We are reminded that this epoch in our own country produced the hammering in of the final iron spikes by a huge workforce of Hephaestuses to complete the transcontinental railroad, thus allowing "manifest destiny" to occur. In an individual birth chart, however, Neptune and Pluto behave along fairly definite patterns in the Second House. Those with Neptune in the Second House are often "spaced out" when it comes to financial issues—money may slip through their fingers like water because they don't really care about it. Like the Chironian types, they may find their best real-world options in the healing or helping professions. Pluto in the Second House is in its house of accidental detriment: these natives may well become self-made millionaires, but, like Midas, they may also have to pay a moral price for their wealth, especially if they have been less than honest in acquiring it.

If Taurus is strongly emphasized in your chart, it is recommended that you familiarize yourself with some of these mythic stories to better understand the energies you are working with. Most of all, remember to honor your body's natural rhythms and tune in to the Moon, for she will intuitively guide your body's soul and life's natural functions by helping you to be aware and focused on your center of gravity at all times.

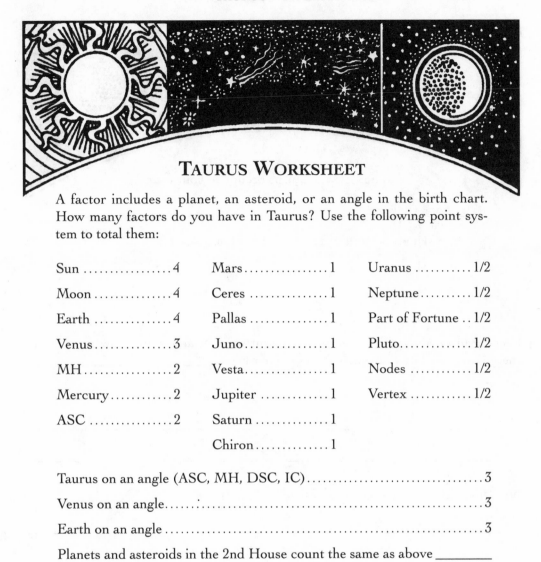

TAURUS WORKSHEET

A factor includes a planet, an asteroid, or an angle in the birth chart. How many factors do you have in Taurus? Use the following point system to total them:

Sun 4	Mars 1	Uranus 1/2
Moon 4	Ceres 1	Neptune 1/2
Earth 4	Pallas 1	Part of Fortune . . 1/2
Venus 3	Juno 1	Pluto 1/2
MH 2	Vesta 1	Nodes 1/2
Mercury 2	Jupiter 1	Vertex 1/2
ASC 2	Saturn 1	
	Chiron 1	

Taurus on an angle (ASC, MH, DSC, IC) 3

Venus on an angle . . . . . . : 3

Earth on an angle 3

Planets and asteroids in the 2nd House count the same as above _____

Taurus, Venus, or Earth as the focal point of a T-square? 2

Taurus, Venus, or Earth involved in a T-square? 1

Total _____

How did you relate to these myths? _____

_____

_____

_____

What house does Taurus occupy in your chart?

_____

10th House—mother   1st House—self

4th House—father   11th House—friends

7th House—mate   5th House—children, lovers

3rd House—sibling

Keeping in mind that these houses represent these relationships, how has Taurus
energy expressed itself through others in your life? _____

_____

_____

_____

What house does Venus occupy and how is it expressed? _____

_____

_____

What house does Earth occupy and how is it expressed? _____

_____

_____

Insights: _____

_____

_____

_____

GEMINI

GEMINI, *The Twins*

SIGN: *Gemini, the 3rd Zodiacal Sign*

MODE: *Mutable* ❧ ELEMENT: *Air* ❧ RULER: *Mercury*

ADDITIONAL MYTHIC ARCHETYPES: *Castor and Pollux*
❧ *the Ashvins (Hindu)* ❧ *Nissyen and Evnissyen (Celtic)*
❧ *Helen and Clytaemnestra (the twin girls)* ❧ *Peter Pan*
❧ *Hermes (Mercury)*

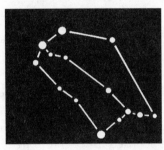

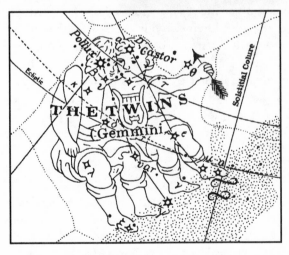

The constellation of Gemini is easily distinguished, for it consists of two stars, side by side, seemingly of equal magnitude. If one looks more closely, however, it becomes apparent that one star is a little bit brighter than the other. This is as it should be, for one of the mythological twins called the Gemini was a son of Zeus, while the other was purely mortal. Zeus came to Leda, the wife of King Tyndareus of Sparta, disguised as a swan. Because she was the most beautiful of women, he seduced her by the banks of a river. Leda gave birth to two sets of twins, one male and one female. Castor and Pollux were the male set of twins, Helen and Clytaemnestra the female. Castor and Clytaemnestra were the children of King Tyndareus, while Pollux and Helen were demigods, children of Zeus. The Gemini Twins, therefore, are more properly part of a quaternity, a fourfold symbol of wholeness which includes male and female, human and divine elements.[1]

Castor and Pollux were inseparable, and, indeed, they are always seen together in the myths; there is little differentiation between them. Castor was renowned for his prowess at horsemanship and chariot-driving; Pollux was the most famous of boxers. The Spartan Games were held in their honor. Curiously enough, the Twins were also the patron deities of sailors, and whenever St. Elmo's Fire was seen casting its eerie glow atop the mainmast, the Greek sailors believed that they had received a visitation from the Twins.[2] Castor and Pollux took part in many of the heroic adventures of Greek mythology, most notably the voyage of Jason and the Argonauts (see Aries).

Castor, the mortal brother, was slain during a war with two other semi-divine twins, Idas and Lynceus. Pollux, mourning, begged Zeus that he not be allowed to outlive his brother. As a son of Zeus, however, Pollux was immortal, and could not die. Hence he ascended into heaven, where he was placed among the constellations along with his brother Castor (it is Pollux, the immortal twin, who is the slightly brighter star). Because of Castor's mortality, it was ordained that the Twins must spend half their time in the underworld as well as in heaven; this, of course, would correspond to the periods when the constellation of Gemini was visible (heaven) or hidden (the underworld).[3]

The Divine Twins are not merely a feature of Greek mythology; they appear wherever the Indo-European languages are spoken. In India they were called the Ashvins, which means "the horsemen." (A constellation is named for them, though not the same one familiar to us.) The Ashvins were the sons of Surya, the sun god; as well as being horsemen, they were also powerful healers.[4] Their connection with horses leads us back to a time before recorded history, for one of the most ancient of Vedic rituals was the *ashvamedha*, or horse sacrifice. This ritual was linked with the myth of the Ashvin twins, indicating that the Divine Twins were worshipped at a very early date; they may well have been the patrons of the common people, the keepers of cattle and horses, the craftsmen and tradespeople of the ancient Indo-European world.[5] This connection with the skilled trades is a part of the Gemini archetype to this very day, for this is the sign of versatility and dexterity *par excellence*, and in medical astrology Gemini rules the hands, those twin instruments of skill and manual accomplishment. We no longer regard the sign as having anything to do with horsemanship, for that archetype is now associated with Gemini's opposite sign, Sagittarius. It is worth remarking, however, that Gemini types often have a love for complicated sports cars as well as the mechanical skills necessary to take care of them. The automobile is the modern equivalent of the horse, and is generally related to the Third House of a horoscope, which is Gemini's natural home. In fact, Gemini and the Third House often refer to all kinds of transportation, but especially short journeys, those that the ancients could make within a few days on horseback and the type the modern world generally makes by auto.

The Dioscuri (Castor and Pollux)

Modern-day Gemini does not retain any strong association as regards healing, which was obviously important in the Hindu myth of the Divine Twins, but the association was still present in Greece. Two well-known Greek gods were Apollo (the Sun) and Hermes (Mercury, our modern ruler of Gemini). In the Olympian rulerships Gemini was linked with Apollo rather than Mercury, and Apollo was the god of healing (see Sun).[6] Even more important is the fact that Apollo is the *brother* of Hermes, and it is Hermes who carries the caduceus, a staff with two serpents intertwined, which is the modern symbol of healing. Apollo also possessed numerous "scientific" skills as well, and this much at least reminds us of Gemini as we know it. Perhaps even more to the point, Apollo was a sun god, and in Vedic India the Divine Twins were sons of the sun.

Today we think of Gemini primarily as a sign of intellect and of duality. The symbolism of the intellect, of course, is derived from its ruling planet, Mercury. The duality of Gemini has to do with the fact that this is a double sign (i.e., twins). Hence it often represents the conflict between the ego and the shadow in any given personality. The ego strives always to take the conscious path, whether founded in the individual will or in the mores of society at large. The shadow, our hidden side, represents all the values we have repressed or refused to acknowledge as our own—values which can be either feral and violent, or spiritual and transcendent, depending upon the value system we have used to shape the conscious ego. The shadow side is always creeping out of darkness and into light in the Gemini-type personality; this is why we think of them as changeable, inconsistent, and potentially treacherous.[7]

Though the myth of Castor and Pollux gives us little information in regards to this duality of shadow and self, the feminine manifestation of the myth is much clearer. As we have remarked, the Gemini Twins were part of a fourfold quaternity—they possess a feminine reflection in the twins Helen and Clytaemnestra. Helen, daughter of Zeus and Leda, is beautiful and passive—she never steps outside the bounds of normal behavior, even when her lack of inner power and resolution triggers the Trojan War. Her more human sister, Clytaemnestra, is possessed of a darker energy—she murders her husband, King Agamemnon, upon his return from the Trojan War. But if she is darker and more violent in temperament, she is also filled with a stronger will. The duality of the two sisters is only too apparent— Helen is "godly" but passive, Clytaemnestra strong but motivated only by her passions and desires. Separately, they can only produce destruction, whether through action or the lack of it. It is only when will is united with spirituality that positive directed action can take place.

The Geminian duality is seen even more clearly in the story of the twins Nissyen and Evnissyen from the Welsh epic *The Mabinogion*.[8] While Nissyen is the eternal peacemaker, Evnissyen touches off a war by brutally maiming the horses of the King of Ireland (this violent scene, so suggestive of the Vedic horse sacrifice, was given a harrowing modern interpretation in Peter Shaffer's play, *Equus*). When the war with Ireland causes destruction to the people of Wales, a remorseful

*A nineteenth-century engraving of the abduction of Helen by Paris, the Trojan Prince,
after the original painting*

Evnissyen brings the victory back to the Welsh by sacrificing himself, leaping into the cauldron of rebirth.

The twin girls, Helen and Clytemnaestra, can also be thought of as the *anima* or feminine nature of their twin brothers, Castor and Pollux. We are inclined to associate Gemini only with the twin boys, while the girls have been virtually ignored, but, as mentioned previously, they are one complete set, and when all four parts are integrated Gemini achieves wholeness. Most likely the reference to boys is due to the fact that Gemini is a masculine, airy sign linked with Jung's thinking type. In classical art, the Gemini Twins are most often portrayed as young children, and the curiosity of the youthful mind is sometimes reckless and intrusive, similar to the behavior displayed by adolescent boys. In any case, most astrological references to Gemini will describe the sign as androgynous, possessing neither male nor female characteristics in abundance. It is true with many Geminis that even as they age, their body frames and personalities reflect youthful, asexual characteristics. Obviously, there are exceptions to this—Marilyn Monroe being one—but for the most part Geminis are best described as *puers* and *puellas*. The *puer aeternus* complex that Jung and Marie Louise von Franz defined literally translates as "eternal youth."[9] The *puer* (male) or *puella* (female) manifestation of this longing to be Peter Pan is noticeable in a few astrological signs, but most strongly in Gemini and its ruling planet Mercury (see Mercury). This is due to the restless, roaming nature of the mind, seeking always to explore uncharted areas and to be constantly stimulated. It is death for a Gemini to grow old, or for a mind to cease its inquiry. And Marilyn Monroe, one of our most famous *puellas*, chose death over the reality of aging.

The third sign of the zodiac is the first of the human signs (i.e., Castor and Pollux). It is the first of the air signs, the realm of mental and social relationships. Often, as was the case with Castor and Pollux, there is a sibling relationship for the Gemini individual to deal with, and more often than not, it is one that challenges rather than supports the Gemini's position. Whether the dueling adversary is an actual twin or simply a sibling, or even an associate, Gemini's abilities are exercised and stimulated, like Aries, by having a sparring partner. But as we have already observed, the sparring takes place mentally or intellectually for the Gemini, as opposed to the more physical or active challenge demanded by Aries.

Sometimes the Gemini process involves the challenge of having a soulmate on another plane, like Castor and Pollux, the mortal one having died. At other times it involves the shadow/light duality that is so characteristic of Gemini, and for still others it involves the innate duality of the mind. "The left hand doesn't know what the right hand is doing" is a phrase which describes one manifestation of mental duality. Another such manifestation is the mind that plays on and on like a radio; one becomes so accustomed to the background noise that there is little, if any, consciousness of what is actually being broadcast. And still another aspect of Geminian duality is a split between the physical world (body) and the mental world (mind) which is perhaps the most common duality experienced in the early stages of human consciousness. External activities are carried out robotically, as if on automatic pilot, while the mind continues its internal chatter, entirely uninvolved with what's actually happening on the outside. Obviously, these are all manifestations of a dysfunctional or afflicted Gemini archetype. More highly evolved Geminis have integrated their duality to such an extent that they are focused and one-pointed in a particular direction. Thus they challenge themselves to explore new and uncharted areas of the human mind.

We owe much of the symbolism of Gemini to its astrological ruler, Mercury (Hermes). Mercury is the trickster who often outwits even himself. Our mythological examples for Gemini involve the interaction of two opposing forces—and whether the duel consists of wrestling with one's own internal light and shadow, or a desire for a place among the stars, there is often in Gemini a longing for something which is not accessible in bodily or earthly form. And it is true that those with a strong Gemini factor (or any of the air signs, for that matter) have a poor relationship with the physical world. Pollux's desire to relinquish his immortality so that he could join his brother reminds us of the centaur Chiron, associated with Sagittarius, Gemini's opposite. He, too, was afflicted with a pain that could not be healed in earthly life, and pleaded that his immortality might cease so that he could leave the earthly plane. We have observed many talented and gifted Geminis whose destiny it was to depart earthly life early.

Mercury, ruler of Gemini

Marilyn Monroe and Judy Garland attained immortality before their early demise, but became even more elevated once freed from the physical plane, where they no longer had to wrestle with the duality of light and shadow that affects so many of Hollywood's stars. The Kennedy brothers, and most notably Gemini John F. Kennedy, seem to dramatize the Castor/Pollux myth. President Kennedy's early exit from life placed him as a bright star in the heavens of American legend, joining his already deceased brother Joseph and being followed by his younger brother, Robert.

In medical astrology Gemini rules the arms, hands, shoulders and lungs. Arms and hands seem appropriate for these mechanically proficient, manually dextrous creatures, but what of the lungs? Gemini is, after all, an air sign, and it is the lungs that receive and expel fresh air for the body. Breath (*prana* in Sanskrit or *ruach* in Hebrew) actually means spirit, and the body's ability to breathe correctly keeps it alive. But even more important is that the intake of fresh air and the expulsion of stale air is what keeps body, mind, and spirit connected and fluid. Gemini's need for extra air is often expressed by smoking, as it forces one to inhale and exhale rhythmically, but a good routine of controlled (yogic) breathing satisfies this need in a much healthier manner.

Planets in Gemini will often express themselves in relationship to the duality theme described above. The ever-present curiosity of the young child's mind seeks to attain new heights of intellectual stimulation and exploration. Jacques Cousteau, a Gemini Sun in the Ninth House (Sagittarius' natural house) has taken exploration to new heights in the 20th century. Many Geminis search restlessly for the ideal life, trying many lifestyles in the process. The Sun, Moon, or Ascendant in Gemini will pose for an individual a life-long struggle to integrate the dual or opposite aspects of his/her nature. Often the opposing factors will be portrayed astrologically by two signs that are prominent elsewhere in the horoscope. For instance, a Gemini with a Taurus Moon and Sagittarius rising may be forever seeking ways to integrate the principles of Taurus and Sagittarius satisfactorily so that both sides seem balanced.

With a Gemini Sun in particular, the solar force is focused upon this dual aspect of one's own inner nature, so that both ends of a dialogue are established whether or not an outside partner exists. When the Moon is here, the natives serve themselves best by reading, holding long conversations with friends, and indulging themselves in new information technology such as playing with the 42-channel remote wand until they realize there's nothing on TV and drive off, quickly but aimlessly, in their cars. Mercury in Gemini is in its dignity. People endowed with this planetary position usually display many gifted qualities in the information field, whether they are professional students, writers, journalists, broadcasters, lecturers, teachers, or story-tellers—even if they just do it for a hobby. Venus in Gemini, as the popular books on astrology maintain, can be flirtatious, but will also charm your socks off. Mars in Gemini gives great energy to the mental and social process and can often be known for its ability to pioneer new avenues of thought. Race-car driving or work with transportation in general can also be fulfilling for those with Mars in Gemini—let's not forget India's twin horsemen.

Ceres and Pallas Athene in Gemini develop and nurture educational skills, both giving much attention to intellectual pursuits in general. The principle difference is that for Ceres in Gemini, the individual may enjoy exercising these skills through teaching or parenting, while with Pallas Athene the brilliance may radiate early in life, resulting in the prodigy. Juno in Gemini people seek to bond with those through whom they can experience mental stimulation and much conversation, and no doubt enjoy a wide variety of subject matters and people in pursuing this process. Vesta in Gemini is wonderful for *focusing* and disciplining one's mentality to one particular area of expertise. Saturn is also able to do this in the sign of the twins.

Head of Mercury depicted on contemporary (1974) Italian currency.
From the Michael A. Sikora collection

Jupiter in Gemini or Saturn in Gemini brings the need for communication and circulation of ideas to the social and sometimes to the lawmaking sphere. Chiron in the Third House is often the "media freak"—too talented or intellectually brilliant for his or her own good, and caught in a world of revolving perspectives until he or she can bring his or her talents into focus. Uranus also shines a little too brightly here, and the power of the intellect may need a great deal of taming (meditation helps) before these natives can emerge as the great writers and communicators they potentially are.

The seven years that Uranus spent in Gemini in its most recent journey through that sign occurred from 1942 to 1949, when the first of the post-war baby-boomer generation was born. These gifted future thinkers are the pioneers of the New Age. These are also the information age wizards who are gifted with computer skills and a mastery of highly sophisticated machinery. These years saw the birth of the computer and the television, two instruments of communication that have contributed greatly to the age of information and high technology. Neptune in the Third House has a desire for information relating to mysticism and the "other world," and may also have a talent for music, poetry, or theater—but, as with all the outer planets in this house, focusing the attention will be an issue. Pluto is a voracious collector of information when in this house. But these individuals must be careful not to invest too much emotional energy in the mental concepts they build out of this information—for all things Plutonian can eventually come crashing down, including one's intellectual assumptions. There is a very strong drive to keep collecting data, nonetheless.

It is worth noting that the two slowest moving planets of our solar system, Neptune and Pluto, who rendezvous in the heavens only once every couple of hundred years, met at the close of the 19th century in Gemini. Around this time the airplane and the automobile were introduced and speeded up the evolution—and certainly the mobility—of humankind in a way which has scarcely been equaled since the invention of the wheel. When the duality of Gemini is united and focused, great accomplishments are possible.

GEMINI WORKSHEET

A factor includes a planet, an asteroid, or an angle in the birth chart. How many factors do you have in Gemini? Use the following point system to total them:

Sun	4	Mars	1	Uranus	1/2
Moon	4	Ceres	1	Neptune	1/2
Earth	3	Pallas	1	Vertex	1/2
Mercury	3	Juno	1	Pluto	1/2
Venus	2	Vesta	1	Nodes	1/2
ASC	2	Jupiter	1	Part of Fortune	1/2
MH	2	Saturn	1		
		Chiron	1		

Gemini on an angle (ASC, MH, DSC, IC) 3

Mercury on an angle 3

Planets and asteroids in the 3rd House count the same as above _____

Mercury or Gemini as the focal point of a T-square? 2

Mercury or Gemini involved in a T-square? 1

Total _____

How did you relate to these myths? _____

_____

_____

_____

_____

What house does Gemini occupy in your chart?

_____

10th House—mother   1st House—self

4th House—father   11th House—friends

7th House—mate   5th House—children, lovers

3rd House—sibling

Keeping in mind that these houses represent these relationships, how has Gemini energy expressed itself through others in your life? _____

_____

_____

_____

What house does Mercury occupy in your chart and how is it expressed?_____

_____

_____

What signs or planets are in your 3rd House and how are they expressed? _____

_____

_____

Insights: _____

_____

_____

_____

Artemis (Diana) of Ephesus, the many-breasted fertility goddess

CANCER

CHAPTER TWENTY-FIVE

CANCER, *The Crab*

SIGN: *Cancer, the 4th Zodiacal Sign*

MODE: *Cardinal* ❧ ELEMENT: *Water* ❧ RULER: *Moon*

ADDITIONAL MYTHIC ARCHETYPES: *Khephra (the Egyptian scarab)* ❧ *the Great Goddess and the Divine Consort* ❧ *Demeter (Ceres)*

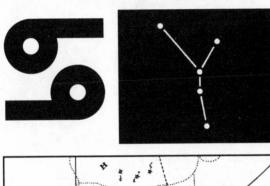

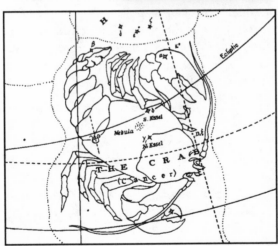

The history and mythology of Cancer is a picture of confusion and contradiction. No one is quite certain what this sign meant to the Babylonians, or even what its symbolic animal was, but to the Egyptians Cancer was the scarab beetle, a sacred totem referring to the soul. The Egyptians began their year during what is now the month of Cancer (July), and Cancer symbolized the soul's point of entry into the body. In esoteric astrology Cancer is also seen as the soul's doorway into incarnation.[1] As we have seen, however, the Egyptians understood their months in terms of the *evening* rising of signs: thus the constellation Cancer, to the Egyptians, was a symbol of the winter solstice, not the summer. The scarab pushes its ball of dung up the slopes of sandhills, then allows it to roll back down again. Similarly, the sun reaches the apex of its southerly motion at the winter solstice, and begins to "roll" back again toward summer—towards life-giving warmth and productivity.[2]

To the Greeks Cancer was initially represented by a turtle or tortoise. This symbol may sound peculiar to us, but in fact, there are many similarities between the

Before Cancer was depicted as a crab, it was known to the Egyptians as a scarab,
illustrated by Diane Smirnow

tortoise and the crab, Cancer's present symbol. Tortoises, like crabs, have hard shells and very soft interiors. Tortoises, like crabs, crawl into their shells when they are frightened, and move at a slow but constant pace. For the Greeks the tortoise symbol for Cancer was linked to the fact that Mercury ruled Cancer in their schema of the twelve Olympians. Shortly after his birth the precocious child Hermes (Mercury) emerged from a cave and beheld a tortoise. Being an extremely clever infant he used the tortoise shell and some cowgut to fashion the first lyre, a stringed instrument which later became associated with Apollo.[3]

At some point in history, perhaps during the Hellenistic Era which followed the death of Alexander the Great and which witnessed a merging of all the ancient Mediterranean cultures, Cancer became associated with the crab and with the Moon. But there was little sentiment involved with lunar rulership in those days, and the Greeks associated that luminary with trade, business, and the rising and falling of the tides which made maritime travel possible. Thus the Roman poet Manilius describes Cancerians as cold-hearted and penurious merchants, greedy for money[4]—an image we do not usually associate with Cancer, although to this day Cancer is known for its ability to make a buck or have something stuffed under the mattress for that rainy day.

In Classical times, the Greeks worked Cancer the Crab into the twelve labors of Hercules. While the hero was engaged in battling a gigantic sea serpent called the Hydra, a huge crab emerged from the deep and fastened its pincers on his heel. Hercules turned around, crushed the crab, and continued his fight with the Hydra. His arch-enemy, the goddess Hera (Juno), placed the crab among the stars as a reward for serving the goddess in her struggle to overcome Hercules.[5]

The true meaning of Cancer, however, can best be understood by considering its position in the seasonal year. Cancer marks the summer solstice, when the longest day of the year (and, of course, the shortest night) occurs. It may seem strange that we should attribute the Moon, symbol of the Great Goddess and the eternal feminine, to this moment when the solar force is at its greatest. But the key idea here is that the sun is *turning back*, beginning its progress into the world of the Nightforce or collective humanity which is the *yin* or feminine component of consciousness and civilization. The solar force or ego has reached its limit, and unbridled individuality must now give way to the needs of collective humanity.

In archaic times (and particularly during the Age of Cancer, c. 8,000–6,000 BC, the time which many scholars identify as the era of Goddess worship), the summer solstice was the day upon which the sun god—or his earthly representative—was ritually slain, sacrificed to the Great Mother. He began his journey into the underworld, just as the ego consciousness begins its journey toward universal consciousness in the Cancerian phase of human life. Thus it is said that Cancer represents one's home and family, for in establishing this small collective unit we, as individuals, begin to allow a little bit of the consciousness of the other into our lives.

The Sun is at its moment of greatest power, while the sign itself is ruled by the Moon. Thus the symbols of Sun and Moon, masculine and feminine, are united in one archetype. We may think of Cancer as the sign of the "mystic marriage," the union of alchemical opposites. In his well-known book, *The Hero With A Thousand Faces*, mythologist Joseph Campbell imaged the hero's journey as a circle.[6] The stages of that heroic journey harmonize quite well with the zodiacal circle, and indeed, the nadir of the circle is attributed to the mystic marriage, just as Cancer is the nadir point of the zodiacal circle. This is the stage where the hero, having traveled to the "other world" which represents the depths of the collective mind, meets the fairytale princess, the sorceress, the magical bride, and is united with her. In primitive ritual, the sun god was often the consort of the Divine Mother, and the priest who played the god's role ritually coupled with the priestess or Divine Mother before his symbolic death. It is through union with the collective or feminine principle that masculine ego consciousness reaches its limit and begins to be absorbed by something different. It is also why males feel both an attraction to and fear of merging with the feminine. At the point of merger, the ego or masculine component of consciousness loses its control, is "swallowed up," and, symbolically speaking, dies in order that consciousness (*yang*) and unconsciousness (*yin*) can be united.

No wonder, then, that Cancerian people are said to be psychic, for they are particularly open to the influx of vast universal forces, which channel themselves into the confines of one's individual consciousness whether or not the Cancerian chooses to be such a channel.

We have remarked that there are essentially four aspects of the Great Goddess, corresponding to the four phases of the moon and to the signs Taurus, Cancer, Virgo, and Scorpio. The first two aspects of the Goddess—those that we encounter in Cancer and Taurus—are strongly related, primarily due to the Moon's important

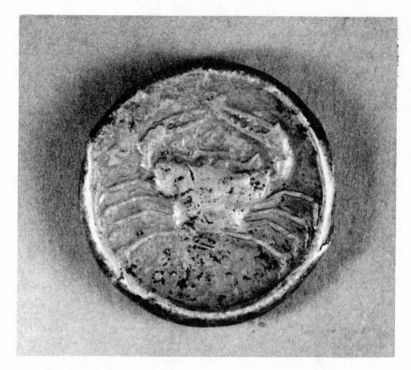

A tetradrachm of Akragas (modern Agrigento), Sicily, 472–420 BC. From the Michael A. Sikora collection

relationship with both signs. In Taurus the Moon is exalted, while in Cancer it is in its dignity. The moon and its constantly changing phases played a large part in the celebrations and rituals of the Goddess era. The Taurean aspect of the Goddess deals with the fertility and abundance of Mother Earth and the female power which was represented by the earth.

Fertility rites and feasts celebrated during the Age of Taurus also dealt with the miracle of conception, the woman's ability to bring forth life from her body. In Cancer it is the relationship between mother and child that is honored and celebrated, a relationship that begins once the egg is fertilized. Researchers claim that the relationship that is established between the fetus and its mother during its nine-month pre-natal development has dramatic and long-lasting effects from birth to adulthood. This is where the mother establishes the relationship to her child and the child is receptive to all input, emotionally and psychically. This is where the umbilical cord is established—and it does not necessarily get cut following birth, at least on the psychic level. Indeed, for some people the psychic umbilical cord remains linked to the mother throughout life, and for those moving through the Cancer experience, this is more often than not the case, whether due to the mother's unwillingness to let go of the child, the child's inability to let go of the mother, or both. Mythic examples of this include Oedipus and Kore (Persephone). In the story of Demeter and her daughter Kore, the goddess of agriculture and the earth, Ceres, who is perhaps exalted in Cancer, condemns the world to an eternal winter in her grief over losing her daughter.

Another similarity between Taurus and Cancer is their mutual need for security, although Taurus needs it in *physical* form and Cancer needs it in the *emotional* realm. But if these signs start out with such a strong relationship to the life-giving functions surrounding birth and the nurturing and care of the infant, it is no wonder that they demand a secure place to be. During pregnancy and the early months of life, especially in ancient times, the infant's and mother's lives were extremely fragile and delicate, and anything that rocked the boat was considered dangerous, a cause for insecurity.

The constellation of the crab was placed into the heavens by Hera for aiding her in her struggle between Hercules and the Hydra. Both Hera and the Hydra are aspects of the pre-Hellenic Great Mother, while Hercules is the archetypal patriarchal or solar hero. Thus, embedded deep within Cancer's psyche may be the need to defend and protect "mother-right," the great feminine which first gave the crab its life, and then its stellar immortality. When mother, family honor, or nest is threatened, Cancer may instinctively respond by pinching the enemy with its claws, as the crab did to Hercules. We see this drama played out in reverse in the animal kingdom where the mother protects her young fiercely—but in the human kingdom the same emotional and psychic messages are nevertheless transmitted, and Cancer types often cherish the assumption and expectation that their young will return the favor and protect them once they are capable of doing so.

Since Cancer is represented by the Great Mother, the real, earthly mother plays no small part in the lives of those who are strongly influenced by that sign. There is often a loving and symbiotic relationship that begins in the womb and continues to the grave. And in the poorly aspected or integrated Cancer individual, it can be the source of psychological problems throughout life. The Great Mother, in such cases, overshadows the individual to such an extent that there is no possibility for individuation. At this point, Cancers become involved in a guilt-ridden dilemma, because their instincts dictate that they should honor the mother for giving them life, while their personal need to individuate is so stifled that they are incited to animosity and rage.

We also know that Cancer rules the breasts and womb in medical astrology—the two biological organs that exist primarily to provide a safe home and nourishment to the young infant. Nourishment, to Cancer, is important throughout life. This is one sign that experiences the most severe eating disorders when afflicted. We recall that Ceres took no food except barley-water when she was grieving over her loss; similarly, her daughter ate nothing in the underworld until just prior to her emergence, when she partook of pomegranate seeds. Strong lunar types may overeat, enjoying the full roundness and radiance of the lunar experience, but they may also use food in a way that is damaging to themselves, compensating for the lack of emotional sustenance in their lives. Bulimia and anorexia, which are related, can often be tied to a dysfunctional planet in Cancer or an ill-nourished Moon, Ceres, Pluto, or any combination thereof in the horoscope.

Of course we associate Cancer primarily with the mother, but the Fourth House or I.C., which is Cancer's domicile, represents the family, the individual's roots, and, as many astrology books maintain—the "nurturing parent" (as opposed to the "domineering" one), though such strict polarization does not often represent reality. Generally speaking, Cancer's place on the wheel represents early family bonding and the effect that such bonding has on the individual's ability to individuate. And, as one Cancer recently observed, "if you take me, you take my family."

Remembering that we are surrounded by water in Cancer (as is the fetus), feeling, sensitivity to the environment, and strong absorption occur here. That, coupled with the fact that Cancer needs a secure place to *be*, accounts for the overriding need in Cancer to constantly search for a place that offers the security it is seeking. Many Cancers have made finding their "true home" their life's quest.

In the Circle of Life (the zodiac), Cancer marks the first stage of experience in the western hemisphere, a region that defines one's relationship to others. With Cancer being the first water sign, it is also emotionally dependent upon relationships, and because of its cardinal nature it is not shy about initiating a relationship when one is not already present. As previously discussed, the first relationship of emotional dependence in any individual's life starts with the mother, as one's entire future depends on it. For this reason, many a Cancer will go through life needing to reiterate the mother/child relationship. In marriage and partnership, for instance, Cancer either needs someone to mother or is in need of someone to mother them. Often, the childless Cancer looks for peers, partners, or projects to mother. But it's more than simply the mother-principle that's at work here. Cancer has a need to feel needed, and in the absence of a child to need it, substitutions will be found.

The moodiness that so many textbooks speak of in regard to Cancer probably has more to do with its relationship to its planetary ruler, the Moon, than anything else. During its 28-day cycle, the moon is constantly changing phases, and it changes signs every two and one-half days. With so much motion, *anyone* could get sea-sick. The other difficulty for Cancer is that cardinal water must, by nature, *initiate* feeling through a process of *merging* with others. Because Cancer is so good at this merging process, the result is often a loss of personal identity. It can also result in a situation wherein Cancer is carrying around everyone else's emotions, yet totally unaware of who and what it is carrying. This too can result in unpredictable moodiness or a total disconnection from who and what one's own purpose is. This results in the loss of one's center of gravity—and that is a most insecure place to be.

In the section entitled "Water" (Chapter Twenty, "The Elements") we spoke of the importance of expressing feelings as a natural outpouring and cleansing process. This process is especially vital for Cancer, due to its cardinal nature, since the ongoing process of absorbing the feelings of the human environment necessitates the purging of those feelings as well. And we're not just talking about absorbing the

Cancer's connection with infants, nurturing, and rulership of the breasts are all shown in this illustration of a woman nursing a child, from Jost Amman's Kunstbüchlin, *printed by Johann Feyerabend, Frankfurt, 1599*

environment and then detaching from it. Cancer has a very difficult time detaching from *anything*, as attested by its claws. Cancer also has difficulty in being objective about what it has just encountered, for at the I.C., or root of the chart, Cancer sits at the most intense point of *subjectivity*, the center of its universe. So *everything out there* potentially affects Cancer in extreme ways on the inner level—perhaps another reason for moodiness. And if there are afflictions to Cancer in the chart, all these more negative traits of insecurity will surface.

Well-aspected Cancer planets in a horoscope contribute to the establishment of nurturing and nourishing relationships throughout life. They will add to the intuitive or psychic qualities that an individual possesses and will also contribute to one's need to establish a solid base of security in life. The Moon will exhibit these qualities most intensely, since it is Cancer's ruling planet and innately understands what Cancer needs. The Sun in Cancer combines solar leadership abilities with Cancer's nurturing qualities and typically shapes an individual who can provide good role models for others. In order for these people to manifest that kind of leadership, however, it is important to integrate feelings absorbed in the womb and during the first seven years of life. Separation from these subconscious feelings is often difficult, even when consciously undertaken. Because the Moon is Cancer's ruling planet, those with the Moon in that sign will embody Cancer's nurturing and intuitive qualities very intensely, as well as its need for security. They balance themselves with food, warm baths, or hot tubs, romance, and moonlight (preferably on the ocean), or, when all else fails, a strong dose of domestic peace and quiet.

Mercury, as the Greeks observed, is a clever and often successful merchant in Cancer. Venus in Cancer is loving and, if negatively aspected, can contribute to "smother-love." Mars in Cancer is easily stimulated in an erotic sense, but its emotional process can get "steamy." Often there is anger towards or from the mother with this position.

Ceres may well be exalted in Cancer; this position leans toward great concern for the family and an exceptionally strong connection between mother and child. Pallas Athene brings wisdom and insight to this sign of feelings, creating a rare blend of insight and compassion—unless Pallas is afflicted, in which case her shield becomes a solid shell of armor. Juno in Cancer, like Ceres, loves the parenting role; though, unlike Ceres, Juno is likely to be more interested in the mating ritual which makes parenthood possible. Vesta will enjoy the Cancer experience, as she is the traditional keeper of hearth and home.

Jupiter performs its typical expansion routine in Cancer—either through family, desiring many children and a strong family experience, or through food, which it may enjoy in excess. Saturn in Cancer or in the Fourth House will typically be carrying a deep wound from infancy—the mothering experience was not a particularly loving, nurturing one, and the family system is often about as dysfunctional as they come. The lifelong process of healing these wounds is what Saturn teaches in

Cancer. Chiron in the Fourth House points also to the need to heal family issues, but like Chiron's wound, the pain may be so deep that healing must take place on a non-physical level.

Uranus in the Fourth House is, for most, a difficult placement, since the Promethean fire of intellect and inner transformation tends to destabilize that soft Cancerian womb. Most of these people grow up in chaotic environments, leave home early, and create homes of their own which are unique to the point of eccentricity. Intuitive abilities are quite strong with this position. Neptune in the Fourth House often has something to do with the actual mother—she may be an artist, an alcoholic, or a mystic—but it is equally indicative of one who must seek security in oneness with the universe itself. Pluto acts with devastating power in this house: it may swallow up the Great Goddess (Ishtar) into the underworld, inducing the Plutonian process of emotional death and rebirth on a regular basis; or it may actually *become* the Dark Mother, using emotional and psychological hooks to gain a silent power over other family members.

The outer planets' transits through Cancer have coincided with some interesting changes in domestic life for families in general. Uranus' seven-year passage through Cancer occurred from 1949 to 1956. Certainly the housing industry and real estate market (Cancer or Fourth House) in America (a Cancer nation, "born" on the 4th of July) experienced a rousing boom in those years, especially with the automation process of labor-saving devices (Uranus) being part and parcel of every home (Cancer)—the American Dream. But what's even more interesting is that the generation of people born with Pluto in Cancer (1919 to 1939) reached their peak child-bearing years during the Uranus in Cancer phase, resulting in the parents' Plutos contacting the childrens' Uranuses in many cases. The reaction that this combination generates is highly volatile and explosive, resulting in the Uranus group introducing and even forcing their unique concepts of mating and parenting upon a group whose generational trademark (Pluto in Cancer) was to hang on for dear life to *everything*, especially tradition and good old family values. In fact, the group with Uranus in Cancer demonstrates a statistical abnormality regarding parenting. This group opted, almost *en masse*, to either totally abandon parenting or postpone their childbearing years to the ages of 35-40, a time when the biological clock is just about to run out. The statistical norm for childbearing in America for the 20th century usually peaks between the ages of 25 and 29.[7] Typically Uranus is too freewheeling and independent to take on the responsibility of parenting, but that strong instinctual Cancer urge to procreate caught up with this generation in the end. The Uranus in Cancer group, coming to parenthood late, has been subjected to further confusion by the need to revolutionize (Uranus) the parenting role (Cancer). This, perhaps, is a reaction against the homogeneous world of the 1950s in which this generation grew up, when children were raised to embody standard American values (Cancer) rather than have their own individuality (Uranus) acknowledged. This group's struggles to deal with parenting are reflected in the recent rash of movies and TV shows about "yuppies with babies"—the Uranus in Cancer generation laughing at itself as it works collectively towards a new, more individualistic or Uranian style of parenting.

And Neptune (the planet which esoteric astrologers associate with Cancer)[8] was in the sign of the crab during the first part of the 20th century (1901–1916), when millions of immigrants were leaving behind their beloved homelands, journeying to Turtle Island (the Native American name for this country and a symbolic link to clever Mercury and his tortoise), a Cancer nation, who would absorb them into her ever-widening womb.

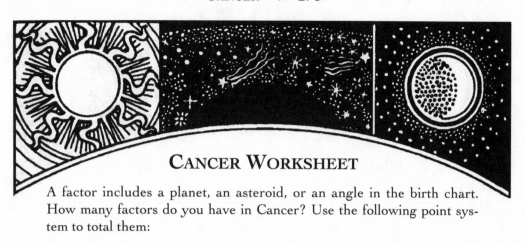

CANCER WORKSHEET

A factor includes a planet, an asteroid, or an angle in the birth chart. How many factors do you have in Cancer? Use the following point system to total them:

Sun 4	Mars 1	Uranus 1/2
Moon 4	Ceres 2	Part of Fortune .. 1/2
Earth 4	Pallas 1	Vertex 1/2
Venus 2	Juno 1	Pluto 2
Mercury 3	Vesta 1	Nodes 1/2
Jupiter 2	Neptune 1	
ASC 2	Saturn 1	
MH 2	Chiron 1	

Cancer on an angle (ASC, MH, DSC, IC) 3

Moon on an angle 3

Ceres or Pluto on an angle 2

Planets and asteroids in the 4th House count the same as above _____

Moon or Cancer as the focal point of a T-square? 2

Moon or Cancer involved in a T-square? 1

Pluto or Ceres involved in a T-square? 1

Total _____

How did you relate to these myths? _____

_____

_____

_____

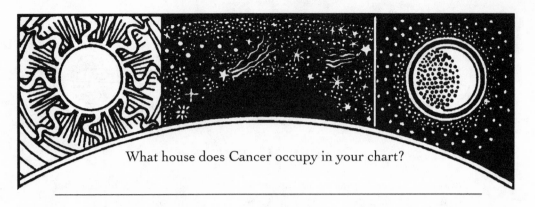

What house does Cancer occupy in your chart?

_____

10th House—mother   1st House—self

4th House—father   11th House—friends

7th House—mate   5th House—children, lovers

3rd House—sibling

Keeping in mind that these houses represent these relationships, how has Cancer energy expressed itself through others in your life? _____

_____

_____

What houses do the Moon, Ceres, and Pluto occupy in your chart and how are they

expressed? _____

_____

What signs or planets are in your 4th House and how are they expressed? _____

_____

_____

Insights: _____

_____

_____

_____

_____

LEO

LEO, *The Lion*

SIGN: *Leo, the 5th Zodiacal Sign*

MODE: *Fixed* ❧ ELEMENT: *Fire* ❧ RULER: *Sun*

ADDITIONAL MYTHIC ARCHETYPES: *Sekhmet (Egyptian)*
❧ *Hercules* ❧ *Atalanta* ❧ *Lugh (Celtic)* ❧ *Rhea*
❧ *Ishtar (Babylonian)*

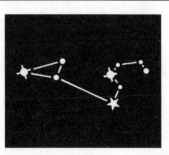

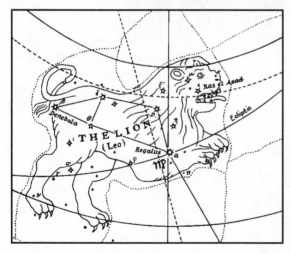

Like Cancer, Leo has a confusing history. The constellation was known to the Babylonians as the Great Dog, and to the Egyptians as the Sickle; how it became the Lion is unclear. The Egyptians worshipped a lion-headed goddess called Sekhmet, who represented the scorching heat of the sun at midday. Since the sun does indeed shine most brightly during the month of Leo, Sekhmet may have been its original archetype.[1]

It was the Egyptians, too, who constructed the Sphinx, which some esotericists believe represents a lion merging with a goddess. In the astrological wheel, this merging is present at the cusp of Leo the Lion and Virgo the Harvest Goddess, and many believe that the building of the Sphinx took place at the turning of the ages between these two greater cycles (c. 10,000 BC). Rudhyar postulates that the Sphinx, or the cusp of Leo and Virgo, represents the first stage of initiation in the disciple's path.[2]

The sun was regarded as the king of the planets even as the lion was the king of beasts. Thus Leo is reputed to be kingly and dominating. The planets circle the sun (their center), and Leo's correspondence in medical astrology is the heart, the central organ of life. Leos often find or place themselves at the center of affairs in their lives, with many of their relationships dependent upon their solar force for leadership, direction, and light. But the solar force of ego or directed will must make compromises with the collective; thus Leo is regarded as a social sign. During the Leo phase of human activity, the individual must find his place in or make his mark upon society in general. Once again, the astrological meaning of the sign is in accordance with the round of the seasonal year, for the sun during its brightest month is analogous to the position of the leader in society.

The sun is the visible symbol of the life-force which animates all sentient beings, the vital power or energy at the core of our existence. As we have seen, however, this solar force is of itself neither good nor bad; it is simply power. When allowed to run wild, without conscious direction, it leads to rampant egotism and the urge to conquer or dominate. This is why dictators are said to represent the negative aspect of Leo. To tame the life-force and bring it under the conscious control of the individual will is a constant theme in mythology and folklore. Jungian psychology sees most dragon-slaying myths in that light.[3] The classical Greeks equated Leo with the first of Hercules' twelve labors, the slaying of the Nemean lion. In this story,

A statue of the goddess Sekhmet at the Temple of Mut in Luxor, Egypt. Photograph by Diane Smirnow

Hercules represents the conscious will gaining control over the vital passions symbolized by the lion. Similarly, the Babylonian hero Gilgamesh comes upon a pride of lions playing in the moonlight, and slays them. And the Tarot card Strength, associated with Leo, depicts an angelic figure, often a female, closing a lion's mouth. The meaning allocated to this card is precisely the same: the taming of the vital force or animal nature by the consciously directed will. This symbol may stem from an Egyptian ritual regarding the taming of lions, a rite of passage each initiate faced in his or her training.[4]

We have observed (see Cancer) how the sun god met his ritual death at the summer solstice in archaic times. During a later phase of antiquity, however, the sun's symbolic sacrifice often took place during the month of Leo, for though the sun shines most brightly at this time, it is the Nightforce which is growing stronger. The Druids celebrated this seasonal change at Lammastide (August 2), which was a funeral for the sun god Lugh as well as a harvest festival. The sun god's death in ritual combat is a recurrent theme in Celtic mythology. It appears in the first branch of the Welsh *Mabinogion*, wherein the hero Pwyll slays Havgan (summer-white) so that Arawn, king of the underworld (winter), may be reinstated as lord of the year. In the *Mabinogion's* fourth branch, the sun-hero Llew Llaw Gyffes, another aspect of the god Lugh, is killed while standing with one foot balanced on a magic cauldron and the other on the back of a goat.[5] In the year 1100, myth impinged ominously on reality when King

Hercules and the Nemean lion, from Jost Amman's Kunstbüchlin, *printed by Johann Feyerabend, Frankfurt, 1599*

William II of England (called Rufus, which means "the red," symbolic color of solar vitality) was slain with an arrow in the New Forest of Hampshire. The circumstances surrounding the king's death were so mysterious that many researchers have concluded that Rufus himself was a pagan and played the role of willing victim in a rite of human sacrifice. The death of William Rufus occurred on Lammas.[6]

As a symbol of the vital power itself, the Sun is an apt and appropriate ruler for Leo. But in the scheme of the twelve Olympians mentioned by the Roman poet Manilius, "Jove, with the Mother of the Gods, himself is Leo's lord."[7] In most mythologies the king of the gods is an archetype of the principle of focused consciousness—thus it is appropriate that Jove or Jupiter should rule over Leo, just as consciousness must rule over instinct. Even today, we often think of Leo people as jovial, projecting an exuberant brand of cheer and good fellowship.

The reference to the Mother of the Gods is a bit more difficult to understand. Astrological historian Rupert Gleadow thought that the title must refer to the goddess Artemis as she was worshipped in Ephesus, a divine mother with many breasts.[8] To us this seems rather unlikely, since the worship of Ephesian Artemis was confined to the coasts of Asia Minor, and especially since it is the goddess Rhea who, according to mythologist Karl Kerenyi, was traditionally called "the mother of the gods."[9] The wife of Cronus (Saturn), Rhea gave birth to Zeus, Poseidon, Hades, Hera, Demeter, and Hestia. Her name seems to be the title by which the Great Goddess was known on the island of Crete, though why she should be associated with Leo is not at all clear.[10] It is perhaps worth noting that another form of the Great Goddess, the Babylonian Ishtar, took the lion as one of her symbolic animals, and is often depicted riding upon its back. Joseph Campbell notes that the goddess Cybele, mother of the slain and resurrected Attis, was known as Mountain Mother, or Mother of the Gods, and was identified with Rhea. Her places of worship were on mountains, and in caves, and her animals were lions.[11]

Yet another Leonine character from Greek myth is Atalanta, daughter of Iasus. Her father, bitterly disappointed that she was a girl, abandoned her on a mountaintop. She was raised by a she-bear in the wild (presumably Artemis in the form of one of her many animal totems), and thus developed hunting and athletic skills surpassing those of any other mortal in the land. She accompanied Jason on the Argo, took part in the Calydonian boar hunt, and was a serious contender in any athletic event. She was not particularly fond of men as mates, though she was fond of having them as competitors in sport. Even though she was challenged by the most skilled athletes, she always equaled or surpassed them, especially in hunting. Many suitors came to seek her hand, so she devised a contest she knew she could win, promising that if anyone could beat her in a foot race, she would take him as her marriage partner. Many tried and many failed, until one day Melanion came along with a plan to defeat her. Three golden apples were placed in her path on the racecourse, and as Atalanta quickly bent down to scoop them up, her speed was slowed just enough so that she could be defeated. She married Melanion, had a child, and, in one version of the myth, the two were eventually turned into lions because of an affront to Zeus.[12] Competitive and competent in sport like Athene and Artemis, goddesses associated with the other fire signs (Aries and Sagittarius respectively), Atalanta represents the fiery, independent, and highly skilled Leo type for whom athletics, games, and adventure are all equally alluring.

The goddess Rhea

Many of our mythological associations with Leo refer to kings and queens, heroes and heroines, who preside over the wild beasts of the jungle and represent fearlessness and courage. Thus, the wisdom in Leo is tied first to one's ability to outwit the beast or enemy, and second, to protect its offspring or kingdom from such enemies. In ancient times kings and tribal leaders typically earned their position as rulers because they displayed such mighty strength and mastery over their challengers that their subjects stood in

A nineteenth-century drawing of Cybele after the original statue in the British Museum

awe of their abilities (as in the case of Napoleon, a Leo, whose name literally means "The Lion"). They were great warriors, and when invading armies came to challenge them, they defended their kingdom by displaying their power—or were defeated and relinquished their position to the new and victorious warrior. Even today it is not uncommon to make our military heroes our leaders; however, this is thankfully much more common in military dictatorships than in democracies. Thus, the second stage of fire (Leo) is linked with the first stage (Aries): the warrior (Aries) becomes king (Leo). The king was the most omnipotent personage in the land, and his marriages were carefully chosen to keep the bloodlines of his descendants pure. The Egyptians strictly maintained such practices, and additionally created continual tests or initiations for royal princes and princesses so that, even when not confronted by an invading enemy from outside, tests were continually administered to insure that the rulers maintained a cleansed and purified inner nature as highly tuned instruments of God. In fact, the Pharaohs were believed to *be* gods.

The Greeks were not so filled with *hubris* as the Egyptians; their gods always resided *above* humanity, on a mountaintop, and when they did mate or mingle with humanity it was at the gods' choosing. The Greeks had their brave and mighty heroes, such as Hercules, whose twelve labors are reminiscent of the sun's progress through the zodiac. A hero might display his powers in seemingly impossible situations, but such a warrior was not made a king. Their kings were persons who embodied wisdom and political savvy. Our modern "kings" and leaders are appointed or elected because they have the most wealth, and thus, it seems, the greatest power.

It is the Sun and Jupiter who preside over Leo, but there is also a very bright star within the constellation of Leo that helps give this fifth stage of the astrological

Lions at Delos, photograph by Ariel Guttman

mandala much of its character. This star is called Regulus, the heart of the lion. To the ancients, this star was one of the "watchers on the horizon," as it is one of a group of four stars that rose at the equinoxes and solstices in Babylonia (the others were Antares, Aldebaran, and Fomalhaut). In the Babylonian sidereal zodiac, Regulus was the star of the summer solstice—the time of year of maximum solar force, thus the association with Leo, the Sun, and *fixed fire*. In the cosmic experience, Leo is the "tamer of the beast" or the "king of the mountain." In the human experience, these lively, high-spirited solar leaders often arouse fear and envy. The association between a person and his or her progeny is usually represented in astrology by Leo or the Fifth House. As if they were kings and

Ramses II offers flowers to the goddess Sekhmet

queens raising perfect thoroughbreds, Leos keep watchful and protective eyes on their children. Ever notice a lion protecting her cubs? Whether we are talking about real, physical children or children of the mind and spirit, Leos' creations are replications of their selves and as such maintain an honored place in their lives. This quality shows up most strongly with a Leo Sun or Moon, while with Leo ascending the natives are on a quest to develop their regal natures. Thus they often find themselves in leadership situations, whether by choice or appointment.

In Cancer, the larger-than-life figure is the mother; in Leo, it is the father: this is due to the respective rulerships of the Moon and Sun. We will encounter a strong connection with the father again in Capricorn as we did previously in Aries. All these fathers are of different natures. In Aries, the father was an original primal source, and perhaps a competitor or even a tyrant to be overthrown. In Leo, we are dealing with those aspects of the father that have an inner, personal, heart connection with the child. In Capricorn the father represents the exterior, public, father/child connection, based on the need for approval. Leo and the Sun are associated with masculine, solar-based heroes, which is often how the father is viewed by the small child. Historically, this connection between father and child reached one of its lowest points during the era of Pluto in Leo (1939–1957), and especially in 1947–48, when Saturn *and* Pluto conjoined in this sign. This is the generation which grew up psychologically fatherless. Even when the father wasn't working or hadn't physically deserted the family, a sense of emotional abandonment was felt by this baby-boomer generation, who themselves have worked for many years to heal that wound or fill that void, often by becoming "super-parents" to their own offspring. The Leonine types in this generation are often very untypical of the familiar, exuberant, enthusiastic Leo described in newspaper horoscope columns. Their inner vitality shines with the dark and mysterious glow of Pluto's underworld realm rather than with the warmth of solar fire. These Leos are like subterranean suns, powerful and brooding. Mick Jagger, with multiple planets (including Pluto and the Sun) in Leo, exemplifies the union of the Sun and Pluto in that sign.

In the era of Neptune in Leo (1920s), art, film, and music (Neptune-ruled domains) produced high-spirited forms of entertainment. The investment world (stocks, bonds, and commodities are ruled by Leo) which had built itself upon Neptunian illusions and fantasies of wealth and power for the greedy suddenly dissolved in 1929 at the "crash."

When the Sun itself is in Leo, it is the definition of one's individuality and the fathering or life-giving qualities that motivate. The Moon, as always, focuses on what makes us feel tranquil or secure; thus Moon in Leo takes its sustenance from days in the sunshine, preferably spent with some heartfelt relationship—a lover or child. These people can center themselves and feel exhilarated through competitive sports, personal creativity, or any of the performing arts. They also feel rejuvenated by tending themselves—buying clothes, jewels, or styling their manes.

A nineteenth-century French Tarot deck showing Strength holding open the mouth of a lion

Mercury in Leo may possess creative skills in the field of speaking or writing, while Venus in Leo more often bends its creativity to the arts of design. Mars, as we have seen, must serve the inner king in order to express itself positively, and in Leo Mars is in the sign of the solar king himself. At best, focused consciousness directs the individual and goals are easily reached, but without proper direction such a native may disperse his energy by chasing after illusory goals. Thus many of these people may pursue a particular career "for the money," but their hearts (the Sun) are not there. Thus they are subject to early burnout or even heart attack.

Ceres in Leo can really be the super-parent, and there is a pride in workmanship and creative projects and, once again, skill in drama or other arts. Pallas Athene possesses a talent for leadership with a built-in "daddy's boy or girl" energy behind it. Juno in Leo is hopelessly devoted to romantic ideas, while Vesta is often focused on both creativity and procreation.

Jupiter in Leo is, of course, the archetypal leader whose power and authority extends into all aspects of life. Jupiter tends to administer its own cosmos, and particularly in the sign of sovereigns, its struggle to remain autonomous prevails. Saturn in Leo is challenged with the task of throwing the yoke of subservience off its back, but ultimately with taking responsibility for its own actions as well. These people may deny their hearts in the process of material acquisitions, and are subject, like Mars in Leo, to heart disease and, most of all, bitterness and resentment. They truly must learn to open their hearts, especially to themselves. Chiron's position in Leo or the Fifth House will help to heal the heart, and this is especially done through the acknowledgment of those close personal relationships that tug at the heart.

A Fifth House Uranus turns on the creative juices; it can produce a supreme artist, or—here in the house of its detriment—a supreme egomaniac. Watch for unusual children in your life if you have Uranus placed here natally! Neptune in the Fifth focuses on the typical Fifth House creativity, especially in terms of acting, painting, or music. Pluto in the Fifth, if afflicted, may bring the generational "fatherlessness" we discussed earlier into high relief for the individual; it may also challenge the native to use his or her creativity in a socially useful way.

We have already mentioned Leo's connection with the heart in medical astrology, and its relationship to the Sun as the "heart" of our solar system. In the human body, the heart represents the vital function of life. In the system of the seven *chakras*, the heart *chakra* is poised strategically at the center, providing the vital link between the lower three *chakras* which represent the instinctual or animal nature, and the upper three centers which represent the divine nature. The heart, or *human*, center allows the individual to combine those two natures and face the most difficult of all challenges—that of keeping the heart open and loving in the continuing soap opera called life. The life force, or *kundalini*, flows up this conduit and, when freely flowing, creates inner harmony and vital energy. In esoteric astrological tradition, the glyph for Leo (♌) is sometimes said to represent this *kundalini* power as it begins to uncoil itself from its slumber at the base of the spine (see Scorpio). One of the largest killers of humanity continues to be heart disease, which occurs when the pathways to the heart have been obstructed for one reason or another. In a highly technological society, where a man's leadership is measured by his wealth and power, the price is often the human heart. At this stage of our personal and planetary evolution, the heart is what's most in need of development, and, as the Age of Aquarius firmly takes root within the consciousness of the planet, the function of its polarity sign, Leo, will be to insure that this is so.

LEO WORKSHEET

A factor includes a planet, an asteroid, or an angle in the birth chart. How many factors do you have in Leo? Use the following point system to total them:

Sun 4	Mars 1	Uranus 1/2
Moon 4	Ceres 1	Neptune 1/2
Earth 3	Pallas 1	Vertex 1/2
Venus 2	Juno 1	Pluto 1/2
Mercury 2	Vesta 1	Nodes 1/2
Jupiter 2	Saturn 1	Part of Fortune . . 1/2
ASC 2	Chiron 1	
MH 2		

Leo on an angle (ASC, MH, DSC, IC) 3

Sun on an angle 3

Planets and asteroids in the 5th House count the same as above _____

Sun or Leo as the focal point of a T-square? 2

Sun or Leo involved in a T-square? 1

Total _____

How did you relate to these myths? _____

_____

_____

_____

_____

What house does Leo occupy in your chart?

_____

10th   House—mother   1st House—self

4th   House—father   11th House—friends

7th   House—mate   5th House—children, lovers

3rd   House—sibling

Keeping in mind that these houses represent these relationships, how has Leo energy expressed itself through others in your life?_____

_____

_____

_____

What house does the Sun occupy in your chart and how is it expressed? _____

_____

_____

What signs or planets are in your 5th House and how are they expressed? _____

_____

_____

Insights: _____

_____

_____

_____

Isis, often associated with the sign Virgo

VIRGO

CHAPTER TWENTY-SEVEN

VIRGO, *The Virgin*

SIGN: *Virgo, the 6th Zodiacal Sign*

MODE: *Mutable* ❧ ELEMENT: *Earth* ❧ RULER: *Mercury*

ADDITIONAL MYTHIC ARCHETYPES: *Kore (Persephone)*
❧ *Demeter (Ceres)* ❧ *Astraea* ❧ *Isis* ❧ *Mary*
❧ *Chiron* ❧ *Hestia (Vesta)* ❧ *Artemis*

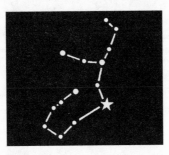

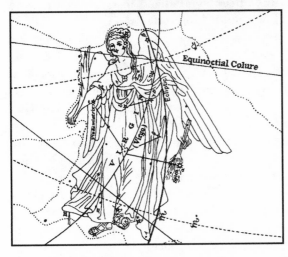

Virgo, along with Taurus, has perhaps the richest mythic associations of any sign. To the Greeks and Romans, Virgo was associated with the goddess Astraea, symbol of justice. She reigned on earth during the Golden Age (see Saturn). When humankind declined to its present state of corruption, she retired from the world in disgust, fixing herself in the heavens where she can still be seen holding the scales of justice (Libra), thus forming an integral unit with the sign which follows.[1]

However, it has always been the myth of Demeter and Persephone which is most strongly associated with Virgo, for Virgo rules the harvest season when Persephone is preparing to leave the world and seek the darkness once again. We have retold this story at some length under the topic of Ceres, and it is worth mentioning that the glyph for Virgo is said to represent the harvest goddess holding grain—and this can only be Demeter (Ceres). That the ancients also associated this particular sign and myth is proved by the fact that Demeter ruled Virgo in the schema of the twelve Olympians.[2]

Head of Demeter with her attributes: sheaves of corn, poppies, and snakes. Illustrated by Diane Smirnow from a photograph of the original terra-cotta bas-relief at the Terme Museum, Rome, Italy

The round of the seasons has always been symbolized in myth as a cosmic drama involving the earth mother and her child. More often than not, the child is male, and serves as the earth mother's lover as well as her son. As we have seen, the consort of the Great Goddess has his time of fruitfulness, followed by his symbolic death and journey into the underworld. The sign Virgo has always been associated with this myth, if only because the turning of the seasons—from summer to the mellow days of autumn which precede winter—occurs during the month of Virgo. In the Persephone myth, however, both the key figures—mother and child—are female. To the Egyptians, Virgo was the goddess Isis with the sun-child Horus on her lap. Medieval Christians saw this same constellation as the Virgin Mary holding the Christ child; and rightly so, for the Christian story is simply the most recent version of the myth of the Great Goddess and her dying child.[3] We live in an astrological age which is permeated with this myth, for Pisces is, in many ways, the dying god, while its opposite sign, Virgo, is the mother. When Michelangelo sculpted the Pieta, he created the mythic image for an entire cycle of history.[4]

If we examine the symbolic associations of Virgo, a particular theme emerges. Virgo concerns the transformation of personality from a childlike or virginal state into a wiser, more mature individuality, represented by the fruition of the harvest. And when we consider Virgo's place in the seasonal round, we would probably conclude, like Rudhyar, that this personal transformation must take place so that we can re-orient ourselves from personal to universal concerns—for Virgo is the final sign in the personal half of the zodiac where the Dayforce predominates.[5] Such a transformation would lead us to perform some manner of devoted service to others; hence Virgo is often called the sign of service. Both transformation and service, symbolically speaking, ought to take place on the physical level because Virgo is, after all, an earth sign, which is why Virgo is believed to have a special concern for health and why Virgo types are so often found among the nurses, therapists, chiropractors, and healers of the world.

But many astrological texts still present the above image of Virgo as an unfulfilled potential—if indeed they mention it at all. By and large, the Virgo type is still represented as cold, fussy, and analytical. Why is this?

Traditionally, Virgo is ruled by the planet Mercury. This planet is exceedingly mental and of the airy realm, being the archetype of the rational mind itself (see Chapter Three, "Mercury"). Mercury functions at its best in purely intellectual realms; which is to say, it does well in air signs. It is somewhat out of harmony with the more practical element of earth. Mercury's intellect applied to the "earthy" level of human existence may produce an excellent watchmaker, dentist, or other technician, but the warmth and naturalness of earth is somewhat stifled by the cerebral outlook of Mercury, and thus Virgos are branded as cold, analytical, and so on. Many astrologers have questioned this narrow view of Virgo, and rightly so. Some have even asserted that Mercury is not an appropriate ruler for this sign, and have

Personification of Mercury, ruler of Virgo, from Nicolas Le Rouge's Le grant kalendrier des bergieres, *Troyes, 1496*

suggested other possibilities among the asteroids or planetoids — Chiron, Ceres, and Vesta being the most noteworthy.[6]

Barbara Hand Clow has suggested Chiron the centaur as Virgo's ruler, due to his highly developed healing skills and knowledge of the human body.[7] While there is no final agreement about which figures belong to which sign, there is agreement that the addition of the four asteroid goddesses and Chiron are archetypes that have greatly expanded the mythic relationships of the signs and rulers of astrology and have supplied needed pieces of the puzzle, heretofore missing.

As we have observed, Mercury does not serve the archetype of a Virgin Goddess symbolism very well. Yet the argument for Mercury can be seen in Virgo's analytical abilities. As we have seen, the stage that Virgo represents in the zodiacal sequence concerns the final or most evolved stage of *individual* development before we reach the first stage of *collective* development in Libra. Thus the Virgo process

involves the breaking down of the entire organism into pieces so that it may assimilate and carry on what is useful for the next stage, or determine what can no longer serve the developing organism and send it to Scorpio for elimination. All of this, of course, requires discrimination, which is Virgo's glorified trait, and Mercury, our mentally proficient youngster, has the equipment to assist in this process.

Mercury, however, is itself a complex symbol. For though the Greeks and Romans knew this deity primarily as a messenger of the gods, and hence as an archetype of the communicating intellect, the medieval alchemists saw Mercury as a symbol of spiritual transformation. To them, Mercury (or, more properly, Mercurius) was both male and female, an androgynous spirit who symbolized the inner vitality inherent in all things living and physical — the inner vital spirit of earth. Hence Mercury was the agency which *transmuted*, or changed, earthly physical reality into something greater than itself — for the awakening of that vital spirit made of the earthly body or physical vehicle a wholeness, a unity of male and female, a synthesis of the four

The Virgin Mary holding the child Jesus — one of the symbols for Virgo. Photograph by Ariel Guttman

elements.[8] This medieval Mercurius is a
fitting symbol for Virgo. Virgo is a feminine sign, and the alchemical Mercurius
is an androgynous being, including the
feminine as well as the masculine (and
indeed, androgyny of some sort is often
attributed to the natives of this sign).
Mercurius is also the spirit which effects
change or transmutation, and Virgo is a
mutable sign. The matter to be transmuted is, according to the alchemists,
"lead" or "earth," i.e., physical reality or
the human body. The theme here is one
which accords perfectly with the higher
aspect of Virgo—transmutation of the
earthly element into a wholeness, a harvest time of the human spirit effected
through the body.

*A nineteenth-century head of Artemis,
another possible association with Virgo,
after a Roman copy of a Greek original*

Thus Virgo types, at their best,
transform their own bodies and minds
through diet, yoga, or other techniques
so that they may attain the kind of
wholeness necessary to truly help or
serve others. We have focused upon the
negative side of Virgo for too long—perhaps because we live now at the end of
the Virgo polarity of the Piscean Age. As we have seen, the authors of the Grail
Legend—who were contemporaries of the alchemists—were aware of the fact that
our civilization was leaning towards the more negative, overly analytical aspect of
its Virgo polarity (see Chapter Twenty, "The Elements," especially the section
"Water"). As we struggle now to clean up and heal a planet endangered by the
excesses of civilization which has replaced spirit with "pure" science, we also find it
necessary to redefine the Virgo polarity of our history and culture, to fashion an
archetype of healing rather than one of cold hard logic.

To the ancients, there were seven planets (five planets and the Sun and Moon)
that had rulership over the zodiacal signs, but, since there are twelve signs, certain
signs had to share planetary rulership. This situation created a zodiacal *mandala* of
"day houses" and "night houses" in which Gemini was Mercury's day house, while
Virgo was Mercury's night house (see Chapter Nineteen, "The Zodiac"). These two
signs "square" each other on the wheel, and are therefore said to operate on two different wavelengths. The association of Mercury to Gemini seems quite fitting in
that both symbols portray youthful, airy archetypes bent on curious exploration and
searching. In Gemini, Mercury's job is to obtain information, no matter what. In

Virgo, then, Mercury's function is to do something with that information. There are really two processes at work in Virgo. The very mental Virgoans handle information and input quite well and are concerned with the ongoing challenges of the mind. These are the Mercury types. But the other type of Virgo is concerned with the realm of earth (Virgo being an earth sign), and these Virgos are primarily concerned with the body of the earth or its microcosm, the human body. Here is where both Ceres and Chiron shine, and share Virgo's love for taking care of one's own body as well as the body of our planet, Earth. An additional archetype worth considering here is Artemis, protectress of childbirth, small animals, and lover of nature, all realms of interest to Virgo.

In Virgo we have reached the third aspect of the Great Goddess, having first encountered her in Taurus, then in Cancer. In Taurus she was celebrated with full round belly and breasts, as giver of life. In Cancer it was her connection with the young infant, i.e., the mother-child relationship, that was adored. Here in Virgo, at the third stage, Demeter must sacrifice her young child to another world, and thus we are witnessing the first stage of severing the bond of mother and child so that the child can enter new realms. In the Holy Mother and Child version of the severing of this bond that is so important in Christianity, the child is sacrificed to the collective spiritual realm of Pisces, where he is finally one with the Father. This, as we have seen, is the archetype of the Virgo/Pisces polarity, the final phase of which humanity is living through at this time. The realm that is entered in the Demeter/Persephone myth is Scorpio, the fourth stage of feminine power, where Kore becomes Persephone, and where a woman is initiated into her own realm of power independent from her mother, and where she may attain the status of crone. But what is most important here is that the archetypes of this story are important to both Virgo and Scorpio, and that the two signs represent shadow images of one another.

Artemis, or Diana

The Virgo needs to journey to the underworld and make the transformation necessary in Scorpio just as much as the Scorpio needs to come up from the underworld and participate in the earthly realm. The sharing of these elements is important in the lives of both signs. The human body and brain must often work themselves to sheer depletion, but they cannot continue this way. Virgos who are addicted to work will often encounter a crisis which forces them to take a sabbatical, re-enacting the Persephone myth by experiencing a crisis and retreating to the cool, dark depths of their personal underworld where healing is possible. Even the glyphs for Virgo and Scorpio resemble one another, Virgo's turning inward and representing the *yin* force while Scorpio's turns outward and portrays a more *yang* aspect. In any case, the story of Persephone forced the rulers of Virgo and Scorpio (Ceres and Pluto) together in a Libra-like compromise (the sign that separates Virgo and Scorpio) that was deemed to be just and fair for all concerned.

In the human body Virgo rules the digestive organs and, in keeping with its association with the harvest season and the final phase of the individual experience, it is a very important turning point in our twelve-fold scheme. In attempting to digest life's process and the five previous stages of individual development that have led up to Virgo, Virgos are constantly reminded that their physical organs are sensitive and vulnerable and must be kept in top shape. While other signs can get away with eating anything and not paying attention to their health, Virgos pay dearly for it. This is especially true if the Moon, Ceres, Saturn, or Vesta are placed in Virgo natally.

Those with the Sun in Virgo naturally focus their attention on fine-tuning the body, mind, or spirit, resulting in a powerful sense of devotion that strives to create a perfect, everything-in-its-place world. People with the Moon in Virgo may find it difficult to nurture themselves—they're too busy fixing everything and everyone around them. They need to appreciate their own achievements, or, best of all, to be able to laugh at their own mistakes.

Mercury in Virgo people will also want to fix everything around them, and use their analytical proficiency in understanding how everything in the world operates. Venus in Virgo natives most assuredly delight in their work, so it is extremely necessary for them to find work that they truly delight in. They also add the element of color and beauty to the sign of fine craftsmanship. Mars in Virgo combines the physical stamina and courage of Mars with the sign that rules physical health. Thus, thorough body maintenance and athletic achievement (perhaps body-building) would appeal. And, given the traditional Martian rulership over iron and other metals, Mars in Virgo types are usually excellent mechanics.

The asteroids Ceres, Pallas, Juno, and Vesta have all been suggested as rulers of Virgo, so it is likely that they would all express their nature most eloquently here, but Ceres and Vesta seem to fit the Virgo archetype particularly well. As we have previously noted, Virgo is the most probable rulership sign for Ceres, giving dedication, honesty, and integrity to the individual. Here, she is highly devoted to the works she performs and the effect her work has on others. Pallas Athene would most likely use her ingenuity and skill in an applied way, perhaps in weaving, sewing, print-making, etc., or work for a social purpose which ranges between the glorious and the obsessive. Juno, let's not forget, is concerned with the mating ritual, and in Virgo would seek to perfect her relationships. Vesta in Virgo must also be exalted: focused consciousness blazes a conduit for spirit and body to meet.

Jupiter's social consciousness may become obsessively concerned with the form and letter of its achievements rather than the spirit, though worldly achievements there should surely be, and in abundance. Saturn in Virgo or the Sixth House tends to be a traditionalist in many things, though certainly a productive one, since Saturn is an earthy planet and Virgo an earth sign. Chiron has been nominated for rulership of Virgo, and it is certainly a powerful influence in that sign or in the Sixth House, though it is equally likely to shape a healer or a hypochondriac. The rebellious power of Uranus is somewhat dampened in the Sixth House, though its scientific or inventive characteristics remain undimmed. Neptune is in accidental detriment in the Sixth House: health (physical or emotional) is often an issue here, though these problems may lead positively to a concern with diet, exercise, yoga, or a helping or healing career. Pluto's obsessive power, when focused in the Sixth House, may produce a native whose sense of order and precision is so developed as to preclude any relaxation or ease, though it also helps the native to focus on a particular goal.

One of the greatest planetary conjunctions of our time took place in Virgo: the conjunction of Uranus and Pluto during the turbulent and revolutionary middle years of the 1960s. This was a pivotal period for humanity, because these planets were, for the first time since the Industrial Revolution, challenging the work-as-routine systems that had been established at that time. In fact, we are governed by the conjunction of those two planets in Virgo until the next conjunction occurs—and that will not happen until the late 21st century. The Virgo conjunction was a warning that earth's resources were being rapidly depleted and drastic measures needed to be taken to reverse the process. Paying little attention to the warning, we continued to abuse the earth until Uranus made the first square to that conjunction in Sagittarius in the mid 1980s, and the world was again reminded and finally started to listen. This process is reminiscent of the story of Demeter, the earth mother who, in mourning for her loss, refused to green the earth. Like Pluto, the dark underworld figure, technology and greed have raped the earth mother, and until she is replenished or made right, we may be facing a greater crisis than we suspect.

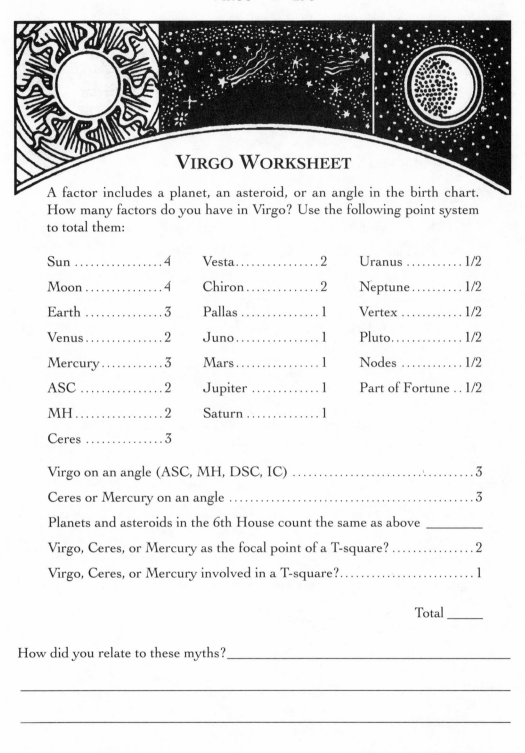

VIRGO WORKSHEET

A factor includes a planet, an asteroid, or an angle in the birth chart. How many factors do you have in Virgo? Use the following point system to total them:

Sun 4	Vesta...............2	Uranus 1/2
Moon 4	Chiron.............2	Neptune.........1/2
Earth 3	Pallas 1	Vertex 1/2
Venus..............2	Juno...............1	Pluto.............1/2
Mercury...........3	Mars...............1	Nodes 1/2
ASC 2	Jupiter 1	Part of Fortune .. 1/2
MH................2	Saturn 1	
Ceres 3		

Virgo on an angle (ASC, MH, DSC, IC) 3

Ceres or Mercury on an angle 3

Planets and asteroids in the 6th House count the same as above _____

Virgo, Ceres, or Mercury as the focal point of a T-square? 2

Virgo, Ceres, or Mercury involved in a T-square?.........................1

Total _____

How did you relate to these myths?_____

_____

_____

_____

_____

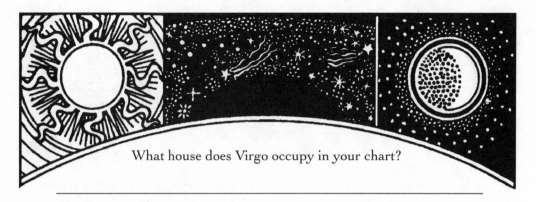

What house does Virgo occupy in your chart?

_____

10th House—mother   1st House—self

4th House—father   11th House—friends

7th House—mate   5th House—children, lovers

3rd House—sibling

Keeping in mind that these houses represent these relationships, how has Virgo energy expressed itself through others in your life? _____

_____

_____

_____

What houses do Ceres and Mercury occupy in your chart and how are they

expressed? _____

_____

What signs or planets are in your 6th House and how are they expressed? _____

_____

_____

Insights: _____

_____

_____

_____

LIBRA

LIBRA, *The Scales*

SIGN: *Libra, the 7th Zodiacal Sign*

MODE: *Cardinal* ❧ ELEMENT: *Air* ❧ RULER: *Venus*

ADDITIONAL MYTHIC ARCHETYPES: *Hephaestus (Vulcan)*
❧ *Maat (Egyptian)* ❧ *Hera (Juno)* ❧ *Pallas Athene (Minerva)*
❧ *Paris, the Trojan Prince* ❧ *Eros and Psyche*

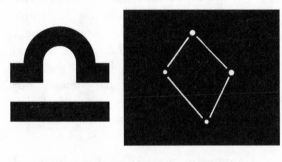

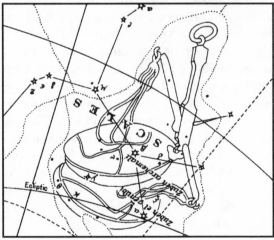

Libra constitutes something of an enigma, inasmuch as it appears to have been inserted into the zodiac at a rather late date. Early Babylonian zodiacs, for instance, contain only eleven signs: the constellation we call Libra was known as the claws of the scorpion, hence a part of Scorpio rather than a separate sign. The Greeks saw this star group as the scales held by Astraea, goddess of justice (see Virgo); here we find it linked with Virgo rather than Libra, but beginning to assume the symbolism which is familiar to us today.[1]

But if Libra was unknown to the Babylonians, it was familiar to the Egyptians. As we have seen, the Egyptians were concerned with the night-time rising of signs, so that Libra would have risen during the month of Aries. This, of course, is the Easter season—and before there was an Easter, there were the ancient New Year festivals associated with the vernal equinox. Thus the Egyptians knew Libra as Chonsu, the Divine Child who symbolized the birth of the New Year, who bore the symbol of the new moon on his head, and whose name means "traveler of the night skies."[2] Our own associations to Libra, however, come from its position on the autumnal rather than the vernal equinox.

As the scales of balance, Libra is the only sign which is represented by a mechanical instrument rather than by some human or animal figure. Perhaps this is why, in the schema of the twelve Olympians, Libra was attributed to Hephaestus (Vulcan), the blacksmith or divine craftsman of the gods.[3] A better rationale for Hephaestus' rulership of Libra may lie in the peculiar circumstances of his birth. The Olympian rulerships were arranged in pairs of male-female opposites; this links Hephaestus with Athene, the Olympian ruler of Aries. Both of these deities were born from a single parent. Athene, as will be remembered, was born from the head of her father Zeus, without feminine intervention. Another mythological tradition asserts that Hephaestus was born of Hera without masculine participation. The daughter, Athene, is the child solely of the father, while the son, Hephaestus, was magically born of the mother. It is perhaps significant that contemporary astrologers now link the asteroids Pallas Athene and Juno (Hera, the mother of Hephaestus) with Libra.

Maat, the Egyptian goddess of law, illustrated by Diane Smirnow

Hephaestus was Aphrodite's husband, although this was not a marriage made in heaven. Nevertheless, both Vulcan and Venus, at one time or another, have been considered Libra's rulers—and they have both been considered Taurus' rulers, as well, for many believe the yet undiscovered planet Vulcan to be associated with Taurus. Because they were divine mates we might see Venus as representing the *anima* of both Taurus and Libra while Vulcan represents the *animus*. As with Virgo, there have been other goddesses and gods suggested for Libra, since it, like Virgo, still has to share a rulership.

The scales in Libra had a deep significance for the Egyptians. It was said that at the time of death the goddess Maat placed the human soul on one scale and a feather on the other. If the scale tipped even slightly, the soul must reincarnate with the goal of releasing the extra weight. Since Libra comes just

The Egyptian god Anubis weighing the souls of the dead. Illustrated by Diane Smirnow

before Scorpio, the sign associated with death—which the Egyptians honored in their eloquent preparations for the afterlife—the prime goal in life was to make the scales balance, or to prepare the soul for its afterlife.

We don't often see modern-day Librans concerned with the weight of their souls. The constant balancing acts they involve themselves in for the sake of partnership, however, may ultimately weigh them down. Libra's scales are constantly weighing and measuring the quality, fairness, or justice of their ongoing relationships. As the sign of the autumnal equinox, Libra represents a transitional moment in the cycle of the seasons. The days and nights are of equal length, so that the energies of the self (day) and the consciousness of "other" or collective humanity (night) stand balanced. This same situation, of course, occurs during the vernal equinox at the beginning of the month of Aries, but with a vital difference. During Aries, it is the Dayforce which is growing stronger. Hence Aries represents an emergent individuality detaching itself from collective humanity. In Libra, the Nightforce is increasing, so that the symbolism here depicts the individual beginning to recognize the needs of others, of the collective.[4] Thus Libra's scales are usually tipped away from the self and toward others. And though the scales may seem a rather impersonal symbol for the sign which we associate with marriage and partnership, they do symbolize the balance of forces which occurs at the equinox.

Athene's balanced decision-making is a fitting archetype for Libra. Helmeted Athene on contemporary (1978) Greek currency. From the Michael A. Sikora collection

The glyph for Libra itself signifies the equinox. Some have imagined that the Libra symbol (♎) represents the beam of a scales, though Cyril Fagan presents a strong case for the origin of the symbol in an Egyptian ideogram called *akhet*.[5] This ideogram depicted the rising of the sun, and its meaning was the horizon or ascendant. In most ancient cultures, the equinoxes and solstices were timed by the observation of the sunrise. Markers were created to gauge the turning points of the year; sometimes whole temples or religious complexes, such as Stonehenge, were dedicated to that purpose.

In medical astrology Libra rules the kidneys, the pair of scales in the body that regulates and balances the workings of the internal system. As a filtering system, the kidneys provide the means by which to keep the body pure of toxic substances that could have serious consequences for the system. This is not unlike Libra's need to filter the experiences of life, or of personal relationships, that might otherwise have similar consequences.

In Libra we become conscious of the need for partnership. Aries is linked with the First House of the horoscopic wheel, and the First House, having to do with beginnings, is often called the house of self. We always begin with consciousness of our unique individuality. Libra is the seventh sign, linked with the Seventh House, and as Aries' polar opposite, constitutes the place on the wheel furthest from self, thus immersed in the "other." This house has always been known as the house of marriage in traditional astrology. Indeed, the first recognition which we, as individuals, have of a larger or collective frame of reference is likely to be a recognition of our need for relationship. Thus Libra's traditional attribution as the sign of love and marriage is well founded, and entirely harmonious with a sign ruled by Venus. But this consciousness of other has a much wider application, for the meaning of the word relationship is not confined to intimate, one-on-one relationships. Any time we, as individuals, must recognize the needs of others, or enter into any kind of a relationship with others, the symbolism of Libra and the autumn equinox is operative. This is why Libran types are believed to be such skilled diplomats, and why Libra is the sign of peace. Because when we come to recognize the needs of others on a truly collective scale, we become conscious of the need to create harmony for humanity at large. This is the symbolism which lies at the root of Libra's famous idealism (as exemplified by Libra natives Mahatma Gandhi and Jimmy Carter, two pacifists dedicated to conflict resolution). Though the average Libran type may be concerned primarily with intimate or romantic relationships, there is always a sense of higher purpose lingering in the background. Libra plants the seeds for a wider vision of humanity, a vision which will come to fruition in the next air sign, Aquarius.

Libra's Venus or Aphrodite is a far cry from Taurus' more earthy goddess. In Taurus she indulged in the raw sensual pleasure principle where eroticism was glorified. Libra's Aphrodite is much more the archetype of aesthetic beauty—a museum piece, beautiful to admire, lovely to flirt with, exciting to tease, and beckoning you to praise, but nearly impossible to touch. And even though Venus, as the goddess of love, fits with the partnership

Astraea (Justice) holding her scales.
Photograph by Ariel Guttman

sign Libra, contemporary astrologers have questioned her rulership of this sign almost as much as they question Mercury's rulership of Virgo. In particular, the asteroids Juno and Pallas Athene have been suggested as rulers of Libra.

Juno (Hera) presided over the institution of marriage and was the wife of Jupiter, the king of the gods. The marriage of Zeus and Hera is a story regarding power struggles in marriage, and indeed, if we are to observe the history of marriage, rarely has it been about love. Historically it has more often taken place as an arranged situation for political, social, or religious reasons. Love is a relatively recent addition to the concept of marriage, making its first appearance in Western culture during the Middle Ages in the form of romances such as *Tristan and Iseult* or Lancelot and Guinevere. And in the upper classes, especially among royalty, marriages are still arranged. Although we associate Venus the love goddess with Libra, Libra has more to do with marriage than love, as attested to by Venus herself in her

Detail of title page showing the Judgment of Paris, presumably by Jost Amman, from the print shop of Sigmund Feyerabend, Frankfurt, 1581

own marriage to Vulcan. Even the Juno-Jupiter union, which was supposedly the archetype for marriage, does not depict a very happy or balanced state. In fact, one modern interpretation of Tristan and Iseult's romance implies that true romance does not happen among married partners at all![6] Juno, because of her rulership over the institution of marriage and her shared power of the heavens with Jupiter, seems a fitting planetary symbol for Libra. But Juno's married life was full of strife, stories of infidelity, mad jealous rages, and revenge upon her husband's lovers. With archetypes like this for marriage, no wonder it's in the state it's in!

With regard to Pallas Athene's rulership over Libra, her wisdom, logic, fairness, and balanced decision-making create a fitting symbol for this sign, especially those Librans who have an excess of air and find cool, detached logic preferable to the emotional entanglements that most close partnerships require. But as a virgin goddess, Athene repudiated partnerships, and Libra's place in the zodiac seems to vibrate in accordance with the partnership theme.

Liz Greene's idea that the Trojan prince Paris symbolizes Libra is also an interesting concept to consider.[7] Paris was asked (as Libras always are) to make a judgment. The judgment concerned a beauty contest in which the contestants were Aphrodite, Hera, and Athene, whom we will recognize as Libra's three planetary rulers. Hera offered Paris "the world;" Athene, the leadership position and victories of a powerful warrior; but Aphrodite, goddess of love and beauty, offered him a gift from her domain, and promised him the most beautiful woman in the world. Paris chose Aphrodite, but the gift was Helen (one of the Gemini quadruplets), a married woman, and her abduction started the Trojan War. In the life of the Libra there is often such a conflict centering on love or beauty. An interesting correlation here is that the city of Paris, known for its love of *love and beauty*, has always beckoned lovers to its heart, and *is* strongly associated with Libra.[8]

And finally, there is one more mythological pair that may be the most fitting archetype yet for Libra, our sign of partnership—Psyche and Eros. Theirs is a story of love (Eros) in search of a soul (Psyche) and a soul in search of love. Eros was Aphrodite's son, the child of the goddess of love. One day it became known that there was a woman more beautiful than Aphrodite herself. Of course, Aphrodite wouldn't have a competitor (especially a mortal), and ordered this woman executed. Her son, Eros, whose usual task was shooting mortals with his magic love arrows, was given the job of making sure that Psyche would meet her death. But when he

Eros, son of Aphrodite

spotted her tied to a rock and blindfolded, he accidentally shot himself with his own arrow; one look at the beautiful Psyche and he was instantly in love. He untied her and carried her off to his castle in the valley. The one thing Eros demanded was that Psyche remain blindfolded when the two of them were together, so that she would not know that she was with the god of love. Soon her sisters came to visit her and, suggesting that she was a fool for remaining blindfolded, admonished her to remove her mask and *look* at her husband, who might even be a monster. In giving in to this nagging fear, Psyche disobeyed the one demand Eros had made, and he instantly fled out the window. Psyche mourned and grieved and prayed to Aphrodite for the return of her lost love. Aphrodite eventually gave in, but demanded of Psyche a series of seemingly impossible tasks which were designed by the goddess of love with the assurance that Psyche could not possibly perform them. But, with the help of the animal kingdom, Psyche completed all the tasks perfectly. Aphrodite had no choice but to reunite the lovers, in a happily-ever-after type of fairytale, to return to their castle in bliss.

This myth is highly symbolic of marriage even in contemporary times. With stars in our eyes we find our mates. After awhile we dare to look and see them as they really are; disillusionment sets in. Whether the separation is emotional or physical, it somehow occurs. The partnership goes through tests, trials, and challenges (Saturn is, after all, esoteric ruler of Libra, and is exalted in that sign) and thus discovers how strong the bond or union actually is. If it's strong, it survives these challenges, and becomes better than ever. Like Eros and Psyche at the end of the story, we are happily reunited as equals in the mating game. Psychologists Erich Neumann and Robert Johnson

Psyche returning from the underworld with the box of beauty which Aphrodite had commanded her to obtain from Persephone

Psyche received onto Olympus — a nineteenth-century engraving after the original painting by Caravaggio

have used this story specifically to depict the basis of feminine psychology.[9] It is offered here as a story not limited to women alone, but one that depicts relationship dynamics in general. It is possible to have the same process occur without a partner. We dare to look under our own masks and see the flaws and imperfections we usually try so desperately to hide. We then set ourselves to the task of self-improvement, which is seemingly impossible and labor-intensive, but yields a fruitful and fulfilling relationship with the self.

Since Libra represents the part of the wheel where we are concerned with the primary mating relationship and the balancing of this relationship with the self, it poses a difficult challenge. Libra has been known for its inability to make a decision because it can see both sides of any issue and strives always to be fair. The most difficult task for the Libra is to see things from a *self-centered* position, and thus it is often too self-sacrificing when concerned with relationships.

In recent times, the term "co-dependent" has been tossed around psychological circles and treatment centers quite liberally as a means of defining the core of many problems in our society and our family structures. And certainly if Libra's positive quality is the ability to relate fairly and equally, then its negative manifestation is co-dependency.

We have observed that Libra or Seventh House individuals strive for balance, fairness, cooperation, harmony, and beauty in life and especially in relationship. Fortunately, all Libras don't have marriages like Juno's, Venus', or Psyche's. But in a world where *concepts* and *ideas* are important, the Libran may keep her or himself so emotionally detached and removed from what's going on at the heart of the union that she or he creates the polarity effect—rage and emotional outburst from the partner such as Juno, Vulcan, and Psyche acted out. Each of these three responded to their dysfunctional relationships in a different way. Vulcan hammered out his anger in his workshop and created beautiful works of art, one of which was a golden net that he used to trap Venus in bed with her lover Mars and thus reveal his own shame and humiliation to all Olympus; Psyche went to work doing menial, labor-intensive tasks as a way of keeping herself focused and balanced while waiting for the return of her lost love; Juno's response to her problem relationship was to strike out at the other *women* who allowed themselves to be involved with a married man, thus revealing her anger towards herself for tolerating her fate as a woman no longer in control of her destiny. The point in Libra, then, is not to eloquently speak of beauty, harmony, and balance as an ideal vision while in the midst of a relationship whose emotional core is a shambles, but to *involve* oneself in the one-on-one process, accepting (rather than projecting) the ugly and imperfect parts *and* taking responsibility for one's own actions in the interplay of opposites that exists in the relationship arena.

Libra is the Sun's "fall" position. The individual ego diffuses itself in favor of the other. On the *mandala* wheel of the houses, Libra occupies the diurnal position of the setting sun, the time of day when, according to the ancients, the sun drove away in his solar chariot to "fall" below the horizon. Its light is lost until the first pre-dawn spark of Aries fire is once again encountered. This corresponds to Libra's position in the seasonal wheel of the year as well. This falling of the Sun symbolizes a psychological truth which portrays Libra as the least self-centered of any sun-sign, tending to encompass the energies of its partners for its source of energy and light.

Moon in Libra types will focus and rejuvenate best in the company of their favorite partner or people—talking, sharing, laughing, discussing. Decorating or remodeling often centers them nicely, as does some form of light exercise in the fresh air—especially when accomplished with a partner, as in tennis. Best of all, they might try to say something impolite or uncompromising once in awhile, just to tip the scale the other way.

Mercury in Libra tends to be the diplomat in verbal and written communications and would probably love a job as an interviewer. Venus in Libra, as we have noted, is in a starring role here, elevating love, beauty, and aesthetics to a fine art. Mars in Libra may assert one's energies on the collective stage by fighting for equal opportunity, equal pay for equal work, etc.

Ceres in Libra individuals tend to be skilled at relating, mediating, and being fair. They, like Mars, may insist on sexual equality in the workplace. Pallas Athene, as we have noted, shines in the fields of mediating, diplomacy, and strategy in this fair-minded sign. Juno in Libra is double-strength, as the asteroid who presides over marriage sits in a sign related to equality and fairness. Vesta may insist on walking a spiritual path within the partnership. Both Juno and Vesta in this sign will look for their "soul-mate."

Jupiter in Libra and Saturn in Libra both are well-suited to careers in the legal system, but regardless of whether it is career-based or not, these natives have the law intertwined in their lives in a most profound way. Chiron in the Seventh House often shows individuals who have been wounded in relationships, and who seek healing by the same means. With Uranus in the Seventh, natives are impelled to seek non-traditional relationships: ordinary partnerships just don't provide the right kind of spark for these individuals. Neptune seeks a soul-mate or spiritual love when in the Seventh. Sometimes this search can become a reality, but these people, more than others, must be on their guard for co-dependent or savior-victim relationships. People with Pluto in the Seventh may seem to swallow their partners up, or be swallowed up by their partners, as Hades swallowed Kore into the earth. Theirs is a love too intense for most, though their ability to make a commitment is also more highly developed than that of ordinary people.

One of the most challenging times for the institution of marriage in recent history was the late 1960s and early 1970s when Uranus and Pluto were both in Libra for a short time. The divorce rate was statistically the highest on record,[10] and if the deities that rule Libra were making a statement about the inequality of the institution of marriage at that time, they were very effective. Many reforms have been instituted since then, and especially from 1972 to 1984, when Pluto was in Libra. Neptune entered Libra in 1942 and stayed there until 1956. This generation of baby-boomers has a unique challenge in regards to relationships. Most of these Neptune in Libra individuals also have Pluto in Leo, and are striving to uphold the sacred institution of marriage and be devoted to their partners (Libra), while fiercely making a statement of self-assertion and individuality (Leo). This is a generation which idealizes relationships, feels empty without them, yet struggles intensely for individual freedom and self-assertion even while involved in them—certainly a curious phenomenon.

LIBRA WORKSHEET

A factor includes a planet, an asteroid, or an angle in the birth chart. How many factors do you have in Libra? Use the following point system to total them:

Sun	4	Juno	2	Uranus	1/2
Moon	4	Saturn	2	Neptune	1/2
Earth	3	Mars	1	Part of Fortune	1/2
Venus	3	Ceres	1	Pluto	1/2
Mercury	2	Vesta	1	Nodes	1/2
MH	2	Jupiter	1	Vertex	1/2
ASC	2	Chiron	1		
Pallas	2				

Libra on an angle (ASC, MH, DSC, IC) 3

Venus or Juno on an angle 3

Planets and asteroids in the 7th House count the same as above _____

Libra, Venus, or Juno as the focal point of a T-square? 2

Libra, Venus, or Juno involved in a T-square? 1

Total _____

How did you relate to these myths? _____

_____

_____

_____

_____

What house does Libra occupy in your chart?

_____

10th House—mother   1st House—self

4th House—father   11th House—friends

7th House—mate   5th House—children, lovers

3rd House—sibling

Keeping in mind that these houses represent these relationships, how has Libra energy expressed itself through others in your life? _____

_____

_____

What houses do Venus and Juno occupy in your chart and how are they

expressed? _____

_____

What signs or planets are in your 7th House and how are they expressed? _____

_____

_____

Insights: _____

_____

_____

_____

_____

A Cretan snake goddess, illustrated by Diane Smirnow

SCORPIO

CHAPTER TWENTY-NINE

SCORPIO, *The Scorpion*

SIGN: *Scorpio, the 8th Zodiacal Sign*

MODE: *Fixed* ❧ ELEMENT: *Water* ❧ RULER: *Pluto*

ADDITIONAL MYTHIC ARCHETYPES: *Mars (Ares)*
❧ *Nergal (Babylonian)* ❧ *Persephone* ❧ *The Cretan Snake
Goddess* ❧ *Inanna (Sumerian)* ❧ *Orpheus and Eurydice*
❧ *Juno (Hera)* ❧ *Shakti (Hindu)* ❧ *Asclepius*

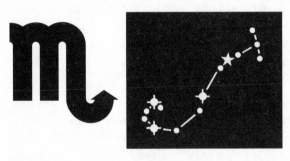

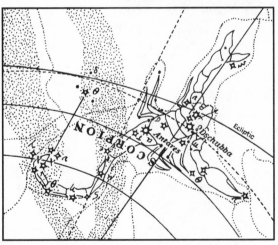

During the month of Scorpio the leaves fall from the trees and the earth begins to "shut down," to prepare for the long sleep of winter. In the ancient nature religions, this was the season in which the goddess or god actually journeyed into the underworld; all things would be empty and cold until the winter solstice marked the beginning of the process of return, leading finally to resurrection in the spring. The Celtic peoples celebrated the Feast of Samhain during this month; the ancient festival survives to the present day as Halloween. On Samhain Eve, the "doors between the worlds" stood open; the connection between humans and elementals — or humans and the spirits of the dead — was intensely heightened. In Latin American countries — and even in Los Angeles and parts of the American Southwest — the first and second of November are honored as the Days of the Dead (*Días de los Muertos*). Families picnic in graveyards and children eat candy fashioned in the shape of skeletons.

It is no wonder, then, that Scorpio is associated with the descent into the underworld. For most of us, this signifies a journey to the very depths of our being—a journey which is inevitably painful, for it forces us to confront our inner demons and psychological complexes. But Scorpio also holds out the promise of resurrection, of returning to the light: thus Scorpio is regarded as a sign of transformation. And certainly it is Scorpio that has always been associated with occult wisdom. Some astrologers have imaged Scorpio as a fourfold process—from angry scorpion to introspective lizard (the underworld sojourn) to soaring eagle (rebirth) to white-winged dove (the Holy Spirit). Dane Rudhyar compared Scorpio to the phoenix, a mythical Egyptian bird which immolates itself on a self-made funeral pyre only to rise reborn from its own ashes.[1]

The connection between Scorpio and the underworld goes back to the very beginnings of astrology. Like the other fixed signs, it appears in the Babylonian *Epic of Gilgamesh*. While Gilgamesh was on his way to Dilmun, the Babylonian other-world, he had to cross forbidding mountains guarded by "the scorpion-men."[2] As early as Sumer, then, Scorpio was the dark guardian at the threshold of the other world, and one had to pass through the gates of darkness in order to reach the world of light. And if the Babylonians linked this sign with the deadly scorpion, they also linked it with the eagle, as is clear from the vision of Ezekiel (see Chapter Twenty-one, "Modalities").

The image of the scorpion requires some consideration, for it is in part because of this rather unlovely and forbidding creature that Scorpio has attained such a dark and negative image in traditional astrology. Though it is true that some natives of this sign possess a temperament (or at least a tongue) which packs the proverbial sting, the scorpion itself has to do with that underworld journey which is the essence of the Scorpio myth. In Egypt, where the evening rising of signs was of paramount importance, Scorpio rose during May. This was the month in which the hot desert winds called the *khamseen* began to blow. Blazing heat blighted the land, threatening crops and other forms of life; scorpions migrated from the desert and became a veritable pestilence.[3] This image of the scorching sun which destroys life is, in fact, the negative or underworld polarity of the sun in general. For if the sun brings life and vitality to the world, it may also bring destruction.

This destructive aspect of the sun was personified by the Babylonians as Nergal, god of war and pestilence. But Nergal was the planet Mars as well—fittingly enough, since the Sun and Mars are linked by their fiery nature, and since Mars is likely to energize the solar qualities of anyone's horoscope, whether for

Scorpion-archer from a boundary stone, Babylon, c. 1140 BC

good or ill.[4] Before Pluto was discovered and named as the ruler of Scorpio, this sign was under the dominion of Mars, both in classical astrology and in the Olympian schema. Here for the first time we come to a sign that has changed its rulership—where the symbolism of the sign has been transformed to represent Plutonian rather than Martian energies. It is true that some astrologers retain the classical Mars rulership for Scorpio, but, following the discovery of Pluto in 1930, most astrologers noted that the archetypal energies which Pluto represented in our contemporary world (the atom bomb, big corporations, depth psychology) seemed to fit symbolically with the sign Scorpio (see Pluto).

The god Nergal was principally known in Babylon for usurping the throne of the underworld (see Mars). The god of war and pestilence stormed the gates of hell, dethroned the goddess who ruled there, and set himself up as lord of the dead.[5] The scorching sun of midday became the sun of darkness, the hidden or midnight sun.

In the story of Hades and Persephone, it is Hades who appears from the underworld in his dark chariot and abducts Persephone, making her his bride to rule with him in the underworld, while in the Babylonian version it is the fiery, masculine deity who goes below and seizes rulership of the underworld from the femi-

Selkhet, the Egyptian scorpion goddess, one of the deities who led the deceased into the afterlife. Illustrated by Diane Smirnow

nine presence. In the Greek version, the underworld is at first ruled solely by a masculine deity, but the netherworld's balance of male and female energies is restored when Hades abducts Persephone. The Greeks understood that the vast, dark, unexplored and unexplained realm of the unconscious and of primordial feeling belonged to the feminine element. Another Greek myth tells how Apollo, the sun god, came to Delphi and made it his home. But the first resident of that sacred place was the Python, a serpentine, feminine deity associated with Gaia, Mother Earth. To claim this region as his own, Apollo had to slay the Python. And though he claimed dominion over the oracle he established at Delphi, it was in fact the slain feminine Python, transformed by death and speaking through a priestess called the Pythoness, who uttered the divine revelations. The masculine and feminine elements operate here in a state of balance. And as we have seen, Pluto in the birth chart is just as much feminine as masculine. Once Persephone joins Hades in the underworld, their energies merge.

Since Mars and Pluto are related in the myth of Nergal, it is no wonder that these two planets share rulership of Scorpio, or that both of them are associated with the myth of the underworld journey. It is also worth noting that the Sun and Mars are both strongly related, in a symbolic way, to the conscious ego, and it is the ego which suffers destruction and transformation in the psychic underworld. The typical Scorpio may indeed have a death wish, or so traditional sources assure us. But what these seemingly obsessed Scorpios *really* or unconsciously seek is not the extinction of the physical body so much as the death and rebirth of consciousness. They may pursue hobbies like race-car driving or skydiving, or they may try to lose themselves in sex or drugs, but at heart they seek inner transformation.

It is through such inner transformation, of course, that we discover wisdom, and Scorpio is consequently a sign of wisdom. To many astrologers, Scorpio is symbolized by the serpent as well as by the eagle, lizard, or scorpion. (And with good reason, for the constellation Serpens is intertwined with Scorpio.) The Serpent Wisdom is a specific kind of knowing—one which includes the deep, unspoken, chthonic mysteries of life, death, and sex. In this respect, Scorpio is truly a feminine or watery sign, for such wisdom can only be obtained through the feelings (water); it is not accessible to logic. The Serpent Wisdom is feminine—the dark, underworld side of the feminine.

Serpents have played a large role in the mythology and ritual of many cultures, yet to this day the sight of one inspires fear and paralysis among some human beings. The snake goddesses who were so prevalent in Crete during the Taurean Age represented the life-giving aspect of the Goddess, but the serpent itself was

Hades' abduction of Persephone, a nineteenth-century engraving after an original painting

worshipped because it was said to hold the secrets of life, death, and rebirth.[6] The gift of prophecy, as well, has always been linked to the Serpent Wisdom, as in Delphi. Cassandra, who was gifted with prophetic vision, is said to have been left as a child with snakes who were found licking her ears. Snakes were also venerated because of their venom. The venom from a snake bite contained a substance that chemically altered brain cells, producing an effect similar to that which psychedelic drugs have on the brain—and inducing in the user a significant alteration of consciousness, including the ability to receive visions in this trance state. Thus, during religious ceremonies serpent venom was used to produce the altered state, to induce dreams, and to provide visions from the gods in much the same way as when shamans enter trance to obtain visionary information regarding the healings they perform. It was also said that they could "enter the world of the dead" in this state, discover and recognize the particular demon (Jungian psychologists and Plato both prefer the less judgmental term *∂aimon*) and then return. It was the discovery and recognition of this demon that saved or cured the individual, much the way a poisonous snake bite can be healed by ingesting the very poison which has infected the sufferer. Scorpios have an ability to access these trance-like states and netherworld regions more easily than most. In fact, the discovery, recognition, and acceptance of one's own demons is a transformative journey which allows the former demons to become totems, or symbols, of empowerment for the individual's healing process. This is why serpents were said to embody wisdom and have always been represented in the healing process. The caduceus, a staff intertwined by two serpents, continues to be the symbol for physicians and medical practitioners today.

Scorpio's process concerns life, death, and rebirth. This is a constant theme in the lives of Scorpio individuals—they typically experience a death or near-death experience, only to be reborn and, like the phoenix, rise from the ashes of their former selves and soar to new heights. This process is seldom undertaken willingly. Scorpio is *fixed* water; therefore it does not usually welcome change. The snake has to bite these reluctant Scorpios first, then their atomic reactors are ready to fire back with a vengeance. Scorpios, like shamans, surgeons, psychotherapists, or hypnotherapists, can help others enter the realm of that netherworld which most of us are unable or unwilling to enter alone.

In Scorpio we reach the fourth stage of the Great Goddess, in which, having descended to the underworld, she emerges as supreme, whole, and transformed. Several mythic archetypes come to mind for this aspect of Scorpio—Ishtar's journey to the underworld in search of her lover Tammuz (see Chapter Four, "Venus," and Chapter Eighteen, "Pluto"), Kore's abduction by Hades (see Chapter Nine, "Ceres"), and Orpheus' descent to the underworld to reclaim his beloved bride, Eurydice. All three stories have one thing in common—the descent involves a partner with whom the journeyer is closely paired. Here in Scorpio we are involved not only with the process of transformation that comes from this journey "down under," but also with the merging with another that never happens more intensely than in Scorpio or its natural house, the Eighth.

In the first water sign, Cancer, we observed the bonding between mother and child. In the second water sign, Scorpio, it is the separation process that is paramount. But if Scorpio is so concerned with merging, how is it that separation is equally significant? In Cancer, the individual was bound or overshadowed by the mother or family unit. In Scorpio, one breaks away from this interdependence, as when Persephone is snatched away from her mother, Demeter, in order to merge as an equal with her masculine counterpart, Hades. This is a major theme in the lives of Scorpios, who are dealing with deep emotional bonding and with the need to maintain some personal control—so that Scorpios will not be controlled by the partner in the same way they were controlled by the family in the earlier, Cancerian phase of the water sign process. In the lives of most Scorpios, particularly when the Sun or Moon is in that sign, a parent has exerted such serious and deliberate control over the individual that his or her life-long struggle is to break free. There is often parental jealousy and rage when the child takes a mate, similar to Demeter's reaction when Persephone was forced to remain with Hades. And there are often jealous bouts between Scorpio and the partner, similar to the squabbles between Juno (an asteroid said to be strongly associated with Scorpio) and her mate, Jupiter. There is a passionate sense of commitment bordering on obsessive need, as with Orpheus, who was so obsessed by his need to have Eurydice at his side that he journeyed twice to the underworld to plead for her return. (Eurydice, it seems, had her life abruptly ended when, in her youth, she was bitten by a poisonous snake.) These are the soap-opera dramas that often fill a Scorpio individual's life, especially when planets in Scorpio are in stressful aspect. Indeed, the transformation of such turbulent energies is paramount in Scorpio's evolutionary cycle.

A nineteenth-century engraving of
Orpheus and Eurydice

The separation and regeneration processes that are so closely associated with the sign Scorpio reflect its rulerships in the body as well. In medical astrology both the sex organs (procreation, regeneration) and the eliminative organs (colon, bladder) are ruled by Scorpio. People with planets in Scorpio (especially those involved in fixed T-squares) often have trouble eliminating the old emotional garbage in their lives and this can have serious effects on the body's ability to eliminate as well.

Whenever a planet appears in Scorpio or in the Eighth House, think of it in terms of being "recycled." The psychic or psychological inheritance of that planet no longer serves the needs of the individual's current evolutionary pattern. These individuals, like Hercules, must do battle with the Hydra (a labor sometimes associated with Scorpio, though it has also been linked to Cancer), and sear off the problem at its root, as Hercules seared off the Hydra's many heads. Because Scorpio is a fixed sign and a water sign, planets appearing therein have most likely established emotional

and psychological patterns for generations in the individual's family tree, and it
is up to this individual to end this pattern
by transforming those energies to a higher plane of consciousness. This is also the
pain of separation that many Scorpios
experience. Whether they are comforted
by their early surroundings or not, there
is attachment, and the breaking of these
attachments is a painful process. The
wrestling with emotional depths and
excesses is encountered in Scorpio as in
no other sign.

Toward the end of Scorpio there is a
constellation called Ophiuchus, pictured
as a giant wrestling with a serpent. The
holder of the serpent is Asclepius, the
healer, honor student of Chiron.[7] Because
this constellation was slightly off the ecliptic when the zodiac we now use was
formed, it was not included as a sign in
our astrological *mandala*. (In fact,
Ophiuchus sits "above" Scorpio.) But
because of the precession of the equinox-

*Personification of Ophiuchus
(Serpentarius), from Hyginus'*
Astronomicon, *Venice, 1482*

es, today the Sun spends more time in this constellation than it actually does in
Scorpio. Thus, before we can finally emerge from Scorpio and enter into the light of
Sagittarius, we must wrestle with this serpent, a process most Scorpios are familiar
with, and one which each handles differently. Asclepius was known for his extraordinary healing abilities and was said to have been able to bring the dead back to life.[8]
Such then is the evolutionary progress in Scorpio from ancient times to modern—
from deadly scorpion to human being gaining control of the secrets of life and death
which the serpent holds, by direct combat with the serpent.

There is also an intimate connection between Scorpio and the mysterious life-
force called *kundalini* (the Serpent Power) in Sanskrit.[9] The *kundalini* is the vital,
animating force within us; it is regarded as an essentially sexual energy. It sleeps at
the base of the spine, and esoteric astrologers are fond of saying that the glyph for
Scorpio itself (♏) represents this Serpent Power, sleeping, coiled and ready to
arise. Awakened by meditation, the *kundalini* travels up a channel in the spinal column. When it reaches the so-called Third Eye in the center of the forehead, all
duality (masculine and feminine polarity) is extinguished and a unified field of consciousness is created. This new center of consciousness can only take shape upon
the "death" of the old ego-bound personality, a personality founded in duality. This
is another facet of the death which Scorpio unconsciously, obsessively seeks.

This serpent power is associated, in India, with the concept of the *shakti*, the feminine polarity of God: in almost all cultures, the Divine Mother is the source of the Serpent Wisdom. Though we are accustomed to think of the feminine or *yin* polarity as passive, the *shakti* is in fact an active force. And because it is also a sexual force, it is often misused. Traditionally, an imbalance in the *kundalini* produces all kinds of sexual problems and deviant behavior—concepts usually associated with the undeveloped or afflicted aspects of Scorpio.[10]

The Sun in Scorpio asks us to separate ourselves from some of the subconscious feelings and patterns we acquired early in life. This process is similar to the one experienced in Cancer—but in Scorpio, the act of separation typically occurs through experiences involving our intimate partners, as with Orpheus. Through these partnerships, the Scorpio will also experience many issues dealing with power. Moon in Scorpio types need to spend days by themselves, indulging in secret activities, researching secret matters. Paradoxically enough, these people tend to be rejuvenated by activities which might seem "heavy" to others—a session with an analyst, hypnotherapist, astrologer, or acupuncturist does wonders for them.

Mercury in Scorpio implies an ability to probe the deep, dark, hidden aspects of human consciousness, as well as a mind that can probe other people's secrets and knows no boundaries. Venus in Scorpio may sometimes be sexually promiscuous, because these people are searching for the *kundalini* awakening through partnership. Mars in Scorpio (like Nergal) must really learn to control its passions, and, like Venus, is interested in sexual exploration; these individuals can also become excellent healers.

Asclepius holding a staff in his left hand, a laurel branch in in his right hand, with a bird perched on his forearm. Bronze coin from Rhegium, Italy, 270–203 BC. From the Michael A. Sikora collection

Ceres in Scorpio reminds us of Demeter searching for Kore; she excels at the grief process and at counseling those who are involved in their own losses. This placement is also good at transforming sorrow into productive channels. Here Ceres is both a healer and a warrior. Because of her association with archaic serpent goddesses, Pallas Athene acquires special importance in Scorpio or the Eighth House. Her healing abilities and the Serpent Wisdom of birth, life, death, and the afterlife will be greatly enhanced. Juno, like Venus, searches for deep sexual union with a mate, and ultimately needs to find the soul-mate. People who have Vesta in the Eighth House or Scorpio may journey to the underworld to collect their own hidden pieces, working as healers, counselors, or therapists with the *kundalini* fire as the primary motivating force in their lives.

Those with Jupiter in association with Pluto or its ruling house or sign will find themselves among the high-rollers at one time or another. They will make money, but they may be given choices in life as to whether to get rich honestly or get to the top by any means available. The Mafia chieftain, the corporate raider, the inaccessible billionaire are all archetypal expressions of a Jupiter-Pluto union. Soul growth may also be at an all-time high for these individuals. Saturn in Scorpio or in the Eighth House or in close aspect to Pluto is, at best, difficult and overwhelming. And yet these are among the finest positions that exist, for these people possess the stamina, will power, determination, and sheer energy to fight all the psychological demons and emotional or physical traumas that have been inflicted upon them in their early (or past) lives. Saturn and Pluto last came together in 1946–48 in Leo, a sign associated with the father. Many esoteric theorists suspect that the bulk of the people born during this conjunction reincarnated directly from the battlefields or concentration camps of World War II. Possessed of sharp and disturbing memories of the horrors of war, coupled with the challenge to stand up and face the enemy directly, this generation fought another war—Vietnam—both at home and abroad. The outgrowth of that horror was that, for the first time, soldiers had to undergo intense therapy to remove the psychic and psychological demons that plagued them as a result of those memories. They also learned to confront their own mortality and their own aging process. Learning to accept old age is one of Saturn's requirements; to gracefully accept it and enter Hades' domain willingly is the true test of Saturnian courage.

In Scorpio or the Eighth House, Chiron is truly the shaman or medicine man. This position forces us to face the lord of the underworld on some level: whether through involvement in the healing arts, through the experience of illness or of our own impending death, the loss of another, or, most commonly, through being forced to confront our own personal underworld in the form of our inner psychological complexes. With an Eighth House Uranus, these same inner complexes are always bubbling up into consciousness; the Uranian urge for liberation pushes all the demons up into the light so that we may slay them. Those with this position may also have some very liberal or unusual notions about sexual expression. Neptune in the Eighth is often a bit of a paradox: these people are likely to be powerfully gifted with psychic awareness, but afraid to accept the gift. Dreams and a general interest in the unconscious may well become conscious for these individuals. Pluto in its own house may be the master manipulator, but it may also show an individual who specializes in transformation. These natives will seek long-term bonding of an intense nature, similar to Hades and Persephone. These people are always astute "natural" psychologists, detectives, and researchers.

As we have seen, Scorpio represents the descent of consciousness into its personal underworld. There, in the depths of our souls, our old ego-consciousness dies so that we may be reborn. The psychological process of death and rebirth has its metaphor in the spiritual, meditative life, where the transformation of personality and the death of ego consciousness are achieved by control of the sexual energy called *kundalini*. Thus Scorpio is one of the deepest and most complex of signs. Anyone who questions this may observe this present era in which we live (1984–1996), a time when the individual and collective goal of humanity and the planet itself is transformation. This is the cycle we pass through every 250 years when the planet Pluto, which is furthest from the sun, makes its passage through its ruling sign, Scorpio, the sign in which it undoubtedly has the most dramatic impact. During its passage through Scorpio, Pluto actually crosses the orbital path of Neptune, so that it is closer to us than its neighbor, as close to the earth and sun as it will ever be. At such times—for instance, during Christ's ministry, the Italian Renaissance, and on the eve of the American Revolution—the world experiences an epoch of accelerated transformation.

SCORPIO WORKSHEET

A factor includes a planet, an asteroid, or an angle in the birth chart. How many factors do you have in Scorpio? Use the following point system to total them:

Sun 4	Vesta...............1	Uranus 1/2
Moon 4	Ceres 1	Neptune..........1/2
Earth 3	Pallas 1	Vertex 1/2
Venus..............2	Juno...............1	Part of Fortune .. 1/2
Mercury...........2	Jupiter 1	Nodes 1/2
MH 2	Saturn 1	Pluto...............3
ASC 2	Chiron.............1	
Mars...............3		

Scorpio on an angle (ASC, MH, DSC, IC) 3

Pluto or Mars on an angle...3

Planets and asteroids in the 8th House count the same as above _____

Scorpio, Pluto, or Mars as the focal point of a T-square?.................2

Scorpio, Pluto, or Mars involved in a T-square? 1

Total _____

How did you relate to these myths?_____

_____

_____

_____

_____

What house does Scorpio occupy in your chart?

_____

10th House—mother   1st House—self

4th House—father   11th House—friends

7th House—mate   5th House—children, lovers

3rd House—sibling

Keeping in mind that these houses represent these relationships, how has Scorpio energy expressed itself through others in your life? _____

_____

_____

_____

What houses do Pluto and Mars occupy in your chart and how are they expressed?

_____

_____

What signs or planets are in your 8th House and how are they expressed? _____

_____

_____

Insights: _____

_____

_____

_____

SAGITTARIUS

CHAPTER THIRTY

SAGITTARIUS, *The Centaur*

SIGN: *Sagittarius, the 9th Zodiacal Sign*

MODE: *Mutable* ✥ ELEMENT: *Fire* ✥ RULER: *Jupiter*

ADDITIONAL MYTHIC ARCHETYPES: *Chiron, the Centaur*
✥ *Artemis (Diana)* ✥ *Hestia (Vesta)*

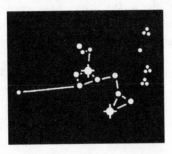

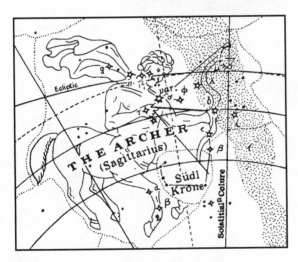

To the Egyptians, Sagittarius was a sign of war, for the full moon in that sign (June) marked the time when the imperial armies began to march. To us, however, Sagittarius is a sign of philosophy rather than war, as befits its position in the yearly cycle. During the month of Sagittarius, the world is locked in the depths of winter. The landscape is quiet, buried under the snow. Activity is at a minimum. Among Native American peoples, this is the time for telling stories, for philosophical reflection. So it is no wonder that Sagittarius is a sign of wisdom and preeminently the sign of the philosopher.

Though the days are just as short during Capricorn, there is a significant difference between the two signs: in Capricorn, the sun has passed the solstice point and the days are growing longer, but in Sagittarius it is the power of the night-time, of collective humanity, which is increasing. So it is fitting that Sagittarius represents the stage in which personal or individual concerns are at a minimum, and universal concerns become all-encompassing. This is why

Sagittarians are said to be lost in abstruse philosophical concepts, neglecting every-day realities while they wander about with their heads in the clouds.

There is an astronomical correlate for this universality: the center of the galaxy is situated in the final degrees of Sagittarius; i.e., from our observation point on the earth, the center of the Milky Way would *appear* to lie near the end of this sign. Thus the darkest days of the year, just before the winter solstice turning point, are tied into a wider frame of reference, with concerns and concepts so vast that they can only be symbolized by the galaxy as a whole.

It is clear, then, how Sagittarius acquired its philosophical symbolism. But this universality is also reflected in myth. Sagittarius is linked with Chiron the Centaur (see Chapter Fifteen, "Chiron"). The centaurs were a race of beings which were half-human and half-horse—their minds and hands had the clarity and dexterity of the human race, while their lower bodies, formed like horses, connected them with the earth and the world of instinct. Chiron, the king of the centaurs, was a philosopher, teacher, and healer. Wounded in the foot by one of Hercules' poisoned arrows, he could not heal himself. But, being immortal, neither could he simply die. Chiron *chose* to die, but for a higher purpose—his sacrifice made it possible for Prometheus, the great awakener, to return to the service of humanity; by way of reward, Chiron was placed in the heavens as the constellation Sagittarius.[1] Here again, as in the seasonal calendar, we meet the theme of the philosopher who sacrifices personal concerns for the sake of the greater whole. Unlike the other centaurs, who were primarily driven by their animal instincts and passions, Chiron had transcended his primal self and dwelt principally in his god-nature. As co-ruler of Sagittarius he represents the stage when we become aware of all three aspects of self: the animal nature driving us from below, the human nature (spirit trapped in a body), and the divine nature.

The Sagittarian arrow is always pointed upward towards the divine, like the gaze of one who is concerned with distant worlds or galaxies—our home in the stars. Many Sagittarians are all too aware of these three natures within them, each with its distinct voice, and they often find difficulty in accepting all three natures as parts of a Self that must be integrated and kept in balance. It is the awareness of these three aspects of one's inner nature as well as the transmission of energy from the animal to the spiritual that makes human beings unique among the creatures of the world. And it is here in Sagittarius that this awareness is tested to its limits—for when one is involved in moving energy from the lower to the upper *chakras* while at the same time continuing to receive excess stimulation from the lower *chakras*, there is a great alchemical process occurring. The typical centaur could scarcely be regarded as a symbol of this process, but Chiron was not a typical centaur.

It is significant that Chiron's wound was in his foot or thigh, thus affecting his mobility. Like Gemini, Sagittarius (which rules the thigh in medical astrology) needs maximum freedom to roam. When that freedom is restricted or obstructed, Sagittarius can feel truly wounded. Chiron lived in a cave, close to the earth, partaking of earth's natural beauty and wisdom. Our Sagittarian friends who have a good deal of earth in their charts will probably relate strongly to Chiron. They may also relate strongly to the wounded healer aspect of this sign, for the awareness of spirit trapped in a body is an important theme for them, and the importance of remembering that they are spirit in body rather than bodies seeking spirit is of utmost concern.

From his cave, Chiron shared his knowledge of celestial phenomena, medicine, herbs, spiritual disciplines, music, and mathematics. This is not unlike the modern-day Chiron type who retreats frequently to the mountains, becomes energized by the earth and the stars, and then longs to share his or her newly

A centaur from an Egyptian sarcophagus, second century AD

acquired wisdom with others. Such a person no doubt has a busy healing or astrological practice, and his or her quest for more knowledge is equaled only by the need to share what has already been learned. Thus, the aspect of Sagittarius that correlates with the wise teacher, philosopher, and healer seems to point strongly to Chiron's association with the sign and its natural astrological house, the Ninth.

We may also regard Chiron as the half-brother of Jupiter, for both were sons of Saturn. Jupiter, of course, is the planet we now associate with Sagittarius. The god Jupiter has no particular connection with high-minded philosophies—that aspect of Sagittarius is better understood by reference to the myth of Chiron and the month's position in the seasonal year. But there is a strong connection between Jupiter and Sagittarius, and one of those connections is best described by reference to the word jovial. Jove, of course, was another name for Jupiter, and those who are of optimistic, enthusiastic temperament are, in many ways, similar to this king of the gods. All things abundant and expansive fall under Jupiter (as do excessive self-indulgence, self-righteousness, and pomposity when the planet is afflicted). Unfailing good humor is another aspect of the Jupiter archetype and a very important one as regards Sagittarius. The typical Sagittarian (if such a creature exists) is generally believed to possess such a happy-go-lucky temperament, fusing broad-minded philosophy with earthy good nature. Since Jupiter succeeded in becoming king of Mount Olympus by tricking his father Saturn and usurping his rule, he represents the fearlessness and leadership aspect of Sagittarius, or the hero (similar to Aries and Leo, the two previous fire signs) who becomes sovereign ruler. This is a fitting archetype for Sagittarians who seem sovereign in their knowingness, even if it's a con.

But other correlations between Jupiter and Sagittarius will also be apparent. It is well-known that Jupiter spent more time pursuing his love affairs than he did governing Mt. Olympus. One question that always arises with Sagittarians is the issue of faithfulness. Committed they are, to their current lover—that's not the issue. But how *long* they can sustain themselves in that commitment is another question. "Till death do us part" is not a credo that Sagittarians hold dear (unless the chart contains strong Juno or Cancer symbolism), and when pushed against the wall to say those words, they usually tremble. Like Geminis, their polar opposites, Sagittarians are forever searching. And in their quest for God, life's meaning, and the answer to every question ever uttered, Sagittarians jump over walls and fences and break down doors; in other words, they always need an escape hatch, *and* are always seeking the next mountain to climb or the next adventure, particularly if it involves the great outdoors.

Sagittarius has always been considered a lucky sign, whether in gambling (which the sign rules) or just in plain living. It is true that there is an aspect of Sagittarius that carries plain old good luck, and with it the faith that everything will turn out for the best. The optimism and inner knowing that Sagittarians possess (some would say guardian angels accompany them on every adventure) may stem from the fact that Jupiter is their ruler, and Jupiter could always make things right, no matter how much trouble one seemed to be involved in, if he deemed the recipient worthy of his efforts. And most of the time, an upward gaze and a prayer to Jupiter was enough to grant the recipient's wish.

The Olympian attribution of Sagittarius is both important and revealing. Manilius writes:

The Hunter's human part Diana rules, but what's of horse is ruled by Vesta....[2]

We often think of Diana/Artemis as a moon goddess, though this is not quite accurate. In late classical times she had lunar associations, though she was always connected with one particular phase of the lunar cycle—the new moon, symbolized by the nymph or maiden (see Chapter Six, "Moon"). Artemis held herself apart from all romantic involvement with men or gods, preferring the freedom to roam wild through the mountains of Arcadia, and to this day it is said that Sagittarians are notoriously gun-shy when it comes to commitment in human relationships, and that they place an unrealistically high value on their personal freedom. However, Artemis should not be regarded as a cold, rather sullen virgin, for her desire to remain apart from the sexual game was not founded on negative withdrawal. Rather, her freedom was the freedom of nature itself, for originally Artemis was the Lady of Wild Beasts, a goddess of the hunt.[3] Her dwelling place was on thickly wooded mountain tops; her totem was the bear. Sagittarius is called the Archer, which is peculiar enough if we think of this sign only in terms of Chiron the centaur, who is not particularly connected with archery. The bow and arrow more properly belong to Artemis, as do the traditions that this sign is athletic, freedom-loving, restless, and inclined towards the outdoors. Artemis, as goddess of the hunt, *protected* animals from being hunted more often than she hunted them herself. The twin sister of Apollo, Olympian ruler of Gemini, she was also the protectress of small children and nature in general. Today's Artemis would no doubt be campaigning to save the whales, the oceans, and the rainforests. She represents the side of

Sagittarius that has achieved wholeness and who voices its compassionate concerns for those that can't speak for themselves. Sagittarian Jane Fonda has demonstrated this aspect of Artemis repeatedly in her career.

Hestia or Vesta was the keeper of the sacred flame or spiritual fire, and thus is related to one's inner passions and sense of devotion. Vesta represents a different type of spiritual awareness. As previously mentioned, the symbolism of the centaur in Sagittarius reflects the aspect of worship that concerns a heavenly type of divinity—thus the arrow and gaze are pointed upward and beyond this earthly dimension. Jupiter resided at the *top* of Mt. Olympus, and to make contact with him one's attention also had to be focused upwards. Vesta is a symbol of the divine fire that resides within, and thus symbolizes the understanding that divinity itself resides within. Temples were erected to

A nineteenth-century engraving of Diana, after the full-length statue by Jean-Antoine Houdon in the Frick Collection, New York

her all over Greece and worshippers, weary of battle, sought her comfort and were renewed by simply being in her energy. This aspect of Sagittarius is reflected by the priest or nun, counselor or friend, who, as agent or direct representative of the God/Goddess energy, is always there with the warm and constant inner radiance that consoles us and inspires us during difficult times.

A Chiron/Artemis combination is perhaps the truest archetype for Sagittarius, and there is, in fact, something distinctly wild about many Sagittarians. They often seem ready to bolt away, especially in social situations. They are uncomfortable in crowds and much more at home in the wilderness. Their love of personal freedom is proverbial and they often have a downright feral sexuality which is more characteristic of wild things than of cultured philosophers. Like Chiron or Artemis, the true Sagittarian has one foot in the primal world of nature. He or she may travel mentally to the heights of Olympus, where Jupiter reigns supreme, but true Sagittarian wisdom is rooted in the earth. This does not mean that Sagittarians are practical; far from it. They have the naivete of wild things, and may seem quite spaced-out in the "real world." But it is their connection with nature that keeps their philosophy from becoming too abstract and which renders their wisdom so quintessentially human.

When the Sun is in Sagittarius, it is the concept of the hero's journey to understand life and existence (i.e., to know God intimately) that keeps the fire raging. The Moon in Sagittarius, on the other hand, needs to approach life with a fairly light touch. These people do well when walking, camping, or merely daydreaming, but they probably do best of all when traveling, exploring new countries—or, if that's impossible, at least a new part of town (especially with their dogs). In short, the Moon in Sagittarius has a strong dose of Artemis in its nature; because of her connection with this sign, we might even consider Sagittarius an exaltation for the Moon, especially when it is new.

Mercury in Sagittarius may lose itself in grand visions and neglect the details, but this position supports the quest for a life purpose and provides the fuel for that quest. Of these people it can be said that travel is in their bones, as is much information about the world. Venus in Sagittarius has been accused of being highly amorous in the early stages of romance, but out the door when commitment is required,

Diana on a stag, from Jost Amman's Kunstbüchlin, *printed by Johann Feyerabend, Frankfurt, 1599*

though this is not always true. What fuels Venus' passion most in this sign is a "traveling companion"—someone with whom these natives can climb new mountains and chart new territories. Mars in Sagittarius puts a lot of energy and personal development into philosophical pursuits, especially the outdoor kind. These people will also be attracted to activities that require very little supervision or rules.

Ceres nurtures one's visions, goals, ideals, dreams, and beliefs. This is one who may become a child of the universe, a teacher, and a visionary. Because Jupiter was Athene's father, Pallas Athene in Sagittarius stresses one's defense of the patriarchal system and one's relationship with the father. Juno in spouse Jupiter's sign reminds us of their volatile relationship, and these individuals need to take a deep look at what they might be getting into before they commit themselves to a serious relationship. Vesta, like the Moon, might be considered exalted in Sagittarius, or at least very well placed. An individual with this position may work to create understanding between different philosophical and religious viewpoints, as well as be highly focused on his or her own individual spiritual development (Mahatma Gandhi had this placement). But there is a danger that commitment to a political or social cause may become so powerful as to suggest fanaticism.

Jupiter in its own sign generally has the makings of a politician or lawyer, and can show the kind of celebrity or fame through which one influences the masses (example: George Bush). Saturn in Sagittarius or the Ninth House links Jupiter with his father, and is said to be favorable for getting ahead in the business and financial world, but it is also true that the tension between these two may result in a conflict between following a material or spiritual path. Another conflict that might arise out of this combination (Jupiter in Saturn's house or sign or Saturn in Jupiter's house or sign, etc.) is doing the *opposite* of what the father wants. Still, when Saturn's worldly practicality is focused on a Jupiterian sense of social or spiritual purpose, the outcome often spells success. This can produce a lawyer or banker.

Chiron, like Jupiter, was a child of Saturn, though Chiron may be considered Jupiter's darker, "animal" brother. Chiron in the Ninth House favors that grand synthesis of knowledge which is Jupiter's greatest gift, for Chiron adds an earthy wisdom to Jupiter's more cerebral speculations. This can produce the healer or physician. Uranus in the Ninth House may endow one with the ability to put even the wildest schemes into action, for one's sense of purpose is focused on Uranian originality. Here we may find the social or political activist, the cult leader (or follower), the innovator or inventor. But the problematical side of Sagittarius—its arrogance and absolutism—is also very likely to raise its head with such contacts.

In former times Jupiter ruled Pisces, a sign now given to Neptune. Hence Neptune's position in the Ninth House or any aspects between Jupiter and Neptune are potentially of major importance. Neptune channels the sense of social purpose implied by the Ninth House into idealistic goals; this position is common among social workers, clergymen, psychotherapists, and other members of the helping professions. There is a strong spiritual drive in these individuals to do what they feel will "please God" or help bring salvation to their own souls. Pluto in the Ninth

Head of Zeus (Jupiter) on a bronze coin of Ptolemy IV, king of Egypt, 221–204 BC.
From the Michael A. Sikora collection

House lends power and purpose—and perhaps obsession—to the spiritual quest itself. Many of these natives grow up in families which espouse rigid religious belief systems. Others grow up in families with no belief system at all. Either way, they are compelled to seek spiritual answers which work for them as individuals, and because of Pluto's power, may also influence the masses in their beliefs (example: Joseph Campbell).

The period that Neptune and Uranus spent in Sagittarius overlapped—from 1970 until 1988 one or both outer planets were in this high-minded sign. Religious cults and gurus flourished during this time like no other in recent history, and it was an accelerated time for air travel, when no distance was too great to journey in search of a quest or ideal. In fact, air piracy, an unfortunate by-product of the time, reached its height during this period as well, making long-distance travel much more risky. Pluto will enter Sagittarius at the turn of the millennium when, hopefully, racial, religious, and political barriers will no longer continue to separate us.

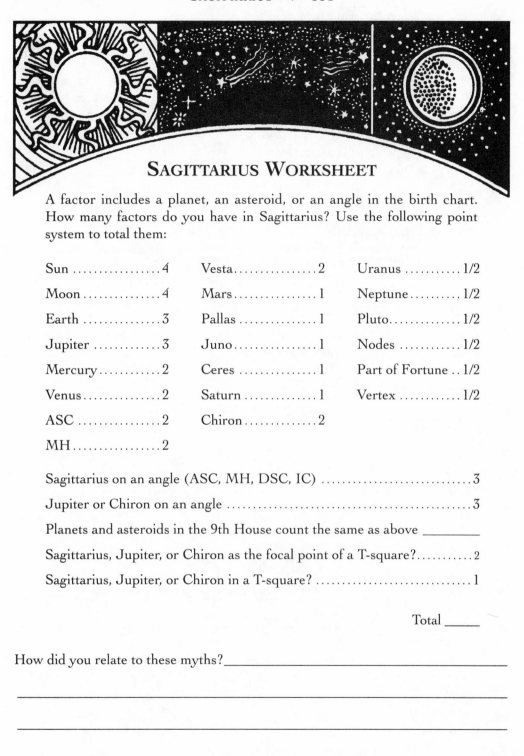

SAGITTARIUS WORKSHEET

A factor includes a planet, an asteroid, or an angle in the birth chart. How many factors do you have in Sagittarius? Use the following point system to total them:

Sun 4	Vesta................2	Uranus 1/2
Moon 4	Mars................1	Neptune..........1/2
Earth 3	Pallas 1	Pluto..............1/2
Jupiter 3	Juno................1	Nodes 1/2
Mercury............2	Ceres 1	Part of Fortune .. 1/2
Venus..............2	Saturn 1	Vertex 1/2
ASC 2	Chiron..............2	
MH................2		

Sagittarius on an angle (ASC, MH, DSC, IC) 3

Jupiter or Chiron on an angle 3

Planets and asteroids in the 9th House count the same as above _____

Sagittarius, Jupiter, or Chiron as the focal point of a T-square?..........2

Sagittarius, Jupiter, or Chiron in a T-square? 1

Total _____

How did you relate to these myths?_____

_____

_____

_____

_____

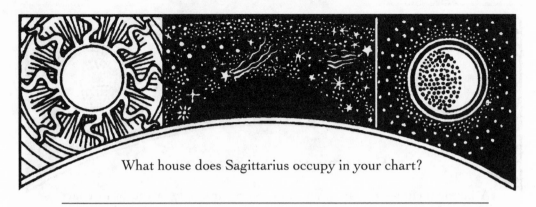

What house does Sagittarius occupy in your chart?

_____

    10th House—mother   1st House—self

     4th House—father   11th House—friends

     7th House—mate   5th House—children, lovers

     3rd House—sibling

Keeping in mind that these houses represent these relationships, how has Sagittarius energy expressed itself through others in your life? _____

_____

_____

What houses do Jupiter and Chiron occupy in your chart and how are they

expressed? _____

_____

_____

What signs or planets are in your 9th House and how are they expressed? _____

_____

_____

Insights: _____

_____

_____

_____

CAPRICORN

CHAPTER THIRTY-ONE

CAPRICORN, *The Goat-Fish*

SIGN: *Capricorn, the 10th Zodiacal Sign*

MODE: *Cardinal* ❧ ELEMENT: *Earth* ❧ RULER: *Saturn*

ADDITIONAL MYTHIC ARCHETYPES: *Hestia (Vesta)* ❧ *Ea (Babylonian)* ❧ *Amalthea* ❧ *Rhea* ❧ *Pan* ❧ *The House of Atreus*

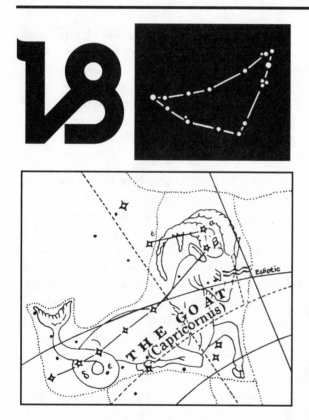

Of the four major turning points of the year, the winter solstice may well be the most significant. Here, at the moment of greatest darkness in the northern hemisphere, the sun "turns back" once again. Having reached its greatest southerly deviation on the eastern horizon, it can be observed to rise a bit farther north as the days slowly begin to lengthen. In the ancient mythological drama of the god or goddess' descent into the underworld, the return to humanity has now begun. And in the journey of individual consciousness, the point of greatest contact with universal consciousness has been reached, the collective wisdom has been assimilated, and the individual begins a symbolic return as a transformed being: the self has become the Self. This is why all gods who represent the higher Self—including Christ—have births celebrated at the winter solstice.

This turning point has been celebrated since at least 3,000 BC. The megalithic tomb of Newgrange in Ireland contains a small stone window through which the winter solstice sun rises, illuminating the interior of the tomb.[1] In megalithic tombs, bones were typically painted with red ochre, a color which symbolized life and vitality, hence the hope of rebirth.

How then did the moment of spiritual rebirth become associated with the goat? The sign has had a long and involved mythic history. Originally it was not the goat, but the "goat-fish," a peculiar image which is now almost forgotten. In ancient Babylon, the god Ea was depicted as a man cloaked with the skin of a fish. He ruled the "waters underneath the earth," the vital power which kept the Tigris and Euphrates rivers flowing, and hence supplied life to the land. Ea rose from the waters of the Persian Gulf and taught wisdom to the people of Sumer. In addition to being cloaked with the skin of a fish, he was called the "antelope of the subterranean ocean."[2] We no longer know the significance of this peculiar attribution, but goats in general and antelopes in particular are often depicted in Mesopotamian art as feeding on the leaves of the Tree of Life.[3] Originally, then, Capricorn was Ea, the bringer of civilization, the fish man who is also, symbolically, the antelope.

Mesopotamian influence on the Egyptians resulted in the fusion of this image with another. When the moon was full in Capricorn (June-July) the waters of the Nile began to rise. Fish became abundant once more, supplying a necessary source of food to Egyptian peasants. Thus the waters flowed up from "beneath the earth" to supply life-giving food (fish) whenever the moon was full in the sign of the goat.[4] Once again the fish and the goat are both linked with the source of human nourishment which may be symbolized by underground waters, the Tree of Life, or the rebirth of the Self.

The Greeks also knew Capricorn as the goat and as a source of nourishment, though they attributed a somewhat different symbolic meaning to this sign. To them, Capricorn was often equated with Amalthea, the goat-nymph who suckled the infant Zeus (Jupiter) when his mother Rhea hid him on the island of Crete to save him from the wrath of his father Cronus (Saturn). As a reward for her service to the future king of the gods, Amalthea was placed in the heavens as the constellation Capricorn.[5]

Half-goat and half-nymph, Amalthea was the sister of the god Pan, hence part of the family of satyrs who are part human and part goat. The British eccentric Aleister Crowley chose Pan, rather than the traditional Devil, to represent Capricorn in his version of the Tarot. Pan is also represented as the Devil in Liz Greene's *Mythic Tarot*.[6] Here is an association which, to us, may seem out of char-

A fish-tailed goat, zodiac figure from a sarcophagus, Thebes, Egypt

acter with the usual interpretation of Capricorn. Pan and his fellow satyrs were devoted to sexual lust and license; in fact the term satyriasis denotes a personality disorder in which the subject (male) is seriously addicted to sexual promiscuity. Our image of Capricorn is much grimmer and more austere than all this, in keeping with its ruler, Saturn. But Saturn himself had an extremely sexual connotation among the ancients. In Rome, the month of Capricorn was the time of Saturnalia, the festival of that particular god. At that time, all social and sexual mores were

Capricorn, from a medieval zodiac illustration

thrown out the window; absolute license and permissiveness prevailed.[7] The pagan winter solstice ritual which marked the beginning of the return of the sun and was celebrated as the Saturnalia was in turn celebrated by the Christians as Christmas, another return of the Son. The original Christmas often lasted for weeks; people took off work, celebrations and feasts were given, gifts were exchanged, and peace reigned. Most religious scholars and historians feel that Christ's birth was celebrated at this time in keeping with the ancient custom of honoring the winter solstice, rather than due to any evidence of his actual birth taking place then—especially since early Christian theologians placed the historical Christ's birth in the spring.

The primal deity Pan was sexually obsessive, and many astrologers know that Capricorn people usually do have a wildly sexual, primitive persona lurking underneath that reserved, wintry exterior. Most natives of this sign are not all that far from the earthiness of the satyrs—though they do keep it well hidden. Greek legend tells of Pan's leap into the Nile to escape the wrath of the giant Typhon. In mid-air his head, which remained above water, became the head of a goat, while his hindquarters became those of a fish; thus the goat-fish was born. This version of the Capricorn story retains the image of the goat-fish, although in the actual constellation the goat appears to be dying, while the fish part is vibrant and alive.[8] Since we celebrate Christ's birth at the winter solstice while the Sun is in Capricorn, it is fitting that the symbol of the goat is merged with that of the fish, a symbol that would come to represent the 2,000 years of Christianity. Since goats are considered symbolic of sexual license and freedom, like Pan, we are dealing symbolically with the fading of this sexuality (the dying goat) in moving to the Piscean Age (the vibrant fish), an age characterized by its *control* of sexuality.

In Capricorn we find the symbolism of wintry withdrawal, latent sexuality, spiritual rebirth, and a powerful sense of purpose all combined. In this context it is interesting to note that the Olympian ruler of the sign was Vesta (Hestia) who, in fact, embodies all of these qualities.[9]

Vesta was, in many respects, an ascetic goddess, embodying the reflective state of withdrawal we associate with winter. Her priestesses, the vestal virgins, were vowed to eternal celibacy. But as we have seen (in Chapter Twelve, "Vesta"), some scholars suspect that the vestal virgins were originally temple prostitutes of the Near Eastern variety, and thus there is good reason to associate Vesta with sexuality.[10] She was the keeper of the hearth-fire, the central fire which was never allowed to wane, and which may be regarded as a metaphor for the "fire within," the same inner fire and sexual power, or *kundalini*, we encountered in Scorpio. It is by control of this inner fire that yogic states of consciousness are attained. By extension, this inner fire may also be seen as a metaphor of the Self, the transcendent personality which is symbolically born at the winter solstice.

The mythic archetypes for Capricorn are therefore diverse, including Vesta, Pan, Amalthea, and Saturn. Vesta and Saturn represent a rigidly stanced, controlled type of individual whose behavior must be impeccable, while Pan and Amalthea, the goats and satyrs, represent the freedom and sexual abandon of the sign. We have seen, however, that in ancient times the symbolism of Saturn and Vesta was not as restricted as was the case during the Hellenistic era (c. 300 BC to 300 AD).

The goddess Rhea, also associated with Capricorn

Still, anyone born in Capricorn must surely have a mixture of these elements within, driven by the passion and wild desire of a satyr but living in an age where such desires must be discreet and carefully doled out for fear of punishment or public humiliation.

Control, or, more precisely, self-mastery, is what Capricorn is really about. When we arrive at this final stage of earth in the astrological *mandala*, we are expected to have gained some mastery over this earthly realm, and this includes the physical appetites. What is expected of Capricorn is behavior and moral fortitude worthy of the final stage of earth.

Saturn's image in astrology is often less than attractive, and this is why Capricorn is associated with stiffness, stuffiness, and rigidity. It (like Virgo, the previous earth sign) has a reputation for coldness, withdrawal, perfection-seeking, and materialism. The need to be in control may also be due to its rulership by Saturn.

A combative relationship with the father occurs in those who have strong

Capricorn or Saturnian themes in their birth chart. In Aries, a fire sign, there was also a necessity to strive against a terrifying, tyrannical father, though in Aries the quest is personal, while in Capricorn it is social or political. In Leo, another fire sign, we encountered the second important relationship with the father, a father that was more in keeping with the symbolism of the sun god; here there was a creative, heart connection (or lack of one) to the father. In Capricorn the father archetype is somewhat different. It represents the connection to the *earth* father, or the influence and direction the father gives to the child in making its way in the world, in providing self-esteem and self-confidence, and finally, in handing over the "kingdom" or rulership to the child. And this is where Capricorns meet their challenge. Uranus was overthrown by

A satyr, illustrated by Gustave Doré

Saturn, and Saturn in fear swallowed his own children. Like Ariens, Capricorns may find themselves swallowed up by a tyrannical father (or mother) who may also represent values such as society, church, or the family system. Whereas Ariens fight free of the father's influence, like Jason or Luke Skywalker (see chapter twenty-two, *Aries*), and thus become individualists, Capricorns are far more easily consumed by other people's value systems. In time they may perpetuate the cycle by becoming overly protective about maintaining their own rule, and thus swallowing their own children in the process. "The sins of the fathers passed on to the sons" seems to reflect this genetic and psychological inheritance of Capricorn.

.Another mythological portrayal of this type of family system, where the sins of the father are paid by the sons, is found in the story of the House of Atreus. The details of the story are carefully recorded in several good texts.[11] Briefly, the story begins with a father who was so bold as to boil his son and serve him at a feast for the gods. This kind of outrage, concluded the gods, must be punished severely. Bringing the son back to life, the gods spared him from the curse that was to follow, and follow it did, down the rest of the family line for several generations, sparing no one. The result was matricide, patricide, infidelity, bloodshed, insanity and, ultimately, resolution. Future generations unknowingly paid dearly for the sins of their forefather but, as with the law of karma (Saturn's domain), what goes around comes around until the debt is cleared.

And it is this wound that seems to afflict most Capricorns—the wound of not getting what they needed from their parents. In turn they worry so much about their own children that, in the process, they try too hard to control them and lose them just the same. Capricorn's children may be projects, work, employees, and even partners—but the bottom line is that their need to maintain control at all times will often drive their associations away. Of course, there is another type of parenting represented in Capricorn—that given by Amalthea and Rhea. Rhea's love for her children was so great, coupled with outrage at the violent acts being inflicted upon them by their father, that she took action, thus saving Zeus from the fate his elder siblings received. By taking the risk to entrust Zeus to the goat-nymph Amalthea, Rhea succeeded in getting her children back. Rhea represents the parent who, though overshadowed by and sometimes weak-willed in the face of a domineering partner, sacrifices whenever possible for the sake of the children. Amalthea, the foster-mother, lovingly nurtured Zeus until it was time to release him back to his family.

Hestia played a part in this family dynamic as well. As the first child of Rhea and Cronus, Hestia was also the first to be swallowed and thus the last to emerge from Cronus' shadow. Jean Shinoda Bolen's portrait of the Hestia childhood suggests that one with this archetype emphasized may never fully overcome the initial loneliness he or she experienced in life.[12] But it is often this kind of loneliness that inspires a person to seek the inner light rather than be immersed in external relationships.

Thus we see that Capricorn and its relationship to the family bears a striking similarity to that of Cancer, its polar opposite, and astrologers have always maintained that the parents of the individual are to be found in the Fourth and Tenth houses of the astrological wheel (the houses which correspond to Cancer and Capricorn). The primary difference is that Cancer, a water sign, is concerned with the *emotional* bond to the family while Capricorn, the *earth* sign, represents a more public image involving individual and family (or society).

The Sun in Capricorn represents the light shining on the mountain top, overseeing humanity's doings just as the gods Uranus, Saturn, and finally Jupiter did from their respective mountain peaks. The lessons these gods learned from occupying such lofty positions certainly indicates that absolute power corrupts absolutely, but in striving for and attaining the topmost positions in life Capricorn fulfills its solar destiny. The Moon is said to be in detriment here, but this is not to say that Capricorn Moon individuals are not sensitive. They are *very* sensitive. The detriment assigned by the ancients probably has more to do with the fact that the hardened, crystallized nature of Capricorn lacks the nourishment and sensitivity required by the Moon in its life-giving process. Most people with the Moon in Capricorn don't feel well nurtured—they have to learn to nurture themselves. Quiet evenings in the warmth and security of their own homes will do wonders for them, just as it does for their opposite type, the Moon in Cancer. Above all, they need to create situations where they can set down their mania for control and just be. At their best, one may develop into an Amalthea or Rhea, the sacrificing parent who does *anything* for his or her children.

Mercury in Capricorn imparts a critical and scientific mind, one who may be interested in the *nature* of things. Venus in Capricorn is loyal beyond belief, and the

Antelope (an early image associated with Capricorn) from a fresco at Knossos, Crete, illustrated by Diane Smirnow

sense of duty and responsibility merges with the love nature. Mars is exalted here, which seems a rather unlikely place for the god of war, except that the military is always connected with political rulership; hence Mars, an energetic planet, does well in ambitious Capricorn.

In Capricorn Ceres becomes the organizer *par excellence*; a person with this planetary placement becomes the mother-figure (or the nurturing father, if male) that everyone else looks to for guidance. Prudence and productivity is favored. Pallas Athene in Capricorn, as in Sagittarius, is the true "defender of the fatherland," of society's rules and regulations; the relationship with the father is strong here as well. Juno in Capricorn, like Venus, is loyal to its commitments in relationship, and while Juno in this sign may wait forever until it finds the *right* mate, it may also stay forever even after there is no longer any basis whatsoever for relating. Vesta in Capricorn is all too likely to limit or restrict sexual expression, and equally likely to enact a genuine Saturnalia by completely giving way to desire. There will probably be tight boundaries and definitions drawn as to when it is appropriate to act this way, in contrast to the individual's typical, more reserved behavior. At its best, Vesta's association with this sign relates to the discipline, dedication to a cause, and tirelessness with which these people perform their tasks. (Vesta in Capricorn people, for instance, would probably only call in sick if they really *were* sick!)

Jupiter in Capricorn brings the father and son together again, this time in a situation where the son (or daughter) usually surpasses the father and ultimately overthrows him in some way, just as Jupiter did to Saturn. If the father/child conflicts are not resolved, this position can usually result in the children cutting themselves off from the father in dramatic ways (like Jupiter throwing Saturn into Tartarus). When they are resolved, there can be an excellent combination of prudence, practicality, and patience (Capricorn) applied to the exuberance, far-reaching vision, and generosity of Jupiter. Saturn in Capricorn is a double-whammy and seems to get Saturn's responsibilities in spades. Laws, traditions, and respect for the past is a big concern here, and it may be said that Saturn in his own sign is capable of honoring these traditions to a fault. Thus one may find people with this placement in positions of respect, leadership, authority, and dominion over others. And of course, with such a position comes the ultimate test of power, the kind which many of our political and religious leaders are facing today with an abundance of outer planets in Capricorn.

Chiron in the Tenth House urges the native to manifest some of Chiron's spirit in his or her relationship with the outer world: teachers (especially at the high school level), healers, and political reformers often have this placement. Uranus in the Tenth House, Capricorn, or aspecting Saturn is complicated and sometimes paradoxical, for again we meet a father-son team who were in opposition to one another's views, and there is apparently a great deal of struggle experienced by those who, throughout life, attempt to reconcile these opposites. Uranus routinely rejects others' rules, and Capricorn is, of course, the sign of law. But Saturn and Uranus were also prolific progenitors, so that the procreative aspects of this combination can also be profound. This may not always imply the creation of biological children; these people tend to give birth to ideas, concepts, inventions, services, and technologies that advance the course of civilization. The thing they must remember is not to get stuck, as both Saturn and Uranus ultimately did, in old ways and methods, refusing to change when the times say change. The next generation may benefit and profit greatly from their creations, but it will also want to make significant changes in keeping with the changing times. When Saturn-Uranus people refuse to change (which is common), they may wind up in the proverbial pit while the rest of the world sails along without them. Every forty-five years or so, these planets come together for a conjunction or rendezvous, a time when political systems and old world leaders may experience castration or dethronement by the people, as in the myth, and when new world orders take form.

Neptune in the Tenth House, Capricorn, or in aspect to Saturn is usually considered a difficult position, because Saturn's relationship to Neptune is very complex and not easily harmonized. Both of these gods (or planets) can experience similar feelings of rejection, fear, guilt, abandonment, and despair all by themselves, and when coupled together these feelings usually multiply. The main conflict between these two gods exists because Saturn is an earth god and dominates the physical, material, rational world and Neptune is a sea god whose domain of the unconscious, mystical, and etheric constitutes a realm which Saturn is not capable of grasping. When a person has these two signs or planets in some type of life-long aspect, one or the other will usually dominate the individual, especially if they were conjunct at birth. Then, when the next conjunction occurs (usually in one's late thirties), the other archetype will emerge, most probably take over, and then eventually harmonize. At that time the individual has a better ability to integrate the two energies, as planetary conjunctions always demand that a compromise be struck. Pluto in the Tenth House occurs often in the charts of extremely successful business people or politicians, though the urge for power may become so strong with this position as to overwhelm the native absolutely (example: Richard Nixon).

From 1984 until 1998, Saturn, Uranus, and Neptune all transit the sign of the goat, and for a short period (1988 to 1990) all three were there simultaneously. No wonder the world is experiencing a breakdown of political traditions which have lasted for decades. The political, economic, and social structures are dissolving or being reformed. And the leaders of these institutions are being tested in their moral fortitude. "Does absolute power corrupt absolutely?" may be the ultimate question of the times.

In Capricorn the solar wheel is turned for the fourth and final time. We achieve a certain mastery in Capricorn—and whether that involves an inner, spiritually directed mastery or outer, publicly governed mastery over others, we have reached the top of the mountain (and the literal top of the wheel astrologically) and at this point must turn our attention ever more strongly to the needs of the collective, a process exemplified in the final two signs, Aquarius and Pisces.

CAPRICORN WORKSHEET

A factor includes a planet, an asteroid, or an angle in the birth chart. How many factors do you have in Capricorn? Use the following point system to total them:

Sun 4	Mars................1	Uranus 1/2
Moon 4	Ceres 1	Neptune..........1/2
Earth 3	Pallas 1	Pluto..............1/2
Venus..............2	Juno................1	Part of Fortune .. 1/2
Mercury...........2	Jupiter 1	Nodes 1/2
MH................2	Saturn 3	Vertex 1/2
ASC 2	Chiron..............1	
Vesta...............2		

Capricorn on an angle (ASC, MH, DSC, IC) 3

Saturn or Vesta on an angle...3

Planets and asteroids in the 10th House count the same as above _____

Capricorn, Saturn, or Vesta as the focal point of a T-square? 2

Capricorn, Saturn, or Vesta in a T-square? 1

Total _____

How did you relate to these myths?_____

_____

_____

_____

_____

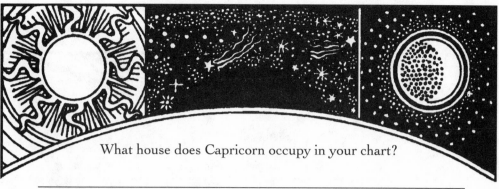

What house does Capricorn occupy in your chart?

_____

10th House—mother   1st House—self

4th House—father   11th House—friends

7th House—mate   5th House—children, lovers

3rd House—sibling

Keeping in mind that these houses represent these relationships, how has Capricorn energy expressed itself through others in your life? _____

_____

_____

_____

What houses do Saturn and Vesta occupy in your chart and how are they

expressed? _____

_____

What signs or planets are in your 10th House and how are they expressed? _____

_____

_____

Insights: _____

_____

_____

_____

Water-bearers from a fresco at Knossos, Crete, illustrated by Diane Smirnow

AQUARIUS

CHAPTER THIRTY-TWO

AQUARIUS, *The Water-Bearer*

SIGN: *Aquarius, the 11th Zodiacal Sign*

MODE: *Fixed* ❧ ELEMENT: *Air* ❧ RULER: *Uranus*

ADDITIONAL MYTHIC ARCHETYPES: *Saturn* ❧ *Juno* ❧ *Osiris,
Isis, and Hapi (Egyptian)* ❧ *Gilgamesh and Utnapishtim
(Sumerian)* ❧ *Ganymede* ❧ *Hebe* ❧ *Prometheus* ❧ *Pandora*

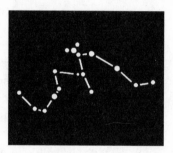

The Nile begins to flood in July, in the month of Leo. This, of course, is the time of year when Aquarius will rise at sunset—or, to put it another way, when the moon will be full in Aquarius. Therefore, it should not surprise us that this sign was originally associated with the flooding of the Nile.[1]

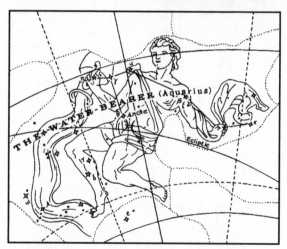

In a symbolic sense, the Egyptians thought of the Nile as the god Osiris, fecundating the goddess Isis who symbolized the Egyptian earth. The myth of Osiris has to do with the death, dismemberment, and the eventual resurrection of this god. One of the holiest shrines of ancient Egypt is the Temple of Elephantine, venerated as the symbolic (though not the actual) beginning of the Nile. Here was kept an especially sacred relic, the lower leg-bone of the god Osiris. Nearby, on the island of Philae, there was a bas-relief depicting Hapi, the god of the Nile, pouring forth the water of life from two vases. The image of Aquarius is, of course, that of the water-bearer pouring forth the waters of life; and the lower leg is associated with that sign in medical astrology.[2] To the ancient Egyptians, then, Aquarius represented the vital spiritual power which renews and fertilizes all things.

The sign had similarly powerful associations among the Babylonians. As we have seen, the four fixed signs of the zodiac recur again and again in Babylonian myth, especially in the *Epic of Gilgamesh* and in the Hebrew *Book of Ezekiel*, which was composed in Babylon during the captivity. Whereas the other three fixed signs are represented by animals, Aquarius acquires a particular distinction inasmuch as it is represented by a human being. In the Gilgamesh epic, this human being has a name and a story.

Osiris

Gilgamesh had lost his closest friend, Enkidu, his companion-in-arms. Seeking to restore Enkidu to life, Gilgamesh went seeking the herb of immortality. The Goddess had sent a bull against him (Taurus) and, during his quest, he conquered a pride of lions (Leo) and passed the gateway where the scorpion-men stood guard (Scorpio). These will be recognized as the first three signs of the fixed cross which Gilgamesh had to master before he could reach the otherworld where dwelt the immortal Utnapishtim, whom we may recognize as Aquarius. Utnapishtim had once been mortal like everyone else, but he alone had listened to the divine voices warning of world destruction. Utnapishtim built a boat and thus saved himself from the massive flood which came to inundate the world. Utnapishtim, of course, is the Sumerian or Babylonian form of Noah, and the flood story in which he plays such a key role is the prototype of the flood story in *Genesis*. Because of his obedience to the divine will, Utnapishtim had been granted eternal life and given keeping over the herb of immortality.

The epic goes on to recount how Gilgamesh wins the herb of immortality only to lose it again—for after all, humankind has not yet attained immortality.[3] But once again we find a mythic figure who is associated with both the flood and with renewal or immortality. Utnapishtim, Hapi, and Osiris all embody the same archetype.

The Greeks told quite a different story. They associated Aquarius with Ganymede, the beautiful Trojan boy who attracted the attention of Zeus (Jupiter). The king of the gods swooped down in the form of an eagle and carried Ganymede away to Mount Olympus to become the cupbearer of the gods.[4] (The other cupbearer was Hebe, the maiden daughter of Hera, who embodied many of her mother's attributes.) The gods subsisted on nectar and ambrosia, and presumably it was ambrosia which Ganymede poured from his cup. Ambrosia is the same word as the Sanskrit *amrita*, which means "the drink of immortality." This, of course, was the same magical substance we have seen placed in the keeping of Utnapishtim. The meaning of Aquarius is intertwined with the concept of a divine substance which nourishes all life. This substance is variously described as the waters of life, a life-giving herb, or a life-giving drink.

One present-day interpretation is that Aquarius rules electricity, and that the glyph for that sign (≈) should be understood as electrical waves rather than water. In our scientific world, we have

Ganymede

come to conceive of the life-giving substance as a vital, electrical quantum of cosmic energy rather than as a magic drink. And we have also come to regard the highly advanced technological aspects of our world as intoxicating—perhaps too intoxicating. Still, without the Aquarian scientific advances that have been ushered in since the days of the discovery of its ruling planet, Uranus, the world would still be somewhat asleep. As we stand poised between the second and third millennia CE, we have already figured out how to extend life (heart, liver, and kidney transplants), how to create life in the laboratory (test tube babies), and how to destroy life in a matter of seconds (atomic power). Certainly, test tube immortality can't be too far behind in this man-plays-God era.

Though Aquarius has always been associated with the waters of life, the actual interpretation of the sign has changed greatly over the centuries—not surprisingly, inasmuch as its rulership has also changed. The Olympian ruler of the sign was Juno, the goddess of marriage—a significator which may seem strange to us today, since we ordinarily think of Aquarians as shying away from marriage because it

King Sety I offers wine before Osiris. Behind Osiris are Isis and Horus

limits their freedom.[5] It is worth remembering, however, that the Olympian ruler-ships were arranged in pairs of opposites, and that Leo, the sign opposite Aquarius, was ruled by Jupiter, Juno's spouse. It is also fitting that, as we approach the Aquarian Age, the principles of freedom and equality are honored above all. Juno's association with Aquarius suggests that humanity will not be lib-erated from its darkness until man and woman are united as equals, in marriage and in all worldly affairs.

In modern astrology, the newly discovered (1781) planet Uranus rules Aquarius. If we examine Uranus closely in myth, we find that his behavior did not at all match the image we currently have of this enlightened sign. Nor do we find much correlation with the ancient ruler, Saturn. What we do find, however, are two gods with incredible life-giving, procreative abilities, the first and second generation gods who fathered all subsequent generations. The problem arose when they could not retire gracefully and let their sons carry on. They held on tightly to their posi-tions of power, for without these positions they felt useless, inadequate. This reminds us of the tremendous creative potential inherent in Aquarius (the ideolo-gists, inventors, artists) and also of their fixity. These future-thinkers and visionar-ies who can move us forward so rapidly may also have great difficulty giving up old ideas, opinions, or positions even when it is time for them to move on. They can remain rigidly attached to a way of thinking forever, and this is probably also why their ruling planet, Uranus, which shatters old and outmoded concepts, is said to create such an earthquake in our lives when it transits something important.

In classical astrology, however, it was Saturn who ruled this sign, and very old astrology texts describe Aquarians in Saturnian terms.[6] This image, too, seems odd to us, for we now regard the Aquarian temperament as the polar opposite of everything traditional or Saturnian. Occasionally, however, one still meets with Aquarians who are cautious, conservative, and melancholy, or quiet, thoughtful, and deep. Ronald Reagan certainly embodies the cautious and conservative side of the Saturnian Aquarian in his philosophy, but demonstrates the Uranian, charismatic side of Aquarius in his personality. On the other hand, Aquarian Abraham Lincoln may be regarded as Saturnian in terms of his appearance, his personal melancholy, and the depth of his thought. His ideas, however, more nearly fit our present-day image of Aquarius as the prophet, the social reformer, and the free thinker. These qualities are characteristic of Prometheus, the divine rebel of Olympus who "steals fire from the gods" (see Uranus).

These changing images of Aquarius illustrate an important point. We may think of the archetypes of the collective unconscious as unchanging; but this is not so. Even the great images sleeping in the mind of all humanity are subject to change. They change gradually over the centuries; but, like the sea-god Proteus who could change his shape at will, they have a flexibility about them which responds to the needs of humanity at a given time. Over the past two hundred years, the collective mind has formulated a new image of Aquarius to fit the coming astrological age. If this sign now represents freedom, the union of science and magic, and the power of individuality harnessed to the service of a greater whole, then these are the qualities that we, collectively, need most.

Thus, as we noted under Uranus, Prometheus is perhaps the most fitting archetype for this sign. It will be remembered that Chiron gave his life so that Prometheus could be released from torment. Here we see an association between Sagittarius or Virgo (Chiron) and Aquarius (Prometheus). Both mythic figures devoted great service to mankind, both suffered, and both desired to be released from their own worldly suffering. There is an aspect to these three signs that is associated with freedom, and especially with the kind of freedom that comes from transcending the body and earthly life. The principle difference is that Sagittarius, the fire sign, seeks *physical* freedom through wide open spaces in which to roam ("don't fence me in"), while Virgo, an earth sign and Chiron's other home, seeks a *spiritual* release from physical demands altogether—the transmutation of the body (earth). Aquarius, the *air* sign, seeks freedom of thought, and if not allowed such intellectual freedom, it feels chained like Prometheus.

Pandora is yet another fitting archetype for Aquarius, and in *The Mythic Tarot* it is Pandora who is portrayed on the Star card, the Tarot's association with astrological Aquarius.[7] Pandora is also related to Prometheus. It was Prometheus' action of stealing fire and giving it to mortals that angered Zeus. As a consequence Zeus instructed the smith-god Hephaestus to create Pandora and her box. Told *not* to open the box, Zeus felt sure she would ignore the command, and thus unleash the ills upon mankind that he placed in the box. Opening the forbidden box got

Pandora, before leaving Mt. Olympus

Pandora into her predicament and this act of curiosity may seem more like Gemini than Aquarius. But there is a difference between the restless curiosity of the young mind in Gemini and the Aquarian curiosity that caused Pandora to open the box. The sealed box is a place of darkness, fear, or ignorance. Thus its opening represents illumination and knowledge. When Pandora opened the box, out came all the ills and pestilence of the world inflicted by the gods on humanity. But the one thing left in the box was hope. It is humanity's hopefulness and also knowledge and illumination which eventually casts out darkness, fear, and ignorance, and is the prime ingredient in healing or transmuting all the ills, whether god-inflicted or man-made.

The air signs, as we have already observed (see Chapter Twenty, "The Elements", section "Air;" Chapter Twenty-four, "Gemini;" and Chapter Twenty-eight, "Libra"), have difficulty maintaining a good relationship with the body. The body refers to both the physical body and earth life in general. Fiery Sagittarius' gaze was always directed upwards, to some distant place, while in Capricorn we reached the mountaintop (Capricorn Martin Luther King: "I have been to the mountaintop!") In Aquarius, the god or goddess is pouring the urn downwards, towards earth, indicating that knowledge exists on the heavenly plane and must be transmitted to earthlings. This, then, is the wavelength to which many Aquarians resonate, and those who have not made proper contact with their information, or who find, like Lincoln, that they have presented it to a world which is not quite ready to receive it, find themselves in a lonely, isolated place, and thus out of harmony with "earth life." Prometheus learned how lonely it can be on top of the mountain.

Aquarius, in the astrological *mandala*, maintains an important relationship with Leo. They are polar opposites and depend upon each other for many key functions. In Leo we observed that the heart was a primary symbol; in Aquarius it is the circulation of the blood. If our circulatory system is malfunctioning, we are not getting enough blood to the heart; thus our vital signs weaken and we may even die. Blood clots are a manifestation of dysfunctional Aquarius energy. The circulation also implies the livelihood of the brain cells in receiving new input. When stimulation to the brain is obstructed, mental stagnation occurs. Thus brain tumors, blood clots, hardening of the arteries, and heart attacks are all related to this Leo/Aquarius polarity. When an individual stops thinking, he stops growing. When he stops growing, he dies. And it is not enough for Aquarius to simply receive information. The urn is facing downward—he must pass that information on to others so that they need not live in darkness.

In Aquarius, where universal rather than personal principles are emphasized, the blazing, fiery temperament of the Sun is in its detriment, for personal will finds little satisfaction in a sign where all are deemed equal. People with the Moon in Aquarius should have no trouble just being—it comes naturally to them. These people like to romp, and need to manifest as much irresponsibility as possible in the process. Depending on their temperament, they may prefer the woods or the big green computer screen, but they need that childlike absorption in play.

Mercury in Aquarius can be brilliant. This kind of genius may be removed from childhood playmates by exhibiting prodigious gifts, such as Hermes inventing the lyre. Venus in Aquarius loves in a fashion which, for many, is too cerebral and detached; but these people genuinely know how to find joy in their relationships in a way which few others ever can. Mars in Aquarius can exhibit brilliance both physically and intellectually, for one's entire system is filled with Uranian creativity. People with this position are likely to be highly individualistic, going against society's grain for the pure pleasure of it.

With Ceres in Aquarius, there is not much of a mothering bond on the emotional level. An early separation from parents or family is likely to produce an independent thinker or doer with brilliance in his or her chosen field. Pallas Athene, like Mercury, can be brilliant in this sign, and is likely to suffer the same isolation from intimate relations with others, but will ultimately be regarded as a leader. And even as Hermes invented the lyre, Athene put her gifts to practical use by inventing the olive tree. Juno was given rulership over Aquarius in the Olympian system, and this is a position that would seem to stress equality in all kinds of human relationships. Vesta might produce a genuine visionary with an erratic but highly charismatic sexual nature.

The Star card from a nineteenth-century French Tarot deck

Jupiter in Aquarius may produce the social reformer, for the sky god's expanded vision ranges even farther than usual in this sign. Even the most conservative of mortals should, with this position, have a mind more open than most. Saturn is in the sign of its old rulership in Aquarius; this position was always associated with leadership, whether political or otherwise, but these leaders have a kind of melancholy born of their mountain-top isolation.

When Chiron is either in the Eleventh House or combined with Uranus or Aquarius, an especially powerful and mythic placement is formed, with a direct bearing on our ability to walk the bridge between Saturn and the outer planets and liberate Uranian energies. From 1952 until 1989 these two planets were in opposition, implying an entire generation for whom the Promethean quest—the liberation of the Self—is of paramount importance. When Uranus is in Aquarius or the Eleventh House, it is in its natural home. The wild-eyed, futuristic idealism, inventiveness and iconoclasm of this planet is at its peak here. Both Prince Charles and his son, Prince William, the future kings of England, have this placement. Prince Charles has already come under fire from the conservatives for some of his non-traditional and very unique concepts. Neptune in the Eleventh House, like Uranus, will certainly give rise to social idealism, though the Neptunian may have trouble bringing his or her vision down to a practical, earthy level. Pluto in the Eleventh may lend its obsessive power either to ideologies or the groups in the native's life; these people will need to identify themselves with *themselves* rather than with friends or philosophies.

Aquarians are said to be ahead of their time, and thus slightly out of sync with the world around them. The Industrial Revolution, a period in history which followed the discovery of Aquarius' ruling planet, Uranus, in 1781, ushered in the so-called Age of Enlightenment—or, at least, the Age of Technology. Ever since that time, astrologers have maintained that we are entering the cusp of the age of Aquarius. And while we are not fully into it yet, we are certainly in transition. Since an astrological age takes around 2,100 years to complete, the cusp can last a couple of hundred years, and it is the cusp or period between two ages that we have been living in since the late 1700s. In the world of today, many Aquarian ideas and inventions (notably those of Aquarians Thomas Edison and Nikola Tesla) have come to light, having the overall effect of making the world seem easier to understand. Aquarian technologies have produced so much information about our world (they do call this the Age of Information), and other worlds, that we no longer need to live in fear of the enemy or of the unknown. And yet many still do. As long as the world's leaders are still concerned with making war, as long as nations of people still live in poverty, in ignorance, and without shelter, as long as people still live in fear of one another, as long as individuals and nations with abundance are hoarding earth's resources and not sharing with those in need, and as long as racial and religious prejudice still exists, we are not yet living in the Age of Aquarius. But the concepts of Aquarius have been coming through more strongly as each new decade unfolds, and humanity is slowly making the great shift which will thwart hunger and disease, create peace and freedom, and dissolve political and racial boundaries, so that we may truly see that each individual is a part of the whole, and is just as important to the whole as each of its parts.

Uranus enters its own sign in 1995 where it will stay for seven years. Neptune will follow, entering Aquarius in 1997, for fourteen years. Based on the higher vibrations of both Uranus and Neptune in this future-oriented, humanitarian sign, the opening years of the third millennium ought to be quite significant in terms of reaching a new spiral of evolutionary accomplishment for humanity.

AQUARIUS WORKSHEET

A factor includes a planet, an asteroid, or an angle in the birth chart. How many factors do you have in Aquarius? Use the following point system to total them:

Sun 4	Mars................1	Uranus 2
Moon 4	Ceres 1	Neptune..........1/2
Earth 3	Pallas 1	Part of Fortune .. 1/2
Venus..............2	Vesta................1	Pluto..............1/2
Mercury...........2	Jupiter 1	Nodes 1/2
MH.................2	Saturn 2	Vertex 1/2
ASC 2	Chiron..............1	
Juno...............2		

Aquarius on an angle (ASC, MH, DSC, IC) 3

Uranus or Aquarius on an angle..3

Planets and asteroids in the 11th House count the same as above _____

Uranus or Aquarius as the focal point of a T-square?.....................2

Uranus or Aquarius in a T-square?.......................................1

Total _____

How did you relate to these myths?_____

_____

_____

_____

_____

What house does Aquarius occupy in your chart?

_____

10th House—mother	1st House—self
4th House—father	11th House—friends
7th House—mate	5th House-children, lovers
3rd House—sibling	

Keeping in mind that these houses represent these relationships, how has Aquarius energy expressed itself through others in your life? _____

_____

_____

_____

What house does Uranus occupy in your chart and how is it expressed?_____

_____

_____

What signs or planets are in your 11th House and how are they expressed? _____

_____

_____

Insights: _____

_____

_____

_____

Siren playing a harp, from Jost Amman's Kunstbüchlin, *printed by*
Johann Feyerabend, Frankfurt, 1599

PISCES

CHAPTER THIRTY-THREE

PISCES, *The Fishes*

SIGN: *Pisces, the 12th Zodiacal Sign*

MODE: *Mutable* ❧ ELEMENT: *Water* ❧ RULER: *Neptune*

ADDITIONAL MYTHIC ARCHETYPES: *Jupiter* ❧ *Venus*
❧ *Cassandra* ❧ *The Lorelei, The Sirens* ❧ *Christ (Dionysus)*
❧ *Odysseus* ❧ *Penelope* ❧ *Perceval*

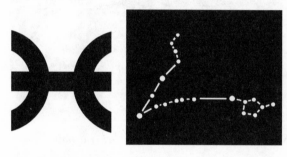

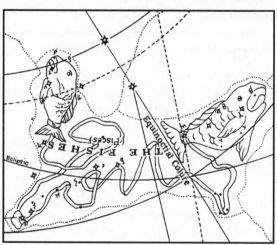

Pisces is one of the earliest signs on record, for the two fishes appear on an Egyptian coffin lid dated c. 2,300 BC. The flooding of the Nile reached its peak when the moon was full in Pisces — Egypt became a veritable ocean.[1]

The ocean has always been the symbolic keynote of Pisces. Today we attribute the sign's rulership to Neptune, who was the god of the sea. Before the discovery of that planet (1846), Jupiter was said to rule Pisces. But if we reach farther back, to the Olympian rulerships common in Plato's time, Neptune (Poseidon) once again appears as the ruler of the sign.[2] And finally, in esoteric astrology Venus rules the sign of the fishes, where she is traditionally said to be exalted.

Neptune was an angry and vengeful god upon occasion. We tend to disregard this violent aspect of the ocean and to associate the sign Pisces with the deep and dreamy aspect of the sea rather than with its storms, but any sailor that has spent much time at sea will tell you that the ocean contains a powerful force not to be taken lightly, and which must be respected. As Carl Jung pointed out, the ocean has always symbolized the group

Dolphin fresco from the Palace at Knossos, Crete. Photograph by Ariel Guttman

mind or, in his terminology, the collective unconscious.[3] The position of Neptune in a chart typically shows the area of life where we are most likely to come into contact with the primordial images and archetypes of the collective unconscious.

Artists and mystics are able to reach into that deep ocean of images and dreams; after all, it is precisely from these depths that they garner the visions, poems, paintings, or symphonies which fascinate and delight the rest of us. It is no wonder, then, that traditional astrological wisdom describes Pisceans as dreamy, mystical, and artistic, for all these individuals are born with at least one foot in the waters of the collective mind. A good example is Piscean visionary Edgar Cayce, who was able to contact an extremely deep stratum of the collective unconscious while he was asleep. Neptune was known for throwing storm clouds and nets of entanglement onto his victims to temporarily confuse them, blind them, and make them lose their way. This, along with the Pisces individual's need to keep rubbing the salt-water from his or her eyes, can contribute to a poor vision or sense of direction on the physical plane for these natives. But we have seen many Pisceans who are tuned into their inner vision and are thus guided to produce the most magnificent artistry and achievements possible to humankind (Michelangelo, Antonio Vivaldi, Albert Einstein).

However, not all Pisceans are inspired to such heights by the cosmic ocean within; instead, many are driven to serious addictions because they are "lost at sea."

Collective consciousness is the polar opposite of individual consciousness; in the Piscean personality, therefore, the individual ego may be quite weak, while the well-spring of universal images is exceptionally strong. Consequently, the Piscean is easily influenced, and may come to believe—from listening to friends, parents, or teachers—that his or her intuitive slant on reality is somehow inappropriate or just plain wrong. Consider Cassandra, who, having been given the gift of vision and prophecy, angered Apollo and was cursed so that nobody paid any attention to her prophetic warnings. Thus she "saw" impending dangers but had no ability or assistance with which to avert them. Many Pisceans "see" things that others are simply not capable of seeing. Therefore, the Pisces is left dangling between two worlds—the earthly realm that appears to be correct according to everyone else—and the cosmic realm, which Pisceans are all too aware of.

This dilemma is embodied in the astrological symbol for Pisces, two fish swimming in opposite directions, but bound together by a cord. Astrologer Robert Hand has pointed out that in reality these fish are not swimming in *opposite* directions as we have always believed.[4] Astronomically there is an east fish and a west fish. The east fish swims upward, away from the ecliptic, toward heaven, while the west fish swims along the plane of the ecliptic. Thus, we may conclude that one fish is seeking spiritual illumination while the other concerns itself with matters of the material plane. This, of course, constitutes the primary conflict and one of the "stormy" areas for the Pisces, who is all too aware of both directions but slightly more comfortable in the heavenly realm than in the physical one. Of course, there are many Pisceans who may surrender to the group definition of reality and often proclaim that only physical reality is "real" or that in this world only money really matters. The sad thing is that such individuals, cut off from their creative and cosmic inheritance, are

A Nereid (sea-nymph) and dolphin

precisely those Pisceans who end up drinking alone in front of the television set while watching science fiction movies at 3:00 am in order to fulfill their desperate need for fantasy. Identifying at either one pole or another is still only halfway to the goal for Pisces. The ultimate objective is to have both fish healthy, energetic, and in touch with their process, swimming merrily along like dolphins—another appropriate Piscean symbol, since these mammalian creatures live in the ocean. In the medical scheme, Pisces governs the feet—an example of the western fish who swims parallel to the material plane and keeps Pisces in a healthy state of balance.

If the collective mind holds deadly perils, it also holds exalted treasures. The Gnostic *Hymn of the Pearl* (c. 200 AD) tells the story of a spiritual seeker who must dive into the ocean to recover a pearl of great price. The poem aptly symbolizes the wisdom and creativity which can be found through contact with the collective unconscious.[5] But mythology also contains numerous stories of individuals—usually men, who have a poor relationship with the unconscious, thanks to our cultural emphasis on intellect—who are seduced by the collective images. The Lorelei, for example, were beautiful maidens who sat on rocks in the middle of the Rhine River, singing magical songs. But all men who harkened to those songs were enchanted and dragged down to their deaths in the murky waters.[6] The story of the sirens who tempted Ulysses and his men is precisely the same, and Slavic mythology tells of a beautiful but deadly creature called the *rusalka*, who performs the same function as the Germanic Lorelei or Greek sirens.[7] In ordinary life, such seduction by the unconscious usually takes the form of drug or alcohol abuse, another internal storm associated with Pisces and its natural house, the Twelfth.

The Piscean Age is, of course, the era in which we are now living. Opinions differ as to precisely when it began or when it will end, though almost everyone agrees that we are very near the end of the cycle, and that its beginning lies somewhere near the onset of the Christian Era. Robert Hand suggests 111 BC, the year when the vernal point reached the first star in Pisces, Alpha Piscium, as an appropriate astronomical beginning of the Piscean Age, while Dane Rudhyar suggests 100 BC[8] and the siderealists, such as Cyril Fagan, Donald Bradley, and most Hindu astrologers, prefer a date near 200 AD or even later.[9] Though it is difficult to argue with the scientific expertise of the siderealists, Hand and Rudhyar accord more with the symbolism of the age. In early Christian times, Christ's symbol was the fish. Early Christians used the fish as their identifying symbol, and it is still used today to symbolize fundamentalist Christianity. And certainly, from a mythic point of view we may regard Christ as a Piscean archetype.[10] One astrological treatise gives a convincing case for Jesus' birth occurring during the month of Pisces, at a time when many other planets lay in that constellation.[11] Throughout the ancient Mediterranean, the eternal round of the seasons was seen in terms of the Mother Goddess and her son or lover. This son or consort of the Divine Mother embodied the power of growth, the energy of the earth itself. We have touched upon various phases of this myth throughout our study of the zodiac, for the cycle of the year itself images the birth, growth, death, and resurrection of this mythic figure, the son

The Crucifixion, the Christian version of the dying son of the Great Mother. By Albrecht Dürer, from the print shop of Hieronymus Hölzel (later Friedrich Peypus), Nuremberg, 1517

of the Great Mother, the harvest god whose names have been legion—Dionysus, John Barleycorn, Christ.

Even as the earth passes through its cycle of spring, summer, autumn, winter, then spring again, so the God (and human life) passes through birth, growth, sacrifice, descent to the underworld, and rebirth. Whatever the historical reality of the Christian story may be, its outlines accord with the myth of the Goddess' dying son, and it is appropriate that Virgo, the sign of the Great Mother, forms the opposite polarity to Pisces, sign of the Divine Son. Medieval Christians thought of the constellation Virgo as the Virgin Mary, and of the star Spica as the Christ child in her lap. As we noted earlier (see Virgo) Michelangelo's Pieta is more than an artistic representation of a single moment in the Christian epic: it is an image of the Divine Mother weeping for her son, the slain Harvest God, as depicted in the story through which that eternal myth has been understood by Westerners for the last two thousand years. It is no wonder that Carl Jung suggested divinizing Mary and thereby replacing the Trinity with a Quaternity which would balance the masculine Father and Son with a feminine Mother and Holy Spirit.[12] Jung's psychology always made good mythic sense.

If universal love and compassion are the cornerstones of Christ's message (despite what interpreters such as Paul and Augustine may have read into it), then that message is in keeping with the sign Pisces. And this may well be where Venus, the goddess of personal *and* divine love, comes into the picture as the ruling planet of Pisces according to the esoteric theorists, and also, according to traditional astrology both Western and Hindu, the planet exalted in this sign. The guilt that humanity has suffered due to its inability to heed that message until it was too late has become a rather unfortunate by-product of this Piscean Age, and seems to afflict the Pisces individual personally. True merging with the collective unconscious involves a surrender of the personal ego. Having become one with all living, what response could we possibly have to the universe around us save compassion? Pisceans not only make the best alcoholics; they make the best counselors,

Dionysus on a modern cast copy of a tetradrachm of Naxos, Sicily, 461–430 BC. From the Michael A. Sikora collection

artists, musicians, world-servers, and mystics. Dane Rudhyar writes that in the Piscean phase of consciousness, the soul must "face the unknown with simple faith."[13] It is no wonder, then, that more than half of the Age of Pisces was known as the Age of Faith. Absolute faith or trust in the universe is the greatest challenge which Piscean individuals face. It is also their greatest strength.

Perhaps there was no greater test of faith than that depicted in the story of Odysseus and his wife Penelope. Odysseus, whose story is eloquently told in Homer's *Odyssey*, is a fitting archetype for all the mutable signs. The most "mercurial" of all Greek heroes, he solves problems with his mind rather than with brute strength; this mental agility is a truly Geminian trait. His wife,

Zeus sitting on his throne, holding a scepter with an eagle perched on his outstretched hand. A tetradrachm of Alexander the Great, 336–323 BC. From the Michael A. Sikora collection

Penelope, embodies the quiet self-containment of Virgo; having told her numerous suitors that she would choose a new husband when she finished weaving a particular cloak, she proceeded to spend the night-time *un*weaving what she had woven by day. Thus, with infinite patience, she awaited the return of Odysseus. Meanwhile, that hero was drifting through unexplored waters, a philosophic adventurer in the Sagittarian mode. But Sagittarius cares little for destinations, and Odysseus takes on a Piscean aspect in his hunger to return home. In this last stage of the astrological *mandala*, the soul, a wandering Odysseus, longs only to return to its place of origin. Odysseus tries always to keep his eye on the goal ahead, but is lost in a sea of confusion and emotional entanglement, beset by delays and challenges.

Odysseus had fought in the Trojan War for ten years, leaving his son and wife at home on the island of Ithaca. Battle-weary and longing for rest, Odysseus set sail after the war, only to encounter one dangerous adventure after another, sailing stormy and uncharted seas. Odysseus had incurred Poseidon's wrath and the god of the oceans was intent on throwing storms and destructive winds in his path at every turn. As a result Odysseus was washed upon one shore after another, and, like Gulliver, encountered every kind of creature imaginable. From lotus-eaters to giants, from cyclops to cannibals, from sirens to witches who turned his men into swine, Odysseus' journey through the twisting, turning, and raging waters kept him in an astral-like world so that the end always seemed further away rather than closer at hand. This is a world that Pisceans often encounter, as they struggle with strange creatures, whether real or imagined, in their own confused, chaotic astral seas. Odysseus, like Hercules, was fated to encounter many labors, the principal difference being that Hercules' use of sheer muscular power enabled him to be victorious, while for Odysseus it was a test of inner strength or faith that, with a pure heart and sincere intentions, he would eventually reach his goal. And for this he was rewarded, for Athene observed his dilemma and enabled him to reach his home. His wife Penelope, whose loyalty had been so sorely tested, had remained steadfast in her faith that he would return. After twenty years with no word of her husband, anyone else would surely have given up hope. But her faith was strong, even in the face of armies of suitors at her door, who took advantage of her situation and her abundant household, with no one to protect her but her son Telemachus. Like Pisceans (or Virgoans) who suffer through victimization by outside forces but seem to have no real power to rid themselves of such parasites, Penelope merely existed, hoping and praying that she would stay free of harm and that her husband would someday come home. Both these tests of faith were rewarded, and, with the help of the gods, Odysseus and Penelope were reunited.

Planets in Pisces in the birth chart attest to the need to swim through the mutable ocean—and some planets are more comfortable in these watery realms than others. In Pisces, the Sun's vital force is directed and expressed in a more universal context. Pisces' personality is so often diluted by its merging with the world around it that the Pisces ego may feel like a tiny raft adrift in a vast sea. Moon in Pisces, like the other water signs, takes a great deal of sustenance from actually being near the ocean. These people also tend to feel warm and nurtured through movies, massage, sensual pleasures in general, and mystical contemplation in particular.

Mercury, the planet associated with logic and mental clarity, is often completely lost in Pisces, having a difficult time keeping up with facts and figures, but excelling at poetry, music, and non-linear forms of communication. As noted, Venus is exalted in Pisces, and here the goddess of love swims in the ocean of universal love and compassion. She is also hopelessly romantic, and a problem here may be victimizing herself for the sake of love. Mars may have some initial difficulty get-

Poseidon on a bronze coin from Syracuse, Sicily, in the reign of Hieron II, 275–215 BC. From the Michael A. Sikora collection

ting used to the water, but this position or a Mars-Neptune aspect can contribute to the making of excellent aquatic athletes, stage performers, and (especially) dancers.

Ceres in Pisces is the archetypal nurse. This planetary position can encourage much devotion to compassionate and selfless service, and, if the individual is not careful, she or he can get stuck in continually rescuing those in need. In Pisces, the gifts of Pallas Athene lean toward the artistic, and her wisdom may take the form of visions. Juno in Pisces may take pity on a partner or marry based on spiritual bonding rather than physical attraction. Vesta in Pisces or with Neptune suggests the mystic or yogi in its focused form, while an unfocused Vesta-Neptune or Vesta in Pisces suggests the lack of boundaries and free-floating qualities typically associated with highly sensitive or traumatized individuals.

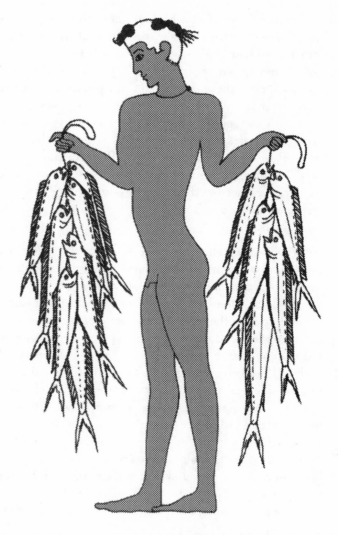

A Piscean illustration by Diane Smirnow after the Fresco of the Fisherman, Akrotiri, Santorini

Jupiter was the ancient ruler of Pisces and still has affinities with that sign. Here his broader, humanitarian outlook applies itself to the selfless service of Pisces in a way that benefits all. Those with Saturn in Pisces or the Twelfth House will probably have to work hard to hold themselves up in the world, as the total ineffectiveness of a father-figure may not have given them very solid grounding, much self-esteem, or direction. Still, because these people have worked so hard at healing their own issues, they can make truly wonderful healers, spiritual counselors, or guides for others. Chiron in the Twelfth House or aspecting Neptune can produce a gifted mystic, though it can also tend to make the native a little bit "spaced out."

Uranus in the Twelfth House activates the unconscious: these people can fight their karmic demons with a truly Promethean strength and, like Prometheus, may find themselves chained or imprisoned because of their visions. They hunger for enlightenment with the fierce energy of the stolen fire, or, if the position is weak or badly afflicted, these individuals may plunge into complexes and addictions with the same fierce determination. Neptune in the Twelfth House may also show problems with various types of addiction when weak, but its strength can also produce the greatest mystics and world-servers, the apostles of compassion (examples: Pope John Paul II and Dorothy Day). Pluto in the Twelfth House acts with relentless power to bring its natives face to face with their own complexes. These people may *try* to run away from their deeper issues, but Pluto will force those issues to the surface again and again. Power complexes are deeply embedded in the psyches of these individuals.

The Greeks tell us that out of Chaos the world was created. Beyond our world and before our world, the universe remains in a state of chaos. It is this chaos, residing just beyond our defined reality, that the Piscean can relate to. But the Greek word "chaos" does not literally mean wild confusion, which is how we are accustomed to define the term. Its ancient meaning was more nearly "the Void"—and this can be understood in the spiritual sense, as it is understood in Tibet. As a symbol of the Void or cosmic ocean, Pisces is the last of the twelve signs, and is said to contain each of the twelve within it. Like a multi-faceted crystal, the Piscean lives inside a twelve-sided geometric figure which encircles him or her. Thus, each time an attempt to take action is made, all twelve windows must be considered. If Libra is lost in a two-sided process of indecision, pity the poor Pisces, lost in twelve! However, the gift of Pisces is not the ability to see clearly from a rational point of view, but rather to look within and answer from the heart, a gift founded upon the belief in a higher power which makes things right. And no matter how out of control humanity seems to get, this underlying theme of the inner savior's reappearance has kept things going for the last 2,000 years—the Piscean era.

Finally let us consider Perceval, the seeker of the Grail, whom we met among the four elements. His name means "the pure fool," and thus aptly describes the state of mystical oneness where the soul does indeed stand naked before God. Pisces also represents the primordial ocean, and it is that unitive oceanic consciousness that Perceval sought when he sought the Grail—becoming one with the great cosmic pulse. Let us hope that by the end of the Piscean Age, the Grail will be fully restored.

PISCES WORKSHEET

A factor includes a planet, an asteroid, or an angle in the birth chart. How many factors do you have in Pisces? Use the following point system to total them:

Sun	4	Mars	1	Uranus	1/2
Moon	4	Ceres	1	Neptune	2
Earth	3	Pallas	1	Part of Fortune	1/2
Venus	3	Juno	1	Pluto	1/2
Mercury	2	Vesta	1	Nodes	1/2
MH	2	Saturn	1	Vertex	1/2
ASC	2	Chiron	I		
Jupiter	2				

Pisces on an angle (ASC, MH, DSC, IC)..................................3

Neptune on an angle..3

Planets and asteroids in the 12th House count the same as above _____

Pisces or Neptune as the focal point of a T-square? 2

Pisces or Neptune in a T-square?...1

Total _____

How did you relate to these myths?_____

_____

_____

_____

_____

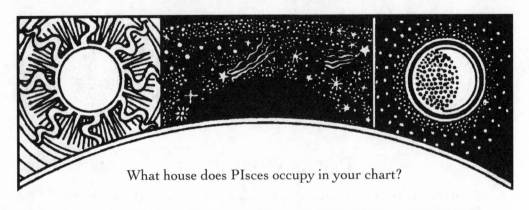

What house does PIsces occupy in your chart?

_____

10th House—mother   1st House—self

4th House—father   11th House—friends

7th House—mate   5th House—children, lovers

3rd House—sibling

Keeping in mind that these houses represent these relationships, how has Pisces energy expressed itself through others in your life? _____

_____

_____

_____

What house does Neptune occupy in your chart and how is it expressed?_____

_____

_____

What signs or planets are in your 12th House and how are they expressed? _____

_____

_____

Insights: _____

_____

_____

Appendix: *Graeco-Roman Deities & Heroes, and Sacred Site Locations*

Greek Deities and Heroes and their Roman Names

Greek	Roman
Aphrodite	Venus
Ares	Mars
Artemis	Diana
Athene	Minerva
Cronus	Saturn
Demeter	Ceres
Dionysus	Bacchus
Eros	Cupid
Hades	Pluto
Hephaestus	Vulcan
Hera	Juno
Heracles	Hercules
Hermes	Mercury
Hestia	Vesta
Odysseus	Ulysses
Ouranus	Uranus
Persephone (Kore)	Proserpina
Poseidon	Neptune
Zeus	Jupiter

Location of Gods' and Goddesses' Sacred Sites

Sun/Apollo:
Rhodes — Helios
Delos — Apollo's birthplace
Delphi — Shrine of Apollo

Moon/Artemis:
Arcadia
Ephesus

Mercury/Hermes:
Mt. Cyllene

Venus/Aphrodite:
Cyprus

Earth/Gaia:
Delphi

Ceres/Demeter:
Eleusis

Pallas Athene:
Lake Triton, Libya — birthplace
Athens

Juno/Hera:
Samos
Argos

Jupiter/Zeus:
Mt. Olympus
Dodona

Chiron:
Mt. Pelion

Neptune/Poseidon:
Sounion

Vulcan/Hephaestus:
Lemnos

Endnotes

INTRODUCTION

1. Gauquelin, Michel, *The Cosmic Clocks*, New York, Avon Books, 1969; and Michel Gauquelin, *Cosmic Influences on Human Behavior*, New York, ASI Publishers, 1978.
2. Sobel, Dava, "Dr. Zodiac," in *Omni*, December, 1989.
3. "Behind The Horoscope," Tony Edwards, BBC, 1980.
4. Jung, Carl G. et al., *Man and His Symbols*, New York, Dell, 1971.
5. Jung, Carl G., "On Synchronicity," in *The Portable Jung*, ed. Joseph Campbell, Harmondsworth and New York, Penguin, 1980.
6. Rudhyar, Dane, *The Astrology of Personality*, Garden City, NY, Doubleday, 1970.
7. Jung, Carl G., "On Mandala Symbolism," in *The Archetypes and the Collective Unconscious (Collected Works*, Vol. 9, I), Princeton, Princeton-Bollingen, 1968.
8. Meyer, Michael, *A Handbook for the Humanistic Astrologer*, Garden City, NY, Anchor-Doubleday, 1974.
9. "Thinking Allowed," Dr. Jeffrey Mishlove, The Institute of Noetic Sciences, PBS, 1990.

Chapter 1. THE PLANETS

1. Ficino, Marsilio, *The Book of Life*, trans. by Charles Boer, Irving, TX, Spring Publications, 1980.
2. Gauquelin, Michel, *The Cosmic Clocks*, ibid., p. 25.

Chapter 2. THE SUN

1. Rendering from the Egyptian by Kenneth Johnson.
2. Stone, Merlin, *When God Was A Woman*, San Diego, CA, Harvest Books, 1976.
3. Neumann, Erich, *The Origins and History of Consciousness*, Princeton, NJ, Princeton-Bollingen, 1973.
4. Graves, Robert, *The Greek Myths*, Baltimore, Penguin Books, 1964, Vol. 1, pp. 80–2.
5. Gray, John, *Near Eastern Mythology*, London, Hamlyn, 1969, p. 20.
6. Cumont, Franz, *Astrology and Religion Among the Greeks and Romans*, New York, Dover, 1960, pp. 55, 74.
7. Jung, C. G., *Mysterium Coniunctionis (Collected Works*, Vol. 14), Princeton, NJ, Princeton-Bollingen, 1974.
8. Bly, Robert, *Iron John*, Reading, MA, Addison-Wesley Publishing Co., 1990, pp. 110–3.
9. Jung, C. G., *Mysterium Coniunctionis*, ibid.
10. Bly, Robert, *Iron John*, ibid., pp. 146–79.
11. Campbell, Joseph, *The Hero With A Thousand Faces*, Princeton, NJ, Princeton-Bollingen, 1973.
12. Gray, John, *Near Eastern Mythology*, ibid., p. 23.

Chapter 3. MERCURY

1. Gray, John, *Near Eastern Mythology*, ibid., pp. 29–33.
2. Gray, John, *Near Eastern Mythology*, ibid., pp. 26–9.
3. Behari, Bepin, *Myths and Symbols of Vedic Astrology*, ed. by David Frawley, Salt Lake City, Passage Press, 1990, pp. 58–64; and James Braha, *Ancient Hindu Astrology for the Modern Western Astrologer*, Miami, Hermetician Press, 1986, p. 241.
4. Kerenyi, Karl, *The Gods of the Greeks*, London and New York, Thames and Hudson, 1951.

Notes to Pages 33–75

5. Behari, Bepin, *Myths and Symbols of Vedic Astrology*, ibid., pp. 177–9.

6. Whitmont, Edward, *The Symbolic Quest*, New York, Harper and Row, 1969, p. 182.

7. Whitmont, Edward, *The Symbolic Quest*, ibid., p. 179.

8. Jung, C. G., *Alchemical Studies (Collected Works*, Vol. 13), Princeton-Bollingen, 1976, pp. 191–250.

9. Jung, C. G., *The Psychology of the Transference*, Princeton, NJ, Princeton-Bollingen, 1969.

Chapter 4. VENUS

1. Hesiod, *Theogony and Works and Days*, trans. M. L. West, Oxford and New York, Oxford University Press, 1988, pp. 8–9.

2. Kerenyi, Karl, *The Gods of the Greeks*, ibid., pp. 68–9.

3. Kerenyi, Karl, *The Gods of the Greeks*, ibid., p. 80.

4. Graves, Robert, *The Greek Myths*, ibid., Vol. 1, pp. 27–30.

5. Gimbutas, Marija, *Goddesses and Gods of Old Europe*, Berkeley and Los Angeles, University of California, 1982, pp. 101–7.

6. Kerenyi, Karl, *The Gods of the Greeks*, ibid., pp. 77–9.

7. Bolen, Jean Shinoda, *Gods in Everyman*, San Francisco, Harper and Row, 1989, pp. 219–50.

8. Graves, Robert, *The Greek Myths*, ibid., Vol. 1, pp. 67–8.

9. Kerenyi, Karl, *The Gods of the Greeks*, ibid., pp. 68, 80.

10. Bolen, Jean Shinoda, *Gods in Everyman*, ibid., pp. 219–50.

Chapter 5. GAIA

1. Lovelock, James, *Gaia: A New Look at Life on Earth*, New York, Oxford University Press, 1975.

2. Rudhyar, Dane, *Astrological Timing*, New York, Harper Colophon, 1972, p. 161–2.

3. Eisler, Riane, *The Chalice and the Blade*, San Francisco, Harper and Row, 1988, pp. 17–8.

4. Gimbutas, Marija, *Goddesses and Gods of Old Europe*, passim.

5. Bailey, Alice, *Esoteric Astrology*, New York, Lucis Publishing Company, 1974.

Chapter 6. MOON

1. Apuleius, Lucius, *The Golden Ass*, trans. by Robert Graves, Harmondsworth, Penguin Books, 1972, pp. 226–7.

2. Leland, Charles, *Aradia: The Gospel of the Witches*, Custer, WA, Phoenix, 1989.

3. Graves, Robert, *The White Goddess*, New York, Farrar, Straus and Giroux, 1974, p. 401.

4. Gimbutas, Marija, *Goddesses and Gods of Old Europe*, ibid., pp. 89–93.

5. Graves, Robert, *The White Goddess*, ibid., passim.

6. Gantz, Jeffrey, trans., *The Mabinogion*, London and New York, Penguin Books, 1976, pp. 91–117.

7. Cunningham, Donna, *Being A Lunar Type In A Solar World*, York Beach, ME, Samuel Weiser, 1982.

8. Rudhyar, Dane, *The Lunation Cycle*, Berkeley and London, Shambala, 1971.

9. Gimbutas, Marija, *Goddesses and Gods of Old Europe*, ibid., pp. 169–71.

Chapter 7. NODES

1. Hawkins, Gerald S., and John B. White, *Stonehenge Decoded*, Garden City, NY, Doubleday, 1965.

2. Ellis Davidson, H. R., *Gods and Myths of the Viking Age*, New York, Bell, 1981, p. 28.

3. Frawley, David, *Gods, Sages and Kings*, Salt Lake City, Passage Press, 1991.

4. Ions, Veronica, *Indian Mythology*, London, Hamlyn, 1967, pp. 111–5.

5. Braha, James, *Ancient Hindu Astrology for the Modern Western Astrologer*, ibid., pp. 33–5.

Chapter 8. MARS

1. Homer, *The Iliad*, various editions.
2. Graves, Robert, *The Greek Myths*, ibid., Vol. 1, pp. 73–4.
3. Gray, John, *Near Eastern Mythology*, ibid., p. 23.
4. Behari, Bepin, *Myths and Symbols of Vedic Astrology*, ibid., pp. 77–80.
5. Bly, Robert, *Iron John*, ibid., pp. 146–79.
6. Bly, Robert, *Iron John*, ibid.
7. Jung, C. G., *Mysterium Coniunctionis*, ibid., passim.
8. Gauquelin, Michel, *The Cosmic Clocks*, ibid., p. 191.
9. Gauquelin, Michel, *Cosmic Influences on Human Behavior*, ibid., p. 89–103.
10. Lewis, Jim, and Ariel Guttman, *The Astro*Carto*Graphy Book of Maps*, St. Paul, MN, Llewellyn, 1989, pp. 153–207.

Chapter 9. CERES

1. Bach, Eleanor, *Ephemerides of the Asteroids — Juno, Pallas, Ceres, Vesta 1900-2000*, Brooklyn, Celestial Communications, Inc., 1973.
2. Dobyns, Zipporah, *Expanding Astrology's Universe*, San Diego, CA, ACS Publications, 1983.
3. George, Demetra, *Asteroid Goddesses*, San Diego, CA, ACS Publications, 1986.
4. Joseph, Tony, *The Archetypal Universe*, unpublished ms., 1984.

Chapter 10. PALLAS ATHENE

1. Graves, Robert, *The Greek Myths*, ibid., Vol. 1, pp. 44–5.
2. Gimbutas, Marija, *Goddesses and Gods of Old Europe*, ibid., pp. 18, 145–51.
3. Bolen, Jean Shinoda, *Goddesses in Everywoman*, New York, Harper and Row, 1985, pp. 75–106; and Demetra George, *Asteroid Goddesses*, ibid., pp. 80–116.
4. George, Demetra, *Asteroid Goddesses*, ibid.
5. Bolen, Jean Shinoda, *Goddesses in Everywoman*, ibid., pp. 75–106.
6. Whitmont, *Symbolic Quest*, ibid.; and Linda Schierse Leonard, *The Wounded Woman*, Boulder and London, Shambhala, 1983.

Chapter 11. JUNO

1. Harrison, Jane Ellen, *Prolegomena to the Study of Greek Religion*, Cambridge, MA, Cambridge University Press, 1922.
2. Gleadow, Rupert, *The Origin of the Zodiac*, New York, Castle Books, 1968, pp. 80–1.
3. Dobyns, Zipporah, *Expanding Astrology's Universe*, ibid., p. 61; and George, Demetra, *Asteroid Goddesses*, ibid., pp. 169–70.
4. Walker, Barbara G., *The Woman's Encyclopedia of Myths and Secrets*, San Francisco, Harper and Row, 1983, p. 484.
5. Graves, Robert, *The Greek Myths*, ibid., Vol. 1, pp. 50–5.
6. Guttman, Ariel, *Astro-Compatibility*, Euclid, OH, RKM Publications, 1986, pp. 11–14.
7. Bolen, Jean Shinoda, *Goddesses in Everywoman*, ibid., pp. 139–67.

Chapter 12. VESTA

1. Eliade, Mircea, *Shamanism: Archaic Techniques of Ecstasy*, Princeton, NJ, Princeton-Bollingen, 1972.
2. Dumezil, Georges, *Archaic Roman Religion*, Chicago and London, University of Chicago Press, 1970, 2 vols.
3. Walker, Barbara G., *The Woman's Encyclopedia of Myths and Secrets*, ibid., pp. 1046–7.
4. Bach, Eleanor, *Ephemerides of the Asteroids — Juno, Pallas, Ceres, Vesta 1900-2000*, ibid.
5. Dobyns, Zipporah, *Expanding Astrology's Universe*, ibid., pp. 60–1; and George, Demetra, *Asteroid Goddesses*, ibid., pp. 124–30.

Notes to Pages 118–166

6. Gleadow, Rupert, *The Origin of the Zodiac*, ibid., pp. 80–1.

7. George, Demetra, *Asteroid Goddesses*, ibid., pp. 124–30.

Chapter 13. JUPITER

1. Gray, John, *Near Eastern Mythology*, ibid., pp. 29–33.

2. Gleadow, Rupert, *The Origin of the Zodiac*, ibid., pp. 80–1.

3. Braha, James, *Ancient Hindu Astrology for the Modern Western Astrologer*, ibid., pp. 27, 65.

Chapter 14. SATURN

1. Hesiod, *Theogony and Works and Days*, ibid., pp. 7–25.

2. Greene, Liz, *Saturn: A New Look at an Old Devil*, New York, Samuel Weiser, 1977.

3. Lilly, William, *An Introduction to Astrology*, Hollywood, CA, Newcastle, 1972 (first published 1647).

4. Ficino, Marsilio, *The Book of Life*, ibid., passim.

5. Gauqelin, Michel, *Cosmic Influences on Human Behavior*, ibid., pp. 120–132.

6. Hesiod, *Theogony and Works and Days*, ibid., pp. 40–2.

7. Perowne, Stewart, *Roman Mythology*, London, Hamlyn, 1969, pp. 42–3.

8. "A Gathering of Men," PBS, 1989.

9. Homer, *The Odyssey*, trans. Robert Fitzgerald, Garden City, NY, Doubleday, 1961.

10. "Gathering of Men," op. cit.

Chapter 15. CHIRON

1. Clow, Barbara Hand, *Chiron: Rainbow Bridge Between the Inner & Outer Planets*, St. Paul, MN, Llewellyn Publications, 1987, pp. 215–27.

2. Stein, Zane, *Interpreting Chiron*, Lansdale, PA, Associates for the Study of Chiron, 1983.

3. Joseph, Tony, *The Archetypal Universe*, ibid.; and Erminie Lantero, *The Continuing Discovery of Chiron*, York Beach, ME, Samuel Weiser, 1983.

4. Graves, Robert, *The Greek Myths*, ibid., Vol. 1, pp. 173–8.

5. Graves, Robert, *The Greek Myths*, ibid., Vol. 2, pp. 113, 148–9.

6. Nolle, Richard, *Chiron: The New Planet in Your Horoscope*, Tempe, AZ, American Federated Astrologers, 1983.

7. Bly, Robert, *Iron John*, ibid., pp. 23, 186.

8. Neihardt, John G., ed., *Black Elk Speaks*, Lincoln, University of Nebraska, 1961.

9. In conversation with the authors, February, 1990, Santa Fe, NM.

10. Nolle, Richard, *Chiron: The New Planet in Your Horoscope*, ibid.

Chapter 16. URANUS

1. Lewis, Jim, and Ariel Guttman, *The Astro*Carto*Graphy Book of Maps*, ibid.

2. Ions, Veronica, *Indian Mythology*, ibid., pp. 14–5.

3. Zaehner, R. C., *The Dawn and Twilight of Zoroastrianism*, New York, G. P. Putnam's Sons, 1961, pp. 65–71.

4. Hesiod, *Theogony and Works and Days*, ibid., pp. 8–9.

5. Greene, Liz, *The Astrology of Fate*, York Beach, ME, Samuel Weiser, 1984, pp. 250–7.

6. Sheehy, Gail, *Passages*, New York, E.P. Dutton, 1974.

Chapter 17. NEPTUNE

1. Graves, Robert, *The White Goddess*, ibid., p. 399.

2. Gimbutas, Marija, *Goddesses and Gods of Old Europe*, ibid., pp. 230–4.

3. Bradshaw, John, *Healing the Shame that Binds You*, Deerfield Beach, FL, Health Communications, Inc. 1988, p. 103.

ENDNOTES ❧ 375

Notes to Pages 173–228

Chapter 18. PLUTO

1. Bolen, Jean Shinoda, *Gods in Everyman*, ibid., pp. 98–123.
2. Green, Jeff, *Pluto: The Evolutionary Journey of the Soul*, St. Paul, MN, Llewellyn, 1985.
3. Greene, Liz, *The Astrology of Fate*, ibid., pp. 36–51.
4. Greene, Liz, *The Astrology of Fate*, ibid., pp. 39–40.
5. Perera, Sylvia Brinton, *Descent to the Goddess*, Toronto, Inner City Books, 1981.
6. Bolen, Jean Shinoda, *Gods in Everyman*, ibid., pp. 98–123.

Chapter 19. THE ZODIAC

1. Gauquelin, Michel, *The Cosmic Clocks*, ibid., pp. 35–41.
2. Gauquelin, Michel, *The Cosmic Clocks*, ibid., pp. 37–8.
3. Campbell, Joseph, *The Hero With A Thousand Faces*, ibid.
4. Rudhyar, Dane, *The Pulse of Life*, Berkeley, Shambala Publications, 1970.
5. Gleadow, Rupert, *The Origin of the Zodiac*, New York, Castle Books, 1968.

Chapter 20. THE ELEMENTS

1. Jung, Emma, and Marie-Louise von Franz, *The Grail Legend*, New York, Putnam's, 1970, pp. 83–4.
2. Douglas, Alfred, *The Tarot*, Harmondsworth and Baltimore, Penguin, 1972, pp. 36–7.
3. Regardie, Israel, *The Tree of Life*, New York, Weiser, 1973, p. 115.
4. Jung, C. G., *Psychological Types* (*Collected Works*, Vol. VI), Princeton, NJ., Princeton-Bollingen, 1974.
5. Whitmont, Edward, *The Symbolic Quest*, ibid., p. 152.
6. Bradshaw, John, *Healing the Shame that Binds You*, ibid., p. 103.
7. Jung, C.G., *Psychology and Alchemy* (*Collected Works*, Vol. 12), Princeton, NJ., Princeton-Bollingen, 1977, pp. 301–2.
8. Jung, C.G., *Psychology and Alchemy* (*Collected Works*, Vol. 12), ibid. pp. 288–316.
9. Kiersey, David, *Please Understand Me*, Prometheus Nemesis Books, Del Mar, CA.
10. Jung, Emma, and Marie-Louise von Franz, *The Grail Legend*, ibid., passim.

Chapter 21. MODALITIES

1. Wilhelm, Richard, trans., *The I Ching*, Princeton, NJ., Princeton-Bollingen, 1970.
2. Frawley, David, personal communication with authors, August, 1990.
3. Jung, C. G., *Psychology and Alchemy* (*Collected Works*, Vol. 12), ibid., passim.
4. Leo, Alan, *Esoteric Astrology*, New York, Astrologer's Library, 1983, p. xvii.
5. Frawley, David, *The Astrology of the Seers*, Salt Lake City, Passage Press, 1990.
6. Mallory, J.P., *In Search of the Indo-Europeans*, London, Thames and Hudson, 1989, pp. 182–5.
7. Gimbutas, Marija, *Goddesses and Gods of Old Europe*, ibid.
8. see Graves, Robert, *The Greek Myths*, ibid., pp. 9–26; also Jane Ellen Harrison, *Prolegomena to the Study of Greek Religion*, ibid.
9. Rudhyar, Dane, *The Pulse of Life*, ibid., pp. 73–8.
10. Campbell, Joseph, *The Hero With A Thousand Faces*, ibid., p. 245.
11. Jung, C. G., *Aion* (*Collected Works*, Vol. 9 II), Princeton, NJ., Princeton-Bollingen, 1975, p. 123.
12. Douglas, Alfred, *The Tarot*, ibid., pp. 113–5.

Chapter 22. ARIES

1. Gleadow, Rupert, *The Zodiac Revealed*, North Hollywood, Wilshire Book Co., 1971, p. 44.
2. Fagan, Cyril, *Astrological Origins*, St. Paul, MN, Llewellyn, 1973, p. 117.
3. Walker, Barbara G., *The Woman's Encyclopedia of Myths and Secrets*, ibid., p. 267.
4. Gleadow, Rupert, *The Zodiac Revealed*, ibid., p. 45.

Notes to Pages 229–277

5. Rudhyar, Dane, *The Pulse of Life*, ibid., pp. 31–8.
6. Graves, Robert, *The Greek Myths*, ibid., Vol. 1, p. 229.
7. Greene, Liz, *The Astrology of Fate*, ibid., pp. 176–83.

Chapter 23. Tᴀᴜʀᴜꜱ

1. Fagan, Cyril, *Astrological Origins*, ibid., pp. 118, 28–32.
2. Gimbutas, Marija, *Goddesses and Gods of Old Europe*, ibid., pp. 89–93.
3. Campbell, Joseph, *Occidental Mythology (Masks of God, Vol. III)*, New York, Viking Press, 1969, pp. 42–92.
4. Fagan, Cyril, *Astrological Origins*, ibid., pp. 112, 118.
5. Gimbutas, Marija, *Goddesses and Gods of Old Europe*, ibid., passim.
6. Sandars, N.K., trans., *The Epic of Gilgamesh*, London and New York, Penguin, 1988, p. 87–8.
7. Eisler, Riane, *The Chalice and the Blade*, ibid., pp. 29–41.
8. Renault, Mary, *The King Must Die*, New York, Pantheon, 1958.
9. Graves, Robert, *The Greek Myths*, ibid., Vol. II, p. 381.
10. Graves, Robert, *The Greek Myths*, ibid., Vol. I, pp. 297, 306.
11. Castillejo, Irene Claremont de, *Knowing Woman*, New York, Harper Colophon, 1973.
12. Hawkins, John Robert, *Transpluto, or Should We Call Him Bacchus, the Ruler of Taurus?*, Dallas, Hawkins Enterprising Publications, 1978.

Chapter 24. Gᴇᴍɪɴɪ

1. Graves, Robert, *The Greek Myths*, ibid., Vol. 1, pp. 206–7.
2. Gleadow, Rupert, *The Zodiac Revealed*, ibid., p. 62.
3. Graves, Robert, *The Greek Myths*, ibid., Vol. I, pp. 245–50.
4. Behari, Bepin, *Myths and Symbols of Vedic Astrology*, ibid.
5. Mallory, J.P., *In Search of the Indo-Europeans*, ibid., pp. 132–7.
6. Gleadow, Rupert, *The Origin of the Zodiac*, ibid., pp. 80–1.
7. Greene, Liz, *The Astrology of Fate*, ibid., pp. 189–96.
8. Gantz, Jeffrey, trans., *The Mabinogion*, ibid., pp. 66–82.
9. von Franz, Marie-Louise, *Puer Aeternus*, Santa Monica, CA, Sigo Press, 1981.

Chapter 25. Cᴀɴᴄᴇʀ

1. According to the neo-Platonic philosopher Porphyry, in his *Cave of the Nymphs* (various eds.).
2. Fagan, Cyril, *Astrological Origins*, ibid., pp. 119–20.
3. Graves, Robert, *The Greek Myths*, ibid., Vol. 1, pp. 63–7.
4. Gleadow, Rupert, *The Zodiac Revealed*, ibid., pp. 71–2.
5. Graves, Robert, *The Greek Myths*, ibid., Vol. II, pp. 108–9.
6. Campbell, Joseph, *The Hero With A Thousand Faces*, ibid., p. 245.
7. U.S. Bureau of the Census, *Statistical Abstract of the U.S.: 1990*, 110th ed., Washington D.C., 1990.
8. Bailey, Alice, *Esoteric Astrology*, ibid.

Chapter 26. Lᴇᴏ

1. Fagan, Cyril, *Astrological Origins*, ibid., pp. 120–1; and Rupert Gleadow, *The Zodiac Revealed*, ibid., p. 81.
2. Rudhyar, Dane, *Astrological Timing*, ibid., pp. 206–08.
3. Neumann, Erich, *The Origins and History of Consciousness*, ibid.
4. Haich, Elizabeth, *Initiation*, Palo Alto, CA., Seed Center, 1974.
5. Gantz, Jeffrey, trans., *The Mabinogion*, ibid., pp. 45–65, 97–117.

6. Bord, Janet & Colin, *Earth Rites*, London, Paladin, 1982, pp. 159–63; and Margaret Murrary, *The God of the Witches*, New York, Oxford University Press, 1970, pp. 162–71.

7. Gleadow, Rupert, *The Origin of the Zodiac*, ibid., p. 80.

8. Gleadow, Rupert, *The Origin of the Zodiac*, ibid., p. 8.

9. Kerenyi, Karl, *The Gods of the Greeks*, ibid., p. 82.

10. Graves, Robert, *The White Goddess*, ibid., p. 85.

11. Campbell, Joseph, *The Mythic Image*, Princeton, NJ, Bollingen Press, 1982, p. 40.

12. Hamilton, Edith, *Mythology*, New York, New American Library, 1969, p. 177.

Chapter 27. VIRGO

1. Gleadow, Rupert, *The Zodiac Revealed*, ibid., p. 89.

2. Gleadow, Rupert, *The Origin of the Zodiac*, ibid., pp. 80–1.

3. Fagan, Cyril, *Astrological Origins*, ibid., pp. 122–3.

4. Greene, Liz, *The Astrology of Fate*, ibid., pp. 257–65.

5. Rudhyar, Dane, *The Pulse of Life*, ibid., pp. 65–73.

6. Clow, Barbara Hand, *Chiron: Rainbow Bridge Between the Inner & Outer Planets*, ibid.; and Demetra George, *Asteroid Goddesses*, ibid.

7. Clow, Barbara Hand, *Chiron: Rainbow Bridge Between the Inner & Outer Planets*, ibid.

8. Jung, C. G., *Alchemical Studies (Collected Works*, Vol. 13), ibid., pp. 191–250.

Chapter 28. LIBRA

1. Gleadow, Rupert, *The Zodiac Revealed*, ibid., p. 100.

2. Fagan, Cyril, *Astrological Origins*, ibid., pp. 123–4.

3. Gleadow, Rupert, *The Origin of the Zodiac*, ibid., pp. 80–1.

4. Rudhyar, Dane, *The Pulse of Life*, ibid., pp. 73–9.

5. Fagan, Cyril, *Astrological Origins*, ibid., p. 124.

6. Johnson, Robert, *We*, New York, Harper and Row, 1983.

7. Greene, Liz, *The Astrology of Fate*, ibid., pp. 220–8.

8. Campion, Nicholas, *The Book of World Horoscopes*, Wellingborough, North Hamptonshire, Aquarian Press, 1988, p. 134.

9. Neumann, Erich, *Amor and Psyche*, Princeton, NJ, Princeton-Bollingen, 1973; and Robert Johnson, *She*, New York, Harper & Row, 1977.

10. Guttman, Ariel, *Astro-Compatibility*, ibid., pp. 11–14.

Chapter 29. SCORPIO

1. Rudhyar, Dane, *The Pulse of Life*, ibid., pp. 79–85.

2. Sandars, N.K., trans., *The Epic of Gilgamesh*, ibid., pp. 98–9.

3. Fagan, Cyril, *Astrological Origins*, ibid., p. 125.

4. Gray, John, *Near Eastern Mythology*, ibid., pp. 23, 34, 43–4.

5. Gray, John, *Near Eastern Mythology*, ibid., p. 23.

6. Stone, Merlin, *When God Was A Woman*, ibid., pp. 198–223.

7. Chartrand, Mark R., *Skyguide*, New York, Golden Press, 1982, p. 170.

8. Hamilton, Edith, *Mythology*, ibid., pp. 279–81.

9. Behari, Bepin, *The Vedic Astrologer's Handbook*, ed. Kenneth Johnson, Salt Lake City, Passage Press, 1992.

10. Garrison, Omar, *Tantra: The Yoga of Sex*, New York, Avon, 1973.

Chapter 30. SAGITTARIUS

1. Bulfinch, Thomas, *Bulfinch's Mythology*, New York, Avenel, 1978, pp. 127–8.

2. Manilius, quoted in Rupert Gleadow, *The Origin of the Zodiac*, ibid., p. 80.

3. Graves, Robert, *The Greek Myths*, ibid., Vol. 1, pp. 83–6.

Notes to Pages 333–365

Chapter 31. CAPRICORN

1. Krupp, E. C., *Echoes of the Ancient Skies*, New York, Plume-Meridian, 1983, pp. 122–5.

2. Gleadow, Rupert, *The Origin of the Zodiac*, ibid., p. 166; and Rupert Gleadow, *The Zodiac Revealed*, ibid., pp. 126–7.

3. Gray, John, *Near Eastern Mythology*, ibid., p. 62.

4. Fagan, Cyril, *Astrological Origins*, ibid., p. 112.

5. Fagan, Cyril, *Astrological Origins*, ibid., p. 113.

6. Crowley, Aleister, *The Book of Thoth*, New York, Lancer, n.d, 105–7; and Juliet Sharman-Burke and Liz Greene, *Mythic Tarot*, New York, Simon & Schuster, Fireside, 1988.

7. Frazer, Sir James George, *The Illustrated Golden Bough*, Garden City, NY, Doubleday, 1978, pp. 189–91.

8. Capt, E. Raymond, *The Glory of the Stars*, Thousand Oaks, CA, Artisan Sales, 1976, pp. 67–8.

9. Gleadow, Rupert, *The Origin of the Zodiac*, ibid., pp. 80–1.

10. George, Demetra, *Asteroid Goddesses*, ibid., pp. 117–23.

11. Especially in three plays by Aeschylus: *Agamemnon*, *The Libation Bearers*, and *The Eumenides*. Sophocles and Euripides each wrote an *Elektra* on the same theme.

12. Bolen, Jean Shinoda, *Goddesses in Everywoman*, ibid., pp. 107–31.

Chapter 32. AQUARIUS

1. Fagan, Cyril, *Astrological Origins*, ibid., pp. 114–15.

2. Lamy, Lucy, *Egyptian Mysteries*, New York, Crossroad, 1981, p. 5.

3. Sandars, N.K., trans., *The Epic of Gilgamesh*, ibid., pp. 97–107.

4. Graves, Robert, *The Greek Myths*, ibid., Vol. 1, pp. 115–18.

5. Gleadow, Rupert, *The Origin of the Zodiac*, ibid., pp. 80–1.

6. Lilly, William, *An Introduction to Astrology*, ibid.

7. Sharman-Burke, Juliet and Liz Greene, *Mythic Tarot*, ibid., pp. 69–71.

Chapter 33. PISCES

1. Fagan, Cyril, *Astrological Origins*, ibid., pp. 115–16.

2. Gleadow, Rupert, *Origin of the Zodiac*, ibid., pp. 80–1.

3. Jung, C. G., *The Portable Jung*, ed. Joseph Campbell, Harmandsworth and New York, Penguin, 1980, p. 330.

4. Hand, Robert, "The Age and Constellation of Pisces," *Essays on Astrology*, Rockport, MA, Para Research, 1982.

5. Jonas, Hans, *The Gnostic Religion*, Boston, Beacon Press, 1963, pp. 112–29.

6. Walker, Barbara G., *The Woman's Encyclopedia of Myths and Secrets*, ibid., p. 549.

7. Mercatante, Anthony S., *The Facts on File Encyclopedia of World Mythology and Legend*, New York, Facts on File, 1988, pp. 564–5.

8. Hand, Robert, *Essays on Astrology*, ibid; and Dane Rudhyar, *Astrological Timing*, ibid.

9. Fagan, Cyril, *Astrological Origins*, ibid.; and David Frawley, *The Astrology of the Seers*, ibid,.

10. Greene, Liz, *The Astrology of Fate*, ibid., pp. 257–66.

11. Jacobs, Donald, "The Chart of Jesus," reproduced in Jeff Green, *Pluto: The Evolutionary Journey of the Soul*, ibid., p. 181.

12. Jung, C. G., "Answer to Job," in *The Portable Jung*, ibid., pp. 639–50.

13. Rudhyar, Dane, *The Pulse of Life*, ibid., p. 108.

Index

Achilles, 143-144
Actaeon, 103, 143
acupuncture, 145, 318
Adler, Alfred, 57, 172
Adonis, 17, 46, 50-51
Aegean, 55, 73, 107
Aeneas, 143
Agamemnon, 124, 253
Age of Aquarius, 55, 283, 353
Age of Cancer, 239, 265
Age of Enlightenment, 353
Age of Faith, 363
Age of Intuition, 1
Age of Pisces, 363
Age of Reason, 1
Age of Taurus, 239-240, 266
Age of Technology, 55, 353
Age of Virgo, 291
Ahura Mazda, 153
air (element), 4, 37, 53, 108, 116,
    170-175, 191-193, 202-212, 217-
    218, 222, 251, 255-258, 289, 297,
    301-302, 306, 330, 345, 349, 351
Ajax, 124
Akhenaten, 17
akhet, 300
alchemy, 23-24, 38-39, 43, 73, 84,
    120, 193-194, 199-200, 203, 219,
    222, 236, 265, 290-291, 324
Aldebaran, 239, 281
Alexander the Great, 73, 212, 264
Alpha Piscium, 360
Amalthea, 333-334, 336, 338
Amazon, or Amazons, 103, 231
ambrosia (see also *amrita*), 25, 73,
    93, 100, 347
America (see also United States), 82,
    152, 157, 171, 177, 232, 271
American Revolution, 320
Amon-Ra, 228
amrita (see also ambrosia), 73, 93,
    347
Anatolia, 55
Anchises, 43
Andrews, Lynn, 121
anima, 43, 219, 231, 255, 298
anima mundi, 43, 219
animus, 245, 298
anorexia, 267
Antares, 281
Antlered God, 56, 62
Antony, Mark, 118
Anu, path of, 181-182
Aphrodite (see also Venus), 10, 38,

41-50, 80, 82, 104, 108, 112, 125,
    153, 156, 164, 188, 241, 298-304
Apollo, 18, 20-24, 28-29, 33, 35, 38,
    44, 58, 66, 110, 123-124, 143, 188,
    214, 235, 253, 264, 313, 326, 359
Apollodorus, 142
Apollonius of Rhodes, 142-143
Apuleius, Lucias, 61-63
Aquarius, 25, 49, 55, 58, 78, 101,
    108, 119, 153, 155, 165-166, 182,
    187-188, 190, 204-206, 213, 218-
    220, 222, 283, 301, 341, 345-355
Aradia, 62
Arawn, 277
Arcadia, 33, 94, 326
Archer, the, 326
Ares (see also Mars), 46, 79-85, 117,
    189, 214, 228, 235, 311
Argo, 229, 231, 278
Argonautica, 142-143
Argonauts, 231, 252
Argos, 107-108, 214
Ariadne, 164-165, 239, 243, 245
Arianrhod, 63-64
Aries, 27-28, 37-38, 49, 58, 81, 184,
    186-188, 196-198, 215-218, 227-
    239, 252, 278, 280-281, 297-300,
    306, 325, 337
Aristotle, 191, 202
Artemis (see also Diana), 18, 63, 67,
    69, 103, 188, 277-278, 287, 291-
    292, 323, 326-328
Asclepius, 125, 142-144, 146, 311,
    317-318
Asgard, 126
ashvamedha, 252
Ashvins, 251-252
Asia, 52, 242, 278
Asia Minor, 278
Astraea, 287, 297, 301
Atalanta, 275, 278
Athamas, 229
Athene (see also Pallas Athene), 79-
    80, 90, 97-105, 110, 120-121, 128,
    137-138, 154, 188, 204, 227-228,
    231-235, 237-238, 247, 257, 270,
    278, 282, 293, 297-302, 306, 318,
    329, 339, 352, 364-365
Athens, 93, 99-100
Atlas, 10, 241
Atreus, House of, 333, 337
Attis, 278
Atwood, Margaret, 57
Augustine, St., 362

Aurelian, Emperor, 24
autumnal equinox, 215, 299
Aztecs, 148

Babylon, Babylonians, 4, 10, 15, 20,
    23, 26-27, 32, 50, 55, 81, 123-124,
    137, 175, 181-182, 184, 212, 227,
    241, 243, 263, 275-276, 278, 281,
    297, 311-313, 333-334, 346
Bacchus (see also Transpluto), 239,
    246
Bach, Eleanor, 90
Balkans, 213, 240
Barleycorn, 362
Beatles, 210
Berlin Wall, 218
Big Dipper, 82, 241
Birth of Venus, 41, 46
Black Elk, 148
Black Sea, 229
Bloom, Molly, 178
Bly, Robert, 24, 82, 84, 124, 137-138
Bode's Law, 89
Bolen, Jean Shinoda, 338
Borsippa, 32
Botticelli, Sandro, 41
Bradley, Donald, 360
Bradshaw, John, 166, 197
Briareos, 109
Brimo, 94
Brimos, 94
Bronze Age, 136
Bryant, Anita, 62, 232
bucrania, 240
Buddhism, 4, 32, 202, 215
Budha (not Buddha), 32
bulimia 267
Bush, George, 116, 245, 329

caduceus, 34-35, 39, 143, 253, 315
Caesar, Julius, 118
Callisto, 125
Campbell, Joseph, 6, 26, 118, 183,
    215, 233, 265, 278, 330
Cancer, 33, 60, 67, 77, 95, 128, 146,
    187, 189, 206, 210, 215-218, 239,
    263-276, 281, 292, 315-316, 318,
    326, 338
Capricorn, 60, 77, 82, 118-119, 136,
    138, 159, 169, 187, 198, 201, 215,
    217-218, 281, 323, 333-343, 351
cardinal signs, 214-218, 222
Carter, Jimmy, 301
Cassandra, 314, 357, 359